Hebrew For Dummies

W9-ASW-434

Useful Questions

Mi (mee; who)

Mah (mah; what)

Matai (mah-*tye*; when)

Eifo (ay-*foh*; where)

Lamah (lah-*mah*; why)

Eich (ech; how)

Kamah Zeh Oleh? (kah-*mah* zeh oh-*leh*; How much does it cost?)

Eifo HaSherutim? (ay-*foh* hah-sheh-roo-*teem*; Where are the restrooms?)

Mah HaSha'ah? (mah hah-shah-*ah*; What's the time?)

Mah Karah? (mah kah-*rah*; What happened?)

Greetings, Goodbyes, and Other Common Phrases

Boker Tov (*boh*-kehr tohv; good morning)

Bevakasha (beh-vah-*kah*-shah; please and you're welcome)

Eich Korim Lecha? (eich koh-*reem* leh-*chah*; What's your name?) (MS)

Eich Korim Lach? (eich koh-*reem* lach; What's your name?) (FS)

Lehitraot (leh-heet-rah-*oht*; see you soon)

Lilah Tov (lye-*lah* tohv; good night)

Mah Shlomcha? (mah shlohm-*chah*; How are you?) (MS)

Mah Shlomech? (mah shloh-*mech*; How are you?) (FS)

Shabbat Shalom (shah-*baht* shah-*lohm*; good Sabbath)

Shalom (shah-*lohm*; hello, good-bye, peace)

Shavua Tov (shah-voo-*ah* tohv; a good week)

Slicha (slee-*chah*; excuse me)

Todah (toh-*dah*; thanks)

Tzohorayim Tovim (tzoh-hoh-rah-*yeem* toh-*veem*; good afternoon)

Hebrew For Dummies®

The Hebrew Alphabet

Letter	Name	Sound
א	Alef	Silent
ב / בּ	Bet	V / B
ג	Gimel	Hard G
ד	Dalet	D
ה	Hay	H
ו	Vav	V
ז	Zayin	Z
ח	Chet	CH (guttural)
ט	Tet	T
י	Yod	Y
כ / ך	Kaf / Final	K
כ / ך	Chaf / Final	CH
ל	Lamed	L
מ / ם	Mem / Final	M
נ / ן	Nun / Final	N
ס	Samech	S
ע	Ayin	Silent
פ / ף	Fay / Final	F
פּ / ף	Pay / Final	P
צ	Tzadi / Final	TZ
ק	Kof	K
ר	Resh	R
שׁ / שׂ	Shin / Sin	SH / S
ת	Tav	T

Vowel	Name	Sound
ְ	Sh'vah	Silent
ִ	Chirik	Long e
ֵ	Tzere	Long a
ֶ	Segol	Eh
ָ	Kamatz	Ah
ַ	Patach	Ah
ֻ or וּ	Shurook	oo
ֹ or וֹ	Cholem	Long o

A Basic Blessing

Remember this great blessing. You can say it any time you experience something new (such as eating the first fruit of the season), or experience something wonderful (it can be a wedding, a new job, a new contract, or whatever). It is a great all-purpose blessing to celebrate the many seasons in our lives.

בָּרוּך ֹתָּה יְָ אֱלֹהֵינוּ מֶלֶך הָעוֹלָם

שֶׁהֶחֱיָנוּ וְקִיְּמָנוּ וְהִגִּיעָנוּ לַזְּמָן הַזֶּה.

Baruch Atah Adonai, Eloheinu Melech Ha'Olam, Sh'hecheyanu, V'Kiyemanu, V'Higianu LaZman HaZeh.

bah-*rooch* ah-*tah* ah-doh-*noye* eh-loh-hay-*noo* meh-lehch hah-oh-*lahm,* sheh-cheh-hee-*yah-noo* veh-kee-yah-*mah-noo* veh-hee-gee-*ah-noo* lahz-*mahn* hah-*zeh.*

Praised are You, the Eternal One our God, Ruler of the Cosmos, who has kept us alive, sustained us, and enabled us to reach this moment.

Copyright © 2003 Wiley Publishing, Inc.
All rights reserved.

Item 5489-1.

For more information about Wiley Publishing, call 1-800-762-2974.

For Dummies: Bestselling Book Series for Beginners

Hebrew

FOR

DUMMIES®

Hebrew
FOR
DUMMIES®

by Jill Suzanne Jacobs

WILEY

Wiley Publishing, Inc.

Hebrew For Dummies®

Published by
Wiley Publishing, Inc.
909 Third Avenue
New York, NY 10022
www.wiley.com

Library of Congress Cataloging-in-Publication Data:

Library of Congress Control Number: 2003101794

ISBN: 0-7645-5489-1

1O/SX/RQ/QT/IN

Manufactured in the United States of America

10 9 8 7 6 5

WILEY   is a trademark of Wiley Publishing, Inc.

About the Author

Jill Suzanne Jacobs is a Jewish educator and writer. She holds a master of arts degree in Jewish education from Hebrew Union College-Jewish Institute of Religion, a bachelor of arts degree in history from UCLA, and has studied at a variety of institutions in Israel, including the Hebrew University of Jerusalem. She teaches and writes in the Boston area, and is part of the editorial team of MyJewishLearning.com, a comprehensive online resource exploring Jewish religion, history, and culture produced by Hebrew College and Jewish Family & Life! Media.

Dedication

This book is dedicated to my teachers. To Rabbi Shelley Waldenberg who taught me the Hebrew letters and a love of all things Jewish. To my Hebrew teachers at UCLA — Yonah Sabar and Nancy Ezer — who taught me the fundamentals of the Hebrew language. To my teachers at Hebrew Union College-Jewish Institute of Religion who taught me to unlock the wisdom of the Hebrew texts of our tradition. To my second-grade teacher, Mrs. Henry, who said I would write a book someday . . . and to my family who knew that I could.

Author's Acknowledgments

This book wouldn't have come into being without the help, love, and support of many people in my life. So many people were there for me along the way that I can't possibly thank them all. Some key players in this endeavor, however, do deserve to be singled out in writing.

My first thanks goes to Sue Mellen, fearless leader (and president) of YourWriters.com (Internet: www.yourwriters.com), who brought this project to me and encouraged me to undertake it.

An incredible debt of gratitude goes to the magnificent team at Wiley. To Natasha Graf, the acquisition editor, for her enthusiasm and patience in teaching me the Dummies ropes. To Marcia Johnson, the project editor, for her hard work, persistence, and brilliant editorial leadership. To Steve Arany for his technical wizardry in working with computer and software issues. And to Ora Leivant, the technical reviewer, who painstakingly reviewed the manuscript.

Hats off to Ziv Hellman — a true *gibor hayil* — who chased down Hebrew word-processing programs in Israel, answered my numerous queries via phone and e-mail, and read nearly every page of this manuscript to help ensure its accuracy and that the Hebrew represented here is indeed reflective of the Hebrew spoken in its native land, the modern-day state of Israel.

A big thank-you to my wonderful and talented colleagues at JFL Media for your enthusiasm and support, for the flexibility in giving me time off when I needed to work on this manuscript, and for the important work that you do — believing, as I do, in the power of Judaism and the media to enhance lives and better the world.

Kudos to the women of the Hadassah Leadership Academy and to my students at *Kehillatenu* for giving me the opportunity *Lilmod U'Lilamed* — to teach and be taught.

Many thanks to my stateside Israeli friends — David Warshavsky, Aron Troen, and Orit Koritsky-Fox for answering my numerous Hebrew related queries. To Rabbi David "Gingi" Wilfond who offered rabbinic advise and wisdom. And to my many Hebrew-loving friends who offered support and encouragement along the way, in particular Michelle Thaler, Jamie Carolan, Sue Hiller, Amy Warshavsky, Esther Schrader, and Nick Anderson.

Thank you, thank you, thank you to my dear roommates, Chitra and Jen, for your companionship and good cheer and for never once complaining about the colossal and unbelievable mess I made in the office.

And *Aharon, aharon, haviv* (*Roughly:* Last but certainly not least) I humbly offer my sincere thanks to God: Unifying Force of the Cosmos, Source of All Harmony. I offer this book as prayer, a prayer for *Shalom* (peace and wholeness) for Israel, the Middle East, and indeed for all peoples that inhabit the earth. *Ken Yehiye Ratzon.* That it be so.

Publisher's Acknowledgments

We're proud of this book; please send us your comments through our Dummies online registration form located at www.dummies.com/register/.

Some of the people who helped bring this book to market include the following:

Acquisitions, Editorial, and Media Development

Project Editor: Marcia L. Johnson

Acquisitions Editor: Natasha Graf

Copy Editor: Mike Baker, Chad R. Sievers

Acquisitions Coordinator: Holly Grimes

Technical Editor: Ora Leivant

Senior Permissions Editor: Carmen Krikorian

Media Development Specialist: Megan Decraene

Editorial Manager: Jennifer Ehrlich

Media Development Manager: Laura VanWinkle

Editorial Assistant: Elizabeth Rea

Cartoons: Rich Tennant, www.the5thwave.com

Production

Project Coordinator: Nancee Reeves

Layout and Graphics: Carrie Foster, LeAndra Johnson, Stephanie D. Jumper, Brent Savage, Jacque Schneider, Jeremey Unger

Proofreaders: Laura Albert, John Tyler Connoley, Betty Kish, Angel Perez

Indexer: Johnna VanHoose

Special Help: Melissa Bennett, Daniel Connelly, John Tyler Connoley, Her Voice Unlimited, LLC

Publishing and Editorial for Consumer Dummies

Diane Graves Steele, Vice President and Publisher, Consumer Dummies

Joyce Pepple, Acquisitions Director, Consumer Dummies

Kristin A. Cocks, Product Development Director, Consumer Dummies

Michael Spring, Vice President and Publisher, Travel

Brice Gosnell, Associate Publisher, Travel

Suzanne Jannetta, Editorial Director, Travel

Publishing for Technology Dummies

Richard Swadley, Vice President and Executive Group Publisher

Andy Cummings, Vice President and Publisher

Composition Services

Gerry Fahey, Vice President of Production Services

Debbie Stailey, Director of Composition Services

Contents at a Glance

Table of Contents

Introduction

● ●

*H*ebrew is an incredible language. And, if you're picking up this book, I'm guessing that you have at least a passing interest in the subject, which thrills me because I think Hebrew is an amazing, fascinating, and beautiful language. To use a phrase that just may reveal my California roots, I'm totally psyched to share my knowledge of Hebrew with you. Whether you're interested in Hebrew because you want to communicate with your Israeli cousins, you want to brush up on the subject so you can understand prayers and other sacred Jewish literature better, or you want to impress your Jewish in-laws, *Hebrew For Dummies* can help.

About This Book

This book is a great place to start regardless of your motivation for picking up or dusting off your Hebrew skills. It won't make you fluent overnight (though wouldn't that be nice?) or turn you into a Biblical scholar, but *Hebrew For Dummies* can give you a solid Hebrew foundation — in both conversational Hebrew and the Hebrew of prayer, sacred texts, and holidays. As if that's not enough, I also share with you my love of things Jewish and the delightful and sometimes quirky culture of the modern state of Israel, where the largest group of Hebrew speakers resides today. But, if you aren't planning on taking a trip to the Middle East, don't worry. Hebrew is alive and well all over the world. You can find plenty opportunities to practice your language skills. (If you're not sure where to turn, I have you covered with some tips on where you can find Hebrew speakers and Hebrew sources right here in North America.) **B'hatzlacha!** (beh-hahtz-lah-*chah;* Good luck! Much success to you!)

Hopefully this book is only the beginning — albeit a good one! You can pick up a language only through constant exposure and repetition. So listen to the CD at the back of this book again and again. Be sure to practice, practice, and (you knew it was coming) practice. Go to places where you hear Hebrew, and speak Hebrew in your home and workplace — teach everyone you know your favorite Hebrew words and expressions. Before you know it, Hebrew will creep into your mind, soul, and heart. And you'll speak it day and night!

Conventions Used in This Book

Here are a couple of conventions that I use in this book for your reading pleasure:

✔ For the most part, I present the Hebrew language in *transliteration* (Hebrew sounds represented with English characters), then provide the pronunciation (how to say the word), and a translation (what the word means in English). In the pronunciation, the stressed syllables are *italicized*.

✔ Because Hebrew language is often gender specific (there are masculine and feminine nouns, verb forms, and so on, see Chapter 2 for an explanation of gender), I've included the following abbreviations wherever necessary:

- Masculine singular (MS)
- Feminine singular (FS)
- Masculine plural (MP)
- Feminine plural (FP)

To help you develop your language skills, *For Dummies* language books include

✔ **Talkin' the Talk dialogues:** Here's where you get to see Hebrew in action. These relatively short, real-life dialogues use the vocabulary and grammatical concepts that I introduce in the book.

✔ **Words to Know blackboards:** Here's where you can find the key words and phrases I introduce. It's all here: the word as it's written in Hebrew, the *transliteration,* the proh-nun-see-*aye*-shun, and the translation.

✔ **Fun & Games activities:** I'm a teacher; I just can't help myself. So at the end of each chapter, I include some fun little exercises to help reinforce your newly acquired Hebrew.

Foolish Assumptions

My father taught me never to assume anything. He even had a little ditty about it that I won't repeat here. But then my editor said that I had to come up with some assumptions about you, the reader. So here they are:

✔ You know no Hebrew — or if you learned Hebrew in religious school, you don't remember a word of it.

✔ You're not looking for a book that will make you fluent in Hebrew; you just want to know some words, phrases, and sentence constructions so that you can communicate basic information in Hebrew.

✔ You don't want to have to memorize long lists of vocabulary words or a bunch of boring grammar rules.

✔ You're inexplicably drawn to all yellow and black books.

✔ You want to have fun and pick up some Hebrew at the same time.

Do any descriptions sound like you? Well, good. I bet you're in good company.

How This Book Is Organized

This book is organized into four parts plus an appendix. The four parts are broken down into chapters. I've organized the chapters around active topics — things you want to *do* (like go to a bank, go to a restaurant, or go to a synagogue). Each chapter gives you the lowdown on the Hebrew you need to know to get by while doing that activity. And, though I know that you don't want to be bogged down by grammar rules, I sneak a grammatical tidbit or two into each chapter. Don't worry: I make these brief excursions as quick and painless as possible.

Part 1: Getting Started

This part of the book starts with the basics. I introduce you to the Hebrew letters and vowels and give you some basic Hebrew vocabulary. I explain how I represent the Hebrew sounds in English letters (so you don't *have to* crack your teeth reading the Hebrew, although I encourage you to try). In Part I, I also give you a basic grounding in Hebrew grammar.

Part 11: Hebrew in Action

Here's where I really get going. In these chapters, I give you basic Hebrew vocabulary to start using in your daily life — when you rise up, when you lie down, in your home, and when you walk (to quote from an important Hebrew prayer). Part II gives you the words to meet and greet, flirt and work, eat and drink, and shop 'til you drop. I also give you vocabulary to use when you go out for a night on the town and when you talk about it on the phone the next day. And I give you all the words you need when you're hanging out at home and cleaning up your place after you've made a mess.

Part III: Hebrew on the Go

Here's where I start to get practical. I cover dealing with money, going to the bank, asking directions, getting around using various forms of transportation (funny thing — I don't mention camels; oh well), and hitting the road for a trip. So, if travel bug has paid you a visit, take a look at Part III. I give you the words and phrases you need for planning the trip. And I also give you some vocabulary for handling — God forbid — an emergency.

Part IV: Sacred Hebrew

Where would Hebrew be without Judaism? In this part, I present the sacred side of the Hebrew language. I tell you all about blessings, prayers, and Jewish holidays.

Part V: The Part of Tens

What would a *For Dummies* book be without one of these? I'll put my top ten lists up against anyone's. In this section, I give you ten Israeli sayings so you can sound like a real **Sabra** (sah-*brah;* native Israeli), plus the top-ten Hebrew sayings heard in the Jewish *Diaspora* (that's everywhere outside of the Land of Israel). I also give you a list of some great reads about the wonderful, wild, and wacky world of Hebrew. But this list wouldn't be complete without the Ten Commandments in Hebrew. It's all here.

Appendixes

Here's all the nuts and bolts. The cogs that make Hebrew run — verb tables and a Hebrew-English/English-Hebrew dictionary. Turn to Part V, and you can also find a listing of the tracks on the CD that comes with this book. And it doesn't stop there. I put the answers to the Fun & Games activities (which you find at the end of each chapter) here too. This is the place to go when you want some information, and you want it fast.

Icons Used in This Book

Sometimes I want to point out something that's especially important or interesting — a grammatical concept, something to remember, a tip to help you with your Hebrew skills, or a bit of insider insight into the wonderful world of Jewish culture. In these cases, I use the following icons that you can find on the left-hand side of the page:

This icon accompanies helpful tips for picking up the Hebrew language.

Think of this icon as that little string around your finger that reminds you of all the little things you gotta do but are prone to forget. This icon flags important concepts that you have to keep in mind while you study Hebrew. You know what they say: God is in the details.

This little guy is by far my favorite icon. When you see this icon, you know that I've taken the opportunity to cram in all sorts of interesting information about the Jewish world — religious and secular — in Israel and the Jewish *Diaspora* (lands outside of Israel).

Ah, grammar. Can't live with it; can't live without it. This icon alerts you to instances where I point out the quirks of the Hebrew language and all those grammar rules that underlie the language's structure.

The audio CD at the back of this book gives you the opportunity to hear Hebrew in action. The CD features native Hebrew speakers bringing to life some of the dialogs from the pages of this book. I bet that you'll be amazed by how beautiful Hebrew can sound.

I really tried to make this foray into Hebrew as painless as possible for you, but every now and then, I felt the need to explain things in technical terms. Don't worry — you can skip the paragraphs marked with this icon and still get all the Hebrew you need for basic conversation.

Where to Go from Here

First the good news: You don't have to read this entire book. In fact, you don't have to read any of it. (But if that's the case, you probably wouldn't have bought it.) Anyway, here's my point: This book is organized so that you can just read the chapters that interest you and skip the rest. At no point in the text do I assume that you've read any of my other scintillating writing in other chapters or sections, and I won't get insulted if you only want to read certain chapters. If you're interested in the religious stuff, then by all means, go straight to Chapters 17, 18, and 19. But if you're interested in the day-to-day stuff, or you just want to know how to ask that cute Israeli guy or girl out on a date, Chapter 3 may be your cup of tea. Just take a look at the Table of Contents and turn to the chapter that most interests you. Go ahead and do it! Read this book out of order. Skip chapters. I won't tell anyone. In fact, I'll never know.

Alright, alright. I do have to add a few exceptions to the read-anything-you-want rule. You'll probably want to read Chapter 1, which gives you an overview of the book. And if you're a grammar geek, you'll looooove Chapter 2. If you aren't a grammar geek (most people despise the stuff, and I can't say that I blame them), you may want to look at Chapter 2 anyway. Here's a tip from someone who knows: After you understand the basics of Hebrew grammar, picking up the rest of the language is a cakewalk. So consider checking out Chapter 2.

Part I
Getting Started

The 5th Wave   By Rich Tennant

"My wife and I are taking the course together.
I figure I only have to learn half as much, since
she finishes all of my sentences anyway."

In this part . . .

Part I welcomes you to the Hebrew language. Here I give you the low down on Hebrew including how to pronounce Hebrew sounds so you sound like a native, how to put Hebrew words into sentences, how to identify the basics of Hebrew grammar and syntax, how to count in Hebrew, and how to communicate in Hebrew with a dash of **Sabra Chutzpah** (sah-*brah* chootz-*pah;* native Israeli attitude)!

Chapter 1

You Already Know Some Hebrew

*B*aruch HaBa! Welcome to Hebrew! In studying Hebrew, you're joining millions of other Hebrew speakers around the world. Its two centers are Israel (of course), and North America, which is home to many Hebrew newspapers, Hebrew-speaking camps and schools, and institutions. You're also speaking the Bible's original language and one of the most ancient languages still spoken today. Furthermore, you're speaking the only language in the history of the world known to have undergone a revival, returning fully to being a spoken language after hundreds — perhaps even two thousand — years of being relegated to correspondence, literature, and the sacred world of prayer and the Bible.

Hebrew was once almost exclusively a holy language — a language of prayers and ritual, of the Bible and other sacred texts, and a language above the humdrum of the everyday. No longer true. That same ancient and holy tongue is now the language of sunbathing on the beach, eating dinner, going to the doctor, and the myriad of everyday life.

All languages are portals — openings to culture and friendship, literature and ideas. Discover any one, and a whole new world opens up to you. Discover Hebrew, and a whole Jewish and Israeli world is yours.

Taking Stock of What's Familiar

If you've ever been to a synagogue or had a bit of Jewish education, you probably already know a little Hebrew. But even if you've never walked through a synagogue's door or studied anything Jewish, you still probably know some Hebrew words. For example, you have probably heard the word *amen.* That word is Hebrew! "Amen" comes from a word meaning faith or belief and people usually say it at the end of a prayer. And the word *Hallelujah?* Hebrew again! The word literally means, "Praise God." Even the word *alphabet* derives from the Hebrew words for the first two letters of its alphabet, *aleph* and *bet.* To see what the Hebrew alphabet looks like, check out the section, "Recognizing Tips to Help You Read Hebrew," later in this chapter.

Of course, you may have heard of other Jewish words, such as **Shlepp** (*shlehp;* to drag or pull) and **Kvetch** (*kvehtsh;* to complain), that are actually Yiddish (the language of the Jews of Eastern Europe combining Old High German, Hebrew, and other languages), that are part of the Israeli vernacular today. You may never even have thought about other words that have Hebrew roots. For example, did you know that *cinnamon* is a derivative of the Hebrew word **Kinamon** (kee-nah-*mohn*) which appears in the Biblical book, The Song of Songs? The English word *dilute* may derive from the Hebrew word **Dal** (dahl), which means weak or thin and first appears in the Biblical book of Genesis.

Some people claim that Hebrew is the mother of all languages. No matter what its history or origin, Hebrew, a language that has its origins in the Fertile Crescent, has crept into North American–spoken English. And this process works in reverse too, as many English words and phrases have crept into the Hebrew language. Interestingly enough — while you as an English speaker may identify these words as "English," some of these words derive from Italian and French, which shows the universality of certain words. But if you say the following words with an Israeli accent, you're speaking Hebrew!

- ✔ Cafe
- ✔ Hamburger
- ✔ Macaroni
- ✔ Pizza
- ✔ Radio
- ✔ Telephone

Incidentally, *The Academy for Hebrew Language,* the institute responsible for creating Modern Hebrew words, did create an authentic Hebrew word for the telephone. The academy called the telephone a **Sach-Rachok** (sahch-rah-*chohk*), which put together the words for conversation and long distance. So telephone translated as "long-distance conversation." Pretty clever, huh? However this word didn't "stick" with the Israeli public. So *telephone* it is.

Introducing The Academy for Hebrew Language

Hebrew, the language of the Bible, is spoken today in Israel and around the world as a modern language. So the question, of course, is where did all these modern words come from? Who decides? The answer is The Academy for Hebrew Language, an institute founded in Israel in 1953 to oversee the language's development, and to create new words — as the need arose — in a manner consistent with Hebrew's historical development. So, although Hebrew is an ancient Biblical language, new words needed to be developed, such as *high tech* (**Ta'ah-siaht-Elit;** tah-ah see-*yat* ee-*leet*) and *start-up company* (**Chevrat Heznek;** chehv-*raht* hehz-*nehk*), *surfboard* (**Galshan;** gahl-*shan*), *jet-lag* (**Ya'efet;** yah-*eh*-feht), and

even — when you've had just a few too many — *hangover* (**Chamarmoret;** chah-mahr-*moh*-reht).

Of course, the Israeli public doesn't accept all the words the Academy invents, although the Academy's decisions are binding for government documents and the offical Israel Broadcasting Authority.

And Israelis aren't above taking matters into their own hands and creating words of their own. In the 1990s, Motorola Israel Corporation introduced wireless phones, coining a new word, *pela-phone*, meaning "wonder-phone." You can learn more about the Academy at: http://hebrew-academy.huji.ac.il/english.html.

Speaking Hebrew Like a Native

When speaking a foreign language, you want to sound as authentic as possible. Use the tips in the following sections to help you start. The most important part of sounding like a native is persistence and practice — and then some more practice! Listen to the CD in this book as much as possible. Spend as much time listening to Hebrew spoken by native speakers whenever you can.

Memorizing vocabulary and certain stock phrases and repeating them to yourself until you can say them at quite a clip is also helpful. In no time at all, you may fool people into thinking you speak Hebrew fluently — or close to it anyway.

Stressing out (not)

The first tip I give you has to do with the way syllables are stressed. In American English, we often stress or place emphasis on the first syllable in each word. For example: "When **speak**ing a **for**eign **lan**guage . . . ." But Hebrew often places the emphasis on the last syllable. So if you were speaking that previous phrase with an Israeli accent, you'd place your emphasis on the last syllable. For example: When speak**ing** a for**eign** langu**age** . . . .

Gesturing like the best of them

Gestures provide the flourishing touch to help you seem like a native speaker. Use the following gestures when speaking in Israel:

✔ When you hold one hand up about shoulder level with the palm upright and all the fingers cupped together in the center of the palm, this means **Rega!** (*reh*-gah; wait a minute).

✔ When you want to catch a cab, point your index finger down at the ground, indicating that you want the cab to stop where you are pointing.

✔ In Israel, the American "thumbs-up" sign has been seen traditionally as an unfriendly gesture that means you're **Brogez** (*broh-gehz*; mad or pissed off at someone).

Interestingly, an extremely recent ad campaign in Israel encourages kids to make a "thumbs-up" sign to drivers when they're crossing the street, with the drivers returning a thumbs-up, as an indication that the drivers acknowledge they see the children and will let them cross without running them over. So thumbs-up is taking on a positive connotation!

Getting out the gutterals

The second piece of advice I can give you has to do with certain Hebrew letters that are pronounced at the back of the throat. Use these tips for pronouncing them:

✔ **Ayin** (eye-*yeen*): This letter makes a barely audible gutteral sound in the back of the throat. For practical purposes, this letter is nearly a silent syllable.

✔ **Chaf** (khahf): This letter makes a sound you don't hear in English. It's a hard *h* sound like you make when you clear your throat.

✔ **Chet** (cheht): This letter makes a strong throaty *h* sound. In this book, this syllable is written as *ch*.

✔ **Reish** (raysh): This letter makes the *r* sound as in *round*. To sound like a native, roll this syllable like a Spanish *r,* and try to produce the sound from the back of your throat.

Find out about the rest of the Hebrew alphabet in the section, "Recognizing Tips to Help You Read Hebrew," later in this chapter.

Opening your mouth to say, "Ah!"

Thirdly, watch the pronunciation of your vowels. When pronouncing the *ah* sound, pronounce that vowel fully. Open your mouth wide and say, "Ah," as if you were at the doctor. Hebrew doesn't have a short *i* sound (like the vowel sound in *sit*), so any time you see an *i,* remember to make it a long sound like *ee* as in *Whoopee!* In Hebrew, *oh* sounds are long like in *over.*

In Hebrew, remember that the language is a Mediterranean language, and as such, has a certain nasal quality to it. More so than English — but actually a lot like French — you use your nasal cavity when making sound. On a less technical tip: When speaking Hebrew, try to fake a French accent! At the very least, your Hebrew will sound better than with an American one!

Counting in Hebrew

Learning how to count is fundamental to the study of any language. Hebrew divides words into masculine and feminine genders (see Chapter 2), and numbers are no different — they have masculine and feminine forms. You may feel a little confused, but don't worry! Table 1-1 gives you the *cardinal numbers* (the numbers you use for counting) from 1 to 10. When you only want to count, without counting objects, use the feminine form. See the section "Counting objects," later in this chapter to find out how to incorporate gender with numbers.

Table 1-1	Counting from 1 to 10	
Number	*Masculine*	*Feminine*
1	Echad (eh-*chad*)	Achat (ah-*chat*)
2	Shnayim (*shnah*-eem)	Shtayim (*shta*-yim)
3	Shlosha (shloh-*sha*)	Shalosh (sha-*lohsh*)
4	Arba'ah (ahr-bah-*ah*)	Arba (*ahr*-bah)
5	Chamisha (chah-mee-*shah*)	Chamesh (chah-*mesh*)
6	Shisha (shee-*shah*)	Shesh (shesh)
7	Shiv'a (sheev-*ah*)	Sheva (*she*-vah)
8	Sh'monah (shmoh-*nah*)	Shmoneh (*shmoh*-neh)
9	Tish'a (teesh-*ah*)	Tay-shah (*tey*-sha)
10	Asarah (ah-sah-*rah*)	Eser (*eh*-sehr)

A people dispersed, a language intact

Hebrew served as the vernacular during the ancient Jewish commonwealth until it was conquered by the Romans in 70 CE (Common Era). Then Jews fanned out across the globe to Asia, Africa, and Europe. Even though they were dispersed, the Jewish people continued to practice their religion — Judaism — and remain literate in their language — Hebrew.

Hebrew continued to be the language of prayer, study, and correspondence for Jewish people. Gradually, Jews adopted the languages of their host countries as their spoken language. They mixed Hebrew with their different host countries'

languages, giving rise to new Jewish languages, such as Ladino, Judeo-Arabic, and Yiddish.

In the 1800s, a movement began to revive Hebrew as a spoken language. Eliezer Ben-Yehuda championed the cause and moved to **Eretz Yisrael** (*eh*-rehtz yees-rah-*ehl;* the Land of Israel) to revive Hebrew, writing the first Modern Hebrew dictionary. Today Hebrew is one of the two official languages in Israel (Arabic being the other official language), and is a living, spoken language for millions of Israelis and other Hebrew speakers across the globe.

Counting objects

The gender of the number you use when you want to count something depends on the noun's gender you're counting. (Sound confusing? Don't worry. You can do it.) Counting objects in Hebrew is easy. Just remember to do the following:

- **Figure out the gender of the noun you're counting:** For example, if you want to talk about *one book,* you first have to figure out if the noun *book* is masculine or feminine. (It's masculine.) So when you count books, you need to use the masculine form of the number.

- **Place the number appropriately** *before* **or** *after* **the noun:** For the number *one,* place the number *after* the noun. So rather than *one book,* you say *book one* (**Sefer Echad;** *seh*-fehr eh-*chad*). But after you get to the number two, place the number *before* the noun. [To make **Sefer** plural in Hebrew, it becomes **S'farim** (sfah-*reem;* books).] So, to say *two books,* you say **Shnai S'farim** (*shnay* sfah-*reem*), for *three books,* say **Shlosha S'farim** (shloh-*shah* sfah-*reem*), for *four books* say **Arba'ah S'farim** (ahr-bah-*ah* sfah-*reem*), and so on.

The number *two* in Hebrew is an exception. When you're specifying two of something, say two boys (**Yeladim;** yuh-lah-*deem*) or two girls (**Yeladot;** yuh-lah-*doht*), and you drop the last syllable (*im*) of the number 2. So you get: **Shnei Yeladim** (two boys) and **Shtei Yeladot** (two girls). Drop the *im* regardless of the noun you're counting.

Counting higher

To form the numbers 11-19, place the second number in front of the ten. For example, eleven in the masculine form is **Echad-asar.** In the feminine form, eleven is **Achat-esrei** (ah-*chaht* es-*reh*). Table 1-2 shows the numbers for 11-19.

Table 1-2		Counting from 11-19
Number	*Masculine*	*Feminine*
11	Echad-asar (eh-*chad* ah-*sahr*)	Achat-esrei (ah-*chaht* ehs-*reh*)
12	Shnaym-assar (shnehym ah-*sahr*)	Shtaym-esreh (shtehym ehs-*reh*)
13	Shlosha-asar (shloh-*sha* ah-*sahr*)	Shlosh-esreh (shlosh-*ehsreh*)
14	Arba'ah-asar (ahr-bah-*ah* ah-*sahr*)	Arba-esreh (ahr-*bah* es-*reh*)
15	Chamisha-asar (chah-mee-*shah* ah-*sahr*)	Chamesh-esreh (chah-*mesh* es-*reh*)
16	Shisha-asar (shee-*shah* ah-*sahr*)	Shesh-esreh (shehsh ehs-*reh*)
17	Shiv'a-asar (sheev-*ah* ah-*sahr*)	Shva-esreh (shvah es-*reh*)
18	Sh'monah-asar (shmoh-*nah* ah-*sahr*)	Shmoneh-esreh (shmoh-*neh* ehs-*reh*)
19	Tish'a-asar (teesh-*ah* ah-*sahr*)	tu-shah-esreh (*tshah*-esreh)

Use the appropriate gender for the ten and the additional number that makes up the compound number.

The multiples of ten (10, 20, 30, and so on) are easy because these numbers are gender neutral. Table 1-3 shows the multiples of 10.

Table 1-3	Counting between Multiples of Ten	
Number	*Hebrew*	*Pronunciation*
20	Esrim	ehs-*reem*
30	Shloshim	shloh-*sheem*
40	Arba'im	ahr-bah-*eem*
50	Chamishim	chah-mee-*sheem*
60	Sheeshim	shee-*sheem*

(continued)

Table 1-3 *(continued)*		
Number	*Hebrew*	*Pronunciation*
70	Shiveem	sheev-*eem*
80	Sh'monim	shmoh-*neem*
90	Tish'im	teesh-*eem*

However, if you want to say something like *twenty-one* or *forty-seven,* you have to pay attention to gender again (see Table 1-4). The pattern for making these numbers is first to state the number in the tens, such as **Esrim** (ehs-*reem;* twenty), and then add the word for *and* (**V';** veh), and then the single number, such as **Echad** (eh-*chad;* one). So *twenty-one* would be **Esrim v'echad** (ehs-*reem* veh-eh-*chad;* twenty-one).

Table 1-4	Counting from 21-29	
Number	*Masculine*	*Feminine*
21	Esrim v'echad (ehs-*reem* veh-eh-*chahd*)	Es-rim v'achat (ehs-*reem* veh-ah-*chat*)
22	Esrim u'shnayim (ehs-*reem* oosh-*nah*-yim)	Esrim u'shtayim (ehs-*reem* ush-*tah*-yeem)
23	Esrim u'shlosha (ehs-*reem* oosh-loh-*shah*)	Esrim v'shalosh (ehs-*reem* veh-shah-*lohsh*)
24	Esrim v'arba'ah (ehs-*reem* veh-ahr-bah-*ah*)	Esrim v'arba (ehs-*reem* veh-ahr-bah)
25	Esrim v'chamisha (ehs-*reem* vah-chah-mee-*shah*)	Esrim v'chamesh (ehs-*reem* veh-chah-*mesh*)
26	Esrim v'shisha (ehs-*reem* veh-shee-*shah*)	Esrim v'shesh (ehs-*reem* veh-*shehsh*)
27	Esrim v'shiv'a (ehs-*reem* veh-sheev- ah)	Esrim v'sheva (ehs-*reem* veh-*sheh*-vah)
28	Esrim u'shmonah (ehs-*reem* ush-moh-*nah*)	Esrim u'shmoneh (ehs-*reem* ush-moh-*neh*)
29	Esrim v'tish'a (ehs-*reem* veh-teesh-*ah*)	Esrim v'tay-shah (ehs-*reem* veh-*teh*-sha)

If you can count to 30, you can count to a million! For all the numbers, you follow the same pattern as Table 1-4. First, state the number that is the multiple of ten (twenty, thirty, forty, and so forth) and then you add **V'** (*veh;* and) plus the single digit. For example, **Shloshim v'ehad** (shloh-*sheem* veh-eh-*chahd;* thirty-one), **Arba'im v'echad** (ahr-bah-*eem* veh-eh-*chahd;* forty-one), and so forth.

To count by hundreds, first say the feminine number of the quantity of hundreds, such as *four* (**Arba**), and then add the word for *hundreds* (**Me'ot**). This pattern continues until a thousand. For example,

100	**Me'ah**	meh-*ah*
200	**Matayim**	mah-*tah*-yeem
300	**Shlosh-me'ot**	*shlohsh*-meh-oht

To count by thousands, first you say the feminine number of the quantity of thousands, and then follow it with the word for *thousands,* **Alafim** (ah-lah-*feem*). This pattern continues until one million. The Hebrew word for one thousand is **Elef** (*eh*-lehf) and the word for two thousand is **Alpayim** (ahl-*pah*-yeem).

1,000	**Elef**	*eh*-lehf
2,000	**Alpyim**	ahl-*pah*-eem
3,000	**Shloshet Alafim**	*shloh*-sheht ah-lah-*feem*
10,000	**Aseret Alafim**	ah-*seh*-reht ah-lah-*feem*
1,000,000	**Mil-*yohn***	meel-*yohn*

Several chapters in this book give you an opportunity to practice using numbers. Check out Chapter 9 to find out how to ask for and give phone numbers, and Chapter 14, which is all about money — don't you love counting money?

Recognizing Tips to Help You Read Hebrew

Hebrew is no ordinary language. Quite the contrary — Hebrew's origins date back more than 3,500 years ago to antiquity and the Hebrew alphabet is quite possibly the first alphabet known to humankind. Hebrew was the language of King David and King Solomon, and the Bible's original language. Furthermore, ancient people called the Phoenicians based their alphabet on the Hebrew alphabet. The Greeks based their alphabet on the Phoenicians' letters. And the Latin letters you're reading right now are derived from the Greeks' letters! So although the Hebrew language may look a little different, only four degrees separate it from what you're used to.

In Jewish circles, using the terms C.E. (Common Era) and B.C.E. (before the Common Era) instead of the terms A.D. (*Ano Do minus;* year of our Lord) and B.C. (Before Christ) is customary. In Hebrew, you say **Lifnei Ha'Sfira** (leef-*nahy* hah-sfee-*rah;* before the counting) and **Acharei Ha'Sfiraha** (ah-chah-*ray* hah-sfee-*rah;* after the counting).

Figuring out the Hebrew alphabet's shapes, sounds, and stories

The Hebrew alphabet is one of the oldest alphabets still in use today. Even though the letters look different than the Latin characters that comprise the English alphabet, don't be intimidated! Just spend some time memorizing the shapes and sounds of these Hebrew letters and reading Hebrew will be easier!

Like many ancient alphabets, you write the Hebrew alphabet from right to left. Hebrew consists of 22 different letters — all consonants. Vowels aren't written within the consonant letters but rather are written in the form of dots and dashes below the consonant letter. For a more complete discussion of Hebrew vowels, see the section, "Those dots and dashes they call vowels," later in this chapter.

The pronunciation I provide in this book is the Sephardic (Mediterranean) pronunciation, which is spoken in Israel today. Ashkenazi (European) pronunciation differs slightly; the vowels have different pronunciations and there are a few consonants that are different as well. I will be using Sephardic pronunciation in this book.

Deciphering the consonant letters
Table 1-5 shows the Hebrew letters and their sounds.

Table 1-5		The Hebrew Alphabet	
Name of the Letter	*Pronunciation*	*Hebrew Character*	*The Sound It Makes*
Aleph	*ah*-lehf	א	makes no sound
Bet	beht	בּ	makes a "B" sound as in "boat"
Vet	veht	ב	makes a "V" sound as in "veterinarian"

Name of the Letter	Pronunciation	Hebrew Character	The Sound It Makes
Gimmel	*gee*-mehl	ג	makes a "G" sound as in "girl"
Dalet	*dah*-leht	ד	makes a "D" sound as in "door"
Hey	hey	ה	makes a "soft H" sound as in "hello"
Vav	vahv	ו	makes a "V" sound as in "video"
Zayin	*zah*-een	ז	makes a "Z" sound as in "zipper"
Chet	cheht	ח	makes a strong guttural "H" sound. In this book, this letter is represented as "Ch."
Tet	teht	ט	makes a "T" sound as in "teaspoon"
Yod	yohd	י	makes a ""Y" sound at the beginning of a word as in "young." This letter also behaves like a vowel at times. I discuss it in the following section about vowels.
Kaf	kahf	כ	makes a "K" sound as in "kite"
Khaf	khahf	כ	makes a strong guttural "H" sound. This letter is represented in this book as "kh."
Lamed	*lah*-mehd	ל	makes an "L" sound as in "lemon"
Mem	mehm	מ	makes an "M" sound as in "mouse"
Nun	noon	נ	makes an "N" sound as in "no" (And you thought only Catholics had nuns.)
Samekh	*sah*-mehch	ס	makes an "S" sound as in "soda"
Ayin	*ah*-yeen	ע	makes a barely audible guttural sound in the back of the throat (For practical purposes as most nonnative speakers can't make this sound, this letter is a "silent letter." You pronounce the vowels that are placed under it, but the letter itself doesn't make a sound.)

Table 1-5			The Hebrew Alphabet
Name of the Letter	**Pronunciation**	**Hebrew Character**	**The Sound It Makes**
Pey	*pay*	פ	makes a "P" sound as in "popsicle"
Fey	*fay*	פ	makes an "F" sound as in "fish"
Tzadi	*tzah-dee*	צ	makes a hard "Tz" sound as the double zz in "pizza." In this book, I represent it with "tz."
Kof	*kohf*	ק	makes this "K" sound as in "Kansas"
Reish	*raysh*	ר	makes the "R" sound as in "round." This letter is actually a "guttural" letter. Roll it like a Spanish "R," and also pronounce it from the back of the throat.
Shin	*sheen*	שׁ	(Not Charlie's brother or Martin's long-lost son) when the dot is on the right side of the letter it makes a "Sh" sound as in "show." In this book, I represent it with "sh."
Sin	*seen*	שׂ	when the dot is on the left side of the letter it makes an "S" sound as in "Sam"
Tav	*tahv*	ת	makes a "T" sound as in "toe"

Those dots and dashes they call vowels

Originally, Hebrew had no vowels. Vowels, in the form of dots and lines under the consonants, were added to the Hebrew writing in the seventh century of the Common Era (C.E.). Before then, people read without vowels. And even today, most books, magazines, and newspapers in Modern Hebrew — not to mention the Torah scroll — are written without vowels.

Modern Hebrew has both long and short vowels. As a general rule, a long vowel can make up one syllable, but a short vowel needs either another vowel or a **Shvah** (shvah; two vertical dots under a consonant) to form a syllable. For more on the **Shvah**, see "Introducing the shvah," later in this chapter.

Vowels are divided into long and short vowels. This categorization doesn't have to do with their pronunciation, but rather with the fact that long vowels are usually found in open syllables — syllables that end with a vowel — while short vowels are usually found in closed syllables — syllables that end with a consonant. However, the **Chirik Maleh** (the long vowel) holds it sound longer than its corresponding short vowel **Chirek Chaser**. Table 1-6 shows the long vowels.

Table 1-6		The Long Vowels	
Name of the Vowel	**Pronunciation**	**Hebrew Character**	**The Sound It Makes**
Chirik Maleh	chee-*reek* mah-*leh*	בִּי	makes the "ee" sound as in "see"
Cholam	choh-*lahm*	בֹ	makes the "o" sound as in "more"
Kamatz	kah-*mahtz*	בָ	makes the "ah" sound as in "saw"
Shuruk	shoo-*rook*	בוּ	makes the "oo" sound as in "mood"
Tzereh	tzay-*reh*	בֵ	makes the "a" sound as in "cape"
Vav Cholam	vahv choh-*lahm*	בוֹ	makes the "o" sound as in "snow"

*Note: In this table, I used the letter **Vet**, so you could see how the vowels look when attached to a consonant. (The vowels are the little squiggles and dots around the **Vet**.) Unlike in English, Hebrew vowels can never be written alone — they are always attached to a consonant.*

Table 1-7 shows the short vowels.

Table 1-7	The Short Vowels		
Name of the Vowel	**Pronunciation**	**Hebrew Character**	**The Sound It Makes**
Chirik Chaser	chee-*reek* chah-*sehr*	בּ	makes the "ee" sound as in "see"
Kamatz Katan	kah-*mahtz* kah-*tahn*	בָ	makes the "o" sound as in "more"
Kubutz	koo-*bootz*	בֻ	makes the "oo" sound as in "mood"
Patach	pah-*tahch*	בַ	makes the "uh" sound as in "nut"
Segol	seh-*gohl*	בֶ	makes the "eh" sound as in "end"

*Note: In this table, I used the letter **Vet**, so you could see how the vowels look when attached to a consonant. (The vowels are the little squiggles and dots around the **Vet**.)*

Sometimes the **Kamatz, Patach, Kamatz Katan,** or the **Segol** is paired with a **Shvah**. This pairing doesn't change the pronunciation.

The **Kamatz Katan** looks identical to the **Kamatz**. For example, if you see something that looks like a **Kamatz** at the beginning of a word, followed by a **Shva**, or between two **Shvas**, it's probably a **Kamatz Katan** and should be pronounced "o."

Introducing the shvah

The **Shva** looks like a colon (:), and you find it underneath letters. Hebrew actually has three types of **Shvahs** (but they all look the same):

- **Shvah Na** (shvah *nah*), which opens a syllable
- **Shvah Nach** (shvah *nahch*), which closes a syllable
- **Shvah Merachef** (shvah mehr-rah-*chehf*), known as the *flying shvah,* which results from two **Shvah Nas** being next to each other in a word

The **Shvahs** don't make their own sound, but are essentially placeholders for the consonant above them. However, the **Shvah Nach** holds the sound for a little bit longer. You can tell a **Shvah Nach** because it usually comes in the middle or the end of a word. A **Shvah Na** is at the beginning of a word or syllable.

Doing it with a dagesh

The little dot that you see in the middle of letters is called a **Dagesh**. For most of the time, this dot doesn't change the pronunciation of the consonant except for three letters. I discuss this point later in this section.

Hebrew has two types of **D'geshim** (dgeh-*sheem;* the plural form of **Dagesh**):

- **Dagesh Kal** (dah-*gehsh kahl*): Appears at the beginning of all words and at the beginning of all syllables in the following letters: **Bet, Gimmel, Dalet, Kaf, Fey,** and **Tav.**

- **Dagesh Chazak** (dah-*gehsh* chah-*zahk*): Appears after the word *the,* which in Hebrew is a prefix consisting of the letter **Hey** and the vowel **Patach** underneath it.

Don't get too hung up on this distinction because all **D'geshim** look the same!

Sometimes in Hebrew, a letter acts like a "weak letter," such as a **Hey** or a **Nun,** disappears in the course of verb conjugation. (By "weak letter," I mean that sometimes it drops out during conjugation.) When a weak letter disappears, a **Dagesh Chazak** appears in the letter that comes after the dropped letter. Also, certain word patterns called **Mishkalim** (meesh-kah-*leem*), where all the words belong to a certain category of words (such as professions, colors, and physical challenges), have a **Dagesh** in one of the letters. For example, words that describe physical challenges, such as blindness and deafness, always take a **Dagesh Chazak** in the middle letter of the word.

Are you totally confused yet? So what difference does adding a Dagesh make? In the Sephardic pronunciation that Israelis and most Hebrew speakers today use, adding a **Dagesh** makes no difference in pronunciation. However, in a few cases, when a **Dagesh** is placed within a letter (always a consonant), it changes the way you pronounce that consonant. For example, when you add a **Dagesh** to the letter **Vet,** the *v* sound becomes a *b* sound, and you pronounce the letter like *bet.* When you pair a **Dagesh** with the letter **Chaf,** the *ch* sound becomes a *k* sound, so the sound of that letter becomes *kaf.* Finally, the letter **Fey** with a **Dagesh** is pronounced *peh.*

Reading and writing from right to left

Hebrew, like other ancient Semitic languages (such as Acadian, Samarian, Ugaritic, and Arabic), is written from right to left. Why? Is there a preponderance of lefties in the region? No!

Hebrew as the holy tongue — don't bite it

Judaism has always regarded Hebrew as a sacred language. Hebrew is often referred to as **Leshon HaKodesh** (le-*shohn* hah-*koh*-desh; the Holy Tongue), and even the Hebrew word for letter, **Ot** (oht) means *sign* or *wonder*. In fact, during the period of its revival as a spoken language, some people objected saying that Hebrew was simply too sacred for saying things like, *take out the garbage.*

Hebrew letters also all have numeric value. A particular form of Jewish numerolgy called **Gematria** (gee-*meht*-ree-yah) plays on the words' numeric values. For example, both the Hebrew word for *wine* (**Yayin;** *yah*-yeen) and

secret (**Sod;** sohd) have the same numerical value. The Talmud has a saying, "When the wine goes in, secrets come out!" Other Jewish sacred writings have claimed that the Hebrew letters are the manifestation of divine energy patterns, and even that the universe's DNA is composed of Hebrew letters.

A 13th-century Jewish mystic Rabbi Abraham Abulafia created a form of Jewish meditation similar to yoga based on the Hebraic forms. And a 16th-century mystic Rabbi Isaac Luria developed another form of meditation based on visualizing the different Hebrew letters.

Maybe you've read the Bible, in particular the part about when Moses comes down from the mountain with the Ten Commandments in hand. And if you haven't read the Bible, then perhaps you've seen the Mel Brooks film version in *History of the World.* When Moses came down from the mountain, what was he holding? A copy of e-mail from the Almighty? A scroll of papyrus? No! He was holding two stone tablets! You may ask: Well, how did the Ten Commandments get on the stone tablets, did Moses have a special pen or something?

Moses chiseled the words in the stone with a mallet. And if he was a rightie, he would have used his dominant hand — his right hand — to pound the mallet onto the stylus he held with his left. And because ancient Hebrew society — like all societies — favored righties, its language was written from right to left. The Phoencians and then the Greeks followed suit. Then for a period of time the Greeks wrote in *both* directions, switching when they got to the end of the tablet/page. That practice makes sense if you think about it; instead of pressing the shift key to go to all the way back, just keep going where you are in the backward direction! Then the Greeks decided left to right would be the standard, but Hebrew kept on writing right to left. Tradition!

If you want some practice reading, check out: http://ejemm.com/aleph/, an online course in Hebrew reading and Jewish values. It features fun interactive activities and audio so you can hear the sounds of the letters. The site can help you read Hebrew in no time!

Fun & Games

Write the sound that each of the following Hebrew characters makes:

בּ _____   ג _____   ל _____   שׁ _____

צ _____   ו _____   ר _____   כ _____

You can find the answers in Appendix C.

Chapter 2

The Nitty Gritty: Basic Hebrew Grammar

. . . .

In This Chapter

▶ Stringing words together into sentences

▶ Getting up close to nouns and adjectives

▶ Looking at personal pronouns

▶ Peeling back the layers of Hebrew verbs and adverbs

▶ Making room for prepositions

. . . .

*B*y birth, Hebrew is part of the Semitic family, along with Arabic, Aramaic, and some other Middle Eastern languages. To this day, the way words are formed, especially verbs, is very similar to other Semitic languages. Hebrew nouns and verbs are marked for gender (feminine or masculine — no neuter), just like their Semitic cousins.

The people who revived Hebrew as a modern language in the 19th and 20th centuries, however, spoke and thought mostly in Yiddish, Russian, German, and other European languages. Those languages became the "adoptive parents" of Hebrew today. You notice their influence most strongly in the pronunciation of Modern Hebrew and in the word order within sentences (syntax).

Making Sense of Hebrew Syntax

The *syntax* (the arrangement of words to make sentences), or **Tachbir** (tahch-*beer*), of a Hebrew sentence is quite different from English. In this section, I run you through the basics of word order — what syntax looks like in English, and how Hebrew is different. I also cover how to say *there is* and *there isn't,* because if you can use this simple sentence construction, you can say a lot — just plug in the noun of your choice, and you'll be speaking Hebrew!

Putting your sentences in order

When you read or hear Modern Hebrew sentences, you may think they're oddly constructed compared to English or any other European language. In English, so much depends on word order. In Hebrew, on the other hand, less depends on word order. For example, in Hebrew you could say either of the following:

- **Memshalah Chadashah Kamah** (mehm-shah-*lah* chah-dah-*shah* kah-mah; *Literally:* government new arises)

- **Kamah Memshalah Chadashah** (*kah*-mah mehm-shah-lah chah-dah-*shah*; *Literally:* arises government new)

Both of these phrases mean the same thing: A new government rises. The order of the words doesn't affect the meaning.

Look at another example in English. *Mollie kissed Fred* isn't the same as *Fred kissed Mollie* is it? Certainly not to Mollie — or for that matter, to Fred.

In Hebrew, sometimes a verb, especially one without an object, comes before its subject, not after it as in English. Under certain conditions, you can identify the *direct object* (person or thing acted upon, as opposed to person or thing doing the acting) because the word **Et** (eht) precedes the direct object. I know it was Mollie who did the kissing whether I say:

- **Mollie Nishkah Et Fred** (*moh*-lee neesh-*kah* eht fred; *Literally:* Mollie kissed Fred)

- **Mollie Et Fred Nishkah** (*moh*-lee eht fred neesh-*kah*; *Literally:* Mollie Fred kissed)

- **Et Fred Nishkah Mollie** (eht fred neesh-*kah moh*-lee; Fred [is] kissed [by] Mollie.)

These sentences, despite their different word order, all mean essentially the same thing: Mollie kissed Fred.

To say *there is* or *there are,* use the word **Yesh** (yehsh) before the noun you want to talk about. To say *there isn't* or *there aren't,* use the word **Ayn** (ayn) before the noun. For example:

- **Yesh Bananot.** (yehsh bah-*nah*-noht; There are bananas.)

- **Ayn Bananot.** (ayn bah-*nah*-noht; There aren't any bananas.)

Now, you can find any noun in this book, put a **Yesh** or an **Ayn** in front of it, and you'll be speaking Hebrew!

Questioning

When you make a question, you don't change the order of the words like in English. You can ask a question in a few different ways. The first is by simply taking a statement and putting a question mark in your voice (by raising your voice at the end of the sentence.) Thus, when asked with the proper intonation, this statement can be a question: **Yesh Chalav BaMakrer**?(yehsh chah-*lahv* bah-mahk-*rehr?;* there's milk in the refrigerator?)

Another way to turn this statement into a question is by adding the word **Nachon** (nah-*chohn;* correct) to the end of the statement. In grammar-speak, this word is called a *tag*. For example: **Yesh Chalav BaMakrer, Nachon?** (yehsh chah-*lahv* bah-mahk-*rehr,* nah-*chohn?;* there's milk in the refrigerator, correct?)

Yet another way to turn a statement into a question is to add the question word, **Ha'im** (hah-*eem*) in front of the sentence. For example: **Ha'im Yesh Chalav BaMakrer?** (hah-*eem* yehsh chah-*lahv* bah-mahk-*rehr;* is there milk in the refrigerator?) This last option is the most formal option, so you won't hear it often.

While Hebrew differs from English in that you don't need to flip the order in a statement in order to make it a question, the word-order flexibility of Hebrew allows the speaker to stress a particular part of the sentence by putting it at the beginning.

For example, if someone just said there are no strawberries in the fridge, you may ask: **Bananot Yesh?** (bah-*nah*-noht yehsh; *Literally:* bananas there are?; but are there bananas?) Or, you may also ask: **Bananot Ayn?** bah-*nah*-noht ehn?; *Literally:* bananas there aren't?; aren't there bananas?)

Recognizing Parts of Speech

In Hebrew, you can recognize the different parts of speech, such as nouns, verbs, and adjectives, by their distinct patterns. However, sometimes a word is *both* a verb and a noun, and adjectives and adverbs can take on many different forms — so I can't offer any easy clues for distinguishing the various parts of speech. You just need to memorize the vocabulary and then you'll know.

Naming nouns

In Hebrew, all nouns are either masculine or feminine. They're conjugated according to number (singular and plural). For example, the noun *book,* a masculine noun, can be conjugated two ways:

Sefer (*seh*-fehr; book)

S'farim (sfah-*reem;* books)

Look at this example of a feminine noun:

Mazleg (mahz-*lehg;* fork)

Mazlegot (mahz-leh-*goht;* forks)

When masculine nouns are conjugated in the plural, they usually have an *im* (eem) ending, and when feminine nouns are conjugated in the plural they usually have an *ot* (oht) ending.

Check out Table 2-1 for some common Hebrew nouns.

Table 2-1	Identifying Some Common Nouns	
Hebrew	*Pronunciation*	*Translation*
Bayit	*bah*-yeet	house
Derech	*deh*-rech	way, road
Ish	eesh	man
Ishah	ee-*shah*	woman
Kesef	*keh*-sehf	money
Mafte'ach	mahf-*teh*-ach	key
Magevet	mah-*geh*-veht	towel
Makrer	mahk-*rehr*	refrigerator
Mazgan	mahz-*gahn*	air conditioner
Mazleg	mahz-*lehg*	fork
Mechonit	meh-choh-*neet*	car
Mitbach	meet-*bahch*	kitchen
Mivreshet	meev-*reh*-sheht	brush
Ochel	*oh*-chehl	food
Sefer	*seh*-fehr	book
Shemesh	*sheh*-mehsh	sun

Directing your objects

In English, when we speak of a direct object, we mean a noun that is acted on by the verb. For example, in the sentence: "He ate a cookie," the word *cookie* is a direct object. In Hebrew, you say this sentence like this:

Hu Achal Ugiah (hoo ah-*chahl* oo-gee-*yah; Literally:* He ate cookie.)

Notice Hebrew doesn't have a word for *a* in this example. The *a* is simply implied.

You can always spot an indirect object in Hebrew because it's always preceded by a preposition. For example, if you want to say, "He gave a boy a cookie." The word *boy* is an indirect object. He is being *given* something, but he isn't directly acted upon. Another test for an indirect object: It can have *to* before it: "He gave a cookie *to* a boy." In Hebrew, you say that phrase this way: **Hu Natan L'Yeled Ugiah** (hoo nah-*tahn* luh-*yeh*-lehd oo-*gee*-yah; *Literally:* He gave to boy cookie.)

Defining definite objects

In Hebrew, you can tell a noun is being used as a definite object (*the* hat as opposed to *a* hat) because it has the prefix **Ha** (hah) attached to the word it modifies. For example, take the noun **Kovah** (*koh*-vah; hat): If you want to indicate that **Kovah** is a definite object, just add the **Ha** prefix: **HaKovah** (hah-*koh*-vah; the hat).

Getting help from the definite article

You can easily spot a definite object by the placement of a definite article **Ha** (hah; the) in front of it. If that definite object is also direct, **Et** (eht) also precedes it. For example, in the following sentence, understand that **Hu Rotzeh** means *he wants,* and then you can figure out the meaning of the entire sentence: **Hu Rotzeh Et HaKovah** (hoo roh-*tzeh* eht hah-*koh*-vah; He wants the hat). Notice the **Et** is in front of the **HaKovah**. (*Note:* **Et** is placed before a *definite* direct object only.) **Et** is kind of like a road sign that says: D.D.O.A: Definite Direct Object Ahead.

Unfortunately, Hebrew doesn't have indefinite articles (*a* or *an*). But Hebrew sentences certainly have indirect objects! Instead, you can tell that an object is nonspecific (*a hat* as opposed to *the hat*) by the omission of **Et** or any other preposition. So if you want to say *he wants a hat* in Hebrew, the sentence looks like this: **Hu Rotzeh Kovah** (hoo roh-*tzeh koh*-vah).

Perfecting your pronouns

When you don't want to name nouns, you can always call in their pinch-hitters, the pronouns (words that stand for the nouns).

Clarifying this and that

Hebrew has a set of pronouns for "this" or "that" that are specialized according to masculine singular, feminine singular, and one lone plural for both masculine and feminine. For example:

Zeh (zeh; this [is]) (MS)

Zot (zoht; this [is]) (FS)

Eleh (ay-*leh;* these [are]) (MP/FP)

These words can function as the subject of an "is" sentence or as adjectives:

- ✔ **Zeh Mafte'ach:** This is a key.
- ✔ **HaMafte'ach HaZeh:** this key

Getting personal

Personal pronouns are nouns that apply to particular people — or, um, *persons*. In English, the personal pronouns are: I, you, he, she, we, and they. In Hebrew, there are four forms for the personal pronoun "you": masculine singular (MS), feminine singular (FS), masculine plural (MP), and feminine plural (FP). The personal pronoun "they," has two forms: masculine and feminine (MP and FP). Table 2-2 shows *subjective case* (when the pronoun serves as the subject of the sentence) personal pronouns in Hebrew.

Table 2-2	Personal Pronouns Used as Subjects	
Hebrew	*Pronunciation*	*Translation*
Ani (MS/FS)	ah-*nee*	I
Atah (MS)	ah-*tah*	you
At (FS)	aht	you
Hu	hoo	he
He	hee	she
Anachnu (MP/FP)	ah-*nahch*-noo	we
Atem (MP)	ah-*tehm*	you
Aten (FP)	ah-*tehn*	you
Hem (MP)	hehm	they
Hen (FP)	hehn	they

Hebrew also has what English calls *objective case pronouns* when a personal pronoun is used as the direct object of a verb (*she saw me*). I'm talking about the English words *me, you, him, her, us,* and *them*. Like other Hebrew pronouns, there are four forms of "you" in the objective case: masculine singular (MS), feminine singular (FS), masculine plural (MP), and feminine plural (FP). Table 2-3 lists the objective case pronouns.

Table 2-3	Personal Pronouns Used as Objects	
Hebrew	*Pronunciation*	*Translation*
Oti (MS/FS)	oh-*tee*	me
Otcha (MS)	oht-*cha*	you
Otach (FS)	oh-*tach*	you
Oto	oh-*toh*	him
Otah	oh-*tah*	her
Otanu (MP/FP)	oh-*tah*-noo	us
Etchem (MP)	eht-*chem*	you
Etchen (FP)	eht-*chen*	you
Otam (MP)	oh-*tahm*	them
Otan (FP)	oh-*tahn*	them

Showing possession

Hebrew, like English, has stand-alone possessive pronouns, such as *mine, yours, his, ours,* and *theirs*. However, you'll notice a few differences. First, the stand-alone possessive pronoun comes after the noun and not before like in English. In addition, if an object has possession, then it has to be a definite object, so you must add the prefix **Ha** (hah; the) to the front of the object. For example, in Hebrew you say **HaKovah Sheli** (hah-*koh*-vah sheh-*lee; Literally:* the hat mine).

In addition, Hebrew differentiates between the singular and plural "your" in both the masculine and feminine form. Check out Table 2-4 to see the differences.

Table 2-4	Stand-Alone Possessive Pronouns	
Hebrew	*Pronunciation*	*Translation*
Sheli	sheh-*lee*	my, mine
Shelcha (MS)	shel-*cha*	your, yours
Shelach (FS)	sheh-*lach*	your, yours
Sheloh	sheh-*loh*	his
Shelah	sheh-*lah*	her, hers
Shelanu	she-*lah*-noo	ours
Shelachem (MP)	sheh-lah-*chem*	your, yours
Shelachen (FP)	sheh-lah-*chen*	your, yours
Shelahem (MP)	sheh-lah-*hem*	their, theirs
Shelahen (FP)	sheh-lah-*hen*	their, theirs

Hebrew doesn't have different words for *my* and *mine.* Both concepts are expressed in the Hebrew word **Sheli** (sheh-*lee;* my, mine). Also, *your* and *yours* are expressed in the same word.

In English, you sometimes pair a pronoun with another noun to show possession. For example, *my teacher, your hat, his paper,* and so on. In Hebrew, you can show that a noun belongs to someone by attaching a suffix to the end of the noun. The suffix changes according to the personal pronoun it represents. However, this is used in spoken Hebrew far less than in classical sources or even formal written Hebrew today. Modern Hebrew speakers today use the suffix with a very limited range of nouns — terms for close relatives, such as **Achot** (ah-*chot;* sister) or **Ben** (behn; son) — and even then very sparingly.

Applying adjectives

In Hebrew, the noun comes first and then the adjective, which is the opposite of English. So, for example, you say **Yaldah Tovah** (yahl-*dah* toh-*vah;* girl good) — meaning *good girl.* You also need to know that adjectives need to match the nouns they modify both in gender and in number. Table 2-5 lists some common adjectives. For more on number and gender, see the section "Understanding Gender and Number," later in this chapter.

Table 2-5	Exploring Some Common Adjectives	
Hebrew	*Pronunciation*	*Translation*
Tov (MS)	tohv	good
Tovah (FS)	toh-*vah*	good
Tovim (MP)	toh-*veem*	good
Tovot (FP)	toh-*voht*	good
Rah (MS)	rah	bad
Ra'ah (FS)	rah-*ah*	bad
Ra'im (MP)	rah-*eem*	bad
Ra'ot (FP)	rah-*oht*	bad
Gadol (MS)	gah-*dohl*	big
G'dolah (FS)	gdoh-*lah*	big
G'dolim (MP)	gdoh-*leem*	big
G'dolot (FP)	gdoh*loht*	big
Katan (MS)	kah-*tahn*	small
K'tanah (FS)	ktah-*nah*	small
K'tanim (MP)	ktah-*neem*	small
K'tanot (FP)	ktah-*noht*	small
Mahir (MS)	mah-*heer*	quick
M'hirah (FS)	meh-hee-*rah*	quick
M'hirim (MP)	meh-hee-*reem*	quick
M'hirot (FP)	meh-hee-*roht*	quick
Iti (MS)	ee-*tee*	slow
Itit (FS)	ee-*teet*	slow
Itiyim (MP)	ee- tee-*yeem*	slow
Itiyot (FP)	ee-tee-*yoht*	slow

In addition, use this adjective pattern: Add an **i** (ee) ending to change a noun into an adjective. For example: **Aviv** (ah-*veev*) is spring (the season), **Avivi** (ah-vee-*vee*) is spring-like; **Yaldut** (yahl-*doot*) is childhood, **Yalduti** (yahl-doo-*tee*) is juvenile. Cool, huh?

Pinpointing Hebrew verbs

The Hebrew verb is an amazing animal! Verbs are conjugated in the present tense according to gender (male and female) and number (singular and plural). In the future and past tenses, verbs have gender, number, and person (first, second, or third). In the imperative (command form), you only have three forms to choose from: masculine singular (MS), feminine singular (FS), and plural (P). When you conjugate a verb, it must match gender and number of the subject. See Appendix A for examples.

Hebrew doesn't have a word for *is* or *are*.

Putting verbs through their tenses

Hebrew has five verb tenses: the infinitive tense (*to* + the verb), the past tense, the present tense, the future tense, and the imperative — command form (as in *shut the door*). In this section, I conjugate **Lichtov** (leech-*tohv;* to write) to show the conjugations because **Lichtov** is a regular verb with no exceptions.

Living in the present

In the present tense, Hebrew verbs are conjugated in four ways: masculine singular, feminine singular, masculine plural, and feminine plural. For example:

Kotev (koh-*tehv;* write) (MS)

Kotevet (koh-*teh*-veht; write) (FS)

Kotvim (koht-*veem;* writes) (MP)

Kotvot (koht-*voht;* writes) (FP)

Puttin' it in the past

In the past tense, Hebrew verbs are conjugated according to number, gender, and person. You can either say the personal pronoun (I, you, he, she, we, you, they), as in **Ani Katavti** (ah-*nee* kah-*tahv*-tee; I wrote), or drop it, in which case the subject is implied, **Katavti** (kah-*tahv*-tee; [I] wrote).

Katavti (kah-*tahv*-tee; [I] wrote)

Katavta (kah-*tahv*-ta; [you] wrote) (MS)

Katavt (kah-*tahvt;* [you] wrote) (FS)

Katav (kah-*tahv;* [he] wrote)

Katvah (kaht-*vah;* [she] wrote)

Katavnu (kah-*tahv*-noo; [we] wrote) (MP/FP)

Ktavtem (ktahv-*tehm;* [you] wrote) (MP)

Ktavten (ktahv-*tehn;* [you] wrote) (FP)

Katvu (kaht-*voo;* [they] wrote) (MP/FP)

Looking to the future

Like the past tense, the future tense also has number, gender, and person, and you can either include the personal pronoun: **Ani Echtov**; ah-*nee* ehch-*tohv;* (I will write) or drop it: **Echtov** ehch-*tohv;* ([I] will write) because it's implied.

Echtov (ech-*tohv;* [I] will write)

Tichtov (teech-*tohv;* [you] will write) (MS)

Ticht'vi (teech-tuh-*vee;* [you] will write) (FS)

Yichtov (yeech-*tohv;* [he] will write)

Tichtov (teech-*tohv;* [she] will write)

Nichtov (neech-*tohv;* [we] will write)

Ticht'vu (teech-tuh-*voo;* [you] will write) (MP/FP)

Yicht'vu (yeech-tuh-*voo;* [they] will write) (MP/FP)

Command performance

To make a command (the imperative mood), you can choose from three forms: *you* (MS), *you* (FS), and *you* (MP/FP). Believe it or not, many Modern Hebrew speakers consider this tense quite rude — as if something an army commander or strict teacher would say. Generally avoid the command tense. Use the future tense instead, which is perceived to be more polite. But if you really want to, you can conjugate the command form like this:

K'tov (kuh-*tohv;* [you] Write!) (MS)

Kitvi (keet-*vee;* [you] Write!) (FS)

Kitvu (keet-*voo;* [you] Write!) (MP/FP)

Looking at some common verbs

The beauty of the Hebrew verb is both its versatility and its simplicity. In Table 2-6, I include some common Hebrew verbs listed in their present tense, masculine singular form.

Table 2-6	Some Common Present-Tense Verbs	
Hebrew	*Pronunciation*	*Translation*
Holech	hoh-*lehch*	goes; walks
Koreh	koh-*reh*	reads

(continued)

Table 2-6 *(continued)*

Hebrew	Pronunciation	Translation
Kotev	koh-*tehv*	writes
Machlit	mahch-*leet*	decides
Madlik	mahd-*leek*	lights
Margish	mahr-*geesh*	feels
M'daber	meh-dah-*behr*	speaks
Mitlabesh	meet-lah-*behsh*	gets dressed
Mitztahref	meetz-tah-*rehf*	joins in
Nichnas	neech-*nahs*	enters
Nose'ah	noh-*seh*-ah	travels
Yoshev	yoh-*shehv*	sits

Detecting adverbs

Like English, most Hebrew adverbs are similar to adjectives — just with different endings. When you use an adjective as an adverb, you don't conjugate it, it just stays in the masculine singular form.

>   **Hu Kotev Yafeh** (hoo koh-*tehv* yah-*feh;* He writes nicely.)

>   **He Kotevet Yefeh** (hee koh-*teh*-veht yah-*feh;* She writes nicely.)

Note that although the pronoun and the verb conjugation changes — in this case from masculine singular to feminine singular — the adverb remains unchanged.

You can also make an adverb by adding the prefix **B'** (buh; in or with) to a noun. For example, **Simcha** (seem-*chah;* happiness) becomes **B'Simcha** (buh-seem-*chah;* gladly).

A third way to make an adverb is to take an adjective and add the suffix **ut** (oot) to the end of it to make a noun. Then you add the prefix **B'** (buh; in or with) in front of the noun to make the adverb. For example: **Adin** (ah-*deen;* gentle) becomes **Adinut** (ah-dee-*noot;* gentleness), and with a prefix **B'** it becomes **B'Adinut** (buh-ah-dee-*noot;* gently).

A fourth way to make an adverb is to add the word **B'Ofen** (buh-*oh*-fehn; in the way of) in front of an adjective. For example: **Otomati** (oh-toh-*mah*-tee;

automatic) becomes **B'Ofen Otomati** (buh-*oh*-fehn oh-toh-*mah*-tee; automatically).

Table 2-7 lists some common adverbs.

Table 2-7	Common Adverbs	
Hebrew	*Pronunciation*	*Translation*
B'Ofen Sadir	buh-*oh*-fehn sah-*deer*	regularly
B'Seder	buh-*seh*-dehr	okay
B'Simcha	buh-sim-*chah*	gladly
B'Sodiyut	buh-soh-dee-*yoot*	secretly
Bimhirut	bim-hee-*root*	quickly, speedily
Bivracha	beev-rah-*chah*	blessedly
Davka	*dahv*-kah	spitefully
Heitev	hei-*tehv*	well
L'at	luh-*aht*	slowly
Maher	mah-*hehr*	quickly
Me'uchar	meh-oo-*char*	late
Mukdam	mook-*dahm*	early
Yafeh	yah-*feh*	nicely

Spotting prepositions

Prepositions are words that show relations between words (*in*, *by*, and *with*, to name a few common English prepositions). In Hebrew, prepositions sometimes stand alone, and sometimes they're attached to another word as a prefix. Table 2-8 breaks them down for you.

Table 2-8	Hebrew Prepositions		
Hebrew Preposition	*Pronunciation*	*Translation*	*Presentation*
Al	ahl	on	stands alone
B'	buh	with/in	prefix

(continued)

Table 2-8 *(continued)*

Hebrew Preposition	Pronunciation	Translation	Presentation
Ehl	ehl	to	stands alone
Im	eem	with	stands alone
L'	luh	to	prefix
Min	meen	from	stands alone
Mi- or Meh-	mee *or* meh	from	prefix

In English, you combine prepositions with nouns to make *prepositional phrases,* such as *in the box, by the river,* or *with a friend.* In Hebrew, if you want to add the word *the* — to form a prepositional phrase — you have to change the vowel sound of the preposition: The *uh* vowel sound becomes an *ah* sound.

So, if a definite direct object is preceded by a preposition, the preposition will include the definite article. For example, "He helped a girl" is: **Hu Azar L'Yaldah** (hoo ah-*zahr* luh-yahl-*dah; Literally:* he helped to girl). The preposition in this case is **L'**. But if you want to say: "He helped *the* girl," you say **Hu Azar La'Yaldah** (hoo ah-*zahr* lah-yahl-*dah; Literally:* he helped to the girl). The preposition **L'** is combined with the definite article in this case and becomes **La** (lah; to the).

Understanding Gender and Number

In Hebrew, all nouns, adjectives and verbs have *gender;* they are classified as either masculine or feminine. Hebrew doesn't have anything gender-neutral. In addition, all nouns, adjectives, and verbs have *number;* they are classified as either singular or plural.

Nouns are classified as either masculine or feminine. Their classification as "masculine" or "feminine" doesn't have anything to do with the masculine or feminine nature of the objects. The classification is somewhat random. You can spot a feminine noun usually by its ending. A feminine noun often has an ending of *ah* (ah) or *it* (eet). However, you can find exceptions to this rule. A good Hebrew-English dictionary classifies masculine nouns with a Hebrew letter **Zayin** (*zah*-yeen) for **Zachar** (zah-*chahr;* masculine) and with a Hebrew letter **Nun** (noon) for **Nekevah** (nuh-keh-*vah;* feminine). Both the masculine and the feminine forms of the nouns have plural forms.

In Hebrew, adjectives come in four forms: masculine singular, feminine singular, masculine plural, and feminine plural. Look back to the section "Applying adjectives" where I discuss adjectives in greater detail.

Nouns and adjectives have to match each other in terms of both gender and number. But, when you have a group of people or things that are both masculine and feminine, you use the adjective's masculine plural form to describe the group. Thus, the masculine plural is for male-only groups and for male-female groups. The feminine plural is for female-only groups — only.

Fun & Games

Take the following statements and turn them into questions:

  1. Statement: **Hu Rotzeh Et Mechonit.**

     He wants the car.

     Question: _____

     Does he want the car?

  2. Statement: **Yesh Magevet.**

     There is a towel.

     Question: _____

     Is there a towel?

Chapter 3

Shalom, Shalom!
Meeting and Greeting

. . . .

In This Chapter

▶ Saying hello in Hebrew

▶ Calling out your name

▶ Introducing the star of the show — you

▶ Chatting with just about everyone

▶ Asking questions: The who, what, where, when, and why

. . . .

*S*halom! If you know this word, which literally means *peace and welfare,* you're ahead of the game because, in Hebrew, you use this word for both hellos and goodbyes, as well as for inquiries about someone's welfare. The many uses of **Shalom** (sha-*lom*) make sense because peace is a central concept in Judaism and an important part of Jewish and Israeli culture. References and hopes for peace fill Jewish prayers, and many popular Israeli songs also express this sentiment.

You can use **Shalom** to say hello, to say goodbye, and to ask **Mah Shlomcha?** (mah shlohm-*chah*), which literally means *How's your peace?* but really asks *How are you?* Hebrew features tons of ways to meet and greet people, and in this chapter, I introduce you to several.

Greeting and Saying Goodbye

Hebrew offers you many choices of ways to say *hello* and *goodbye.* Here are a few things to say in greeting:

✔ **Shalom.** (shah-*lohm;* Hello; peace.)

✔ **Mah Ha'Inyanim?** (mah hah-in-yah-*neem;* How are things?)

✔ **Mah Nishmah?** (mah neesh-*mah;* What's up?)

✔ **Mah Shlomcha?** (mah shlohm-*chah;* How are you? *Literally:* How is your welfare?) (MS)

✔ **Mah Shlomech?** (mah shloh-*mehch;* How are you? *Literally:* How is your welfare?) (FS)

✔ **Mah Shlom'chem?** (mah shlohm-*chehm;* How are you?) (MP/FP)

Ah, but parting is such sweet sorrow. When you have to hit the road, use one of these phrases to say goodbye:

✔ **Shalom.** (shah-*lohm;* Peace.)

✔ **Kol Tuv.** (*kohl* toov; Be well.)

✔ **L'hitraot.** (leh-heet-rah-*oht;* See you soon.)

Greeting all day long

In Hebrew, as in every other language, the time of day you greet a person often determines what you say. But Hebrew throws a bit of a twist into the standard mix. It also contains particular greetings that depend on whether you greet someone before or after the *Jewish Sabbath.* The Sabbath starts when the sun *begins to set* on Friday night, and it ends about 25 hours later at sundown on Saturday night when the sun *has completely set.*

In the morning, you can say **Boker Tov** (*boh*-kehr tohv; good morning). If someone greets you in this manner, you can say **Boker Tov** right back to him or her, or you can say **Boker Or** (*boh*-kehr ohr; morning light). In the afternoon, you can say **Tzohora'im Tovim** (tzoh-hoh-*rye*-eem toh-*veem;* good afternoon). In response, you can simply repeat the same words back.

The pattern of simply repeating the greeting as a reply holds true for all the time-sensitive greetings. The morning greeting is the only exception because you can reply with either **Boker Tov** or **Boker Or.**

So, in the evening, you can say **Erev Tov** (*eh*-rehv tohv; good evening) whether you're greeting someone or responding to another person's salutation. At night, you can say **Lilah Tov** (*lye*-lah tohv; good night). And, if someone is headed off to bed, you can wish him or her **Chalomot Paz** (cha-loh-*moht* pahz; golden dreams)!

Got that? Good. Now I want to outline the Sabbath-related greetings. All day Friday and during the Sabbath, greeting people with the words that wish them a peaceful Sabbath is customary: **Shabbat Shalom** (shah-*baht* shah-*lohm;* peaceful Sabbath). When the sun sets on Saturday night (and you can see three stars in the sky), the Sabbath is over. On Saturday nights and even on Sundays, it's customary to greet people with a cheery **Shavu'a Tov** (shah-*voo*-ah tohv), wishing them a *good week.*

The Book of Genesis describes each day as beginning in the evening: "There was evening; there was morning; a first day." Therefore, days and holidays on the Jewish calendar begin in the evening with the setting sun and last until the sun is completely set 25 hours later. The duration is 25 hours to err on the side of safety. It should be exactly 24 hours, but rabbis added the extra hour so that we'll never start the Sabbath too late or end the Sabbath too early.

Replying to a greeting

Knowing how to say hello and goodbye is a great start. But, if you want to get past the initial hello, you need a few more phrases in your back pocket (like what to say when someone asks how you're doing). Who knows? These phrases could be the start of a beautiful friendship. Responses to greetings include:

- **Shlomi Tov.** (sh-loh-*mee* tohv; My welfare is good.)
- **Etzli B'seder Gamur.** (ehtz-*lee* buh-*seh*-dehr gah-*moohr*; With me, things are completely okay.)
- **B'seder.** (beh-*seh*-dehr; Okay.)
- **Mamash Tov.** (mah-*mahsh* tohv; Really good.)
- **Lo Kol-Kach Tov.** (loh kohl-*kahch* tohv; Not so good.)

Talkin' the Talk

Michal and Kobi are old friends. They've just run into each other downtown, and they're both busy with errands on Friday before **Shabbat** starts. They quickly say hello and then dash off to complete their shopping. (Track 2)

Kobi: **Michal! Shalom! Mah Shlomech?**
mee-*chahl!* shah-*lohm!* mah sh-loh-*mehch?*
Michal! Hello! How are you?

Michal: **Shalom Kobi! Mah Ha'Inyanim?**
shah-*lohm koh*-bee! mah hah-in-yah-*neem?*
Hello, Kobi! How are things?

Kobi: **Ani Mamash Beseder.**
ah-*nee* mah-*mahsh* beh-*seh*-dehr.
I am very well.

Michal: **Aizeh Yofi. Az, Ani Chayevet LaRutz.**
ay-*zeh yoh*-fee. ahz, ah-*nee* chah-*yeh*-veht lah-*rootz.*
Terrific. Well, I've got to run.

Kobi: **Gam Ani. Le'hitraot!**
gahm ah-*nee*. leh-heet-rah-*oht!*
Me too. See you soon!

Michal: **Shabbat Shalom. Kol Tuv.**
sha-*baht* shah-*lohm. kohl*-toov.
A peaceful Sabbath. All the best.

Kobi: **Shabbat Shalom.**
sha-*baht* shah-*lohm.*
A peaceful Sabbath.

Words to Know

B'Seder	buh-<u>seh</u>-der	okay
Kacha-Kacha	<u>kah</u>-chah <u>kah</u>-chah	so-so
Mamash	mah-<u>mahsh</u>	quite, really
Rah	rah	bad
Tov	tohv	good

Putting a name to a face

One surefire way to jumpstart conversations is to ask people their names. Use these phrases to ask someone's name:

- **Mah Shmech?** (mah sh-*mehch;* What's your name?) (FS)

  Mah Shim'cha? (mah sheem-*chah;* What's your name?) (MS)

- **Eich Kor'im Lach?** (ehch kohr-*eem* lahch; What do they call you?) (FS)

  Eich Kor'im L'cha? (ehch kohr-*eem* leh-*chah;* What do they call you?) (MS)

The response:

- **Sh'mi . . .** (sh-*mee;* My name is . . .)

- **HaShem Sheli . . .** (hah-*shehm* sheh-*lee;* My name is . . .)

- **Kor'im Li . . .** (kohr-*eem* lee; They call me . . .)

You may have noticed that there are two different ways of saying *My name is*. The first way, **Sh'mi,** is what we call in Hebrew an *inflection* where two words (in this case *name* and *my*) are put together in one word. Kind of like when *do* and *not* become one word, *don't*. The second way of saying *My name is,* **HaShem Sheli,** literally means *the name mine*. In Hebrew, unlike English, possessive pronouns come *after* the noun.

Talkin' the Talk

Gadi and Tzipi have just met each other at a party thrown by some friends. As they stand near the munchies, they chat briefly and get acquainted. (Track 3)

Gadi: **Shalom.**
shah-*lohm.*
Hello.

Tzipi: **Shalom.**
shah-*lohm.*
Hello.

Gadi: **Eich Kor'im Lach?**
ehch kohr-*eem* lahch?
What do they call you?

Tzipi: **Kor'im Li Tzipi.**
kohr-*eem* lee tzee-pee.
They call me Tzipi.

Gadi: **Zeh Shem Yafeh.**
shehm yah-*feh.*
A nice name.

Tzipi: **Todah. Mah Shim'cha?**
toh-*dah.* mah sheem-*chah?*
Thanks. What's your name?

Gadi: **Sh'mi Gadi.**
sh-*mee gah*-dee.
My name is Gadi.

Gadi: **Mamash Nekhmad Le'hakir Otach.**
mah-*mahsh* nech-*mahd* leh-hah-*keer* oh-*tahch.*
It's a real pleasure meeting you.

Tzipi:	**Gam Lee.**
	gahm lee.
	For me as well.

Making Grand Introductions

One of the best ways to meet people socially or professionally is to have someone else introduce you. When you begin to make friends, bringing your friends together to meet each other is also nice. And, if you think that two people *really* need to meet because you want to make a **Shiduch** (shee-*dooch;* match), you *really* want to know what you're doing.

In Judaism, introducing people to their **Basherte** (bah-*shehrt;* intended one) is considered a great act of **Chesed** (*cheh*-sehd; kindness). In fact, one Jewish adage teaches that a person who makes three such matches is assured a place in heaven.

Introducing yourself

At times, you may be at a party, a bus station, or even a cafe when you see someone you'd like to get to know. But what do you do if no one is around to introduce the two of you? Well, don't be shy! Just take the bull by the horns and introduce yourself. All you need are the words, and here they are:

- ✔ **Shalom. Ani . . .** (shah-*lohm* ah-*nee;* Hello. I am . . .)

- ✔ **Efshar L'hakir Ot'cha?** (ehf-*shahr* leh-hah-*keer* oht-*chah;* Is it possible to meet you?) (MS)

    Efshar L'hakir Otach? (ehf-*shahr* leh-hah-*keer* oh-*tach;* Is it possible to meet you?) (FS)

- ✔ **Slicha. Atah Me'od Mukar Li.** (slee-*chah.* ah-*tah* meh-*ohd* moo-*kahr* lee; Excuse me. You look very familiar.) (MS)

    Slicha. At Me'od Mukeret Li. (slee-*chah.* aht meh-*ohd* moo-*keh*-reht lee; Excuse me. You look very familiar.) (FS)

Introducing others

Introducing people and getting introduced is always fun. The formal way of introducing two people in Hebrew is **Na L'ha'kir Et . . .** (nah leh-hah-*keer* eht; Please be acquainted with . . .). The customary response is **Na'im Me'od** (nah-*eem* meh-*ohd;* very pleasant).

How my friend's grandmother invented a Hebrew word

Hebrew is a very gendered language. Saying something completely gender neutral is almost impossible. Take, for example, the word *rabbi*, the Jewish clergy. In English you just call a rabbi "Rabbi." Whether the person is a man or a woman, the title remains the same.

When my friend got married, the rabbi who officiated at her wedding was a woman. My friend's Israeli grandmother wanted to address this "woman of the cloth" in Hebrew. The Hebrew word for a *male* rabbi is **Rav** (rahv), but she realized that she didn't know the proper Hebrew word for a *female* rabbi. Upon returning to Israel,

she did some research and found out that an official word for a woman rabbi didn't exist.

So my friend's clever grandmother took it upon herself to invent a Hebrew word for a woman rabbi. She came up with **Rabah** (rah-*bah*) as one possible way to feminize the word. She wrote to **Ha'Akademiah La'Lashon Ha'Ivrit** (hah-ah-kah-*dehm*-yah la-lah-*shohn* hah-eev-*reet;* the Hebrew Language Academy) and made her suggestion. And wouldn't you know it? The academy agreed with her suggestion and made **Rabah** the official Hebrew word for a woman rabbi. Hebrew history in the making.

Israeli society is a very informal society, so if you visit Israel, you find yourself on a first-name basis with people right away. You only use formal titles like Mr. or Mrs. in the most formal situations, like if you're attending a party at the **Beit HaNasi** (bayt hah-nah-*see;* president's house).

Words to Know

Efshar . . .	ehf-<u>shahr</u>	Is it possible . . .
L'hakir	leh-hah-<u>keer</u>	to meet, to become acquainted with
Na	nah	please
Na'im Me'od	nah-<u>eem</u> meh-<u>ohd</u>	very nice, very pleasant
Slicha	slee-<u>chah</u>	excuse me

Hebrew is a biblical language, so certain words have, well, biblical connotations. In English, saying that you know someone is perfectly acceptable, and the meaning is quite innocent. But, if you say that you know someone in Hebrew, people will understand the statement to mean that you *know* the person *biblically.* (And perhaps you do, but that subject isn't usually the topic of polite conversation in Hebrew or English.) So when you're speaking Hebrew, just be sure to say that you're *acquainted with* someone — **Ani Makir/Makirah Oto/Otah** (ah-nee mah-*keer*/mah-kee-*rah* oh-*toh*/oh-*tah;* I am acquainted with him/her).

Talkin' the Talk

Ya'ara and Natan are both mutual friends of Shulamit. They are all at a party on **Motze'ei Shabbat** (moh-tze-*ay*-shah-*baht;* Saturday night). As everyone is mingling together, Shulamit decides to introduce her two friends to each other. (Track 4)

Shulamit: **Bo Natan. Ani Rotzah L'hakir L'cha Mishehi.**
boh nah-*tan.* ah-nee roh-*tzah* leh-hah-*keer* leh-*chah* mee-sheh-hee.
Come, Natan. I want to introduce to you somebody.

Natan: **Tov, Todah.**
tohv, toh-*dah.*
Okay, thank you.

Shulamit: **Bo'i Ya'arah. Yesh Li Mishehu Lehakirir Lach.**
boh-ee ya-ah-*rah.* yehsh lee *mee*-sheh-hoo leh-hah-*keer* lahch.
I have someone to introduce to you.

Ya'ara: **Yofi. Ani Ba'ah.**
yoh-fee. ah-*nee bah*-ah.
Fine. I am coming.

Shulamit: **Natan, Na L'hakir Et Ya'ara.**
nah-*tan,* nah leh-ha-*keer* eht yah-ah-*rah.*
Natan, please get to know Ya'ara.

Natan: **Na'im Me'od.**
nah-*eem* meh-*ohd.*
Very pleasant.

Shulamit: **Ya'ara, Zeh Natan.**
yah-ah-*rah,* zeh nah-*tan.*
Ya'ara, this is Natan.

Ya'ara:	**Na'im L'hakir Otcha.**
	nah-*eem* leh-hah-*keer* oht-*chah.*
	Nice to meet you.
Natan:	**Ha'Oneg Kulo Sheli.**
	hah *oh*-nehg koo-*loh* sheh-*lee.*
	It's my pleasure.

Getting Better Acquainted

After you meet someone and get past the introductions, you may want to get to know him or her better. But knowing where to start can be difficult because you're starting with a blank slate. In this section, I fill you in on some of the basics. I cover finding out if someone speaks English (which you may want to avoid doing so you can *really* practice speaking Hebrew), asking where someone is from, and telling your new acquaintance how you feel. You'll be mixing and mingling and meeting and greeting in no time.

Finding out who speaks English

Sometimes inquiring minds just gotta know, and you may want to know if someone speaks English. Practicing your Hebrew is necessary, but at times, you may want to express something complicated or satisfy a need to hear some of your **S'fat Em** (s-*faht* ehm; mother tongue).

The following sentences can get you started:

- ✔ **Ha'im Atah Medaber Anglit?** (hah-*eem* ah-*tah* meh-dah-*behr* ahn-*gleet;* Do you speak English?) (MS)

  Ha'im At Medaberet Anglit? (ha-*eem* aht meh-dah-*beh*-reht ahn-*gleet;* Do you speak English?) (FS)

- ✔ **Eizoh Safah Atah Medaber?** (ay-*zoh* sah-*fah* ah-*tah* meh-dah-*behr;* What language do you speak?) (MS)

  Eizoh Safah At Medaberet? (ay-*zoh* sah-*fah* aht meh-dah-*beh*-reht; What language do you speak?) (FS)

- ✔ **Ani Lo Medaber Ivrit.** (ah-*nee* loh meh-dah-*behr* eev-*reet;* I don't speak Hebrew.) (MS)

  Ani Lo Medaberet Ivrit. (ah-*nee* loh meh-dah-*beh*-reht eev-*reet;* I don't speak Hebrew.) (FS)

✔ **Ani Meveen Ktzat Ivrit.** (ah-*nee* meh-*veen* k-*tzaht* eev-*reet;* I understand a little Hebrew.) (MS)

Ani Meveenah Ktzat Ivrit. (ah-*nee* meh-vee-*nah,* k-*tzaht* eev-*reet;* I understand a little Hebrew.) (FS)

The following list shows you the Hebrew words for some commonly spoken languages:

✔ **Aravit** (ah-rah-*veet;* Arabic)

✔ **Russit** (roo-*seet;* Russian)

✔ **Sepharadit** (sfah-rah-*deet;* Spanish)

✔ **Tzarfatit** (tzar-fah-*teet;* French)

✔ **Yevanit** (yeh-vah-*neet;* Greek)

Words to Know

Anglit	ahn-<u>gleet</u>	English
Ivrit	eev-<u>reet</u>	Hebrew
Ktzat	k-<u>tzaht</u>	a little
Medaber (MS)	meh-dah-<u>behr</u>	speak
Medaberet (FS)	meh-dah-<u>beh</u>-reht	speak
Meveen (MS)	meh-<u>veen</u>	understand
Meveenah (FS)	meh-vee-<u>nah</u>	understand
Safah	sah-<u>fah</u>	language

Talking about where you come from

Whenever I meet someone, one of the first things I want to know is where they're from. I want to know their nationality. I want to know whether they grew up in a big city or a little town. I want to know if they live in the country or a suburb. It's a great starting point for a longer conversation.

To ask people where they're from in Hebrew, you say

Me'a'yin Atah? (meh-*ah*-yeen ah-*tah;* Where are you from?) (MS)

Me'a'yin Aht? (meh-*ah*-yeen aht; Where are you from?) (FS)

But, if you want to know where in Israel a person is from, the customary questions are

Me'ayin Atah BaAretz? (meh-*ah*-yeen ah-*tah* bah-*ah*-rehtz; Where are you from in the land?) (MS)

Me'ayin At BaAretz? meh-*ah*-yeen aht bah *ah*-rehtz; Where are you from in the land?) (FS)

To respond to these questions, you can just say **Ani Me . . .** (ah-*nee* meh; I am from . . .) and fill in the blank with some of the following phrases:

- **Africa** (*ahf*-ree-kah; Africa)
- **Artzot HaBrit** (ahr-*tzoht* hah-*breet;* the United States)
- **Asia** (*ahs*-yah; Asia)
- **Europa** (ay-*roh*-pah; Europe)
- **Drom Amerika** (d*rohm* ah-*meh*-ree-kah; South America)
- **Chalal** (chah-*lahl;* outerspace)

Or perhaps you just want to tell people that you live in the **Ha'Ir** (hah-*eer;* city) or a **Parvar** (pahr-*vahr;* suburb).

When you're in Israel, and people suspect you may not be a native, they may ask you if you come from **Chutz La'Aretz** (chootz-lah-*ah*-rehtz; Literally: outside of the land), which means abroad or anywhere but Israel. People also use the acronym of this word, **Chul** (chool).

Words to Know

Chutz La'Aretz	chootz lah-<u>ah</u>-rehtz	abroad
Ir	eer	city
Karov	kah-<u>rohv</u>	close
Me'a'yin	meh-<u>ah</u>-yeen	from where
Parvar	pahr-<u>vahr</u>	suburb

Chatting about how you feel

When all else fails in your attempt to strike up a conversation (and even if it doesn't), talking about how you feel and asking how another person feels can occupy a conversation for hours. To ask people how they feel, you say

- ✔ **Eich At Margisha?** (ehch aht mahr-gee-*shah;* How do you feel?) (FS)

- ✔ **Eich Atah Margish?** (ehch ah-*tah* mahr-*geesh;* How do you feel?) (MS)

- ✔ **Eich Aten Margishot?** (ehch ah-*tehn* mahr-gee-*shoht;* How do you feel?) (FP)

- ✔ **Eich Atem Margishim?** (ehch ah-*tehm* mahr-gee-*sheem;* How do you feel?) (MP)

Table 3-1 presents some important words to talk about how you're feeling.

Table 3-1	Words to Describe How You Feel	
English	*Hebrew for a Male Speaker*	*Hebrew for a Female Speaker*
curious	Sakran (sahk-*rahn*)	Sakranit (sahk-*rah-neet*)
happy	Same'ach (sah-*meh*-ach)	S'mecha (s-meh-*chah*)
sad	Atzuv (ah-*tzuv*)	Atzuva (ah-tzoo-*vah*)
scared	Mefuhad (meh-foo-*chahd*)	Mehfuchedet (meh-foo-*cheh*-det)
sick	Choleh (choh-*leh*)	Cholah (choh-*lah*)
tired	Ayef (ah-*yehf*)	Ayefah (ah-yeh-*fah*)

If you're hot or cold, you don't say *I am hot* or *I am cold* in Hebrew. Instead you say *There is hot to me* and *There is cold to me.* Because of the way the sentence is constructed, you don't have to worry about masculine and feminine ways of saying this. You just say:

- ✔ **Cham Li.** (chahm lee; I'm hot.)

- ✔ **Kar Li.** (kahr lee; I'm cold.)

Extending and Responding to Invitations

The Hebrew word *to invite* is **L'hazmin** (leh-hahz-*meen*). If you want to invite someone somewhere you can say

> ✔ **Efshar L'hazmin Ot'cha?** (ef-*shar* leh-hahz-*meen* oht-cha; May I invite you?) (MS)
>
> **Efshar L'hazmin Otach?** (ef-*shar* leh-hahz-*meen* oht-*ach;* May I invite you?) (FS)
>
> ✔ **Ani Yachol L'hazmin Ot'cha?** (ahi *nee* yah-*chol* leh-hahz-*meen* oht-*cha;* Can I invite you?) (MS)
>
> **Ani Yecholah L'hazmin Otach?** (ah-*nee* yeh-*chohl* leh-hahz-*meen* oh-*tach;* Can I invite you?) (FS)

If you want to accept an invitation, you can say **Ken, Ani Esmach La'Vo. Todah** (kehn, ah-*nee* ehs-*mahch* lah-*voh.* toh-*dah;* Yes, I'd be happy to come. Thanks.). But, if you would like to politely decline, you can say

> **Todah Al Ha'Hazmana, Aval Ani Lo Yachol.** (toh-*dah* ahl hah-hahz-mah-*nah,* ah-*vahl* ah-*nee* loh yah-*chohl;* Thanks for the invitation, but I can't come.) (MS)
>
> **Todah Al Ha'Hazmana, Aval Ani Lo Y'chola La'Vo.** (toh-*dah* ahl hah-hahz-mah-*nah,* ah-*vahl* ah-*nee* loh yeh-choh-*lah* lah-*voh;* Thanks for the invitation, but I can't come.) (FS)

Asking for a date

They say love is a universal language, but if you want to ask someone out on a date in Hebrew, a few words and phrases may be helpful. In Hebrew, the word for *date* is **P'gisha** (p-gee-shah), which literally means *meeting*. Because this word also has the connotation of a business meeting, people in Israel often just use the English word *date* when it's a romantic meeting of sorts. Here are some phrases you can use to make an amorous advance:

✔ **Efshar Lehazmin Otach LeKos Kafeh?** (ehf-shahr leh-hahz-*meen* oh-*tach* leh kohs kah-*feh;* Can I take you out for a cup of coffee?) (any gender to a female)

✔ **Efshar Lehazmin Otchah LeKos Kafeh?** (ehf-shahr leh-hahz-*meen* oht-*chah* leh kohs kah-*feh;* Can I take you out for a cup of coffee?) (any gender to a male)

✔ **Ani Makir Otach Me'aifo Shehu?** (ah-*nee* mah-*keer* oh-*tahch* meh-ay-foh-sheh-*hoo;* Do I know you from somewhere?) (a male to a female)

✔ **Ani Makirah Otcha Me'aifo Shehu** (ah-*nee* mah-keer-*ah* oht-*chah* meh-ay-foh-sheh-*hoo;* Do I know you from somewhere?) (a female to a male)

If someone invites you to their house, you may also want to ask what you can bring.

> **Mah Ani Yachol L'havie?** (mah ah-*nee* yah-*chol* leh-hah-*vee;* What can I bring?) (MS)

> **Mah Ani Yechola L'havie?** (mah ah-*nee* yeh-choh-*lah* leh-hah-*vee;* What can I bring?) (FS)

Asking Questions: The Who, What, Where, When, Why, and How

An old saying says, "Curiosity killed the cat, but information brought him back." By simply reading this book, you're displaying a healthy curiousity about the world around you. And I'm guessing that you want to ask many questions about that world in Hebrew, too. Here are some basic question words to start you off:

- **Eich** (ehch; how)
- **Eifo** (*ay*-foh; where)
- **Lamah** (*lah*-mah; why)
- **Mah** (mah; what)
- **Matai** (mah-*tye;* when)
- **Mi** (mee; who)

Asking yes or no questions

When you speak in Hebrew, you can indicate that you're asking a question by the tone of your voice. So, for example, you can say "There's pizza in the refrigerator" and mean it as a statement. Or you can put a question mark in your voice and use the exact same words in the same order, and people will understand that you're asking a question. This concept is generally only true for questions that someone can answer with a simple yes or no.

Another way to indicate that you're asking a "yes or no" question is to start your question with the question word **Ha'im** (hah-*eem*). This handy word can be used to signal any yes or no question you can think of. All you need to do is simply put **Ha'im** in front of a statement to turn it into a question.

- ✔ **Ha'im Atah Medaber Russit?** (hah-*eem* ah-*tah* meh-dah-*behr* roo-*seet;* Do you speak Russian?)

- ✔ **Ha'im At Mi'California?** (ha-*eem* aht mee-kah-lee-*fohr*-nee-yah; Are you from California?)

Forming negative questions

If you want to ask a "negative question" — questions that end with phrases like *didn't she?* or *aren't you?* — use the Hebrew word for *no,* **Lo** (loh), or *there isn't,* **Ayn** (ayn). These words are not interchangeable because they have different meanings. Both **Lo** and **Ayn** are placed before the object they are modifying in the sentence. For example:

- ✔ **Ayn Oogiyot?** (ayn oo-gee-*yoht;* No cookies?)

- ✔ **Ha'im Ayn Oogiyot?** (hah-*eem* ayn oo-gee-*yoht;* There aren't any cookies?)

- ✔ **Atah Lo Makir Otah?** (ah-*tah* loh mah-*keer* oh-*tah;* You don't know her?)

- ✔ **Ha'im Atah Lo Makir Otah?** (hah-*eem* ah-*tah* loh mah-*keer* oh-*tah;* You don't know her?)

If you want to say the actual English equivalent of *didn't he?* or *aren't you?* (in grammar-speak this is known as a *tag*), simply add the Hebrew word to mean *correct,* **Nachon** (nah-*chohn*), at the end of the sentence.

- ✔ **Atah Same'ach, Nachon?** (ah-*tah* sah-*meh*-ahch, nah-*chohn;* You're happy, aren't you?)

- ✔ **At Garah B'Ir, Nachon?** (aht *gah*-rah buh-*eer,* nah-*chohn;* You live in a city, don't you?)

Words to Know

Ayn	ayn	there isn't
Eich	ehch	how
Eifo	ay-foh	where
Ha'im	hah-eem	if
Hazmanah	hahz-mah-nah	invitation
Ken	kehn	yes
Lamah	lah-mah	why
L'Hazmin	leh-hahz-meen	to invite
Lo	loh	no
Mah	mah	what
Matai	mah-tye	when
Mi	mee	who
Nachon	nah-chohn	correct
Yesh	yehsh	there is

Fun & Games

Match the Hebrew word with its correct translation.

1. **Eich** _____   A. how
2. **Eifo** _____   B. what
3. **Lamah** _____   C. when
4. **Mah** _____   D. where
5. **Matai** _____   E. who
6. **Mi** _____   F. why

Part II
Hebrew in Action

The 5th Wave   By Rich Tennant

"Most of these phrases can stand by themselves.
Dropping in the occasional 'y'all',
is entirely optional."

In this part . . .

This part lets you put Hebrew to work in your daily life. Chatting with friends, eating, drinking, shopping, working or relaxing at the office, and wiling away your precious free time — I cover it all so you can do it in Hebrew! **Bilui Naim** (bee-loo-*y* nah-*eem;* have fun!)

Chapter 4

Getting to Know You: Making Small Talk

. . . .

In This Chapter

▶ Starting a conversation with simple questions

▶ Discussing your family

▶ Weathering the storm

▶ Working on your occupational vocabulary

▶ Exchanging contact information

. . . .

I don't know about you, but I love meeting new people. Every person is a world unto himself or herself, and there's so much to explore in each world. One of the most pleasant ways to get to know someone is to engage in small talk: Weather, jobs, and family all make great fodder for conversation.

Shootin' the Breeze

Casual conversation can really help pass the time. And who knows where such conversation may lead? You can use the following questions to strike up a conversation with just about anyone — just about anywhere. (And for the particulars on how to construct a question, flip back to Chapter 2.)

✔ **Atah Choshev SheYered Geshem?** (ah-*tah* choh-*shehv* sheh-yeh-*rehd geh*-shehm; Do you think it will rain?) (MS)

At Choshevet SheYered Geshem? (aht choh-*sheh*-**v**eht sheh-yeh-*rehd geh*-shehm; Do you think it will rain?) (FS)

✔ **Atah Nasui?** (ah-*tah* nah-soo-*ee;* Are you married?) (MS)

At Nesua? (aht neh-soo-*ah;* Are you married?) (FS)

✔ **Ben Kamah Atah?** (ben *kah*-mah ah-*tah;* How old are you?) (MS)

Bat Kamah Aht? (baht *kah*-mah *aht;* How old are you?) (FS)

✔ **Eifo Ani Yachol Limtzo Mis'ada Tova?** (*ay*-foh ah-*nee* yah-*chohl* leem-*tzoh* mees-ah-*dah* toh-*vah;* Where can I find a good restaurant?) (MS)

Eifo Ani Yecholah Limtzo Mis'ada Tova? (*ay*-foh ah-*nee* yeh-choh-*lah* leem-*tzoh* mees-ah-*dah* toh-*vah;* Where can I find a good restaurant?) (FS)

✔ **Eizeh Muzikah Atah Ohev?** (*ay*-zeh *moo*-zee-kah ah-*tah* oh-*hev;* What kind of music do you like?) (MS)

Eizeh Muzikah At Ohevet? (ay-*zeh* moo-zee-kah aht oh-*heh*-vet; What kind of music do you like?) (FS)

✔ **Me'ayn Atah Ba'Aretz?** (meh-*ayin* ah-*tah* bah-*ah*-rehtz; Where are you from in Israel?) (MS)

Me'ayn At Ba'Aretz? (meh-*ayin* aht bah-*ah*-rehtz; Where are you from in Israel?) (FS)

✔ **Me'Eifo Atah?** (meh-*ay*-foh ah-*tah;* Where are you from?) (MS)

Me'Eifo At? (meh-*ay*-foh aht; Where are you from?) (FS)

✔ **Me'od Cham HaYom, Nachon?** (meh-*ohd* chahm hah-*yohm* nah-*chohn;* It's quite hot today, isn't it?)

✔ **Slicha, Mah Ha'Sha'ah?** (slee-*chah* mah hah-shah-*ah;* Excuse me, what is the time?)

✔ **Yesh L'cha Achim V'Achayot?** (*yesh* leh-*chah* ah-*cheem* veh-ah-chah-*yoht;* Do you have brothers and sisters?) (MS)

Yesh Lach Achim V'Achayot? (yesh *lach* ach-*eem* veh-ah-chah-*yoht;* Do you have brothers and sisters?) (FS)

In the list above, I include the phrase for *How old are you?* Although asking someone's age may be taboo in North America, feel free to ask this question when you're in Israel. People not only ask you about your age, but they also inquire about your salary, how much you paid for your house, and other personal matters! Israelis want to know how many children you have and whether you're married. If you're not married, some folks will offer to introduce you to a nice single boy or girl. And, if you're in Israel during election time, feel free to ask anyone and everyone for whom they are voting. They'll tell you! So ask away!

As you may have noticed, I also list two ways of asking someone where they're from. Use the **Me'ayin Atah Ba'Aretz?** version when you know the person is from Israel, and the **Me'Eifo Atah?** version when the individual could be from somewhere outside of Israel.

But what if someone asks *you* one or more of the questions from the list above? Keep reading; I tell you how you can answer back.

Talking About Yourself and Your Family

Whenever I meet people, I'm always curious about their **Mishpacha** (meesh-pah-*chah;* family) and where they grew up. Where were they born? Where are their **Horim** (hoh-*reem;* parents) from? How many brothers and sisters do they have? People have interesting stories, and you can always uncover a lot about new acquaintances by asking some simple questions about their family. Table 4-1 gives you the Hebrew names for bunch family members. (Flip back to Chapter 3 to find out how to ask people where they're from.)

When you talk to Jewish people about their families, you can learn a lot about Jewish and Israeli history. Jews are a people who have wandered the globe, and every family has tales of their trials, tribulations, and joys.

Table 4-1		All in the Family
Hebrew	*Pronunciation*	*Translation*
Aba	*ah*-bah	father
Ima	*ee*-mah	mother
Ben	ben	son
Bat	baht	daughter
Ba'al	*bah*-al	husband
Ishah	ee-*shah*	wife
Ach	ahch	brother
Achot	ah-*choht*	sister
Yeladim	yeh-lah-*deem*	children
Saba	*sah*-bah	grandfather
Savta	*sahv*-tah	grandmother
Neched	*neh*-chehd	grandson
Nechdah	nech-*dah*	granddaughter
Dod	dohd	uncle
Dodah	*doh*-dah	aunt
Ben-Dod (MS)	ben-*dohd*	cousin
Bat-Dod (FS)	baht *dohd*	cousin

(continued)

Table 4-1 *(continued)*

Hebrew	Pronunciation	Translation
Cham	chahm	father-in-law
Chama	chah-*mah*	mother-in-law
Gis	gees	brother-in-law
Gisah	gee-*sah*	sister-in-law

Talkin' the Talk

 Shira and Maya are sitting next to each other on a flight to Israel. The two women strike up a conversation to pass the time. (Track 5)

Shira: **Shalom. Ani Shira. Eich Korim Lach?**
          shah-*lohm.* ah-*nee shee*-rah. eich kohr-*eem* lahch?
          Hello. I'm Shira. How do they call you?

Maya: **Naim L'hakir Otach, Shira. Korim Li Maya.**
          nah-*eem* leh-hah-*keer* oh-*tahch, shee*-rah. kohr-*eem*
          lee *mah*-yah.
          Nice to meet you, Shira. They call me Maya.

Shira: **Naim Me'od Maya. Lamah At Nosa'at L'Yisrael? Yesh
          Lach Mishpacha Sham?**
          nah-*eem* meh-*ohd mah*-yah. *lah*-mah aht no-*sah*-aht
          le-yees-rah-*ehl?* yesh lahch meesh-pah-*chah* shahm?
          Very nice [to meet you], Maya. Why are you traveling
          to Israel? Do you have family there?

Maya: **Ken. Ha'Horim Sheli Garim Sham. V'At? Me'Eifo At?**
          ken. ha-hoh-*reem* sheh-*lee* gah-*reem* shahm. veh-aht?
          meh-*ay*-foh aht?
          Yes. My parents live there. And you? Where are you
          from?

Shira: **Ani Mi'Yisrael. Aval HaBen Sheli Gar B'Artzot Ha'Brit.**
          ah-*nee* meh-yees-rah-*ehl.* ah-*vahl* hah-*ben* sheh-*lee*
          gahr beh-ahr-*tzoht* hah-*breet.*
          I'm from Israel. But my son lives in the United States.

Maya: **Me'ayin At B'Aretz?**
          meh-ah-*yeen* aht bah-*ah*-rehtz?
          Where are you from in Israel?

Shira:	Ani MeZichron Ya'akov.
	ah-*nee* meh-zeech-*rohn* yah-ah-*kohv*.
	I'm from Zichron Ya'akov.

Israelis and Jews who live in the Diaspora often refer to Israel as **Ha'Aretz** (hah-*ah*-rehtz), which means simply *the land*.

Chatting About the Weather

Whether it's hot and humid or cool and breezy, the **Mezeg Ha'Avir** (*meh*-zehg hah-ah-*veer;* weather) is always a good — and safe — topic of conversation. Because it affects everyone, the weather is a great way to start up a conversation. Try any of the following:

- **Norah Cham HaYom, Nachon?** (noh-*rah* chahm hah-*yohm* nah-*chohn;* It's quite hot today, isn't it?)

- **Norah Kar HaYom, Nachon?** (noh-*rah* kahr hah-*yohm* nah-*chohn;* It's quite cold today, isn't it?)

- **Yom Yafeh, Nachon?** (yohm yah-*feh* nah-*chohn;* It's a nice day, isn't it?)

The easiest way to find out about weather conditions is to tune into a **Tachazit Mezeg Ha'Avir** (tah-chah-*zeet meh*-zehg hah-ah-*veer;* weather forecast) where you're likely to hear some of these words:

- **Anan** (ah-*nahn;* cloud)
- **Barak** (bah-*rahk;* lightning)
- **Geshem** (*geh*-shehm; rain)
- **Keshet** (*keh*-sheht; rainbow)
- **Lachut** (lah-*choot;* humidity)
- **Ra'am** (*rah*-ahm; thunder)
- **Ru'ach** (*roo*-ach; wind)
- **Se'arah** (seh-ah-*rah;* storm)
- **Sheleg** (*sheh*-lehg; snow)
- **Shemesh** (*sheh*-mehsh; sun)

To say *It is . . .* in Hebrew, just use the word **Zeh** (zeh; it *or* this). There is no *is* in Hebrew, so if you want to say something like *It is hot today,* you just say **Zeh Cham HaYom** (zeh hahm hah-*yohm;* It's hot today). Just follow this pattern: **Zeh . . . HaYom** (It is . . . today). You can use the following words to fill in the blank:

✔ **Cham** (chahm; hot)

✔ **Kar** (kahr; cold)

✔ **Me'unan** (meh-oo-*nahn;* cloudy)

✔ **Me'unan Chelkit** (meh-oo-*nahn* chel-*keet;* partly cloudy)

✔ **Yored Geshem** (yoh-*rehd geh*-shehm; raining)

✔ **Yored Sheleg** (yoh-*rehd sheh*-lehg; snowing)

Talkin' the Talk

 It's a hot day in the middle of an Israeli summer. Sivan and Tal are sitting at the beach discussing the weather. (Track 6)

Sivan: **Norah Cham Hayom, Nachon?**
noh-*rah* chahm hah-*yohm,* nah-*chohn?*
It's quite hot today, isn't it?

Tal: **Ken, Mamash Cham Li. Lefachot Ayn Lachut B'Chof HaYam.**
kehn, mah-*mahsh* chahm lee. le-fah-*choht* ayn lah-*choot* buh-*chohf* hah-*yahm.*
Yes, it's quite hot. At least there's no humidity at the beach.

Sivan: **Ken, Ani Lo Nehenet MiLachut. Norah Lach Ba'Ir.**
ken, ah-*nee* loh neh-heh-*neht* me-lah-*hoot.* noh-*rah* lach bah-*eer.*
Yes, I don't enjoy humidity. It's very humid in town.

Tal: **Ken, Ani Yode'a. Yesh Lanu Sharav Achshav.**
kehn, ah-*nee* yoh-*deh*-ah. yesh *lah*-new shah-*rahv* ahch-*shahv.*
Yes, I know. There's a heat wave now.

Sivan: **Nachon. Atah Yode'a Matai Zeh Yipasek?**
nah-*chohn*. ah-*tah* yoh-*deh*-ah mah-*tye* zeh
yee-pah-*sek?*
That's true. Do you know when it will end?

Tal: **L'fee Tachazeet Mezeg Ha'Avir, Zeh Yitkarer B'Od Yomayim.**
le-*fee* tah-chah-*zeet meh*-zehg hah-ah-*veer,* zeh yeet-kah-*rehr* beh-*ohd* yoh-*mye*-eem.
According to the weather forecast, it will get colder in two more days.

Sivan: **Yofi!**
yoh-fee!
Great!

Rain, rain go away: Fun Hebrew expressions with the word *rain*

Judaism is an agricultually-based religion, which explains why Hebrew has so many expressions with the word *rain.* Hebrew features a special word for the first rain of the year, **Yoreh** (yohr-*reh*), and the last rain of the season, **Malkosh** (mahl-*kohsh*). Here are some expressions that contain the Hebrew words **Geshem** (*geh*-shehm; rain) and **Matar** (mah-*tahr*, rainshower):

✔ **Bein SheYerdu Geshamim U'vein SheLo Yerdu** (*bayn* sheh-yehr-*doo* geh-shah-*meem* oo-*vayn* sheh-loh yehr-*doo;* rain or shine)

✔ **She'ayno Mechapes Machseh Bise'arah** (sheh-*ay-noh* meh-chah-*pehs* mahch-*seh* bee-seh-*ah-rah;* not to know enough to come out of the rain)

✔ **V'arubot Ha'shamayim Niftachu.** (ve-ah-roo-*boht* hah-shah-*mah*-yeem neef-*tah*-choo; The sky opened up.)

Rain is so important that once a year on the Jewish holiday of **Sh'mini Atzeret** (shmee-*nee* ah *tzeh*-reht), which falls roughly in September or October, Jews recite a special prayer for rain. **Sh'mini Atzeret** caps off the week-long Jewish harvest holiday, **Sukkot,** with prayers for a rainy season in Israel.

There's even a Hebrew prayer to recite when you see a **Keshet** (*keh*-sheht; rainbow) as a reminder of the Biblical promise between God and humanity never to flood the world again:

> **Baruch Atah Adonai Eloheinu Melech Ha'Olam, Zocher Et Ha'brit Ve'ne'eman B'vrito V'kayam B'ma'amaro.**
>
> bah-*rooch* ah-*tah* ah-doh-*nai* eh-loh-*hey*-noo *meh*-lehch hah-oh-*lahm,* zoh-*chehr* eht ha-*breet* veh-neh-eh-*mahn* bivree-*toh* ve-kah-*yahm* beh-mah-ah-mah-*roh.*
>
> Praised are You the Eternal One our God, who remembers the covenant and keeps promises.

Speakin' slang with the best of 'em!

When you're speaking Hebrew and you really want to sound like a native speaker, being able to throw in some slang is handy! If you want to say that you think things are *cool*, you can say that everything is **Magniv** (mahg-*neev*) or **Sabbaba** (sah-*bah*-bah). But if things aren't going your way, it's a **Basah** (*bah*-sah, bummer). Here's a tricky one: If you think something is really fantastic, you may declare that it's **Chaval Al Ha'zman** (chah-*vahl* ahl haz-*mahn*), which literally means *a waste of time*. (Hey, I don't make up the slang; I just report it.)

If something is really terrible, you can say it's **Al Ha Panim** (ahl hah-pah-*neem*), which literally means *on the face*, as in falling flat on your face.

And, if you think someone is about "to go nuts" you say they are going **L'hitcharfen** (le-heet-char-*fen*; to go crazy). Here's a good one: **L'Hitkarnef** (leh-heet-kahr-*nehf*) literally means *to act like a rhinoceros,* but figuratively means to *ignore what's around you.* This slang expression is based on a character who dressed like a rhinoceros in an avant-garde Israeli play from many years ago. And now for my all-time favorite: If you want to hang out on Tel Aviv's main drag, Dizengoff Street (named after the city's first mayor), there's an actual Hebrew verb for that — **L'hizdangef** (le-heez-dahn-*gef*; to hang out on Dizengoff street).

Words to Know

Anan	ah-<u>nahn</u>	cloud
Cham	chahm	hot
Geshem	<u>geh</u>-shem	rain
Kar	kahr	cold
Keshet	<u>keh</u>-sheht	rainbow
Lachut	lah-<u>choot</u>	humidity
Mezeg Ha'Avir	meh-<u>zehg</u> hah-ah-<u>veer</u>	weather
Sheleg	<u>sheh</u>-lehg	snow
Shemesh	<u>sheh</u>-mehsh	sun

Six Days You Shall Labor: Talking About Work

You can tell a lot about someone by what he or she does for a living. Work takes up much of our waking hours, and people are often passionate about their chosen profession (if they're lucky). You can find out a lot about people by asking them what they do for a living. You can ask someone **Bemah Atah Oved** (MS)/**At Ovedet** (FS)? (beh-*mah* ah-*tah* oh-*vehd*/aht oh-vehd-*eht;* What do you do for work?), or you can say **Mah Ha'Miktso'ah Shelcha** (MS)/**Shelach** (FS)? (mah hah meek-*tzoh*-ah shel-*chah*/she-*lach;* What's your profession?) Table 4-2 contains some occupations that either you or your conversation partner may hold. Check it out! (And for additional work-related words, check out Chapter 10.)

Table 4-2	Calling in the Professionals	
Hebrew (M/F)	*Pronunciation (M/F)*	*Translation*
Ach/Achot	ach/ah-*choht*	nurse
Chaklai/Chakla'it	Chahk-*lahy*/chah-klah-*eet*	farmer
Ro'eh Cheshbon/ Ro'at Cheshbon	roh-*eh* chehsh-*bon*/ roh-*aht* chesh-*bon*	accountant
Chashmelay/ Chashmela'it	chahsh-meh-*lahy*/ chash-meh-lah-*eet*	electrician
Itonai'i/Itonai-it	ee-toe-*nahy*/ee-toe-nah-*eet*	journalist
Mazkir/Mazkirah	maz-*keer*/maz-kee-*rah*	secretary
Mehandes/ Mehandeset	meh-hahn-*dehs*/meh-hahn-*deh*-set	engineer
Menahel/Menahelet	meh-nah-*hel*/meh-nah-*heh*-let	manager
Moreh/Morah	moh-*reh*/moh-*rah*	teacher
Nehag/Naheget	neh-*hag*/nah-*heh*-get	bus driver
Orech Din/Orechet Din	oh-*rech*-deen/oh-*reh*-chet deen	lawyer
Oved Sotziali/ Ovedet Sotzialit	oh-*vehd* sohtz-*yah*-lee/ oh-*veh*-det sohtz-*yah*-leet	social worker

Table 4-2 (continued)

Hebrew (M/F)	Pronunciation (M/F)	Translation
Rakdan/Rakdanit	rahk-*dahn*/rahk-dah-*neet*	dancer
Rofeh/Rof'ah	roh-*feh*/rohf-*ah*	doctor
Shoter/Shoteret	shoh-*tehr*/shoh-*teh*-ret	police officer

Talkin' the Talk

 Nadav and Aviva have just met and struck up a conversation at a party. Because he wants to keep the conversation going, Nadav asks Aviva what she does for a living. (Track 7)

Nadav: **Mah Ha'Miktzoah Shelach?**
mah hah-meek-*tzoh*-ah sheh-*lach?*
What's your profession?

Aviva: **Ani Itona'it. Be'Mah Atah Oved?**
ah-*nee* ee-toh-nah-*eet.* beh-*mah* ah-*tah* oh-*vehd?*
I'm a journalist. What do you do for work?

Nadav: **Ani Mehandes.**
ah-*nee* meh-hahn-*dehs.*
I'm an engineer.

Aviva: **Yafeh Me'od. Atah Neheneh MiZeh?**
yah-*feh* meh-*ohd.* ah-*tah* neh-heh-*neh* mee-zeh?
Very nice. Do you enjoy it?

Nadav: **Ken. Zeh Me'od Me'anyen. Eich Ha'avodah Shelach?**
kehn. zeh meh-*ohd* meh-ahn-*yehn.* ahch hah-ah-voh-*dah* sheh-*lach?*
Yes. It's very interesting. How's your work?

Aviva: **Ani Me'Od Ohevet Et Zeh. Ani Mamash Ohevet Lichtov.**
ah-*nee* meh-*ohd* oh-*heh*-vet et zeh. ah-*nee* mah-*mahsh* oh-*heh*-vet leech-*tohv.*
I like it very much. I really like to write.

Nadav: **Kol HaKovod!**
kohl ha-kah-*vohd!*
Good for you!

Words to Know

Avodah	ah-voh-<u>dah</u>	work
Kol HaKavod	kohl hah-kah-<u>vohd</u>	Good for you!
Miktso'a	meek-<u>tsoh</u>-ah	profession

Getting Addresses and Phone Numbers

Telling someone where you live and giving out your telephone number are often the key to continuing social contacts after you get past the nice-to-meet-you phase. You may want to carry around a **Kartis Bikur** (kahr-*tees* bee-*koor;* business card) to make the process a little easier, just in case. (For more information on talking on the phone, take a look at Chapter 9. Also, check out Chapter 15 where I discuss giving directions.)

Asking and telling where you live

To ask someone where he or she lives, just say

> **Eifo Atah Gar?** (*ay*-foh ah-t*ah gahr;* Where do you live?) (MS)
>
> **Eifo At Garah?** (*ay*-foh *aht gah*-rah; Where do you live?) (FS)

Any of the following phrases are appropriate responses:

- ✔ **Ani Gar . . .** (ah-*nee gar* buh; I live in . . .) (MS)

  Ani Garh B' . . . (ah-*nee gah*-rah buh; I live in . . .) (FS)
- ✔ **Ani Gar Ba'Ir.** (ah-*nee* gar buh-ear; I live in the city.) (MS)

  Ani Garah Ba'Ir. (ah-*nee gah*-rah buh-ear; I live in the city.) (FS)
- ✔ **Ani Gar B'Parvar.** (ah-*nee* gar buh-pahr-*vahr;* I live in a suburb.) (MS)

  Ani Garah B'Parvar. (ah-*nee gah*-rah buh-pahr-*vahr;* I live in a suburb.) (FS)

Depending on how well you know the person and the circumstances, someone may ask you for your **K'tovet** (*ktoh*-veht; address). Jump to Chapter 13 to find out how to talk about your address in Hebrew.

Minding your manners

In Hebrew, there's no word for tact! But here are some words in case you want to be polite anyway.

✔ **Bevakasha.** (beh-vah-kah-*shah;* Please *and* You're welcome.)

✔ **Ha'Oneg Kulo Sheli.** (ha-*oh*-nehg koo-*loh* sheh-*lee;* The pleasure is all mine.)

✔ **Slicha.** (slee-*chah;* Excuse me.)

✔ **Todah.** (toh-*dah;* Thank you.)

Asking and giving a phone number

If someone asks you **Mah Mispar HaTelephone Shelcha (MS)/Shelach (FS)?** (mah mees-*pahr* hah-*teh*-leh-fohn shel-*chah*/sheh-*lach;* What's your telephone number?) or **Efshar Levakesh Et Mispar HaTelephone Shelcha (MS)/Shelach (FS)?** (ef-*shar* leh-vah-*kesh* eht mees-*pahr* hah-teh-leh-*fohn* shel-cha/shel-ach; May I ask for your telephone number?), you can respond by saying **Mispar HaTelephone Sheli Hu . . .** (mees-*pahr* hah-*teh*-leh-fohn sheh-*lee* hoo; My telephone number is . . .).

When you're giving out phone numbers, knowing how to count in Hebrew will probably be very useful. Flip back to Chapter 1 for that information.

Fun & Games

Match these family members with the Hebrew words that identify them:

A. _____

B. _____

C. _____

D. _____

E. _____

Aba, Ima, Achot, Ach, Savta

Chapter 5

Eat! Eat! You're So Thin!

*J*ews have been called the "People of the Book." Another title that can also apply is the "People of the Palate." A large part of the culture and religion revolves around food. What would **Shabbat** (shah-*baht;* Jewish Sabbath) be without **Challah** (chah-*lah;* braided egg-bread) on Friday night? What would **Pesach** (peh-*sach;* Passover) be without yummy **Matzah** (mah-*tzah;* unleavened bread)? And what would a good Jewish mother be without her chicken-soup recipe?

In this chapter, I provide plenty of vocabulary about meals and food including special foods eaten on Jewish holidays. With this chapter in hand, you can figure out how to place an order in a restaurant and how to shop for food at the grocery store in Hebrew. You can also uncover some terms for **Kashrut** (kahsh-*root;* Jewish dietary laws) and some basic blessings to say before you eat. **B'Teavon** (buh-teh-ah-*vohn;* Healthy appetite)!

Jewish Love Means Never Having to Say "I'm Hungry"

A great way to find out about any culture is through its food, and Jewish culture is no different. Jewish cuisine springs from ancient traditions and bears the imprint of Jewish wanderings around the globe. Within the Jewish community, distinctive foods of both **Ashkenazi** (European) and **Sephardic** (Mediterranean) origin are common. These dishes often make their way from one generation to the next. Many dishes are associated with a particular holiday on the Jewish calendar. If you ask any Jewish person about his or her memories of Jewish holidays, I guarantee you that food will be part of the picture.

In much of Jewish culture, food is an expression of love. In Israeli culture in particular, offering food is part of the gracious hospitality for which the warm Middle Eastern culture is known. In Israeli homes, you can usually find dishes of **Egozim** (eh-goh-*zeem;* nuts) and **Garinim** (gahr-ee-*neem;* seeds) in the public gathering rooms just waiting for guests to stop by.

Hunger and thirst pangs aren't in your future as long as you're in a Jewish household. The following food-related words and phrases will serve you well when you want to talk about food:

- **O'chel** (*oh*-chehl; food)
- **L'Echol** (leh-eh-*chohl;* to eat)
- **Ochel** (oh-*chehl;* eat) (MS)
  Ochelet (oh-cheh-*leht;* eat) (FS)
- **Ochlim** (och-*leem;* eat) (MP)
  Ochlot (ohch-*loht;* eat) (FP)
- **Leha'achil** (leh-hah-ah-*cheel;* to feed)
- **Ma'achil** (mah-ah-*cheel;* feed) (MS)
  Ma'achila (mah-ah-*chee-lah;* feed) (FS)
- **Ma'achilim** (mah-ah-*chee-leem;* feed) (MP)
  Ma'achilot (mah-ah-chee-*loht;* feed) (FP)

In the list above, I note that **Ochlim** and **Ma'achilim** are masculine plural forms. But these words are also used for a group of people made up of both males and females.

Quieting a growling stomach

When **Ohchel** is the subject, the first thing you need to know how to express is hunger. I just happen to have a few handy phrases:

- **Ani Ra'ev.** (ah-*nee* rah-*ehv;* I'm hungry.) (MS)
  Ani Ra'evah. (ah-*nee* reh-eh-*vah;* I'm hungry.) (FS)
- **Anachnu Ra'evim.** (ah-nahch-*noo* reh-eh-*veem;* We are hungry.) (MP)
  Anachnu Ra'evot. (ah-*nahch-noo* reh-eh-*voht;* We are hungry.) (FP)

Taming a wild thirst

Atah Tzameh? (ah-*tah* tzah-*meh;* Are you thirsty? *Literally:* You must be thirsty!) After you've eaten, you probably want a **Sh'tiah** (shuh-tee-*ah;* drink). Master the phrases in the following list, and you'll never go thirsty.

- **Ani Tza'meh.** (ah-*nee* tzah-*meh;* I'm thirsty.) (MS)

  Ani Tzme'ah. (ah-nee tzuh-*meh-ah;* I'm thirsty.) (FS)

- **Anachnu Tzme'im.** (ah-*nahch*-noo tz-*meh-eem;* We're thirsty.) (MP)

  Anachnu Tzme'ot. (ah-*nahch*-noo tz-*meh-oht;* We're thirsty.) (FP)

You can easily turn the phrases I introduce into questions. Just put a verbal question mark in your voice when you use these phrases, or add the word **Ha'im** (hah-*eem;* if) before the phrases. Check out Chapter 3 where I talk about forming questions a little more.

Words to Know

O'chel	<u>oh</u>-chehl	food
Ra'ev (MS)	rah-<u>ehv</u>	hungry
R'evah (FS)	reh-eh-<u>vah</u>	hungry
Sh'tiah	shuh-tee-<u>ah</u>	drink (noun)
Tza'meh (MS)	tzah-<u>meh</u>-ah	thirsty
Tzme'ah (FS)	tzmeh-<u>ah</u>	thirsty

Getting Down to Business: Food, Glorious Food!

Eating is an important part of everyone's day. Without food, your days would be numbered. But the Jewish culture (like many cultures) places a particular emphasis on food that makes it central to Jewish life — both in Israel and the

Diaspora (the lands outside of Israel where Jews have made their home). In this section, I dish out the facts on the main meals people eat every day — breakfast, lunch, and dinner. (And you didn't think that I'd forget about snacks, did you?) I provide the lowdown on the foods that many folks commonly eat and some information on special Jewish food customs.

Starting the day with breakfast

You know what they say: Breakfast is the most important meal of the day! In Hebrew, *breakfast* is called **Aruchat Boker** (ah-roo-*chaht* boh-kehr; *Literally:* morning meal). In the morning, many people can't function without a cup of **Cafeh** (kah-*feh;* coffee). Or maybe your morning isn't complete without a cold, refreshing glass of **Mitz Tapuzim** (*meetz* tah-poo-*zeem;* orange juice). Do you like a hearty breakfast with **Beitzim** (bay-*tzeem;* eggs), or do you prefer simpler foods like a **Lachmania** (lahch-mah-nee-*yah;* roll) or some **Yoghurt** (you know how to pronounce this one; yogurt). If you're in Israel, you may want to do as Israelis do and have a typical Israeli breakfast of **Agvaniot** (ahg-vah-nee-*yoht;* tomatoes) and **Melafefonim** (meh-lah-feh-foh-*neem;* cucumbers). No, I'm not kidding!

Here are some other common foods you may eat for breakfast:

- **Chalav** (chah-*lahv;* milk)
- **Chavitah** (chah-vee-*tah;* omelet)
- **Dysah** (dye-*sah;* cereal)
- **Meetz** (*meetz;* juice)
- **Perot** (pehr-*roht;* fruit)

Enjoying lunch

For many people, **Aruchat Tzohorayim** (ah-roo-*chaht* tzoh-hoh-*rah*-eem; lunch) is the quickest meal of the day. You can grab a **Sendvitch** (send-*veech;* sandwich) and eat it on the fly. Or you can always gobble down some reheated **Pasta Im Rotev** (*pahs*-tah eem *roh*-tehv; pasta with sauce) at your desk. But lunch doesn't always have to be eaten at a heartburn-inducing pace. You can easily enjoy it with friends and family. On *Shabbat,* the Jewish Sabbath, lunch is the focal point of Saturday afternoon, and it often lasts for hours. Several courses are served including **Marak** (mah-*rahk;* soup) or a special slow-cooked stew called **Chamin** (chah-*meen*). **Chamin** is prepared before the Sabbath. It then has plenty of time — all night and the next morning — to simmer to perfection.

Shakshuka: An "all mixed up" Israeli egg dish

A popular egg dish in Israel is called **Shakshuka**, which is an appropriate name. The word is an onomatopoeia, which is a fancy way of saying the word *sounds* like exactly what it *means*. **Shakshuka** is literally the sound something makes when it gets all mixed up. You make the dish by taking tomatoes, garlic, tomato paste, olive oil, salt, and paprika and mixing them all up while heating them in a pan. When these ingredients are hot, you crack a few eggs and add them to the pan. The eggs cook right in the sauce. You serve the dish directly from the pan. It's quite **Ta'im** (tah-*eem;* delicious)!

Here are some additional foods you may eat for lunch:

- ✔ **Dag** (dahg; fish)
- ✔ **Falafel** (fah-*lah*-fehl; fried chickpea paste in pita bread)
- ✔ **Hambuger** (*hahm*-boo-gehr; hamburger)
- ✔ **Naknikiah** (nahk-nee-kee-*yah;* hot dog)
- ✔ **Peetza** (*pee*-tzah; pizza)
- ✔ **Salat** (sah-*laht;* salad)

Eating dinner

Ah, dinner! Hopefully the workday is done and you can enjoy your meal. For Jewish families in North America — like their non-Jewish compatriots — dinner is the focal meal of the day. During dinner, you may have several courses. Perhaps **Marak** and **Salat** — familiar foods from lunch — are on the menu, followed by **Basar** (bah-*sahr;* meat) or, if it's a special occasion, **Hodu** (*hoh*-doo; turkey). Usually dinner also includes some kind of **Yerakot** (yeh-rah-*koht;* vegetables) and perhaps some **Orez** (*oh*-rehz; rice). And don't forget **Kinuach** (kee-*noo*-ahch; dessert)!

In Israel, however, Mediterranean culture predominates, and dinner is usually lighter fare because lunch serves as the main meal of the day.

Here are some other items you may have for **Aruchat Erev** (ah-roo-*chah* eh-rev), which literally means *evening meal:*

- ✔ **Afunah** (ah-foo-*nah;* peas)
- ✔ **D'la'at** (*dlah*-aht; squash)

- **Gezer** (*geh*-zehr; carrots)
- **Kishuim** (kee-shoo-*eem;* zucchini)
- **Kruvit** (kroo-*veet;* cauliflower)
- **Of** (ohf; chicken)
- **Oogah** (oo-*gah;* cake)
- **Tapuach Adamah** (tah-*poo*-ahch ah-dah-*mah;* potatoes)
- **Tered** (*teh*-rehd; spinach)
- **Yayin** (*yah*-yeen; wine)

Raiding the refrigerator

The irresistible snack! You can say *snack* many ways in Hebrew. You can call this indulgence an **Arucha Kalah,** (ah-roo-*chah* kah-*lah;* light meal) or a **Hatif** (chah-*teef; Literally:* something snatched), or you can say simply that you **Zolel Ben Ha'aruchot** (zoh-*lehl* bayn hah-ah-roo-*choht;* devour between meals). But whatever you say, snacking is always fun.

Here are some foods that you may eat for a snack, including both foods that are **Bari** (bah-*ree;* healthy) and **Lo Kol-kach Bari** (loh kohl-*kahch* bah-*ree;* not so healthy):

- **Glidah** (glee-*dah;* ice cream)
- **Oogiot** (oo-gee-*yoht;* cookies)
- **Sh'kedim** (sh-kay-*deem;* almonds)
- **Shokolad** (shoh-koh-*lahd;* chocolate)
- **Sucariot** (soo-kahr-ee-*yoht;* candy)
- **Tapuach** (tah-*poo*-ahch; apple)
- **Tzimukim** (tzee-moo-*keem;* raisins)

And ladies and gentleman and children of all ages, may I introduce to you the all-time Israeli favorite snack food — drum roll, please — **Garinim** (gahr-ee-*neem;* seeds)! You can buy **Garinim** by the kilo in little sidewalk stores in Israel. In most Israeli homes, people keep a stash to serve their friends when they pop by unexpectedly.

Going to Shabbat dinner

The main meal of the week (and a festive one at that) in Jewish households in Israel and around the world is the Friday night dinner, **Aruchat Shabbat** (ah-roo-*chaht* shah-*baht*). The meal begins after sundown. Because **Aruchat Shabbat** is the focal point of the week, families often set the table with a **Mapah Levanah** (mah-*pah* leh-vah-*nah;* white tablecloth) and their prettiest dishes. Atop the table sits the **Kos L'Kiddush** (kos leh-kee-*doosh;* Kiddush cup), which is held when the blessing over the Sabbath day is said. Before the meal, Jewish people sing a song to welcome Sabbath angels and follow it with **Brachot** (brah-*choht;* blessings) over the **Yayin** (yah-*yeen;* wine) and **Lechem** (leh-*chehm;* bread).

In some traditional households, people ritually wash their hands — called **Netilat Yadaim** (neh-tee-*laht* yah-dye-*eem*) — before consuming bread. Traditionally, Sabbath-dinner foods include **Of** (ohf; chicken), **Tzimis** (tzi-*mehs;* a stew made with carrots), and sometimes **Basar** (bah-*sahr;* red meat). Eating **Dag** (dahg; fish) on **Shabbat** is also a traditional practice. One of the reasons for this custom is connected to the **Gematria** (geh-mah-tree-*ah;* numerology) of the fish. In **Gematria,** each Hebrew letter is assigned a numerical value. And the numerical values of the letters in the Hebrew word for fish total seven. And **Shabbat** is the seventh day of the week!

On a typical **Shulchan Aruch L'Shabbat** (shool-*chahn* ah-rooch leh-shah-*baht;* a table set for **Shabbat**), you may also find:

- **Kapit**, **Kapiyot** (kah-*peet,* kah-pee-*yoht;* teaspoon, teaspoons)
- **Kos, Kosot** (kohs, koh-*soht;* cup, cups)
- **Kos L'Kiddush** (kohs leh-kee-*doosh;* the Kiddush cup over which a special blessing for the Sabbath is recited)
- **Mapah Levanah** (mah-*pah* leh-vah-*nah;* white tablecloth)
- **Mapit, Mapiot** (mah-*peet,* mah-pee-*yoht;* napkin, napkins)
- **Mazleg, Mazlegot** (mahz-*lehg,* mahz-leh-*goht;* fork, forks)
- **Prachim** (prah-*cheem;* flowers)
- **Sakin, Sakinim** (sah-*keen,* sah-kee-*neem;* knife, knives)
- **Tzalachat, Tzalachot** (tzah-*lah*-chaht, tzah-lah-*choht;* dish, dishes)

People often say **HaShulchan Haya Amus Be'Ochel** (hah-shool-*chahn* hah-*yah* ah-moos beh-*oh*-chehl; The table was loaded with food!) on Friday nights because of the sheer amount of food present.

Words to Know

Arucha	ah-roo-<u>chah</u>	meal
Aruchat Boker	ah-roo-<u>chaht</u> <u>boh</u>-kehr	breakfast
Aruchat Tzohorayim	ah-roo-<u>chaht</u> tzoh-hoh-<u>rah</u>-eem	lunch
Aruchat Erev	ah-roo-<u>chaht</u> <u>eh</u>-rehv	dinner
Arucha Kalah	ah-roo-<u>chah</u> kah-<u>lah</u>	light meal
Kinuach	kee-<u>noo</u>-ahch	dessert

Matching Adjectives and Nouns

In Hebrew, the adjective comes *after* the noun, unlike the adjective-noun pattern in English, in which the adjective usually comes before the noun. As if that little twist doesn't make things challenging enough, the noun and adjective must match in gender (masculine or feminine) and number (plural or singular). For example:

- **Mapah** (mah-*pah;* tablecloth) (FS)
- **Levanah** (leh-vah-*nah;* white) (FS)
- **Mapah Levanah** (mah-*pah* leh-vah-*nah;* white tablecloth) (FS)
- **Mapot** (mah-*poht;* tablecloths) (FP)
- **Levanot** (leh-vah-*nah;* white) (FP)
- **Mapot Levanot** (mah-*pah* leh-vah-*nah;* white tablecloths) (FP)
- **Perach** (*peh*-roht; flower) (MS)
- **Yafeh** (yah-*feh;* pretty) (MS)
- **Perach Yafeh** (*peh*-rahch yah-*feh;* pretty flower) (MS)
- **Prachim Yafim** (prah-*cheem* yah-*feem;* pretty flowers) (MP)

All nouns are either masculine or feminine. Many nouns and adjectives ending with an *ah* or *it* are feminine, and most other words are masculine. But notice that I said *most,* not *all.* You just have to know whether a word is masculine or feminine, and the only way to know for sure is to memorize every word — sorry. Hebrew-English dictionaries use the Hebrew letter *zayin* for masculine and the Hebrew letter *nun* for feminine to note a word's gender. English translations usually have an "m." for masculine and an "f." for feminine. (In this book, I use an "MS" and an "FS," for the same purpose.) To find out more about this fascinating subject (and other Hebrew grammar tidbits), take a look at Chapter 2.

Basic blessings

The phrase **Achalta, V'Savata, U'Verachta** (ah-chahl-*tah,* veh-sah-vah-*tah,* oo-veh-rahch-*tah;* You shall eat, and you shall be satisfied, and you shall bless) comes from the Book of Deuteronomy. From this verse comes the religious obligation to recite a blessing after eating.

Bread has special status in Judaism. On the Jewish New Year, people throw breadcrumbs from their pockets; Passover features an eight-day bread fast; and a special ritual is conducted before and after eating bread. When folks sit down to a meal that features **Lechem** (*leh*-chehm; bread), they recite a lengthy prayer afterwards called **Birkat HaMazon** (beer kaht-hah-mah-*zohn; Literally:* Blessing over the food). When they don't eat bread, they traditionally recite another prayer at the end called **Brachah Achronah** (brah-*chah* ahch-roh-*nah;* last blessing).

As Judaism developed, rabbis decided that if people were required to say a blessing *after* a meal, they should recite a blessing *before* they eat as well. Here are a few basic blessings you say before eating:

✔ **Over bread: Baruch Atah Adonai Eloheinu Melekh HaOlam, HaMotzi Lechem Min HaAretz.** (bah-*rooch* ah-*tah* ah-doh-*nahy* eh-loh-*hay*-noo *meh*-lehch hah-oh-*lahm,* hah-moh-*tzee leh*-chehm meen hah-ah-rehtz; Praised are You, the Eternal One our God, Ruler of the Cosmos, who brings forth bread from the earth.)

✔ **Over wine: Baruch Atah Adonai Eloheinu Melekh HaOlam, Boreh P'ri HaGafen.** (bah-*rooch* ah-*tah* ah-doh-*nahy* eh-loh-*hay*-noo meh-lehch hah-oh-*lahm,* boh-*reh* pree hah-*gah*-fehn; Praised are You, the Eternal One our God, Ruler of the Cosmos, Creator of the fruit of the wine.)

✔ **Over fruit: Baruch Atah Adonai Eloheinu Melekh HaOlam, Boreh P'ri Ha'Etz.** (bah-*rooch* ah-*tah* ah-doh-*nahy* eh-loh-*hay*-noo meh-lehch hah-oh-*lahm,* boh-*reh* pree hah-ehtz; Praised are You, the Eternal One our God, Ruler of the Cosmos, Creator of the fruit of the tree.)

✔ **Over vegetables: Baruch Atah Adonai Eloheinu Melekh HaOlam, Boreh P'ri Ha'Adamah.** (bah-*rooch* ah-*tah* ah-doh-*nahy* eh-loh-*hay*-noo *meh*-lehch hah-oh-*lahm,* boh-*reh* pree hah-ah-dah-*mah;* Praised are You, the Eternal One our God, Ruler of the Cosmos, Creator of the fruit of the earth.)

Note: The prayer over the bread is considered to be a sort of a mega-blessing. If you have a meal where bread is served, you can just bless the bread and consider everything else blessed.

Adjectives can be conjugated to be either masculine singular, masculine plural, feminine singular, or feminine plural. Another important thing to know is that nouns and adjectives need to match both in terms of number (singular or plural) and gender (male or female). Nouns and adjectives in the singular form are made feminine singular by adding a *ah* sound, masculine plural by adding a *im* sound and feminine plural by adding a *ot* sound. For example:

- **Gadol** (gah-*dohl;* big) (MS)
- **G'dolah** (gdoh-*lah;* big) (FS)
- **G'dolim** (gdoh-*leem;* big) (MP)
- **G'dolot** (gdoh-*loht;* big) (FS)
- **Katan** (kah-*tahn;* small) (MS)
- **K'tanah** (k-tah-*nah;* small) (FS)
- **K'tanim** (k-tah-*neem;* small) (MP)
- **K'tanot** (k-tah-*not;* small) (FP)

Talkin' the Talk

 Yaniv and Maya are a married couple. They've invited their friend, Hilah, over for Friday night Shabbat dinner. She has just arrived. (Track 8)

Hilah:	**Shabbat Shalom!** shah-*baht* shah-*lohm!* Good Sabbath!
Yaniv & Maya:	**Shabbat Shalom!** shah-*baht* shah-*lohm!* Good Sabbath!
Maya:	**Bo'oo, Neshev.** boh-*oo,* neh-*shev.* Come, let us sit down.
Hilah:	**HaMapah HaLevanah Kol-Kach Yafah.** hah-mah-*pah* hah-leh-vah-*nah* kohl-*kahch* yah-*fah.* The white tablecloth is so pretty.
Maya:	**Todah Rabbah! Efshar La'Tet Lach Mashehu, Hilah?** toh-*dah* rah-*bah!* ehf-*shahr* lah-*teht* lahch *mah*-sheh-hoo, hee-*lah?* Thank you very much! Can I give you something, Hilah?

Hilah:	**Ken, Tni Li Dag, Of, Orez, V'Tered.** kehn, tni *lee* dahg, ohf, *oh*-rehz, veh-*teh*-rehd. Yes, give me fish, chicken, rice, and spinach.
Maya:	**At Rotzah Yayin Adom, Yaniv?** aht roh-*tzah yah*-yeen ah-*dohm*, yah-*neev?* Would you like some red wine, Yaniv?
Yaniv:	**Ken, Todah Rabbah.** kehn, toh-*dah* rah-*bah.* Yes, thanks very much.
Maya:	**Bete'avon L'chulam!** beh-teh-ah-*vohn* leh-choo-*lahm!* Good appetite everyone!
Yaniv & Hilah:	**Bete'avon!** beh-teh-ah-*vohn!* Good appetite!

The Hebrew verb **Latet** (lah-*teht;* to give) is an irregular verb. It has three Hebrew letters in the root: *nun, tav, nun.* (Flip back to Chapter 1 to see what these Hebrew letters look like.) However, in the infinitive, future, and command forms, the *nun* disappears. The following table shows the conjugation of the verb **Latet** in infinitive, present, future, and imperative tenses.

Verb Tense	Hebrew	Pronunciation	English
Infinitive	Latet	lah-*teht*	to give
Present	Noten (MS)	no-*tehn*	give
	Notenet (FS)	no-teh-*neht*	give
	Not'nim (MP)	not-*neem*	give
	Not'not (FP)	not-*noht*	give
Future	Ti'ten (MS)	tee-*tehn*	will give (you)
	Ti'tni (FS)	teet-*nee*	will give (you)
	Ti'tnu (MP/FP)	teet-*noo*	will give (you)
Imperative	Ten (MS)	tehn	Give!
	T'ni (FS)	t'*nee*	Give!
	T'nu (MP/FP)	t'*noo*	Give!

Taking Your Grocery List to the Market

Because the main festive meal of the week takes place on Friday night, grocery shopping in Israel and in traditional Jewish households around the world often takes place on Thursday or Friday mornings.

In order to buy your weekly **K'iyot** (kuh-nee-*oht;* groceries), you can go to any of the following places:

- ✔ **HaSuper** (hah-*soo*-pehr; supermarket)
- ✔ **Makolet** (mah-*koh*-leht; little neighborhood grocery store)
- ✔ **Shuk** (shook; open air market)

You may also want to swing by a **Ma'afiah** (mah-aha-fee-*yah;* bakery) for these items:

- ✔ **Lechem** (*leh*-chehm; bread)
- ✔ **Oogiot** (oo-gee-*yoht;* cookies)
- ✔ **Oogot** (oo-*goht;* cakes)

And what meal would be complete without a trip to the **Shochet** (shoh-*cheht;* butcher) for kosher

- ✔ **Basar** (bah-*sahr;* meat; beef)
- ✔ **Basar Taleh** (bah-*sahr* tah-*leh;* lamb)
- ✔ **Dag** (dahg; fish)
- ✔ **Of** (ohf; chicken)

When you get to the **HaSuper,** you may have some of these items on your shopping list:

- ✔ **Yerakot** (yeh-rah-*koht;* vegetables)
  - • **Agvania** (ahg-vah-nee-*yah;* tomato)
  - • **Batzal** (bah-*tzahl;* onion)

- **Chasah** (*chah*-sah; lettuce)
- **Chatzilim** (chah-tzee-*leem;* eggplant)
- **Gezer** (*geh*-zehr; carrot)
- **Melafefon** (meh-lah-feh-*fohn;* cucumber)
- **Tapuchei Adamah** (tah-poo-*chey* ah-dah-*mah;* potatoes)
- **Teras** (*tee*-rahs; corn)
- **Tered** (*teh*-rehd; spinach)

✔ **Perot** (peh-*roht;* fruit)

- **Afarsek** (ah-fahr-*sehk;* peach)
- **Agas** (ah-*gahs;* pear)
- **Ananas** (ah-nah-*nahs;* pineapple)
- **Banahnah** (bah-*nah*-nah; banana)
- **Mishmesh** (mish-*mesh;* apricot)
- **Petel** (*peh*-tehl; raspberry)
- **Shezif** (shef-*zeef;* plum)
- **Tapuach** (tah-*poo*-ahch; apple)
- **Tapuz** (tah-*pooz;* orange)
- **Toot-Sadeh** (toot sah-*deh;* strawberry)
- **Uchmaniot** (ohch-mah-nee-*yoht;* blueberries)

✔ **Mutzarei Halav** (moo-tzah-*ray* chah-*lahv;* dairy products**)**

- **Beitzim** (bay-*tzeem;* eggs)
- **Chalav** (chah-*lahv;* milk)
- **Chem'ah** (chehm-*ah;* butter)
- **G'vinah** (guh-vee-*nah;* cheese)
- **Shamenet** (shah-meh-*neht;* sour cream)
- **Shoko** (*shoh*-koh; chocolate milk)
- **Yoghurt** (*yoh*-gurt; yogurt)

Talkin' the Talk

The following conversation takes place in a bustling **Shuk** (shook; open-air market) on **Yom Shishi** (yohm shee-*shee;* Friday) as everyone is busy buying food for Shabbat. Sivan is shopping for vegetables for her Shabbat dinner and approaches a **Mocher** (*moh*-chehr; seller). (Track 9)

Sivan: **Shalom. Ani Rotzah Li'Knot Kamah Yerakot. Haim HaYerakot Tri'im?**
shah-*lohm.* ah-*nee* roh-*tzah* leek-*noht* kah-*mah* yeh-rah-*kot.* hah-*eem* hah-yeh-rah-*koht* tree-*eem?*
Hello. I want to buy some vegetables. Are the vegetables fresh?

Mocher: **Bevakasha, Geveret. HaYerakot Me'od Tri'im. Rak Higi'u HaYom Min HaKibbutz! Mah At Rotzah?**
beh-vah-kah-*shah,* geh-veh-*reht.* Hah-yeh-rah-*kot* meh-*ohd* tree-*eem.* rahk hee-gee-*oo* hah-*yohm* meen hah-kee-*bootz!* Mah aht rohtz-*ah?*
Please, miss. The vegetables are very fresh. They just arrived today from the Kibbutz! What would you like?

Sivan: **Ani Rotzah Shnei Kilo Agvaniot, Shnei Kilo Gezer, V'Shlosha Kilo Melefefonim.**
ah-*nee* rohtz-*ah* shnay kee-*loht* ahg-vah-nee-*yoht,* shnay kee-*loh* geh-*zehr,* veh-shloh-*shah* kee-*loh* meh-lah-feh-foh-*neem.*
I want two kilos of tomatoes, two kilos of carrots, and three kilos of cucumbers.

Mocher: **Hineh HaYerakot Shelach Geveret. Zeh Tish'a VaChetzi Shekalim.**
hey-*nay* hah-yeh-rah-*koht* sheh-*lahch* geh-veh-*reht.* zeh teesh-*ah* vah-cheh-*tzee* shkah-*leem.*
Here are your vegetables, miss. That is nine and one-half shekels.

Sivan: **Yofi! Todah! Shabbat Shalom.**
yoh-fee! toh-*dah.* Shah-*baht* shah-*lohm.*
Great! Thanks! Good Sabbath.

Mocher: **Todah Lach, Kol Tuv.**
toh-*dah* lahch, *kohl* toov.
Thank you. All the best.

Words to Know

K'niot	knee-<u>yoht</u>	groceries
Kol Tuv	<u>kohl</u> toov	all the best
Perot	peh-<u>roht</u>	fruit
Shabbat Shalom	shah-<u>baht</u> shah-<u>lohm</u>	a peaceful Sabbath
Tari	tah-<u>ree</u>	fresh
Yerakot	yeh-rah-<u>koht</u>	vegetables
Yofi	<u>yoh</u>-fee	great, wonderful, beautiful

Dining in a Restaurant

Sometimes you just don't want to cook. When you develop an allergic reaction to pots, pans, and mixing spoons, going out to a **Misadah** (mees-ah-*dah;* restaurant) is always fun. You can peruse the **Tafrit** (tahf-*reet;* menu) and be served by a **Meltzar** (mehl-*tzahr;* waiter) or a **Meltzarit** (mehl-tzah-*reet;* waitress). At the end of the meal, you get a **Cheshbon** (chesh-*bohn;* bill), which isn't as bad as a pile of dirty dishes.

Here are some phrases you can use when ordering food in a restaurant:

- **Efshar Lekabel Tafrit B'Vakasha?** (ehf-*shahr* leh-*kah*-behl tahf-*reet* beh-vah-kah-*shah;* May I have a menu please?)
- **Ani Rotzeh L'Hazmin.** (ah-*nee* roh-*tzeh* leh-hahz-*meen;* I would like to order.) (MS)

  Ani Rotzah L'Hazmin. (ah-*nee* rohtz-*ah* leh-hahz-*meen;* I would like to order.) (FS)
- **Haim Ha'Ochel Tari?** (hah-*eem* hah-*oh*-chehl tah-*ree;* Is the food fresh?)
- **Mah Atah Mamlitz?** (mah ah-*tah* mahm-*leetz;* What do you recommend?) (MS)

  Mah At Mamlitzah? (mah aht mahm-lee-*tzah;* What do you recommend?) (FS)

You can also ask whether the food is **Metugan** (meh-too-*gahn;* fried), **Afui** (ah-foo-*ee;* baked), **Tzalui** (tzah-loo-*ee;* grilled) or **Me'udeh** (meh-oo-*deh;* steamed).

Keeping things kosher

You may have heard someone say that they "keep kosher." In Hebrew, that person would say **Ani Shomer (MS) / Shomeret (FS) Al Kashrut** (ah-*nee* shoh-*mehr*/shoh-meh-*reht* ahl kahsh-*root;* I keep kosher). This declaration means that the person observes Jewish dietary laws written in the Torah, which rabbis later interpreted and extrapolated. These dietary laws include abstaining from forbidden foods, such as pork and shellfish, not mixing **Chalav** (chah-*lahv;* milk) with **Basar** (bah-*sahr;* meat), and only eating foods prepared with kosher utensils. Thus, Jews who observe these laws often buy prepared foods that have a **Hechsher** (hech-*shehr*), a seal that ensures a rabbi has inspected the food and certified it kosher.

Kosher homes have two sets of dishes — one for **Chalavi** (chah-lah-*vee;* dairy) meals and another for **B'sari** (buh-sah-*ree;* meat) meals. If the meal contains neither meat nor milk (when it features foods like vegetables, rice, and even fish), it's called **Parve** (*pahr*-veh) and may be eaten with either milk or meat. In a kosher restaurant, the menu is either **Chalavi** or **B'sari**.

Talkin' the Talk

Dining in a restaurant is great. Oren, a bachelor, hates to cook. So he often goes out to eat. Here's what he says when the food server approaches his table.

Oren:	**Efshar Lekabel Tafrit B'vakashah?** ehf-*shah* leh-kah-*behl* tahf-*reet* beh-vah-kah-*shah?* May I have a menu, please?
Meltzarit:	**Ken Adoni. Hineh HaTafrit.** kehn ah-doh-*nee.* Hee-*nay* hah-tahf-*reet.* Yes, sir. Here is the menu.
Oren:	**HaKol Nir'eh Li Mamash Taim. Me'od Kasheh Li Livchor.** hah-*kohl* nir-*eh* lee mah-*mahsh* tah-*eem.* meh-*ohd* kah-*sheh* lee leev-*chohr.* Everything looks quite delicious. It's very difficult to choose.
Meltzarit:	**HaDag Shelanu HaYom Mamash Metzuyan. Ze Bah im Gezer V'Orez.** hah-*dahg* sheh-lah-*noo* hah-*yohm* mah-*mahsh* meh-tzoo-*yahn.* zeh bah eem *geh*-zehr veh-*oh*-rehz. Our fish today is quite excellent. It comes with carrots and rice.

Oren: **Haim HaDag Metugan?**
          hah-*eem* hah-dahg meh-too-*gahn?*
          Is the fish fried?

Meltzarit: **Ken, V'Zeh Me'od Taim.**
          kehn, veh-*zeh* meh-*ohd* tah-*eem.*
          Yes, and it's very tasty.

Oren: **Yofi! Zeh Nishmah Li Metzuyan. Ani Rotzeh
          L'Hazmin Dag, Im Gezer VeOrez.**
          yoh-fee! zeh neesh-*mah* lee meh-tzoo-*yahn.*
          ah-*nee* roh-*tzeh* leh-hahz-*meen* dahg, eem
          geh-zehr veh-*oh*-rehz.
          Great! That sounds excellent. I want to order fish
          with carrots and rice.

Meltzarit: **Ani M'yad Mevi'ah L'cha, Adoni.**
          ah-*nee* mec-*yahd* meh-vee-*ah* leh-*chah,* ah-doh-*nee.*
          I'll bring it to you right away, sir.

Words to Know

B'hechlet	beh-nehch-<u>leht</u>	absolutely
Im	eem	with
Mamash	mah-<u>mahsh</u>	quite
Meltzar	mehl-<u>tzahr</u>	waiter
Meltzarit	mehl-tzah-<u>reet</u>	waitress
Me'od	meh-<u>ohd</u>	very
Metzuyan	meh-tzoo-<u>yahn</u>	excellent
Misadah	mees-ah-<u>dah</u>	restaurant
Tafrit	tahf-<u>reet</u>	menu
Ta'im	tah-<u>eem</u>	tasty, delicious

In Israel, as in many North American and European cities, meeting friends in cafes is a popular pastime. When the weather is good, many cafes have out-door seating where you can watch the people go by as you enjoy some coffee and dessert. Speaking of coffee, an Israeli **Tafrit** usually contains several different kinds of coffee:

- **Cafeh Filter** (kah-*feh fil*-tehr; filtered coffee — the filter is placed on top of the cup and brought to your table while it's brewing)
- **Cafeh Hafuch** (kah-*feh* hah-*fooch;* café latte)
- **Cafeh Kar** (kah-*feh* kahr; iced coffee)
- **Cafeh Nemes** (kah-*feh* nah-*mehs;* instant coffee)
- **Tay** (tay; tea)

You can also order coffee **Im Cafein** (eem kah-feh-*een;* with caffeine) or **Ntul Cafein** (n-*tool* kah-feh-*een;* without caffeine).

When asking someone if they like their food, it is common in Israel to ask **Taim L'cha?** (MS) (tah-*eem* leh-*chah; Literally:* Is it tasty to you?) or **Taim Lach?** (FS) (tah-*eem* lahch). The answer (if you like the food) is **Ken, Zeh Taim Li** (kehn zeh tah-eem *lee;* Yes, it is tasty to me).

Talkin' the Talk

Dor and Yael have met for coffee at a popular cafe. They're finishing their coffee and dessert, and they ask the **Meltzar** for their **Heshbon.** (Track 10)

Yael: **Ha'Ochel Haya Ta'im L'cha?**
hah-*oh*-chehl hah-*yah* tah-*eem* leh-*chah?*
Did your food taste good?

Dor: **Ken, Zeh Haya Mamash Ta'im Li. Nehenet M'Ha'Glidah Shelach?**
kehn, zeh hah-*yah* mah-*mahsh* tah-*eem* lee. Neh-neh-*neht* meh hah-glee-*dah* sheh-*lahch?*
Yes, it was delicious. Did you enjoy your ice cream?

Yael: **Ken, HaGlidah Hayitah Mamash Tovah.**
kehn, hah-glee-*dah* hah-y-*tah* mah-*mahsh* toh-*vah.*
Yes, the ice cream was quite good.

Dor: **Tov! Meltzar! HaCheshbon B'vakashah!**
       tohv! mehl-*tzahr!* hah-chehsh-*bohn* beh-vah-kah-*shah!*
       Good! Waiter! The bill please!

Meltzar: **Hene HaCheshbon, Adoni.**
       hee-*nay* hah-chesh-*bohn,* ah-doh-*nee.*
       Here is the bill, sir.

Dor: **Todah. Yael, Ani Mazmin.**
       toh-*dah.* yah-*ehl,* ah-*nee* mahz-*meen.*
       Thanks. Yael, my treat.

Yael: **Todah Rabbah L'cha.**
       toh-*dah* rah-*bah* leh-*chah.*
       Thank you very much.

Meltzar: **Atah Tzarich Odef?**
       ah-*tah* tzah-*reech* oh-*dehf?*
       Do you need change?

Dor: **Lo, Ze Bishveilcha.**
       loh, zeh beesh-veel-*chah.*
       No, that's for you.

Meltzar: **Todah, Adoni.**
       toh-*dah,* ah-doh-*nee.*
       Thanks, sir.

Words to Know

Ani Mazmin (MS)	ah-<u>nee</u> mahz-<u>meen</u>	my treat
Ani Mazminah (FS)	ah-<u>nee</u> mahz-mee-<u>nah</u>	my treat
Cheshbon	chehs-<u>bohn</u>	bill
Glidah	<u>glee</u>-dah	ice cream
Ta'im Li.	tah-<u>eem</u> <u>lee</u>	This is delicious.

Fun & Games

Here's a set table. Using the words below, can you identify all the things in the picture?

| Kapit | Mapit | Mazleg | Sakin |
| Mapah Levanah | Marak | Of | Yayin |

Chapter 6

Going Shopping

. . . .

In This Chapter

▶ Finding your shopping destination

▶ Getting dressed

▶ Clothing yourself for all seasons

▶ Making sure your clothes match

. . . .

*H*ow many times has this happened to you? You have a closet full of clothes but nothing to wear. You have only one solution to this malady: Hit the stores! In this chapter, I talk about all the different places where you can buy clothes, and all the words you need to dress yourself. You've heard the saying: Clothes make the man (or woman)! So dress for success!

Exploring Places to Shop

Now that you want to buy some clothes, the question becomes where to get them. You can go to a

▬ **Chanut Kol-Bo** (chah-*noot kol*-bo; department store)

▬ **Kanyon** (kan-*yohn;* shopping mall)

▬ **Merkaz Knyiot** (mehr-*kahz* knee-*yoht;* shopping center)

▬ **Midrachov** (meed-reh-*chohv;* outdoor shopping mall, usually lined with cafes and cute little shops)

▬ **Shuk HaPishpeshim** (shook hah-peesh-peh-*sheem;* flea market)

Bargains galore at the flea market

One of my favorite places to shop in Israel is the **Shuk HaPishpeshim** (shook hah-peesh-peh-sheem; flea market) in Old Jaffa. You can find it by walking down the main road of Old Jaffa, Tel Aviv-Jaffa Way, and looking for the signs. There you find cavernous alleys with sellers hocking everything from fine leather to cheap T-shirts to pots and pans. You have to bargain, and it's great fun! I've found great bargains. The dresses I bought there never fail to bring in compliments.

Selecting the Perfect Outfit

The word to dress oneself in Hebrew is **Lehitlabesh** (le-heet-lah-behsh). In general, you **Lovesh** (loh-vehsh; wear) **Begadim** (beh-gah-deem; clothes). However, in Hebrew, you use specific verbs when you wear a **Kovah** (koh-vah; hat), **Na'alyim** (nah-ah-lye-eem; shoes), **Garbayim** (gahr-bye-eem; socks), a **Sha'on** (shah-ohn; watch), a **Chagorah** (chah-go-rah; belt), **Mishkafyim** (meesh-kah-fah-eem; glasses), an **Anivah** (a-nee-vah; necktie), or **Tachsheetim** (tach-shee-teem; jewelry).

For example, the verb you use to talk about wearing a hat is **Lachavosh** (lah-chah-vosh; to wear a hat). For words like **Chultzah** (chool-tzah; shirt), **Michnasyim** (meech-nah-sah-eem; pants), **Simla** (seem-lah; dress), **Chatza'it** (chah-tzah-eet; skirt), **Tachtonim** (tahch-toh-neem; underwear), and **Chaziah** (chah-zee-yah; bra) you use the same verb, **Lovesh**.

> **Hu Chovesh Kovah.** (hoo choh-vehsh koh-vah; He wears a hat.)
>
> **He Choveshet Kovah.** (hee choh-veh-shet koh-vah; She wears a hat.)
>
> **Hem Chovshim Kovah.** (hem chohv-sheem koh-vah; They wear a hat.) (MP)
>
> **Hen Chovshot Kovah.** (hen chohv-shot koh-vah; They wear a hat.) (FP)

When you want to talk about wearing shoes, use the verb **Lin'ol** (lin-ohl; to wear shoes).

> **Hu No'el Na'alyim.** (hoo noh-el nah-ah-lye-eem; He wears shoes.)
>
> **He No'elet Na'alyim.** (hee noh-eh-let nah-ah-lye-eem; She wears shoes.)
>
> **Hem No'elim Na'alyim.** (hem noh-ah-leem nah-ah-lye-eem; They wear shoes.) (MP)
>
> **Hen No'elot Na'alyim.** (hen noh-ah-lot nah-ah-lye-eem; They wear shoes.) (FP)

To talk about wearing socks, use the verb **Ligrov** (lig-*rohv;* to wear socks).

> **Hu Gorev Garbayim.** (hoo goh-*rehv* gahr-*bye*-eem; He wears socks.)
>
> **He Gorevet Garbayim.** (hee goh-*reh-veht* gahr-*bye*-eem; She wears socks.)
>
> **Hem Gorvim Garbayim.** (hem gohr-*veem* gahr-*bye*-eem; They wear socks.) (MP)
>
> **Hen Gorvot Garbayim.** (hen gohrv-*oht* gahr-*bye*-eem; They wear socks.) (FP)

To talk about wearing glasses, use the verb **Leharkiv** (leh-har-*keev;* to wear glasses).

> **Hu Markeev Mishkafayeem.** (hoo mar-*keev* meesh-kah-*fye*-eem; He wears glasses.)
>
> **He Markeevah Mishkafayeem.** (hee mahr-kee-*vah* meesh-kah-*fye*-eem; She wears glasses.)
>
> **Hem Markeevim Mishkafayeem.** (hem mahr-kee-*veem* meesh-kah-*fye*-eem; They wear glasses.) (MP)
>
> **Hen Markeevot Mishkafayeem.** (hen mahr-kee-*voht* meesh-kah-*fye*-eem; They wear glasses.) (FP)

To talk about wearing a belt, use the verb **Lachgor** (lach-*gohr;* to wear a belt).

> **Hu Choger Chagorah.** (hoo choh-*gehr* chah-goh-*rah;* He wears a belt.)
>
> **He Chogeret Chagorah.** (hee choh-geh-*reht* chah-*goh-rah;* She wears a belt.)
>
> **Hem Chogrim Chagorah.** (hem chohg-*reem* chah-goh-*rah;* They wear a belt.) (MP)
>
> **Hen Chogrot Chagorah.** (hen chohg-*roht* chah-goh-*rah;* They wear a belt.) (FP)

To talk about wearing a watch or jewelry, use the verb **La'anod** (lah-ah-*nohd;* to wear jewelry).

> **Hu Oned Sha'on.** (hoo oh-*nehd* shah-*ohn;* He wears a watch.)
>
> **He Onedet Sha'on.** (hee oh-*neh*-deht shah-*ohn;* She wears a watch.)
>
> **Hem Ondim Sha'aon.** (hem ohn-*deem* shah-*ohn;* They wear a watch.) (MP)
>
> **Hen Ondot Sha'on.** (hen ohnd-*doht* shah-*ohn;* They wear a watch.) (FP)

Words to Know

Anivah	ah-nee-*vah*	tie
Chagorah	chah-goh-*rah*	belt
Chalifa	chah-lee-*fah*	suit
Chatza'it	chah-tzah-*eet*	skirt
Chazyah	chah-zee-*yah*	bra
Chultzah	chool-*tzah*	shirt
Garbyim	gahr-*bye*-eem	socks
Kovah	*koh*-vah	hat
Michnasayim	meech-nah-*sah*-yeem	pants
Mishkafayeem	meesh-kah-*fey*-eem	eyeglasses
Na'alyim	nah-ah-*lye*-eem	shoes
Sha'on	shah-*ohn*	watch
Simla	seem-*lah*	dress
Tachtonim	tach-toh-*neem*	underwear

Be very careful not to confuse the word for pants **Michnasayim** (mich-nah-*sah*-yeem) with the word for eyeglasses **Mishkafyim** (meesh-kah-*fey*-eem)! I know someone who did this once — with very embarrassing results. He forgot his glasses on the bus, so he went to the central bus station's information desk to ask for help. He carefully explained to the clerk how he had forgotten his glasses, how he had taken them off while he was on the bus, folded them, and placed them beside him. But he didn't say **Mishkafyim** (meesh-kah-*fey*-yeem; glasses), he said **Michnasayim** (mich-nah-*sah*-yeem; pants)! The clerk thought he was very strange indeed!

Judaism has a blessing for everything, even clothes! The traditional blessing for wearing new clothes the first time is:

Baruch Atah Adonai Eloheinu Melech HaOlam, Maïbish Arumim.

bah-*rooch* ah-*tah* ah-doh-*nai* eh-loh-*hey*-nu *meh*-lech hah-oh-*lam*, mal-*beesh* ah-roo-*meem*.

Praised are You the Eternal One our God who clothes the naked.

Talkin' the Talk

Orit is shopping for new clothes in the **Kol-Bo** (kohl-*boh;* department store). A saleswoman named Maya offers to help her.

Maya: **Shalom Geveret. Efshar La'Azor Lach?**
shah-*lohm* ge-*vai*-ret. ef-*shahr* lah-ah-*zor lach?*
Hello, Miss. May I help you?

Orit: **Ken, Todah Ani Mechapeset Begadim. Ani Rotzah Chultzah, Michnahsayim, Simlah, V'chatza'it.**
kehn, toh-*dah* ah-nee meh-chah-*peh*-set bgah-gah-*deem.* ah-nee roh-*tzah,* chool-tzah, meech-nah-*sah*-eem, seem-*lah,* veh-chah-tzah-*eet.*
Yes, Thank you. I am looking for clothes. I want a shirt, pants, a dress, and a skirt.

Maya: **Yofie. Aizeh Tzva'im At Ohevet?**
yoh-fee. *ay*-zeh tz-vah-*eem* aht oh-*heh*-vet?
Great. What colors do you like?

Orit: **Ani Ohevet Chum, Shachor, Ve'Lavan.**
ah-*nee* oh-*heh*-vet choom, shah-*chohr,* veh-lah-*vahn.*
I like brown, black, and white.

Maya: **Mah HaGodel Shelach?**
mah hah-*goh*-del sheh-lach?
What is your size?

Orit: **HaGodel Sheli Shlosheem-Ve'Shesh.**
hah-*goh*-del sheh-*lee* shloh-*sheem* veh-*shehsh.*
I'm a size 36.

Maya:	**Tov. Ani Me'Yad Avi Et Ha'Begadim Shelach Le'Chadar Ha'Halbasha.**
	Tohv. ah-*nee* meh-*yahd* ah-*vee* eht hah-bgah-gah-*deem* she-*lach* leh-cha-*dahr* hah-hal-bah-*shah.*
	Good. I'll bring the clothes to the dressing room right away.

Some people love to shop. Others hate it. But if you want to be well dressed, shopping is a task that you just have to do. You know the routine: Go to a **Chanut** (chah-*noot;* store) and grab a bunch of **Begadim** that you like. Grab your correct **Godel** (*goh*-dehl; size) and take a look at the **Mechir** (meh-*cheer;* price). You don't want anything too **Yakar** (yah-*kahr;* expensive)!

Maybe a sale is going on and the **Mechir** is really **Zol** (zohl; inexpensive). You need to find a **Chadar Halbasha** (chah-*dahr* hal-bah-*shah;* dressing room) **Limdod** (leem-*dohd;* to try on) all your **Begadim.** You don't want **Begadim** that are too **Rafu'im** (reh-foo-*eem;* loose) or too **Tzmudim** (tzh*moo-deem;* tight).

When you've made your choice, find a **Kupah** (koo-*pah;* cash register) so you can pay for you new purchases. **Titchadesh (MS)/Titchadshi (FS)!** (teet-chahd-*desh*/teet-chahd-*shee;* May you be renewed by your new purchase!)

Words to Know

Chadar Halbasha	cha-<u>dar</u> hal-bah-<u>shah</u>	dressing room
Godel	<u>goh</u>-del	size
Kupah	koo-<u>pah</u>	cash register
Limdod	leehm-<u>dohd</u>	to try on
Mechir	meh-<u>cheer</u>	price
Odef	<u>oh</u>-def	change
Rafui	rah-<u>foo</u>-<u>ee</u>	loose
Tzamud	tzah-<u>mood</u>	tight
Yakar	yah-<u>kahr</u>	expensive
Zol	<u>zohl</u>	inexpensive

Styling Your Clothes Around the Seasons

Of course, when you buy clothes, you want to dress for the season. Whether you are wearing **Begadim Yom Yomiyim** (beh-gah-*deem yohm*-yoh-mee-*yeem;* casual clothes), **Levush Chagigi** (leh-*voosh* chah-gee-*gee;* dressy clothes), or even your **Bigdei Shabbat** (beeg-*day* shah-*baht;* Sabbath clothes, the Hebrew equivalent of "Sunday Best"), or if you live in a climate with four seasons, you want to have all kinds of clothes handy for the different weather.

Fall fashion

Ah, fall — when the air is crisp and the leaves are colorful! On the Jewish calendar, fall is the time of the High Holidays, including Rosh HaShanah and Yom Kippur — the Jewish New Year and the Day of Atonement. Fall is a time for new beginnings. It's also a great time to get some new clothes. The following Hebrew words are a few fall items you may want to have on hand:

- **Afudah** (ah-foo-*dah;* vest)
- **Me'il-Geshem** (meh-*eel geh*-shem; raincoat)
- **Me'il Katzar** (meh-*eel* kah-*tzar;* jacket or short coat)

The winter look

Winter! What a magical time of year. If your home area receives snow, this time can be especially fun — and cold! Thus you need to bundle up! I include some special winter clothing you want to take out of storage when the temperatures start hovering around freezing:

- **Kfafot** (*k-fah*-foht; gloves)
- **Kovah** (*koh*-vah; hat)
- **Magafayim** (mah-gah-*fye*-eem; boots)
- **Me'il** (meh-*eel;* coat)
- **Tza'if** (tzah-*eef;* scarf)

Talkin' the Talk

 Dani and Orit are about to play in the **Sheleg** (*sheh*-leg; snow). Before they go, they make sure they have everything they need. (Track 11)

Dani:	**O.K. Anachnu Holchim Le'Yom Sheleg. At Muchanah?**
	oh-*kay.* ah-nach-*noo* hol-*cheem* leh-*yohm* sheh-leg. aht moo-chah-*nah?*
	Are you ready for a day in the snow?
Orit:	**Ken. Ani Muchanah. Ani Gorevet Garbayim MiTzemer, Ani Noelet Magafayim, Ani Loveshet Me'il Cham**
	kehn. ah-*nee* moo-chah-*nah.* ah-*nee* goh-*reh*-vet garh-*bah*-yeem mee-*tzeh*-mer, ah-*nee* noh-*eh*-let mah-gah-fye-*eem,* ah-*nee* loh-*veh*-shet meh-*eel* chahm.
	Yes, I am wearing wool socks, boots, and a warm coat.
Dani.	**Yofi. Yesh Li Tza'if Ve'Kfa'fot. Al Tishkachi Et Ha Kovah Shelach!**
	yoh-fee. yaysh-*lee* tzah-*eef* ook-fah-*foht.* Al teesh-keh-*chee* eht hah *koh*-vah sheh-*lahch!*
	Great. I have a scarf and gloves. Don't forget your hat!
Orit:	**Tov SheHizkarta Li!**
	tohv sheh-heez-*kahr*-tah *lee!*
	Good that you reminded me!

Spring attire

Spring is wonderful! The days grow longer and warmer. Trees and flowers begin to bloom. And we can finally stop wearing those wool gloves and toss off that heavy coat in favor of a lighter jacket. You can now wear:

- **Chultzah im Sharvulim K'tzarim** (*chool-tzah eem shahr-voo-leem k-tzah-reem;* short-sleeved shirt)
- **Mitria** (meet-ree-*yah;* umbrella)

Summer wear

The dog days of summer! Long sunny days! Ice cream cones! And, of course, the clothes you can wear only on the hottest days of the year:

- ✔ **Beged Yam** (*beh*-gehd *yahm;* bathing suit)
- ✔ **Michnahsayim K'tzarim** (mich-nah-*sah*-yeem ktzah-*reem;* shorts)
- ✔ **Mishkafay-Shemesh** (meesh-kah-*fay sheh*-mesh; sunglasses)
- ✔ **Sandalim** (sahn-dah-*leem;* sandals)

When you put two nouns together to form one word, you have a dependent relationship or a compound noun. In Hebrew, you call this compound a **Smichut** (smee-*choot*). A good example in English is the word *fireplace*. Basically, two words combine to make up one word. In Hebrew, when both nouns are singular, putting them together in **Smichut** (smee-*choot*) is easy. For example, the word for swimsuit in Hebrew is **Beged Yam** (*beh*-gehd *yahm*), which literally means *sea suit*. ***Note:*** In Hebrew, the order is opposite of what it is in English. In the previous example, **Beged** means clothes or suit while **Yam** means sea. So literally that phrase means *clothing of the sea*. Furthermore, if the nouns have only one syllable, their pronunciation remains the same. One exception is the word for room **Cheder** (*cheh*-dair). In **Smichut, Cheder** becomes **Chadar** (chah-*dar*). Hence, the Hebrew word for *dressing room* is **Chadar Halbashah** (chah-*dar* hahl-bah-*shah*). If the first word in the **Smichut** is masculine plural, the final ***mem*** (a Hebrew letter — take a look at Chapter 1 for more about the Hebrew letters) drops off. For example, *sunglasses* is **Mishkafei Shemesh** (meesh-kah-*fey sheh*-mesh). One more tidbit: If you want to add the word *the* (**Hah;** hah) to a **Smichut,** put it in front of the second noun. For example:

- ✔ **Beged HaYam** (*beh*-gehd hah-*yahm;* the bathing suit)
- ✔ **Chadar Ha'Halbashah** (chah-*dar* hah-hahl-bah-*shah;* the dressing room)
- ✔ **Mishkafei HaShemesh** (meesh-kah-*fey* hah-*sheh*-mesh; the sunglasses)

Talkin' the Talk

 Dani and Orit are getting ready to go to the beach on a hot summer day. Before they go, they make sure they have everything. (Track 12)

Dani: **Norah Cham HaYom! Tov She'Ani Lovesh Michnasyim K'tzarim.**
noh-*rah* chahm hah-*yohm*! tohv sheh-ah-*nee* loh-*vesh* mich-nah-*sye*-eem ktzah-*reem*.
It's hot today! I'm glad I'm wearing shorts.

Orit: **Ken. Simlah B'li Sharvulim sheli V'HaSandalim Sheli Tovim Li BaShemesh.**
kehn. hah-seem-*lah* buh-*lee* shahr-voo *leem* veh-hah-san-dah- *leem* toh-*veem* lee bah-*sheh*-mehsh.
Yeah. My sleeveless dress and sandals feel good in the hot sun.

Dani:	**Yesh Lach Et Mishkafei HaShemesh Shelanu?**
	yehsh lahch eht meesh-kah-*fay*-hah-sheh-mesh sheh-*lah*-noo?
	Do you have our sunglasses?
Orit:	**Ken. Yesh L'cha Et HaMagafayim Ve'Ha'Krem Neged Shizuf?**
	kehn. yehsh leh-*chah* eht hah-mah-gah-*fye*-eem ve-hah-kreme *neh*-gehd shee-*zoof*?
	Yes. Do you have the towels and the sunblock?
Dani:	**Ken. Yesh Li. Ve'Gam Yesh Li Et Bigdei HaYam. Ani Gam Chovesh Kovah.**
	kehn. yehsh *lee*. veh-*gahm* yehsh-*lee* eht beeg-*day* hah-*yahm*. ah-*nee* gahm choh-*vehsh* koh-*vah*.
	Yes. I have them. I have the swimsuits, too. And I'm also wearing a hat.
Orit:	**Tov SheHizkarta Li! Ani Gam Rotzah Lachvosh Kovah.**
	tohv sheh-heez-*kahr*-tah *lee!* ah-*nee* gahm roh-*tzah* lach-*vohsh koh*-vah.
	It's good that you reminded me again! I also want to wear a hat.

Words to Know

Beged Yam	beh-gehd yahm	swimsuit
Kfafot	kfah-foht	gloves
Kovah	koh-vah	hat
Me'il	meh-eel	coat
Metria	meet-ree-yah	umbrella
Mishkafay Shemesh	meesh-kah-fay sheh-mehsh	sunglasses
Tza'if	tzah-eef	scarf

Garbing yourself for God

Jews have several ritual garments that they wear. In Orthodox circles, only men wear these garments. However, increasingly in non-Orthodox settings and even in some liberal Orthodox communities, you also find women wearing them. Observant Jews wear a prayer shawl, or a **Talit** (ta-*leet*), during morning prayers and on Yom Kippur, the Day of Atonement. The **Talit** (ta-*leet*) is a rectangular garment with **Tzi'tzit** (tzee-*tzeet;* fringes) on its four corners. The fringes are tied in such a way that they're symbolic of the 613 **Mitzvot** (meetz-*voht;* commandments) that Jews are obligated to observe.

Jews cover their heads as a sign of respect. Hence, men and some women cover their heads with a "skull-cap" or **Kipah** (kee-*pah*). Some observant Jews wear a **Talit Katan** (tah-*leet kah-tahn*), which is a four-cornered garment under the shirt. Each corner of the garment has **Tzi'tzit** (tzee-*tzeet;* fringes). Some people tuck their **Tzi'tzit** in their clothes, while others leave them hanging out so they see them and remember their religious obligations.

When you use a sentence with a definite direct object after a verb, you must precede the object with the word **Et** (eht). For example: **Ani Rotzah Lir'ot Et HaKovah** (ah-*nee* roh-*tzah* leer-*ot* eht hah-*koh*-vah; I want to see the hat).

Color Me Beautiful

When you buy **Begadim** (bgah-*deem;* clothes), look for the **Tzva'im** (tzvah-*eem;* colors) that look best on you. Some people like **Tzva'im Mavrikim** (tzvah-*eem* mahv-ree-*keem;* bright colors), and others don't. Here are the colors:

- **Adom** (ah-*dohm;* red)
- **Kachol** (kah-*chohl;* blue)
- **Katom** (kah-*tohm;* orange)
- **Lavan** (lah-*vahn;* white)
- **Segol** (seh-*gohl;* purple)
- **Shachor** (shah-*chor;* black)
- **Tzahov** (tzah-*hohv;* yellow)
- **Varod** (vah-*rohd;* pink)
- **Yarok** (yah-*rohk;* green)

Heads, shoulders, knees, and toes: Modesty rules

If you're going to an Orthodox synagogue or neighborhood, you want to take note of the dress code and dress appropriately. Of course, many shades of orthodoxy exist from the ultra-Orthodox who observe Jewish law stringently and are somewhat suspicious of the modern world, to the modern Orthodox who are dedicated to both Jewish law and being part of the modern world. In general, in Orthodox settings, women should wear a dress or skirt that covers their knees and sleeves that cover their shoulders or elbows. Men should cover their head. In the ultra-Orthodox neighborhood of Mea She'arim in Jerusalem, signs request that all who enter the neighborhood abide by the dress code. And if you visit the **HaKotel** (*hah-koh-tel;* the Western Wall) in the Old City of Jerusalem, men are given head coverings and women skirts before they approach Judaism's holiest site.

If you want to tell someone that you like his or her hat, shirt, or shoes, use a Biblical phrase and say that the object "finds favor in your eyes." For example: **HaKovah Shelach Motzeh Chen B'Einai!** (hah-*koh*-vah sheh-*lach* moh-*tzeh* chen buh-ay-*nye;* I like your hat!) (Literally: Your hat finds favor in my eyes.)

Getting More Than (and Less Than) You Bargained For

Remember Sally in *Harry Met Sally* when she went to a restaurant? She wanted a little more of this, less of that, the least of that other thing, and so forth. You too can be fussy in Hebrew, if only you know the right words. In this section, I tell you how to say words like *more than, less than, the most,* and *the least.* So you can tell people exactly what you want!

Making comparisons

If you want to say something is bigger, taller, more beautiful, and so forth, use the word **Yoter** (yoh-*tair*) either before or after the adjective.

Adjective	*Comparative*
Tov (tohv; good)	**Yoter Tov** (yoh-*tair* tohv; better)
Gadol (gah-*dohl;* big)	**Gadol Yoter** (gah-*dohl* yoh-*tair;* bigger)

If you want to say something is less in some way, use the Hebrew word **Pachot** (pah-*choht*) in front of the adjective.

Adjective	*Comparative*
Tov (tohv; good)	**Pachot Tov** (pah-*choht* tohv; not as good)
Gadol (gah-*dohl;* big)	**Pachot Gadol** (pah-*choht* gah-*dohl;* not as big)

If you want to say something is *more than* or *less than* something else, use the Hebrew word **Mi** (mee) to make the comparison. For example, if a **Yeled** (*yeh*-lehd; boy) is bigger than a **Yaldah** (yahl-*dah;* girl) say it like this:

✔ **HaYeled Yotair Gadol Mi'Ha'Yaldah.** (hah-*yeh*-led yoh-*tehr* gah-*dohl* *mee*-hah-yahl-*dah;* The boy is bigger than the girl.)

✔ **HaYaldah Pachot G'dolah Mi'HaYeled.** (hah-yahl-*dah* pah-*choht* g-doh-*lah* *mee*-hah-*yeh*-lehd; The girl is not as big as the boy.)

Measuring up

Finding your right size can be tough any time you go shopping. But if you're shopping in Israel, the problem is compounded because clothing sizes aren't the same as the United States. The clothes in Israel use the European system. When in Israel, use the following charts to help you find your size:

Use the approximate equivalents for women's clothing:

United States	4	6	8	10	12	14	16	18	20
Israel	34	36	38	40	42	44	46	48	50

For men's jackets and suit sizes, use these rough conversions:

United States	38	40	42	44	46	48	50
Israel	48	50	52	54	56	58	60

If you want to ask how big something is, or inquire about its size, use **Mah HaGodel?** (*mah*-hah-*goh*-dehl; What's the size?).

For more information on numbers, peruse Chapter 1.

Speakin' in hyperbole

If you want to say something is *the most, the biggest, the most expensive, the prettiest,* and so on, use the Hebrew word **Hachi** (ha-*chee*) in front of the adjective.

> **HaChultza HaChi Yafah BaChanut.** (hah-chool-*tzah* hah-*chee* yah-*fah* bah-chah-*noot;* the prettiest shirt in the store.)

> **Ha'Michnasayim Ha'Chi Yekarim BaChanut.** (*hah*-meech-nah-*sah*-eem hah-*chee* yeh-kah-*reem bah*-chah-*noot;* the most expensive pants in the store.)

Fun & Games

These four people are dressed in fall, winter, spring, and summer clothes. Can you match the correct Hebrew word with the correct article of clothing? Using the vocabulary in the word bank, write the correct words in the space provided.

Chultzah, Simla, Kovah, Mishkafay-Shemesh, Me'il Katzar, Tza'if, Kfafot, Mitria, Chagorah, Michnasayim, Garbayim, Na'alyim, Magafayim, Sandalim, Beged Yam

A. _____	F. _____	K. _____
B. _____	G. _____	L. _____
C. _____	H. _____	M. _____
D. _____	I. _____	N. _____
E. _____	J. _____	O. _____

Chapter 7

Having Fun Hebrew Style

In This Chapter

▶ Keeping track of the time

▶ Chatting about fun activities: Key vocabulary words

▶ Attending movies, museums, the theater, and concerts

▶ Going to the zoo

This chapter is about having fun. Whether you want to go to the movies, check out a museum, or see the animals at the zoo, you can do it using Hebrew!

Before you dash out to have a day of fun or a night on the town, you need to figure out some basics first, including how to tell time and how to say the days of the week in Hebrew. After all, you need to know when the fun begins.

Counting the Hours and Minutes

Whether you're chronically early, always late, or right on time, you want to know the time of day. If you don't have a watch, you can ask a passerby by saying, **"Slicha, Mah HaSha'ah?"** (slee-*chah* mah hah-shah-*ah*?; Excuse me, what is the time?) If you want to know the time of a specific event, you can ask **"B'Aizo Sha'ah . . ."** (buh ay-*zoh* shah-ah; At what time [does such-n-such occur?])

Telling time like an American

Hebrew speakers use two different systems for telling time. One way is similar to the way in the United States, which uses the time of a standard clock from 1 to 12. Israelis commonly use the 24-hour clock or military time. For more on the 24-hour clock, see the sidebar, "Using the 24-hour routine," later in this chapter.

Using the 24-hour routine

To avoid any misunderstanding, Israelis often use the 24-hour system of telling time. You notice this style of telling time on any timetable, such as when a movie starts, when a bus arrives or leaves, or when a bank or business remains open.

In this system, after you reach 12, you just keep adding to it. So 1 p.m. in this system is 13, 2 p.m. is 14, 3 p.m. is 15 and so on. In the 24-hour system, you don't say "a quarter to" or "ten minutes to." You always state the hour and then the minutes afterwards. For example:

- ✔ **Ha'Sha'ah Arbah'esrei V'Asarah** (hah-shah-*ah* ar-bah-es-*reh* vuh-ah-sah-*rah;* The hour is 14 and ten minutes). This corresponds to 2:10 p.m.

- ✔ **Ha'Sha'ah Esrim-Ve'Achat VaChetzi** (hah-shah-*ah* es-*reem* ve-ah-*chaht* vah-*cheh*-tzee; The hour is 21 and a half). This corresponds to 9:30 p.m.

- ✔ **Ha'Sha'ah Shesh-Esrei V'Chamishim** (hah-shah-*ah* shaysh-es-*reh* ve-chah-mee-*sheem;* The hour is 16 and 50). This corresponds to 4:50 p.m.

On the hour

Saying the time at the top of the hour is easy. You just say: **HaShah'ah . . .** (hah-shah-*ah;* The hour is . . .), and then say the number of the correct hour. Use the feminine form of numbers when telling time. (See Chapter 1 for more details about numbers and counting.)

On the half hour

If you want to say half-past the hour, the hour comes first and then the expression **Vachetzi** (vah-*cheh*-tzee). For example, 3:30 is **Shalosh VaChetzi** (shah-*lohsh*-vah-*cheh*-tzee; three and a half).

You may also hear **Ushloshim** (oo-shlo-*sheem*). For example, **Shalosh Ushloshim** is an alternative to **Shalosh VaChetzi** as an expression for 3:30, meaning "three and thirty."

On the quarter hour

If you want to express that the time is either 15 minutes before or after the hour, you need these expressions:

- ✔ **Reva Le...** (*reh*-vah luh; It's a quarter to . . .)
- ✔ **vaReva** (vah-reh-vah; and a quarter . . .)

When you say "a quarter to," the hour comes after the expression. However if you want to say "a quarter after," you state the hour first and then the expression. For example:

✔ For 2:45, you say **Reva Le'Shalosh** (*reh*-vah leh-shah-*lohsh;* a quarter to three).

✔ For 3:15, you say **Shalosh VaReva** (shah-*lohsh* vah-*reh*-vah; three and a quarter).

A few minutes before or after the hour

Sometimes, time doesn't neatly divide itself into half and quarter hours. In such cases, you can use the same preceding patterns, substituting the times in terms of minutes before or after the hour. For example:

✔ For 2:50, you say **Asarah L'Shalosh** (ah-sah-*rah* leh-shah-*lohsh;* ten to three).

✔ For 3:10, you say **Shalosh V'Asarah** (shah-*lohsh* veh-ah-sah-*rah;* ten after three).

Knowing the time of day

No matter what time of day it is, you need to know the correct Hebrew words. Use the following terms to know what time of day it is:

✔ **Acharei-haTzohorayim** (ah-chah-*ray*-ha-tzoh-hoh-*rah*-yeem; afternoon)

✔ **Boker** (*boh*-kehr; morning)

✔ **Erev** (*er*-rehv; evening)

✔ **Lilah** (*lye*-lah; night)

✔ **Tzohorayim** (tzoh-hoh-*rah*-yeem; noon)

Relating time to the past, present, and future

Sometimes when you're talking about time, you don't speak of events in terms of their exact **Ta'arich** (tah-ah-*reech;* date) or point in time. Instead, you speak of time relative to the present. Hence, you speak of **Etmol** (eht-*mohl;* yesterday), **Shilshom** (shil-*shohm;* the day before yesterday), **Emesh** (*eh*-mehsh; last night), **Machar** (mah-*char;* tomorrow), and **Machratayim** (mach-ra-*ta*-yeem; the day after tomorrow). You can also talk about **HaShavu'a She'avar** (ha-shah-*voo*-ah sheh-ah-*vahr;* last week) and **HaShavua Ha'bah** (ha-shah-*voo*-ah ha-*bah;* next week). And if you're feeling particularly nostalgic, you can talk about **HaShanah She'Avrah** (ha-shah-*nah* sheh-av-*rah;* last year). And, of course, you always have **HaShanah Ha'ba'ah** (ha-shah-*nah* hah-bah-ah; next year)!

The Hebrew infinitive for "to be" is **Lehityot** (le-hee-*yoht*). Check out Table 7-1 to see how to conjugate this important verb in the past and future tenses. Lehityot doesn't have a present tense, however. It is implied in the pronoun. So when you want to say, for example, "I am," in Hebrew, all you need to say is **Ani** (ah-*nee;* I).

Table 7-1	Conjugating Lehityot (le-hee-yoht; to be)		
English Verb	**Hebrew Verb**	**Pronunciation**	**Gender**
Past Tense			
I was	Hayiti	hah-*yee*-tee	
you were	Hayita	hah-*yee*-tah	(MS)
you were	Hayit	hah-*yeet*	(FS)
he was	Haya	hah-*yah*	
she was	Haytah	hei-*tah*	
we were	Hayenu	hah-*yee*-noo	(MP/FP)
you were	Hayeetem	hah-*yee*-tehm	(MP)
you were	Hayeeten	hah-*yee*-tehn	(FP)
they were	Hayu	hah-*yoo*	(MP/FP)
Future Tense			
I will be	Eheyeh	eh-heh-*yeh*	
you will be	Tiheyeh	teh-he-*yeh*	(MS)
you will be	Tiheyi	tee-hee-*yee*	(FS)
he will be	Yehiyeh	yee-hee-*yeh*	
she will be	Tiheyeh	tee-he-*yeh*	
we will be	Nehiyeh	nee-he-*yeh*	(MP/FP)
you will be	Tehiyu	te-hee-*yoo*	(MP/FP)
they will be	Yehiyu	yee-hee-*yoo*	(MP/FP)

A couple of other tidbits about the infinitive **Lehiyot** include the following:

✔ Two popular Israeli expressions using this verb are: **Yehiyeh Tov** (yeh-hee-*yeh tohv;* Things will get better), and **Mah Yiheye** (*mah* yeh-hee-*yeh;* What will be, or What's going to happen) — when pronounced fast, *mah yihyeh.*

✔ The Hebrew equivalent of "Once upon a time" uses this verb. The expression is: **Hayo Haya** (hah-*yoh* ha-*yah*).

Words to Know

Boker	<u>boh</u>-kehr	morning
Chatzi Sha'ah	chah-<u>tzee</u> shah-<u>ah</u>	half an hour
Daka	dah-<u>kah</u>	minute
Emesh	<u>eh</u>-mehsh	last night
Erev	<u>eh</u>-rehv	evening
Etmol	eht-<u>mohl</u>	yesterday
Lailah	<u>lye</u>-lah	night
Machar	mah-<u>chahr</u>	tomorrow
Machratayim	mach-rah-<u>tah</u>-eem	day after tomorrow
Rega	<u>reh</u>-gah	moment
Sh'niya	sh-nee-<u>yah</u>	second
Sha'ah	shah-<u>ah</u>	hour
Shavua	shah-<u>voo</u>-ah	week
Shilshom	shil-<u>shohm</u>	day before yesterday
Ta'arich	tah-ah-<u>reech</u>	date
Tzoharayim	tzoh-hoh-<u>rah</u>-yeem	noon
Z'man	z-<u>mahn</u>	time

CULTURAL WISDOM

Israelis are excellent multitaskers. When an Israeli is in the middle of something, but wants to indicate to you that he or she will pay attention to you in "just a moment" and you should just wait a bit, he or she may cup the fingers of his or her hand and shake it at you. When you see this, it means **Rak Rega** (*rahk reh*-gah; just one moment).

Talkin' the Talk

 Natan is waiting for the bus on a Sunday morning. He forgot to wear his watch today, so he asks the man standing next to him for the time. (Track 13)

Natan:	**Slicha, Adoni. Mah Ha'Sha'ah?**
	slee-*chah* ah-doh-*nee*. mah-hah-shah-*ah?*
	Excuse me, sir, what's the time?
Man:	**Ha'Sha'ah Shmoneh VaChetzi.**
	hah-shah-*ah* sh-*moh-neh* vah- *cheh*-tzee.
	The time is eight-thirty.
Natan:	**Todah Rabbah Lecha Adoni.**
	toh-*dah* rah-*bah* leh-*chah* ah-doh-*nee.*
	Thank you very much, sir.
Man:	**B'vakasha.**
	beh-*vah*-kah-*shah.*
	You're welcome.
Natan:	**B'Aizo Sha'ah Ha'otobus Amur L'Hagi'ah?**
	beh-ay-*zoh* shah-ah hah-oh-toh-*boos* ah-*moor* leh-hah-*gee*-ah?
	When is the bus supposed to come?
Man:	**Od Chamesh Dakot.**
	ohd chah-*mesh* dah-*koht.*
	In five more minutes.

Having fun with Israeli slang

Hebrew has several ways to express having a good time. The word for fun in Hebrew is **Kef** (*kehf*). If something is really fun, you may want to comment that it is **Kef Lo Normali** (kehf loh nor-*mal-ee;* Fun beyond the norm). Or you may want to say **Oi, Yoi, Yoi. Kamah SheZeh Nechmad!** (*oi, yoi, yoi,* Kah-*mah* sheh-*zeh* nech-*mahd;* Wow! That was so pleasant). If you want to say "to have fun," you can say **Lekayef** (leh-kah-*yehf*) or you can tell someone **La'asot Chaim** (lah-ah-*soht* chah-*yeem*), which means literally, "to make life." If you want to tell someone to have a good time, the expression is **Bilui Na'im!** (bee-*looy* nah-*eem*).

All day on **Yom Shishi** (*yohm* shee-*shee;* Friday) and also on **Yom Shabbat** (*yohm* shah-*baht;* Saturday) the customary greeting is **Shabbat Shalom** (shah-*baht* shah-*lohm;* a peaceful Sabbath). When **Shabbat** (shah-*baht;* the Sabbath) is over on **Motze'ei Shabbat** (moh-*tza-ay* shah-*baht;* Saturday night), you should wish people a **Shavu'a Tov** (shah-*voo*-ah t*ohv;* a good week).

Discovering the Days in a Week

In Hebrew, the only day that has an official name is the Sabbath, which falls on the seventh day of the week — Saturday. That day is called **Shabbat** (shah-*baht*). Friday afternoon is then called **Erev Shabbat** (*eh*-rehv shah-*baht;* Shabbat afternoon), while Friday evening is **Leil Shabbat** (*layl* shah-*baht;* Shabbat evening). Take a look at Chapter 1 where I cover all the numbers. The rest of the days of the week are numbered as follows:

- ✔ **Yom Rishon** (*yohm* ree-*shohn;* the first day, Sunday)
- ✔ **Yom Sheni** (*yohm* shay-*nee;* the second day, Monday)
- ✔ **Yom Shlishi** (*yohm* sh-lee-*shee;* the third day, Tuesday)
- ✔ **Yom Revi'i** (*yohm* reh-*vee-ee;* the fourth day, Wednesday)
- ✔ **Yom Chamishi** (*yohm* chah-mee-*shee;* the fifth day, Thursday)
- ✔ **Yom Shishi** (*yohm* shee-*shee;* the sixth day, Friday)

In traditional Jewish households around the world, **Yom Shishi** is often a hectic day preparing for **Shabbat.** Everyone is out buying the items they need for the day of rest. People often buy **Prachim** (prah-*cheem;* flowers) to adorn the dinner table) to help emphasize the festive nature of the day.

According to the Hebrew calendar, days begin in the evening, so the Jewish Sabbath actually starts with sunset on Friday night. The time, of course, varies during the year. So in the winter, **Shabbat** can start as early as 3 p.m., and in the summer **Shabbat** may not start until as late as 8 p.m. **Shabbat** lasts a total of 25 hours from the time the sun begins to set on **Erev Shabbat** until it has completely set **Motze'ei Shabbat** (moh-tze-*ay* shah-*baht;* Saturday night) and you can see three stars in the sky.

The workweek in Israel runs from the Sunday to Friday. However, Friday is a half-day and increasingly more and more companies in Israel are converting to a five-day workweek and Friday is considered part of the weekend.

Catching Some Culture

So you want to go out for a good time. So what do you want to do? The opportunities abound! How about a movie? Perhaps you want to hear live music or take in some live theater. Or maybe you want to nurture your aesthetic side and spend some time strolling through a museum. You just have to choose. And if you want to say it in Hebrew, keep on reading and I show you how.

Visiting museums and art galleries

If you want to go somewhere to nurture your **Nefesh** (*neh*-fehsh; soul), a **Muze'on** (moo-zeh-*ohn;* museum) is a wonderful place to go. Wandering the quiet **Misderonot** (mees-de-roh-*noht;* halls) and examining the works of **Ohmanut** (oh-mah-*noot;* art) or artifacts of **Arche'ologia** (ar-che-oh-*log*-yah; archeology) always inspires. I always love to catch the latest **Tetzugah** (tetz-oo-*gah;* exhibition) and stroll through the **Galeriat Omanut** (gah-lehr-*yaht* oh-mah-*noot;* art gallery), and even take some **Siyrum Mudrachim** (see-yoo-*reem* mood-rah-*cheem;* guided tours) if they're offered. But before you go, check out **She'ot HaMuze'on** (sheh-*oht* hah-moo-zeh-*ohn;* the museum hours) because you don't want to arrive to closed doors!

Words to Know

Galeriat Ohmanut	gah-lair-<u>yaht</u> oh-mah-<u>noot</u>	art gallery
Muze'on	moo-zeh-<u>ohn</u>	museum
She'ot Ha'Muze'on	sh-<u>oht</u> hah-moo-zeh-<u>ohn</u>	museum hours
Siyurim Mudrachim	see-your-<u>eem</u> moo-drah-<u>cheem</u>	guided tours
Tetzugah	teh-tzoo-<u>gah</u>	exhibition

Going to the movies

I like all kinds of **S'ratim** (srah-_teem;_ movies). I'm happy to see a **Seret Drama** (_seh_-reht _drah_-mah; a dramatic film) or a **Seret Bidur** (_seh_-reht bee-_door;_ a comedy). Believe it or not, I love a good **Seret Pe'ulah** _(seh_-reht pe-oo-_lah;_ action film), and if it's not too scary, I'm even up for a **Seret Metach** (_seh_-reht _meh_-tach; thriller).

Some people choose movies if they like the **Bamai** (bah-_mahy;_ director) or the **Mefik** (meh-_feek;_ producer) while others like to go see their favorite **Sachkan** (sach-_kahn;_ actor) or **Sachkanit** (sach-kah-_neet;_ actress). If one of the actors is particularly **Mefursam** (meh-foor-_sahm;_ famous), he or she can often have a big draw at the box office.

When you go to a **Kolno'a** (kohl _noh_-ah; movie theater), you need to buy a **Kartis** (kahr-_tees;_ ticket) at the **Kupah** (koo-_pah;_ box office). In Israel, sometimes you have **Mekomot Mesumanim** (meh-koh-_moht_ meh-soo-mah-_neem;_ assigned seats). Also in Israel, movies have **Pirsomot** (peer-soh-_moht;_ commercials) before the show and a **Hafsakah** (hahf-sah-_kah;_ intermission)! So if you forget to go to the **Sherutim** (sheh-roo-_teem;_ bathroom) before the show, you can go during the intermission.

Words to Know

Bamai	bah-<u>may</u>	director
Hafsakah	hahf-sah-<u>kah</u>	intermission
Kartis	kahr-<u>tees</u>	ticket
Kolno'a	kohl-<u>noh</u>-ah	movie theater
Kupah	koo-<u>pah</u>	box office
Mefursam	meh-four-<u>sahm</u>	famous
Mehfik	meh-<u>feek</u>	producer
Sachkan	sach-<u>kahn</u>	actor
Sachkanit	sach-kah-<u>neet</u>	actress
Seret	<u>seh</u>-reht	movie
Sherutim	sheh-roo-<u>teem</u>	restrooms

To sound like a native, use slang. Israeli slang uses expressions that use the Hebrew word for film, **Seret** (*seh*-reht). One expression, **Ayzeh Seret** (ay-*zeh seh*-reht), which literally means "what a movie," is used when you want to say that something is really great. **K'var Hayiti BaSeret HaZeh** (kv*ahr* hah-*yee*-tee ba-*seh-reh*t hah-*zeh;* I've already been in this movie), is the Hebrew equivalent of "Been there, done that."

Enjoying live entertainment: music and theater

You may also want a real treat and spend an evening at the **Te'atron** (tay-aht-*rohn;* live theatre). Israel has its own national theater company **HaBima** (hah-*bee*-mah; the stage). Theater is an incredible art form. In Israel, a country whose national anthem, **HaTikvah** (hah-teek-*vah*) means "the hope," theater plays an important role in continuing to shape and define the country's national identity and chronicling its hopes and dreams for the future.

Wherever you are, you get a thrill watching the **Sachkanim** (sach-kah-*neem;* actors) perform on a **Bimah** (bee-*mah;* stage) and joining in a thunderous **Mechi'at Kapa'im** (meh-chee-*aht* kah-*pah*-eem; applause) as the **Masach** (mah-*sach;* stage curtain) falls.

I love **Muzikah** (*moo*-zee-kah; music). One of my favorite things to do is go to a **Mo'adon** (moh-ah-*dohn;* night club) to hear a **Hofa'ah Chayah** (hoh-fah-*ah* chah-*yah;* live show). Even if I've never heard of the **Lehakah** (leh-hah-*kah;* band), I'm happy to go and just soak up the atmosphere.

I love to hear **Zamarim** (zah-mah-*reem;* singers) who have written the **Milim** (mee-*leem;* words) and **Lachan** (*lah*-chan; melody) to their own **Shirim** (shee-*reem;* songs). And if the music is **Akusti** (ah-*koos*-tee; acoustic), well then, all the better.

At a **Hofa'ah Chayah,** you may hear several **Naganim** (nah-gah-*neem;* musicians) who like **LeNagen B** (leh-nah-*gehn* buh; to play [an instrument]) many types of **Klay-Negina** (k-lai-neh-gee-*nah;* instruments).

Instruments may include:

- ✔ **Chalil** (chah-*leel;* flute)
- ✔ **Chemet Chalilim** (*cheh*-meht cha-lee-*leem;* bagpipes)

- **Geetara** (gee-*tah*-rah; guitar)
- **Klee HaKashah** (klee hah-kah-*shah;* percussion)
- **Kinor** (kee-*nohr;* violin)
- **Klidim** (klee-*deem;* keyboards)
- **Tupim** (too-*peem;* drums)

Watching Israeli films on video and DVD

A great way to practice your Hebrew is to rent some Israeli films with English subtitles. You can accustom your ear to an authentic Israeli accent and also discover a little about Israeli culture. I recommend the following flicks:

- **HaKayitz Shel Aviya** (Ha-*kah-yeetz* shehl ah-vee-*yah; Aviya's Summer*): This moving film is about a widow and her young daughter who have made their way to Israel after surviving the Holocaust. The true story presents a touching picture of life in Israel's early years of independence. The film is presented through the author's eyes when she was a little girl. And the author, Gila Almagor, plays the part of her mother in the movie. Winner of the Silver Bear Award from the Berlin International Film Festival.

- **Micha'el Sheli** (michah-*el* sheh-*lee; My Michael*): This classic Israeli film based on the novel by acclaimed Israeli author Amos Oz takes place in the divided city of Jerusalem in the 1950s.

- **Bluz La'Chofesh Ha'Gadol** (blooz lah-*choh*-fehsh hah-gah-*dohl; Late Summer Blues*): Nearly two decades after this film was first released, it still paints a touching portrait of Israeli youth coming of age amid the tensions of war. This powerful film set in 1970 during the War of Attrition, chronicles the lives of seven Israeli teenagers during the summer following their high school graduation before their compulsory army service.

- **Shirat HaSirena** (shee-*raht* hah-see-*reh*-nah; *Song of the Siren*): On the eve of the 1991 Gulf War as her family dons gas masks and sits in a sealed room, sassy Talia dumps her boyfriend in front of everyone. Against the backdrop of air-raid sirens and Iraqi Scud missiles falling on Tel Aviv, a young Israeli woman looks for love. A box-office smash hit in Israel.

- **Afula Express** (ah-*foo*-lah ex-*prehs; Pick a Card*): A lighthearted comedy set in Israel in the late 1990s during the heyday of the Oslo Accords. A time when peace really seemed possible. The film follows the shenanigans of a young man who wants to be a career magician — only he's no good at doing tricks. Winner of six Israeli Academy Awards.

You can purchase many of these films at www.1worldfilms.com/israel.htm. Or you can ask your local video store to keep them in stock!

Words to Know

Bimah	bee-_mah_	stage
Hofa'ah Chayah	hoh-fah-_ah_ cha-_yah_	live show
Klee Negina	klee neh-gee-_nah_	instrument
L'Nagen	leh-nah-_gehn_	to play [an instrument]
Lehakah	leh-hah-_kah_	band
Mo'adon	moh-ah-_dohn_	club
Muzikah	_moo_-zee-kah	music

Talkin' the Talk

Shulie and Nomi are **Shutafot** (shoo-tah-_foht_; roommates). They're sitting around their **Dirah** (dee-_rah;_ apartment) one evening trying to decide what to do. Shulie suggests that they go to a **Mo'adon** (moh-ah-_dohn;_ club) to hear a really cool band called **Esta** (_ehs_-tah). (Track 14)

Nomi: **Mah At Rotzah La'Asot Ha'Erev?**
mah _aht_ roh-_tzah_ lah-ah-_soht_ hah-_eh_-rehv?
What do you want to do this evening?

Shulie: **Bah Li Lishmo'a _Muzikah._**
bah lee leesh-moh-ah moo-zee-kah.
I feel like listening to music.

Nomi: **Mi Mofi'ah BaMo'adon BaShchunah?**
mee moh-_fee_-ah bah-moh-ah-_dohn_ bah-shuh-choo-_nah?_
Who is playing at the neighborhood club?

Shulie: **Yesh Lehakah Metzuyenet beshem Esta.**
yehsh leh-hah-_kah_ meh-tzoo-_yeh_-net be-_shehm_ ehs-tah.
There's an excellent band called Esta.

Nomi:	**Yofie! Shamati She'Hem "Chaval Al Ha'Zman"!**
	yoh-fee! shah-*mah*-tee sheh-*hem* chah-*vahl* ahl hah-*zmahn.*
	Great! I heard they're amazing!
Shulie:	**Nachon. Yesh La'Hem Tupim, Chalil, Guitarah, Klidim, Kinor V'Afilu Chemet Chalilim.**
	nah-*chohn.* yehsh lah-*hem* too-*peem* chah-*leel,* gee-*tah*-rah, klee-*deem* kee-*nor,* ve-ah-*fee*-loo *cheh*-meht chah-lee-leem.
	That's right. They have drums, a flute, a guitar, keyboards, a violin, and even bagpipes.
Nomi:	**Bo Nelech!**
	boh neh-*lech!*
	Let's go!

Esta is a real Israeli band, and the group is excellent. The musicians are a world-fusion band that bring together the sounds from many different musical traditions. They're worth checking out! Plus I can't imagine a better way to learn some Hebrew.

You can learn more about this incredible band at www.estamusic.com or www.israel-music.com. You can find Esta's CDs along with plenty of other awesome Israeli music!

The Animals Went on the Ark Two by Two: Visiting the Zoo!

The **Gan Chayot** (*gahn* chah-*yoht;* zoo) is a wonderful place to spend the afternoon with your family or friends. Check out Table 7-2 to see some of the animals you may see at the zoo.

Table 7-2	Animals You May See at a Zoo	
Hebrew	*Pronunciation*	*English Translation*
Arieh	ahr-*yeh*	lion
Dag	dahg	fish
Dov	dohv	bear

(continued)

Table 7-2 *(continued)*

Hebrew	Pronunciation	English Translation
Jeerafah	jee-*ra*-fah	giraffe
Karnaf	kahr-*nahf*	rhinoceros
Kipod	kee-*pohd*	porcupine
Kof	kohf	monkey
Peel	peel	elephant
Sus Ha'Ye'or	soos hah-yeh-*ohr*	hippopotamus
Tzav	tzahv	turtle
Tzipor	tzee-*pohr*	bird

And although you may not see these animals at the zoo, you may have a **Chatul** (chah-*tool;* cat) or a **Kelev** (*keh*-lehv; dog) as pets! And if you're visiting a farm, you may see a **Parah** (pah-*rah;* cow), a **Sus** (soos; horse), a **Chazir** (chah-*zeer;* pig), and maybe even a **Tarnegol** (tahr-neh-*gohl;* rooster).

Spicing Up Your Sentences with Adverbs

Hebrew doesn't have a single formula for changing *adjectives* (words that describe a noun) into *adverbs* (words that describe a verb). In English, for example, *slow* becomes *slowly, hungry* becomes *hungrily, angry* becomes *angrily.* In Hebrew, you just put the phrase **B'Ofen** (buh-*oh*-fehn; *Literally:* in the manner of) in front of the adjective to change it to an adverb. For example:

- **Kavu'a** (kah-*voo*-ah; permanent) becomes **B'Ofen Kavu'a** (buh- *oh*-fehn kah-*voo*-ah; permanently)

- **Mahair** (mah-*hehr;* quick) becomes **B'Ofen Mahir** (buh-*oh*-fen mah-*heer;* quickly)

You can also convert an adjective to an adverb by preceding the noun with **B'** (with) For example:

- **Adin** (ah-*deen;* gentle) becomes **B'Adinut** (buh ah-dee-*noot; Literally;* with gentleness; gently)

- **Mahair** (mah-*hehr;* quick) becomes **B'imhirut** (bim-hee-*root; Literally;* with quickness; quickly)

Some adverbs are adjectives used in their masculine singular form. You may see some adjectives used in the following way:

- ✔ **Chazak** (chah-*zahk;* strong)
- ✔ **Kasheh** (kah-*sheh;* difficult)
- ✔ **Metzuyan** (meh-tzoo-*yahn;* excellent)
- ✔ **Norah** (noh-*rah;* terrible)
- ✔ **Rah** (rah; bad, badly)
- ✔ **Tov** (tohv; good, and well)
- ✔ **Yafeh** (yah-*feh;* pretty)
- ✔ **Yashar** (yah-*shar;* straight)

For more on making masculine and feminine adjectives, take a look at Chapter 2.

Fun & Games

See the pictures of different **Ba'alei Chaim** (bah-ah-_lei_ chah-_yeem_; animals). Using the word list, write the correct name of the animal under its picture.

Arieh, Chatul, Dag, Kelev, Parah, Peel, Sus, Sus Ha'Ye'or, Tarnegol, Tzipor

Chapter 8

Enjoying Your Free Time: Hobbies, Sports, and Other Fun Activities

In This Chapter

▶ Talking about your interests

▶ Taking pleasure in sports as a spectator or participant

▶ Having fun in the great outdoors

▶ Dancing up a storm

All work and no play can make you a very dull boy or girl. The antidote, of course, is to have a good time! Sports, hobbies, and interests are all great ways not only to have fun, but also to meet people and restore energy. I believe that everyone should have at least one instrument and one sport that they play, and at least one other interest that they pursue. They make you well rounded. In this chapter, you discover how to talk about your recreational passions: the sports you love, the hobbies you adore, and the myriad of activities you like to do whenever you find the time. **Bilui Naim** (bee-*looy* nah-*eem;* Have fun!).

Chatting About Your Hobbies

Our hobbies and interests make great fodder for conversation. In this section, I tell you what words you need to know in order to gab away with your friends and family about what you enjoy!

Amassing an amazing collection

Some people like to collect anything and everything. If you stuff items in a box or under your bed, we call you a pack rat. But if you take the items you collect and put them on display, then we call it a **Tachbiv** (tahch-*beev;* hobby). One also may call it a **Sha'ashu'a** (shah-ah-*shoo*-ah; amusement), or even a **Shiga'on** (shee-gah-*ohn;* madness). Truth be told, collecting is an enjoyable activity, always searching for your next great find to add to your mix. You can tell people what you like to collect by saying the following:

- ✔ **Ani Osef . . .** (ah-*nee* oh-*sehf;* I collect . . .) (MS)

  Ani Osefet . . . (ah-*nee* oh-*seh*-feht; I collect . . .) (FS)

- ✔ **Ani Me'unyan B . . .** (ah-*nee* meh-oon-*yahn* beh; I am interested in . . .) (MS)

  Ani Me'unyenent B . . . (ah-*nee* meh-oon-*yeh*-neht beh; I am interested in . . .) (FS)

At the end of the phrases, you can name the item you like to collect. For example, you may collect any of the following:

- ✔ **Atikot** (ah-tee-*koht;* antiques)
- ✔ **Bubot** (boo-*boht;* dolls)
- ✔ **Bulim** (boo-*leem;* stamps)
- ✔ **Matbe'ot** (mat-be-*oht;* coins)

Creating things with your hands

Making things with your hands isn't only fun, but also satisfying. Gazing upon some item you created with your own hands is very rewarding. So you're probably not surprised that many hobbies revolve around different types of handicraft. In Hebrew, you can tell someone about your favorite hobby by using one of the following phrases:

- ✔ **HaTachbiv Sheli . . .** (hah-tach-*beev* sheh-*lee;* My hobby is . . .)
- ✔ **Tachbivi . . .** (tach-bee-*vee;* My hobby is . . .)

At the end of the phrase, you tack on what it is you like to do. For example:

- ✔ **Avodat Etz** (ah-voh-*daht ehtz;* woodworking)
- ✔ **Bishul** (bee-*shool;* cooking)
- ✔ **Gananut** (gah-nah-*noot;* gardening)
- ✔ **Isuf** (ee-*soof;* collecting)
- ✔ **Tziur** (tzee-*yoor;* painting)
- ✔ **Umanut** (oo-mah-*noot;* craft)

In Hebrew, you can show possession — indicate that something belongs to someone — by attaching a particle to the end of the object. In grammar-speak, this particle is known as a *personal-possessive suffix.* The suffixes are as follows:

i (ee; my, mine)

chah (chah; you, yours) (MS)

ech (ehch; you, yours) (FS)

o (oh; his)

ah (ah; her, hers)

nu (noo; our, ours)

chem (chehm; your, yours) (MP)

chen (chehn; your, yours) (FP)

am (ahm; theirs) (MP)

an (ahn; theirs) (FP)

After you attach the preceding suffixes to words, they look like the following list (in this case I use the word for hobby):

Tachbivi (tahch-bee-*vee;* my hobby)

Tachbivcha (tahch-beev-*chah;* your hobby) (MS)

Tachbivech (tahch-bee-*vehch;* your hobby) (FS)

Tachbivo (tahch-bee- *voh;* his hobby)

Tachbivah (tahch-bee-*vah;* her hobby)

Tachbivnu (tahch-bee-*vei*-noo; our hobby)

Tachbivchem (tahch-beev-*chem;* your hobby) (MP)

Tachbivchen (tahch-beev-*chen;* your hobby) (FP)

Tachbivam (tahch-bee-*vam;* their hobby) (MP)

Tachbivan (tahch-bee-*van;* their hobby) (FP)

Another way of showing possession is to state the object followed by the *ownership phrase,* such as *mine, yours,* or *ours.* You can use the personal suffix or the ownership phrase for any and all nouns. For example: **HaTachbiv Sheli** (Hatach-*beev* sheh-*lee;* my hobby).

If you're speaking about more than one person who possesses the certain object, or if you're talking about more than one object, the *word stem* changes just a wee bit. If the object ends with the letter **Hey** (hey), then the **Hey** (hey) disappears and is replaced with a **Tav** (tahv).

Talkin' the Talk

 Ziv and Hod, are discussing their hobbies as they wait for the bus. (Track 15)

Ziv: **Mah Atah Ohev La'asot BaZman HaPanui Shelcha?**
mah ah-*tah* oh-*hev* lah-ah-*soht* bah-z'*mahn* hah-pah-noo*y* shel-*chah*?
What do you like to do in your free time?

Hod: **Ani Osef Bulim. Ve Ani Gam Osek B'Avodat Etz K'Tachbiv.**
ah-*nee* oh-*sef* boo-*leem*. veh ah-*nee* gahm oh-*sehk* buh-ah-voh-*daht ehtz* kuh-tach-*beev*.
I collect stamps. And I also do woodworking as a hobby.

Ziv: **Eizeh Ketah! Gam Ani Osef Bulim. Tachbivi Bishul.**
ay-*zeh keh*-tah! gahm ah-*nee* oh-*sef* boo-*leem*. tach-*bee-vee* bee-*shool*.
Wow! I also collect stamps. Cooking's my hobby.

Hod: **Shiga'on.**
shi-gah-*ohn*.
Awesome.

Words to Know

Atikot	ah-tee-<u>koht</u>	antiques
Bishul	bee-<u>shool</u>	cooking
Bubot	boo-<u>boht</u>	dolls
Bulim	boo-<u>leem</u>	stamps
Gananut	gah-nah-<u>noot</u>	gardening
Matbe'ot	maht-beh-<u>oht</u>	coins
Tachbiv	tahch-<u>beev</u>	hobby
Tziur	tzee-<u>oor</u>	painting

Playing and Watching Sports

Whether you're a spectator or a participant, sports are a great way to let off some steam. In this section, I share some key sports words and equip you with the lingo for chatting about your favorite sports.

Kickin' to score in soccer

In many parts of the world, you find many **Ohadim** (oh-hah-*deem;* fans) of **Kadur Regel** (kah-*dur reh*-gel; soccer). The World Cup final is practically a national holiday in some countries with the workplaces clearing out for soccer-loving fans to cheer on their favorite **Kvutza** (kvoo-*tzah;* team). Many international soccer matches have the **Yetzi'im** (yeh-tzee-*eem;* stands) packed as people root and cheer on their favorite **Sachkan** (sach-*kahn;* player), yelling: **Hu Gadol, Hu Gadol, Hu Gadol** (hoo gah-*dohl,* hoo gah-*dohl,* hoo gah-*dohl;* He's great, he's great, he's great).

The literal translation of soccer, **Kadur Regel,** is *football* — which is what the sport is referred to everywhere but North America. If you want to talk about *football* that is the popular American game, you have to specify **Kadur Regel Amerikani** (kah-*dur reh*-gehl ah-mer-ee-*kah*-nee), which literally means *American football.* Check out Table 8-1 for terms you use on a soccer field.

Table 8-1	Common Soccer Terms	
Hebrew	*Pronunciation*	*Translation*
Be'ita Chofshit	beh-ee-*tah* chof-*sheet*	free kick
Beitat Onshin	beh-ee-*taht* ohn-*sheen*	penalty kick
Chalutz (MS)	cha-*lootz*	forward
Chalutza (FS)	cha-loo-*tzah*	forward
Itztadion	itz-tahd-*yohn*	stadium
Kadur	kah-*dur*	ball
Kashar (MS)	kah-*shar*	midfielder
Kasheret (FS)	kah-*she*-reht	midfielder
Keren	*keh*-ren	corner kick
Lehavki'a	leh-hav-*kee*-ah	to score a goal
Magen (MS)	mah-*gehn*	defender

(continued)

Table 8-1 *(continued)*		
Hebrew	*Pronunciation*	*Translation*
Magina (FS)	mah-gee-*nah*	defender
Nivdal	neev-*dahl*	off sides
Sho'er (MS)	shoh-*ehr*	goalkeeper
Sho'eret (FS)	*shoh-eh*-reht	goalkeeper

Shooting for three in basketball

Kadur-Sal (kah-*dur* sahl; basketball) is a great game to play and watch. If you're a **Sachkan Gavoha** (sach-*kahn* gah-*voh*-hah; taller player), you have a distinct advantage over a **Sachkan Namuch** (sach-*kahn* nah-*mooch;* short player). Of course, height doesn't make much of a difference if you're a **Sahkan Garu'ah** (sach-*kahn* gah-*roo*-ah; terrible player)! Look at Table 8-2 for some common basketball terms.

Table 8-2	Common Basketball Terms	
Hebrew	*Pronunciation*	*Translation*
Averah	ah-vee-*rah*	foul
Kadur Chozer	kah-*dur* choh-*zehr*	rebound
Lekader	leh-kah-*dehr*	to dribble
Migrash	meeg-*rahsh*	court
Pesek Zman	*peh*-sehk z-*mahn*	timeout
Sal	sahl	basket
Tze'adim	tzeh-ah-*deem*	traveling
Zrikat Onshin	zeh-ree-*kaht* ohn-*sheen*	free throw

Swinging away at baseball

Ah! **Kadur Basis** (kah-*dur* bah-*sees;* baseball)! That great American pastime! At baseball games, you can sit in the **Yetzi'im** (yeh-tzee-*eem;* stands), get some

Botnim (boht-*neem;* peanuts) or **Beygeleh** (*bay*-geh-leh; pretzels), a nice cold **Birah** (*bee*-rah; beer) or **Soda** (*soh*-dah; soda), and cheer on your favorite **Kvutzah.** Table 8-3 provides some terms you use on a baseball diamond.

Table 8-3	Common Baseball Terms	
Hebrew	*Pronunciation*	*Translation*
Basis	bah-*sees*	base
Glisha	glee-*shah*	slide
Kadur Gavoha	kah-*dur gah-voh*-hah	fly ball
Kadur Karkah	*kah*-dur *kahr*-kah	ground ball
Kashar	kah-*shahr*	shortstop
K'fafat Chovet	*k-fah*-faht *choh*-veht	batting glove
Kvutzat Ha'Bayit	*kvoo-tzaht hah-bye*-eet	home team
Machbet	mach-*beht*	baseball bat
Magish	mah-*geesh*	pitcher
Safsal	sahf-*sahl*	bench
Shofet	shoh-*feht*	umpire
Tnuffah	tnoo-*fah*	swing

Going for Jewish gold

Who says Jews can't jump? Believe it or not, the Jewish people have their own Olympics of sorts. Called the **Macabiah** (mah-kah-bee-*yah*) after the hero of the **Chanukah** (chah-noo-*kah*) story, Judah the Maccabee, this worldwide Jewish sporting event was founded in 1895. Since 1957, the **Macabiah** has been held every four years in Israel, bringing together Jewish athletes from all over the world to celebrate their shared culture, history, and values, and to compete in the sports that they love. The 16th Maccabiah games were held in Israel July 2001, and the next games are scheduled for the summer of 2005. Among the more famous alumni of this illustrious Jewish sporting extravaganza are: swimmer Mark Spitz, gymnast Mitch Gaylord, National Basketball Association stars Ernie Grunfeld, Dolph Schayes, and Danny Schayes, golfer Bruce Fleisher, tennis pros Brad Gilbert and Dick Savitt, and World Cup soccer star Jeff Agoos.

Taking a dip in the pool

I love **Lischot** (lees-*choht;* to swim). Swimming is the best **Hitamlut** (heet-ahm-*loot;* exercise) because it's a great workout for your **Guf** (goof; body). What more could you want? Plus it's fun! In the **Kayitz** (*kah*-yeetz; summer), I love to swim **Bachutz** (bah-*chootz;* outdoors) in an **Agam** (ah-*gahm;* lake). When the weather turns cooler, then it's the **Brechat-s'chiya** (brei-*chaht*-schee-*yah;* swimming pool) for me — preferably one indoors. When you're swimming, you may want to try out these strokes:

- **Mischeh Chazeh** (mees-*cheh* chah-*zeh;* breast stroke)
- **Mischeh Chofshi** (mees-*cheh* chohf-*shee;* freestyle)
- **Mischeh Gav** (mees-*cheh gahv;* back stroke)
- **Mischeh Parpar** (mees-*cheh* pahr-*pahr;* butterfly stroke)

Working up a sweat playing other sports

Of course, the sports I mention are by no means exhaustive. Sports are great because something is available for everyone. If you don't like **Tacharut** (tah-chah-*root;* competition), plenty of sports allow you to go solo. And of course, you can play plenty of sports just for fun. Table 8-4 lists some other popular sports.

Table 8-4	Other Popular Sports	
Hebrew	*Pronunciation*	*Translation*
Galgiliot	gahl-gee-*lee-yoht*	in-line skating
Galshan	gahl-*shahn*	surfboarding
Glisha B'Sheleg	guh-lee-*shah* buh-*sheh*-lehg	skiing
Goalf	goh*lf*	golf
Hachlaka Al Ha'Kerach	hach-lah-*kah* ahl hah-*keh*-rahch	ice skating
Kadur Af	kah-dur-*ahf*	volleyball
Kadoret	kah-*doh*-reht	bowling
Rechiva Al Ofanayim	reh-*chiva* ahl oh-fah-*nah*-yeem	bicycling
Ritzah	ree-*tzah*	running

Words to Know

Hitamlut	heet-ahm-<u>loot</u>	exercise
Itztadion	itz-tahd-<u>yohn</u>	stadium
Kadur	kah-<u>door</u>	ball
Kadur Regel	kah-<u>dur</u> <u>reh</u>-gehl	soccer
Kadur Sal	kah-dur <u>sahl</u>	basketball
Kvutzah	k'voo-<u>tzah</u>	team
Migrash	meeg-<u>rahsh</u>	court
Ohadim	oh-hah-<u>deem</u>	fans
Ritzah	ree-<u>tzah</u>	running
Sal	sahl	basket
S'chiyah	s'chee-<u>yah</u>	swimming

Talkin' the Talk

Gal and Sivan are waiting for the bus. While they're waiting, they talk about sports. (Track 16)

Gal:
: **Le'an Aht Nosa'at?**
  leh-*ahn* aht noh-*sah*-aht?
  Where are you going?

Sivan:
: **Ani No'sa'at La'Migrash Ba'Ir Le'sachek Kadur-Sal.**
  ah-*nee* noh-*sah*-aht lah-meeg-*rahsh* bah-e*ar* leh-sah-*chek* kah-*dur sahl*.
  I'm going to a court in the city to play basketball.

Gal:
: **Kol HaKavod! Ani Nosa'at Le'sachek Kadur-Regel.**
  kohl hah-kah-*vohd!* ah-*nee* noh-*sah*-aht leh-sah-*chek* kah-*dur reh*-gehl.
  Good for you! I'm going to play soccer.

Sivan:	**Aizeh Tafkid Aht?**
	ay-*zeh* tahf-*keed aht?*
	What position do you play?
Gal:	**Ani Sho'eret.**
	ah-*nee* shoh-*eh*-reht.
	I'm a goalie.

Venturing Outdoors for Some Fun

The outdoors is a wonderful place for recreation. The outdoors isn't only a great place to get some fresh air, but also a wonderful way to renew your soul. Some useful words for talking about nature include:

✔ **Emek** (*eh*-mehk; valley)

✔ **Etz** (etz; tree)

✔ **Har** (hahr; mountain)

✔ **Midbar** (meed-*bahr;* desert)

✔ **Nahar** (nah-*hahr;* river)

✔ **Sela** (*seh*-lah; rock)

✔ **Yam** (yahm; sea)

A wise rabbi, Rabbi Nachman of Bratslav, advised his disciples that they should make it their practice to spend time in nature every day. Table 8-5 refers to some outdoors activities.

Table 8-5	Popular Outdoors Activities	
Hebrew	**Pronunciation**	**Translation**
Dayig	*dah-yeeg*	fishing
Glishat Chevel	glee-*shaht cheh*-vehl	rappelling
Glishat Mayim	glee-*shaht mah*-yeem	water skiing
Haflaga	haf-lah-*gah*	boating
Machna'oot	mach-nah-*oot*	camping

Hebrew	Pronunciation	Translation
Tipus Chofshi	tee-*poos* chohf-*shee*	free climbing
Tipus Metzukim	tee-*poos* meh-tzoo-*keem*	rock climbing
Tiyul	tee-*yool*	hiking

While enjoying the great outdoors, and you want to express gratitude to God for the glory of nature, recite these Hebrew blessings:

✔ When you see amazing natural phenomena, such as tall mountains or big rivers, you can say **Baruch Atah Adonai, Melech Ha'Olam, Oseh Ma'aseh B'reishit** (bah-*rooch* ah-*tah* ah-doh-*nay* meh-lech hah-oh-*lahm* oh-*seh* mah-ah-*seh* buh-ray-*sheet;* Praised are You God, Sovereign of the Cosmos, Maker of the Works of Creation). Flip to Chapter 18 if you want to see what this blessing looks like in Hebrew.

✔ When you see the ocean, you can say **Baruch Atah Adonai Melech Ha'Olam, Oseh Et Ha'Yam Ha'Gadol** (bah-*rooch* ah-*tah* ah-doh-*nay* meh-lech hah-oh-*lahm* oh-*seh* eht hah-*yahm* hah-gah-*dohl;* Praised are You, God, Sovereign of the Cosmos, Maker of the great ocean).

Boogieing 'til You Drop

Do you like **Lirkod** (leer-*kohd;* to dance)? I love to dance, and I also love to watch it. I love **Lirkod** at a **Mo'adon** (moh-ah-*dohn;* club) all night!

I also enjoy going to a **Hofa'ah** (hoh-fah-*ah;* show) to see a **Lehakat Machol** (leh-hah-*kaht* mah-*chohl;* dance group). I like everything from **Rikud Balet** (ree-*kood* bah-*let;* ballet) to **Machol Achshavi** (mah-*chohl* ahch-shah-*vee;* modern dance). I enjoy watching the **Rakdanim** (rahk-dah-*neem;* dancers) move in time to the **Ketzev** (*keh*-tzehv; rhythm) of the music.

Machol (mah-*chohl*), the Hebrew word for a kind of rhythmic dancing in which the body moves joyously in concert with a specific musical rhythm, shares the same root with the Hebrew word for forgiveness — **Mechila** (meh-chee-*lah*). Rabbi Mordechai Gafni teaches that at first glance these two concepts, dancing and forgiveness, seem disparate. But both acts require a certain giving over of the self, a moving in harmony with an outside force.

CULTURAL WISDOM

Taking a spin around the dance floor:
Folk dancing, Israeli-style

Dance has always been an integral part of Jewish culture. Dance was the response of the ancient Israelites after crossing the Sea of Reeds. And who hasn't been to a Jewish wedding and danced all night?

Today, **Rikudei-Am** (ree-koo-*day ahm;* folk dancing) is a quintessential Israeli art form bearing the imprint of the Jewish people and their wanderings across the globe. A cross section of the Israeli population participates in more than 300 Israeli folk dance circles around the country. The dance steps include the Yemenite step (which depicts the way one would move barefoot on hot sand) the Tcherkessia (from Russia), the Debka (an Arabic step), and moving in circle-form reflective of the Hora, a closed-circle dance with origins in Romania.

Israeli folk dancing spans the globe in 37 countries with sessions taking place in cities as far flung as Tokyo, New York City, Amsterdam, and Los Angeles. An annual international folk-dance festival held each summer in the Galilee development town of Karmiel draws more than 250,000 devotees from all over the world. Workshops and performances are held during the day. When the sun goes down, the outdoor dancing begins and continues until the sun begins to rise the next morning. The dancers then warily climb Karmiel's hills back to their rented rooms to catch some sleep before the revelry resumes.

Keeping up with the latest dances is an art in itself. Those that miss a chunk of sessions find themselves watching on the sidelines, leaving no middle ground in Israeli dancing. Outside of beginner circles, you're in or you're out. In Israel, folk-dance sessions draw close to a thousand people, and clubs in cities, such as Los Angeles and New York City, draw crowds in the hundreds.

Shoulder-to-shoulder dancers twist and turn, moving in time to popular Israeli music they represent a unique and authentic Israeli cultural phenomenon: a true **Kibbutz Galuyot** (kee-*bootz* gah-loo-*yoht;* ingathering of the exiles) — creating an art form that is both ancient and timeless; a reflection of the land and modern state that Jews the world over call home.

Fun & Games

Using the word list, identify the activities in the picture. **Bilui Naim** (bee-*looy* nah-*eem;* have fun)!

Kadur-Basis, Kadur-Regel, Rikud, S'chiya, Tiyul

Chapter 9

Talking on the Phone

. . . .

In This Chapter

▶ Beginning a phone conversation

▶ Leaving a message

▶ Using the phone to make plans

▶ Reviewing the past tense made easy

. . . .

Where would we be without telephones? In our phone-addicted society, you can find a phone in almost every major room in a house, in almost every office, and on almost every street corner. And now with the advent of cellular phones, you can find a phone in almost every pocket too. Telephones are everywhere, so figuring out how to speak on one is an important part to picking up any new language. In this chapter, I give you the essential phrases that you need in order to have a **Sichat Telefone** (see-*chat teh*-leh-fohn; telephone conversation) in Hebrew.

The word that people commonly use in Hebrew for the English word *telephone,* **Telefone** (*teh*-leh-fohn), wasn't the word that the Academy for Hebrew Language created. The *Academy for Hebrew Language* is the supreme institute for the Hebrew language that makes decisions about modern Hebrew grammar and coins new Hebrew words as the need arises. No, telephones didn't always exist, so someone had to create a Hebrew word for the concept. The Academy created a Hebrew word for *telephone* — **Sach-Rachok** (sach-rah-*hohk*), which literally means *long-distance conversation.* Clever, huh? However, the term didn't stick with the Hebrew-speaking public, so **Telefone** it is.

Dialing Up the Basics

Having a conversation on the phone in Hebrew is great, but you need to start at the beginning. In this case, the beginning is simply nailing down the various Hebrew words associated with the actual telephone equipment:

▮ ✔ **Telefone** (*teh*-leh-fohn; telephone)

▮ ✔ **Telefone Tziburi** (*teh*-leh-fohn tzee-boo-*ree*; public telephone)

✔ **Telekart** (*teh*-leh-kahrt; phone card; used in public telephones)

✔ **Pelefone** *or* **Telefone Selulari** (*peh*-leh-fohn *or teh*-leh-fohn seh-loo-lah-*ree;* cell phone)

✔ **Oznit** (ohz-*neet;* telephone receiver)

✔ **Kav HaTelefone** (kahv hah-*teh*-leh-fohn; telephone line)

Finding someone's number

In the United States, if you want to find someone's **Mispar Telefone** (mees-*pahr teh*-leh-fohn; phone number), you dial 411. In Israel you can dial 144. When you reach the **Merkazan** (M) / **Merkazanit** (F) (mehr-kah-*zahn*/mehr-kah-zah-*nit;* operator), he or she will generally ask you for the person's **Shem Mishpacha** (shem mees-pa-*chah;* family name), **Shem Prati** (shem prah-tee; first or private name), and perhaps the **Ir** (ear; city) in which the person lives. You can also try the **Madrich Telefone** (mah-*dreech teh*-leh-fohn; phone book), or if you're looking for a particular business or service, the **Dapei Zahav** (dah-*pay* za-*hahv;* yellow pages) may be helpful.

Telling someone to call you

You can always find someone's phone numbers, but sometimes, simply asking him or her to call you is easier. In Hebrew, you have several options when you want to ask someone to give you a call:

✔ **TarimTelefone** (tah-*reem teh*-leh-fohn; *Literally:* pick up the phone) (MS)

  Tarimi Telefone (tah-ree-*mee teh*-leh-fohn; *Literally:* pick up the phone) (FS)

✔ **Ten Li Tziltzul** (tehn *lee* tzil-*tzool;* give me a ring) (MS)

  Tni Li Tziltzul (tnee *lee* tzil-*tzool;* give me a ring) (FS)

✔ **Talfen Elahy** (tahl-*fehn* eh-*lie;* phone me) (MS)

  Talfeni Elahy (tahl-feh-*nee* eh-*lie;* phone me) (FS)

Using a public phone in Israel

In Israel, you can't simply drop coins into a public phone. All public phones in Israel are operated with a magnetic card called a **Telecart** (*teh*-leh-kahrt; phone card) that you can buy at numerous stores or at your hotel. They're sold in different time increments. You simply insert one of these cards into a slot on the **Telefone Tziburi** (*teh*-leh-fohn tzee-boo-*ree;* public phone) before placing your call.

Talkin' the Talk

Shira and Nomi have just met for lunch. After lunch Shira asks Nomi if she would call her.

Shira:	**Tzaltzeli Elahy.** tzahl-tzeh-*lee* eh-*lahy.* Give me a ring.
Nomi:	**Tov. Ani Atalfen Lach.** tohv. ah-*nee* ah-tahl-*fehn* lach. Good. I'll phone you.
Shira:	**HaMispar Telefone Sheli Shesh, Echad, Shesh, Sheva, Sheva, Sheva.** hah-mees-*pahr* teh-leh-fohn sheh-*lee* shaysh, eh-*chahd,* shaysh, *sheh-*vah, *sheh*-vah, *sheh*-vah. My telephone number is six, one, six, seven, seven, seven.

Words to Know

Dapei Zahav	dah-<u>pay</u> zah-<u>hahv</u>	yellow pages
Kav HaTelefone	kahv hah-<u>teh</u>-leh-fohn	telephone line
Madrich Telefone	mahd-<u>reech</u> <u>teh</u>-leh-fohn	phone book
Pelafone	<u>peh</u>-leh-fohn	cell phone
Telefone	<u>teh</u>-leh-fohn	telephone
Telefone Tziburi	<u>teh</u>-leh-fohn tzee-boo-<u>ree</u>	public telephone

Asking for People and Getting the Message

In this section, I provide vocabulary and useful expressions that you can use when you want to speak to someone on the phone or leave a message.

When you call someone on the **Telefone,** the person on the other end of the **Kav HaTelefone** (kahv hah-teh-leh-*fohn;* telephone line) generally says either **Hello** (I'm guessing you've figured out the pronunciation and translation for this one) or **Shalom** (shah-*lohm;* peace).

Talkin' the Talk

 Chaim and Michal are beginning a **Sichat Telefone** (see-*chaht teh-leh-fohn;* phone conversation). (Track 17)

Chaim: **Shalom.**
shah-*lohm.*
Hello.

Michal: **Shalom. Medaberet Michal. Efshar LeDaber Im Chaim?**
shah-*lohm.* meh-dah-*beh*-reht mee-*chah*l. ef-shahr le'dah-*behr* eem chah-*eem?*
Hello. This is Michal speaking. May I speak to Chaim?

Chaim: **Medaber.**
meh-dah-*behr.*
Speaking.

Leaving a message

Sometimes the person with whom you want to speak is simply not at home. When that happens, you can leave a **Hoda'ah** (hoh-dah-*ah;* message).

Talkin' the Talk

Michal is calling her boyfriend, Chaim. He's not home, so she leaves a message with his sister, Shira.

Shira: **Shalom.**
shah-*lohm.*
Hello.

Michal: **Shalom. Ha'im Chaim Nimtza?**
shah-*lohm.* hah-*eem* chah-*yeem* neem-*tzah?*
Hello. Is Chaim there?

Shira:	**Hu Ayno Nimtza Ka'et.**
	hoo ay-*no* neem-*tzah* kah-*eht*.
	He's not here right now.

Michal:	**Efshar L'hash'ir Hoda'ah?**
	ef-*shahr* le-hahsh-*eer* hoh-dah-*ah*?
	May I leave a message?

Shira:	**B'vadai.**
	beh-vah-*dye*.
	Certainly.

Michal:	**Todah. Tagid Lo She Michal Hitkashra.**
	toh-*dah*. tah-*geed* loh sheh mee-*chahl* heet-kahsh-*rah*.
	Thanks. Tell him Michal called.

Shira:	**Tov. Ani Emsor Lo.**
	tohv. ah-*nee* em-*sor* loh.
	Good. I'll tell him.

Michal:	**Todah Rabbah Lach.**
	toh-*dah* rah-*bah* lach.
	Thank you very much.

Shira:	**Ayn B'Ad Mah.**
	ayn be'*ahd mah*.
	It's nothing.

The wonders of technology

Back in the olden days, if you called people and they weren't home, the phone just rang and rang. You figured out that they weren't there, and you just called them back later. Or, if the line was **tafus** (tah-*foos*; busy), you simply hung up and called back. Well, no more. Now everyone seems to have **Sicha Mamtinah** (see-*chah* mahm-tee-*nah*; call-waiting), and a lot of folks even have **Sherut Akov Acharei** (she-*root*-ah-*kohv* ah-cha-*rey*; call forwarding), so your phone calls follow you everywhere. Why people want others to be able to constantly track them down is beyond me, but hey, who am I to question it? If you like knowing who's calling before you **Merim Telefone** (meh-*reem* teh-leh-fohn; to pick up the phone), you definitely need **Sicha Mezuhah** (see-*chah* me-zoo-*hah*; caller-ID). And, if you miss a call because you're running up the stairs and fail to grab the phone in time, you can always use **Chiug Chozer Automati** (chee-*yoog* choh-*zair* oh-toh-*mah*-tee; auto-redial) — also popularly known as **Nudnik** (*nood*-neek), which literally means pest!

Words to Know

B'vadai	beh-vah-<u>dye</u>	certainly
Efshar	ehf-<u>shahr</u>	May I? (Literally: Is it possible?)
Hoda'ah	hoh-dah-<u>ah</u>	message
Ka'et	kah-<u>eht</u>	right now
Tafus	tah-<u>foos</u>	busy

Dealing with answering machines and other annoyances

Technology! It's a part of life. This section goes over how to deal with the wonders of telephone technology.

Reaching an answering machine

In this technology driven society, it's amazing that we actually speak to each other at all. I usually find myself speaking to a friend's **Meshivon** (meh-shee-*vohn;* answering machine) more often than I speak to the person. Here's an example of an outgoing message you may hear on an answering machine:

> **Shalom. Higa'tem Le'Mispar Shesh Echad Sheva, Shesh Echad Sheva Chamesh. Ari V'Shalvi Aynam Nimtzaim Ka'et. Na LeHash'ir Hoda'ah Acharei Ha'Tziftzuf.**
>
> shah-*lohm.* hee-*gah*-tem le-mees-*pahr* shaysh eh-*chad sheh*-vah, shaysh eh-*chad sheh*-vah chah-*mehsh.* ah-ree veh-*shahl*-vee ay-*nahm* neem-tzah-*eem* kah-*eht.* nah le-hahsh-*eer* hoh-dah-*ah* ah-chah-*ray* hah-tzeef-*tzoof.*
>
> Hello. You have reached (telephone) number 617-6175. Ari and Shalvi aren't here right now. Please leave a message after the beep.

Dealing with voice mail

If you fail to reach a real live person when you place a call, you may find yourself wading through a barrage of **Ta Koli** (tah koh-*lee;* voice mail) instructions asking you to choose from a **Tafrit** (tahf-*reet;* menu) of options. When this happens, I generally press **Efes** (eh-fehs; zero) in hopes of reaching the **Merkazan**(M) / **Merkazanit**(F) (mehr-kah-*zahn*/mehr-kah-zah-*neet;* operator). Here's an example of an automated message you may hear in Hebrew:

Zo He Hoda'ah Mukletet. Im Birtzoncha L'Hagi'a L'Machleket Ha'Begadim Hakesh Echad. L'Machleket Ha'Ochel Hakesh Shta'im.

zo hee hoh-dah-*ah* mook-*leh*-teht. eem beer-tzohn-*chah* leh-hah-gee-*ah* le-mach-*leh*-ket hah-be-gah-*deem* hah-*kehsh* eh-*chahd*. le-mach-*leh*-ket hah-*oh*-chel hah-*kehsh* sh-*tah*-yeem.

This is a recorded message. If you want to reach the clothing department press one. For the food department, press two.

Dumping the dreaded telemarketer

To me, no phone frustrations are worse than the **Meshavek B'Telefone** (meh-shah-*vek* buh-*teh*-leh-fohn; telemarketer) who disturbs you at home by trying to sell you some wonderful product or service like siding for your house or a fifth mortgage. **Chutzpah** (chootz-*pah;* Such nerve)! Here's an example of something you may hear in Hebrew when you pick up the phone and a tele-marketer is on the line:

Shalom. Ratzinu L'anyen Ot'cha B'Chofesh B'Chinam.

shah-*lohm*. rah-tzee-*noo* leh-ahn-*yehn* oht-*chah* buh-*choh*-fesh buh-chee-*nahm*.

Hello. We wanted to interest you in a free vacation.

If you want to be polite, you can answer in the following fashion:

Ayn Li Zman L'Daber Achshav. Atah Yachol Lishlo'ach Li Mashehu BaDo'ar?

ayn lee zmahn leh-dah-*bear* ach-*shahv*. ah-*tah* yah-*chohl* leesh-*loh*-ach lee *mah*-sheh-hoo buh-*doh*-ahr?

I don't have time to speak right now, can you send me something in the mail?

Or if you're feeling less polite, you can **LiTrok Et Ha'telefone** (leet-*rohk* eht hah-*teh*-leh-fohn; to slam down the phone) or simply **LeNatek Et Ha'sikha** (le-nah-*tek* eht hah-see-*cha;* to hang up). Or if you're feeling particularly silly, you can answer with the line my uncle always uses when these folks call:

Hu Ayno Nimtza Kahn Yotair. Hu Avar Le'Sin. Atah Rotzeh Et Mispar Ha'Telefone Shelo Sham?

hoo ay-*noh* neem-*tzah* kahn yoh-*tehr* hoo ah-*vahr* leh-*seen*. ah-tah roh-*tzeh* et mees-*pahr* hah-*teh*-leh-fohn sheh-*loh* shahm?

He doesn't live here anymore. He moved to China. Would you like his phone number there?

Words to Know

HaKesh	hah-<u>kehsh</u>	to press (or to dial)
Hoda'ah Mukletet	hoh-dah-<u>ah</u> mook-<u>leh</u>-teht	recorded message
Kahn	kahn	here
Meshivon	meh-shee-<u>vohn</u>	answering machine
Merkazan (MS)	mehr-kah-<u>zahn</u>	telephone operator
Merkazanit (FS)	mehr-kah-zah-<u>nit</u>	telephone operator
Meshavek B'Telefone	meh-shah-<u>vek</u> buh-<u>teh</u>-leh-fohn	telemarketer
Na	na	please
Sham	shahm	there
Ta Koli	tah koh-<u>lee</u>	voice mail
Tziftzuf	tzeef-<u>tzoof</u>	beep

Making Arrangements Over the Phone

The phone is a useful instrument for conducting your social life, but you use it for other purposes as well — discussing business, calling the doctor to make an appointment, calling a hotel to make a reservation, and so on. Dealing with businesses on the phone requires some specific language. Check it out.

Using the **Telefone** to make a **Hazmana** (hahz-mah-*nah;* reservation) at a **Misada** (mees-ah-*dah;* restaurant) or a **Malon** (mah-*lohn;* hotel) is easy. And, if you're not feeling well, you may want to make a **Tor Etzel Ha'Rofeh** (tor *eh*-tzel hah-roh-*feh;* appointment at the doctor). Here are some words you can use in these situations.

- ✔ **L'Hazmin Hazmana** (leh-hahz-*meen* hahz-mah-*nah;* to make a reservation)
- ✔ **L'Hazmin Tor** (leh-hahz-*meen* tor; to make an appointment)

Check out Chapter 7 for more on talking about and telling time, two useful concepts when making reservations or appointments. And take a look at Chapter 10 for more stuff on work life, Chapter 5 for information on eating in a restaurant, and Chapter 16 for dealing with illnesses and other emergencies. No matter what kind of arrangement you need to make over the phone, I have you covered.

Talkin' the Talk

Hod is calling Elephant Solutions, a **Chevrat Heznek** (chehv-*raht* hehz-*nek;* start-up company) in Jerusalem. He reaches a **Mazkirah** (mahz-kee-*rah;* secretary). Hod asks her to transfer him to the correct **Shluchat Telefone** (shloo-*chaht teh*-leh-fohn; extension number). (Track 18)

Mazkirah: **Shalom. Chevrat Pil. Efshar Lehamtin Rega?**
shah-*lohm.* cheh-*vraht* peel. ehf-*shahr* leh-hahm-*teen reh*-gah?
Hello. Elephant Company. Can you wait a moment?

Hod: **Ken.**
kehn.
Yes.

Mazkirah: **Ani Mitnatzelet She'Garamti Lecha Lechakot. Efshar La'azor Lecha?**
ah-*nee* meet-nah-*tzeh*-leht sheh-gah-*rahm*-tee leh-*chah* leh-chah-*koht.* ehf-*shahr* lah-ah-*zohr* leh-*chah?*
I'm sorry I kept you waiting. May I help you?

Hod: **Ken. Efshar Ledaber Im Adon Hellman? Mispar HaShlucha Shelo Efes, Efes, Chamesh.**
kehn. ehf-*shahr* le-dah-*bear* eem ah-*dohn* helman? mees-*pahr* hah-shloo-*chah* sheh-*loh* eh-fes, eh-fes, chah-*mehsh.*
Yes. May I speak with Mr. Hellman? His extension number is zero, zero, five.

Mazkirah: **Ani Mi'yad Ma'avirah Otcha LaShlucha Shelo.**
ah-*nee* mee-*yahd* mah-ah-veer-*rah* oht-*chah* lah-sh-loo-*chah* sheh-*loh.*
I'll transfer you right now to his extension.

Hod: **Todah Rabbah Lach.**
toh-*dah* rah-*bah* lahch.
Thank you very much.

Words to Know

Hazmana	hahz-mah-<u>nah</u>	reservation
Mispar Shlucha	mees-<u>pahr</u> sh-loo-<u>chah</u>	extension number
Shluchat Telefone	shuh-loo-<u>chaht</u> <u>teh</u>-leh-fohn	telephone extension
Tor	tohr	appointment

Talking About the Past: How Was Your Shabbat?

In the course of a conversation, most people often talk about the past. With all the everyday hustle and bustle, folks often need to catch each other up on what's going on in their lives. Calling a friend on the phone is an easy way to catch up. When you talk about what has already happened to you, you speak in the past tense. In Hebrew, the past tense is created by attaching a *suffix* — or ending — to the root of the verb. Check out Table 9-1 for a list of verb suffixes. (**Note:** There is no suffix for *he*.) For more information on all this grammar stuff, take a look at Chapter 2.

Table 9-1	Verb Suffixes	
Suffix	*Pronunciation*	*English Translation*
Ti	tee	I
Ta (MS)	tah	you
T (FS)	t	you
Ah	ah	she
Nu	noo	we
Tem (MP)	tehm	you
Ten (FP)	tehn	you
U	oo	they

Here's an example of a past-tense verb conjugation using the Hebrew infinitive **LeTalfen** (leh-tahl-*fehn;* to phone). (An infinitive is the form of the verb that expresses action — to do something — without referring to a person. *To phone, to walk,* and *to sleep* are all examples of infinitives.)

Hebrew	Pronunciation	Translation (Gender)
Tilfanti	til-*fahn*-tee	I phoned
Tinlfanta	til-*fahn*-tah	you phoned (MS)
Tilfant	til-*fahnt*	you phoned (FS)
Tilfen	til-*fehn*	he phoned
Tilfenah	til-feh-*nah*	she phoned
Tilfenu	til-feh-*noo*	we phoned
Tilfantem	til-*fahn*-tehm	you phoned (MP)
Tilfanten	til-*fahn*-tehn	you phoned (FP)
Tilfenu	til-feh-*noo*	they phoned

When you speak in the past tense in Hebrew, you often don't need to use the words *I* or *you* when speaking in the first or second person because the pronoun is understood within the context of the conversation. For example:

✔ **Matai Tilfanta?** (mah-*tye* til-*fahn*-tah; When did [you] call?)

✔ **Tilfanti Ba'Boker.** (til-*fahn*-tee bah-*boh*-kehr; [I] called in the morning.)

The Hebrew past tense is the equivalent of four different past-tense forms in English: the simple past, immediate past, past perfect, and past progressive. Pretty cool, huh? You only have to figure out one set of rules instead of four. Makes things easier when you're trying to learn Hebrew. So, **Ani Tilfanti** (ah-*nee* til-*fahn*-tee; I called) can mean all of the following:

✔ I called.

✔ I just called.

✔ I have called.

✔ I was calling.

Fun & Games

Here are some questions commonly asked on the phone. Match them up with the correct responses.

She'elot (sheh-eh-*loht*; questions)

1. **Efshar Ledaber Im Chaim?** (May I speak to Chaim?)

2. **Efshar L'hash'ir Hoda'ah?** (May I leave a message?)

3. **Ha'im Chaim Nimtza?** (Is Chaim there?)

Tshuvot (*tshoo-voht*; possible answers)

A. **Hu Ayno Nimtza Ka'et.**

B. **B'vadai.**

C. **Medaber.**

Chapter 10

At the Office and Around the House

The Torah says "Six days you shall labor and do *any* kind of work." Why, you may ask, does the text say *any* kind of work? Because *any* kind of work — even busywork — is preferable to idleness. As my mother says, "Hard work is good for you!" Ideally, **Avodah** (ah-voh-*dah;* work) should be more than something that just takes up our time. It provides our livelihood. For many, our work is a calling — a way of contributing to the world. In this chapter, I fill you in about all the good "work" words you need to know. I also talk about the little sanctuary you create when you aren't working: your home.

Finding Your Way Around Your Job

If you work **Misra Me'leh'ah** (mees-*rah* meh-leh-*ah;* full-time), your **Misrad** (mees-*rahd;* office) is almost a second home. So why not personalize your **Mekom Avodah** (muh-*kohm* ah-voh-*dah;* workspace), so the place screams you? I like to put up **T'munot** (te-moo-*noht;* pictures), decorate my **Machshev** (mach-*shehv;* computer) with **Madbekot** (mahd-beh-*koht;* stickers) and place on my **Shulchan Avodah** (shool-*chahn* ah-voh-*dah;* desk) a **Kishut** (kee-*shoot;* trinket) or two. You also need to have all the **Tziud** (tzee-*yood;* supplies) you need to get your job done.

Supplying your office

When you're setting up a work area, whether at home or at an office, have these items close at hand:

- **Madpeset** (mahd-*peh*-set; printer)
- **Mechonat Faks** (meh-choh-*naht fahks;* fax machine)
- **Telefone** (*te*-leh-fohn; telephone)

Aside from the machinery, I keep my desk stocked with the following supplies:

- **Atev** (ah-*tehv;* bulldog clip)
- **Dafdefan** (dahf-deh-*fahn;* notepad)
- **Devek** (*deh*-vehk; glue)
- **Eht** (eht; pen)
- **Iparon** (ee-pah-*rohn;* pencil)
- **Machak** (*mah*-chahk; eraser)
- **Mehadek** (meh-hah-*dehk;* paperclip)
- **Seret Davik** (*seh*-reht dah-*veek;* tape)
- **Shadchan** (shahd-*chahn;* stapler)
- **Tipex** (*tee*-pehx; liquid paper)

If you've run out of **Tipex,** or misplaced your **Eht** for the umpteenth time, you can always ask your colleagues if they have one you can use. For example, you may say:

Yesh Lecha Tipex? (*yehsh* le-*chah tee*-pehx; Do you have liquid paper?) (MS)

Yesh Lach Tipex? (*yehsh lach tee*-pehx; Do you have liquid paper?) (FS)

Talkin' the Talk

Shulamit is working at the office. She has misplaced all her pens again and is about to go into a meeting where she must take notes. So, she asks an **Amita** (ah-mee-*tah*; colleague) if she can borrow a pen from her. (Track 19)

Shulamit: **Slicha, Efshar Lehash'il Li Eht?**
slee-*chah,* ehf-*shahr* leh-hahsh-eel lee eht?
Excuse me, can you loan me a pen? (*Literally:* Is it possible to loan to me a pen?)

Colleague: **Ken. Henei.**
kehn. hee-*nay*.
Yes. Here it is.

Shulamit: **V'Gam Yesh Lach Dafdefan?**
ve'*gahm yehsh lahch* dahf-deh-*fahn*?
And do you also have a notepad?

Collegue: **Bevadai. Kchi.**
beh-vah-*dye*. kchee.
Certainly. Take it.

Words to Know

Avodah	ah-voh-<u>dah</u>	work
Amit (MS)	ah-<u>meet</u>	colleague
Amita (FS)	ah-mee-<u>tah</u>	colleague
Eht	eht	pen
Iparon	ee-pah-<u>rohn</u>	pencil
Machak	<u>mah</u>-chahk	eraser
Machshev	mahch-<u>shev</u>	computer
Misrad	mees-<u>rahd</u>	office
Misrah M'leah	mees-<u>rah</u> meh-lay-<u>ah</u>	full-time position
Shadchan	shahd-<u>chahn</u>	stapler
Shulchan Avodah	shool-<u>chahn</u> ah-voh-<u>dah</u>	desk

Searching for the perfect job

Searching for the perfect **Avodah** (ah-voh-*dah;* work) can be a full-time job in and of itself. It can also be fun. Job searching is exciting to see all the available possibilities. Plus, you can get away with **Hithalelut** (heet-hah-leh-*loot;* bragging)!

When you go in for your **Re'ayon** (reh-ah-*yohn;* interview), be prepared to talk about your **Nisayon** (ne-sah-*yohn;* experience) and have a copy of your **Korot Chaim** (koh-*roht* chah-*yeem;* resume). And before you accept any job, make sure you check out the **Maskoret** (mahs-*koh*-reht; salary) and the **Hatavot** (hah-tah-*vot;* benefits)!

Some of the **Hatavot** you want to hear about are:

- **Bituach Bri'ut** (bee-*too*-ach bree-*ooht;* health insurance)
- **Chufsha** (choohf-*shah;* vacation)
- **Mas Hachnahsah** (*mahs* hach-nah-*sah;* income tax)
- **Maskoret** (mahs-*koh*-reht; salary)
- **Pensia** (*pens*-yah; pension)
- **Sha'ot Nosafot** (shah-*oht* noh-sah-*foht;* overtime)
- **Tashlum Sha'ot Nosafot** (tahsh-*loom* shah-*oht* noh-sah-*foht;* overtime pay)

Whatever your **Miktzoa** (meek-*tzoh*-ah; profession), hopefully you're a **Charutz** (chah-*rootz;* hard worker) (MS) or **Charutzah** (chah-roo-*tzah;* hard worker) (FS) and you won't lose your job. You don't want to contribute to the growing problem of **Avtala** (ahv-tah-*lah;* unemployment). But if you do lose your job — and it happens to the best of us — don't be an **Atzlan** (ahtz-*lahn;* lazy person) (MS) or an **Atzlanit** (ahtz-lah-*neet;* lazy person) (FS). Get out there and look for work!

Talkin' the Talk

Nurit and Ya'ir are meeting at a coffee shop and their conversation turns to their work. (Track 20)

Ya'ir:	**Eich Holech Lach Ba'Avodah?** ehch hoh-*lech* lahch buh-ah-voh-*dah?* How's it going with you at work?
Nurit:	**Lo Kol-Kach Tov.** loh kohl-*kahch* tohv. Not so good.
Yair:	**Lamah?** *lah*-mah? Why?

Nurit: **Ha'Avodah Atzmah He B'Seder, Aval Ani Lo Ohevet Et Ha'Menahel Sheli.**
hah-ah-voh-*dah* ahtz-*mah* hee beh-*sed*-der, ah-*vahl* ah-*nee* loh oh-*heh*-veht eht hah-meh-nah-*hel* sheh-*lee*.
The work itself is okay, but I don't like my boss.

Yair: **Basa! Mah Ta'asee?**
bah-sah mah tah-ah-*see?*
Bummer! What are you going to do?

Nurit: **Ha'Emet, Ani B'Chipus. Atah Yode'ah Mashehu She'Mat'im Li?**
hah-eh-*meht,* ah-nee beh-chee-*poos.* ah-*tah* yoh-*deh*-ah *mah*-sheh-hoo sheh-maht-*eem lee?*
Truth, I'm looking. Do you know of something suitable for me?

Words to Know

Atzlan (MS)	ahtz-<u>lahn</u>	lazy person
Atzlanit (FS)	ahtz-lah-<u>neet</u>	lazy person
Avtala	ahv-tah-<u>lah</u>	unemployment
Hatavot	hah-tah-<u>voht</u>	benefits
Korot Chaim	koh-<u>roht</u> chah-<u>yeem</u>	resume
Nisayon	nee-sah-<u>yohn</u>	experience
Maskoret	mahs-<u>koh</u>-reht	salary
Menahel (MS)	meh-nah-<u>hel</u>	manager
Menahelet (FS)	meh-nah-<u>heh</u>-leht	manager
Miktzoa	meek-<u>tzoh</u>-ah	profession
Re'ayon	reh-ah-<u>yohn</u>	interview

Goofing off at work

You're at a **Misrah** (mees-rah; job) **MiTaysha Ad Chamesh** (mee-*tay*-shah ahd chah-*mesh;* from nine-to-five) and during your weekly 40 hours, you run out of tasks to do. **Oy-Va-a-Voy** (oye-vah-ah-voye; Oh no). What are you to do? Look busy? You can **Liglosh BaReshet** (leeg-lohsh buh-*reh*-sheht; surf the Web). Or maybe you want **Ledaber BaTelefone** (leh-dah-behr bah-teh-leh-fohn; to speak on the phone). You can always try **Lesader Et Shulchan Ha'Avodah** (leh-sah-*dehr* eht shool-*chahn* hah-ah-voh-*dah;* to straighten up your desk). Or maybe you want **Leflartet** (leh-flahr-*teht;* to flirt) with that cute **Amit** (M)/**Amita** (F) (ah-*meet*/ah-mee-*tah;* co-worker). And then you can choose that favorite Israeli (and American) pastime: **Lishtot Kafeh** (leesh-*toht* ca-*faeh;* drinking coffee). In Hebrew, this scenario is called **Tayshah-Chamesh-Efes** (*tay*-shah-chah-*mesh*-eh-fehs; nine-five-zero). You work 9-to-5 but accomplish nothing.

The word ***Eht*** (eht) means *with*. (***Note:*** This word is different from the Hebrew word for pen, "Eht" which is spelled with an *ayin* and a *tet* while the word for *with* is spelled with an *aleph* and a *tav.*) When you combine **Eht** with a personal pronoun, such as me, you, him, her, us, or they (in Hebrew grammar-speak this is called *inflecting*), it takes on the forms in the following list:

Iti (ee-*tee;* with me)

Itcha (eet-*chah;* with you) (MS)

Itach (ee-*tahch;* with you) (FS)

Ito (ee-*toh;* with him) (MS)

Ita (ee-*tah;* with her) (FS)

Itanu (ee-*tah*-noo; with us) (any gender)

Itchem (eet-*chehm;* with you) (when talking to lots of people, male or a mixed-group)

Itchen (eet-*chen;* with you) (FP)

Itam (ee-*tahm;* with them) (MP)

Itan (ee-*tahn;* with them) (FP)

You can also use **Eht** in combination with suffixes that indicate different pronouns to mean *to me, to you,* and so forth. It's inflected as follows:

Oti (oh-*tee;* me)

Otchah (oht-*chah;* you) (MS)

Otach (oh-*tach;* you) (FS)

Oto (oh-*toh;* him) (MS)

Ota (oh-*tah;* her) (FS)

Otanu (oh-*tah*-noo; us)

Ehtchem (eht-*chem;* you) (MP, but also used for a mixed bunch of people)

Ehtchen (eht-*chen;* you) (FP)

Otam (oh-*tahm;* them) (MP, but also used for a mixed bunch)

Otan (oh-*tahn;* them) (FP)

You also use **Eht** (that can be modified to be MS, FS, MP, or FP) when you want to indicate that something is *the same*. Of course, with Hebrew, this word must match gender and number:

- ✔ **Oto Ha'Yeled** (oh-*toh* hah-*yeh*-lehd; the same boy)
- ✔ **Ota Ha'Yalda** (oh-*tah* hah-yahl-*dah;* the same girl)
- ✔ **Otam Ha'Yeladim** (oh-*tahm* hah-yeh-lah-*deem;* the same boys)
- ✔ **Otan Ha'Yeladot** (oh-*tahn* hah-yeh-lah-*doht;* the same girls)

Words to Know

Drishot	dree-<u>shoht</u>	requirements
Hachshara	hahch-shah-<u>rah</u>	training
Iton	ee-<u>tohn</u>	newspaper
Kishurim	kee-shoo-<u>reem</u>	qualifications
Moda'ot Drushim	moh-dah-<u>oht</u> droo-<u>sheem</u>	want ads

Looking for jobs in all the right places

A good place to look for a job is to search the **Iton** (ee-*tohn;* newspaper) for **Mo'da'ot Drushim** (moh-dah-*oht* droo-*sheem;* want ads). The ads generally start off with the word **Darush** (dah-*roosh* (MS); wanted) or **D'Rusha** (d-roo-shah (FS); wanted). The ad may also specify **Kishurim** (kee-shoo-*reem;* qualifications), **Drishot** (duh-ree-*shoht;* requirements), and **Hachshara** (hach-shah-*rah;* training). Other phrases you may see are: **Na Lifnot I . . .** (nah leef-*noht* le; please respond to . . .) and **Na Lishloach Et Korot Hehcha'im Le . . .** (nah leesh-*loh*-ach eht koh-*roht* heh-chah-*yeem* le; please send your resume to . . .).

Hanging Out at Home

Home is your refuge from the hustle and bustle of the outside world. In Jewish tradition, every home has the potential of being a **Mikdash Me'at** (meek-*dash* meh-*aht;* mini-sanctuary). The Jewish value of **Sh'lom Bayit** (sh-*lohm bah*-yeet; peace within the home) is an important concept. Thus, the items that we bring into our homes, and the ways that we behave within those walls have the potential to bring the sacred into our everyday lives. In this section, I tell you about all the stuff you need — both sacred and everyday — to make your house a home.

Looking through the rooms

How many **Chadarim** (chah-dahr-*eem;* rooms) does your **Dirah** (dee-*rah;* apartment) or **Bayit** (*bah*-yeet; house) have? Do you have plenty of space where you live? Or do you want some more elbowroom? Whether you live in an apartment or house, your dwelling probably has these rooms:

- **Ambatia** (ahm-*baht*-yah; bathroom)
- **Aron** (ah-*rohn;* closet)
- **Chadar Sheinah** (chah-*dar* shay-*nah;* bedroom)
- **Mitbach** (meet-*bach;* kitchen)
- **Pinat Ochel** (pee-*naht oh*-chel; breakfast nook)
- **Prozdor** (prohz-*dohr;* hallway)
- **Salon** (sah-*lohn;* living room)

And if you're fortunate, your property may have some of these features as well:

- **Gader** (gah-*dehr;* fence)
- **Ginah** (gee-*nah;* yard)
- **Mirpeset** (meer-*peh*-seht; balcony)
- **Musach** (moo-*sahch;* garage)

At the entrance of a traditional Jewish home, you may find a small amulet called a **Mezuzah** (meh-zoo-*zah*) containing within it a central Jewish prayer. Around the entrance, you may also find a **Birkat Habayit** (beer-*kaht* hah-*bah*-yeet; blessing for the home). On the eastern wall, you may find a **Mizrach** (meez-*rahch*), which literally means "east" and is usually a decorative picture. Jews place it on the eastern wall because that is the direction of Judaism's holy city, Jerusalem, and the direction Jews face during prayer. However, if you live in Israel, then you place the **Mizrach** on the wall facing Jerusalem, so if you live five kilometers north of Jerusalem, then you place it on the southern wall.

Words to Know

Ambatia	ahm-<u>baht</u>-yah	bathroom
Bayit	<u>bah</u>-yeet	house
Chadar Sheinah	chah-<u>dahr</u> shay-<u>nah</u>	bedroom
Mirpeset	meer-<u>peh</u>-seht	balcony
Mitbach	meet-<u>bahch</u>	kitchen
Salon	sah-<u>lohn</u>	living room

Furnishing your humble abode

After you move into your home, you need **Rihut** (reeh-*hoot;* furniture). You can buy it new, troll the yard sales, or see what you can bum off family and friends. I'm always surprised to see what people have sitting around in their **Martef** (mahr-*tehf;* basement) or **Aliyot Gag** (ah-lee-*yoht gahg;* attics) that they are happy to give away. What do you need?

- **Kiseh no'ach** (kee-seh *noh*-ach; easy chair)
- **Kiseh** (kee-*seh;* chair)
- **Madaf S'Farim** (mah-*dahf* sfah-*reem;* bookshelf)
- **Mitah** (mee-*tah;* bed)
- **Sapah** (sah-*pah;* couch)
- **Shulchan** (shool-*chahn;* table)

Then, of course, you have all the electrical conveniences that are part of modern-day living. How did we ever get along without them?

- **Kirayim** (kee-*rah*-yeem; stove)
- **Makrer** (mahk-*rair;* refrigerator)
- **Mazgan** (mahz-*gahn;* air-conditioner)
- **Mechonat K'visa** (meh-choh-*naht* kvee-*sah;* washing machine)
- **Mikrogal** (meek-roh-*gahl;* microwave)
- **Tanur** (tah-*noor;* oven)

✔ **Tanuron** (tah-nooh-*rohn;* toaster oven)

✔ **Televizia** (teh-leh-*viz*-yah; television)

Words to Know

Kirayim	kee-<u>rah</u>-yeem	stove
Kiseh	kee-<u>seh</u>	chair
Mikrogal	<u>meek</u>-roh-gahl	microwave
Mitah	mee-<u>tah</u>	bed
Sapah	sah-<u>pah</u>	couch
Shulchan	shool-<u>chahn</u>	table
Tanur	tah-<u>noor</u>	oven

Doing the sponjah! Housecleaning the Israeli way!

When I got my first apartment in Israel, an Israeli friend came over to help me **Lesader Et Ha'Makom** (lee-sah-*dehr* eht hah-mah-*kohm;* to straighten up the place). He found me trying to wash the floor, pushing a damp **Smartoot** (smahr-*toot;* rag) about the **Ritzpa** (reetz-*pah;* floor) with a **Magav** (mah-*gahv;* squeegee). He scolded me, saying I didn't know how to clean house properly, promptly grabbed a **Dli** (dlee; bucket), and filled it with hot soapy water. Then he dumped all the hot soapy water on the floor! Expertly he wrapped the **Smartoot** around the **Magav** and wisked the soapy water down the **Petach Nikooz** (*peh*-tach neeh-*kooz;* drain opening) in the middle of the floor.

Believe it or not all (or most) Israeli houses are built this way, and Israelis wash their floors in this manner. This method is called **La'Asot Sponja** (lah-ah-*soht* spon-jah; to do the sponjah). It's actually quite effective. Israelis wonder how we **Chulnikim** (*chool*-nee-keem; foreigners) ever manage to get our floors clean. If you inspect the wooden feet of furniture in Israeli homes, you notice that they're often a bit swollen. That's what happens to wood from sitting in all that hot, soapy water. But if you don't want to go through all this hassle every time you want the floor clean, you can always use your **Matateh** (mah-tah-*teh;* broom)!

Residing in an Apartment

Wherever you live, if in the **Ir** (eer; city) or a **Parvar** (pahr-*vahr;* suburb), or if you're new to town, you may need to find a new **Dirah** (dee-*rah;* apartment) — unless, of course, you're a student and you live in the **Me'onot** (meh-oh-*noht;* dorms). Do you want to live **Levad** (leh-*vahd;* alone) or with **Shutafim** (shoo-tah-*feem;* roommates)? Do you have a **Mechonit** (meh-choh-*neet;* car) and thus need a **Mekom Chanaiah** (meh-*kohm* chah-nah-*yah;* parking spot)? Or are you car-free and prefer to live near **Tachbura Tziburit** (tach-boo-*rah* tzee-boo-*reet;* public transportation)?

Hunting for your very own flat

When you're **Mechapes** (MS)/**Mechapeset** (FS) (meh-chah-*pes*/meh-chah-*peh-set;* looking for an apartment), you first want to decide in which **Shchunah** (shchoo-*nah;* neighborhood) you want to live. You want to know if the **Dirah** is on **Komah Rishonah** (koh-*mah* ree-shoh-*nah;* the first floor) or **Komah Elyonah** (koh-*mah* ehl-yoh-*nah;* an upper floor).

What Americans call the first floor is the **Komat Karka** (koh-*maht kahr*-kah; ground floor) in Israel. Furthermore, when Israelis say the **Komah Rishona** (koh-*mah* ree-shoh-*nah;* first floor), they mean what Americans call the second floor.

If the **Binyan** (been-*yahn;* building) has many **Komot** (koh-*moht;* floors), you may want to inquire about a **Ma'alit** (mah-ah-*leet;* elevator). Of course, you need to ask how much the **S'char Ha' Dirah** (s'*chahr* hah-dee-*rah;* apartment rent) is. When you sign the **Chozeh S'chirut** (choh-*zeh* s'chee-*root;* rental contract), you also need to provide a **Check Pikadon** (check pee-kah-*dohn;* deposit check) and a document guaranteeing that you have the ability to pay rent month after month called a **Shtar Arevut** (sh-*tahr* ahr-reh-*voot;* guarantee).

In Israel, a "two-room" house means a **Chadar Sheinah** (chah-*dahr* shay-*nah;* bedroom) and a **salon** (sah-*lohn;* living room), different from the United States where "two-rooms" often just refers to the bedrooms. For more on the names of rooms in dwelling places, check out the section, "Looking through the rooms," earlier in this chapter.

Talkin' the Talk

Rina is looking for an apartment. She and her realtor are discussing what type of apartment she wants. (Track 21)

Realtor: **Kamah Chadarim At Rotzah?**
kah-*mah* chah-dah-*reem* aht- roh-*tzah?*
How many rooms do you want?

Rina: **Ani Rotza Shnei Chadarim.**
ah-nee roh-*tzah* sh-*nay* chah-dah-*reem.*
I want two rooms.

Realtor: **Ichpat Lach Im Zeh B'Komah Elyonah, V'Ayn Ma'alit?**
eech-*paht lach* eem zeh beh-koh-*mah* ehl-yoh-*nah*
vuh-*ayn* mah-ah-*leet?*
Does it matter to you if it's on an upper floor and there's no elevator?

Rina: **Lo, Zeh Lo Ichpat Li. Ani Tze'iera V'Gam Zeh Bari LeTapes BaMadregot.**
loh. zeh loh eech-*paht* lee. ah-*nee* tze-ee-*rah* vuh-
gahm zeh bah-*ree* le-tah-*pehs* buh-mahd-reh-*goht.*
No, that doesn't matter to me. I'm young and it's also healthy to climb stairs.

If you want to ask someone if something matters to them, you use the Hebrew phrase **Ichpat** (eech-*paht*) and you inflect the personal pronoun with a **Lamed** (lamed) which means *to*. Inflecting basically means combining the words together. For example:

Ichpat Li (eech-*paht lee;* it matters to me)

Ichpat L'Cha (eech-*paht* leh-*chah;* it matters to you) (MS)

Ichpat Lach (eech-*paht lach;* it matters to you) (FS)

Ichapt Lo (eech-*paht loh;* it matters to him) (MS)

Ichpat Lah (eech-*paht lah;* it matters to her) (FS)

Ichpat Lanu (eech-*paht lah*-noo; it matters to us)

Ichpat Lachem (eech-*paht* lah-*chehm;* it matters to you) (MP or for a bunch of people)

Ichpat Lachen (eech-*paht* lah-*chen;* it matters to you) (FP)

Ichpat Lahem (eech-*paht* lah-*hem;* it matters to them) (MP or mixed plural)

Ichpat Lahen (eech-*paht* lah-*hen;* it matters to them) (FP)

Giving your apartment some flair

After you settle in your new **Dirah,** you probably want to spruce it up! Colorful **Shtichim** (shtee-*cheem;* rugs) always help to brighten up the place, and **Tzmachim** (tzmah-*cheem;* plants) can really make the place seem like home. Even some **Dagim** (dah-*geem;* fish) in a little **Akvarium** (ahk-*vahr*-yoom; aquarium) add a nice touch. Hanging some **Omanut** (oh-mah-*noot;* art) on the **Kirot** (kee-*roht;* walls), including **Posterim** (pohs-ter-eem; posters), can be pleasant and homey. Of course, don't forget **T'munot** (tmoo-*noht;* pictures) of your family and friends and plenty of funky **Magnetim** (mag-*neh*-teem; magnets) for the **Makrer** (mahk-*rair;* refrigerator). Speaking of which, Hebrew magnetic poetry is a really good idea. You can even buy it on the Web at www.hebrewmagnets.co.il/.

Keeping your apartment safe

You don't want to have a **Bayit Saruf** (*bah*-yeet sah-*roof;* burnt-down house), or a **Shoded** (shoh-*dehd;* thief) or **Rotze'ach** (roh-*tzeh*-ach; murderer) break in! **Chas V'Chalilah** (chahs-veh-chah-*lee*-lah; heaven forbid)! So you need to take some precautions. You need to do the following steps to protect your dwelling:

- ✔ **Lechabot Eht Ha'Ohr** (leh-chah-*boht* eht hah-*ohr;* to turn off the light)
- ✔ **Lin'ol Et Ha'Delet** (leen-*ohl* eht hah-*deh*-leht; to lock the door)
- ✔ **Lisgor Et Ha'Chalon** (lees-*gohr* eht hah-chah-*lohn;* to close the window)
- ✔ **Lisgor Et Ha'gaz** (lees-*gor* eht hah-*gahz;* to close the gas valve)

Danger on the roof!!!

One year when I was living in Israel, the **Dirah** (dee-*rah;* apartment) I was sharing with two **Shutafim** (shoo-tah-*feem;* roommates) (**Shutafot** is the word to use for female roommates, but in this case, I was living with a man and a woman so I use the form that works for either male plural or mixed gender) had the kind of heating system that required you to order a vat of **Gahz** (gahz; fuel) from the local gas company, **Paz Gaz** (pahz gahz), which literally means golden gas. The gas man came out and installed this large tank of **Gahz** right on top of our **Gag** (gahg; roof)! I was a little disconcerted, to say the least. "What happens," I sensibly asked my **Shutafa** (shoo-tah-*fah;* roommate (FS), "if **Barak** (bah-*rahk;* lightning) strikes the **Gahz** while we are all in the **Dirah?**" "Well," my **Shutafa** replied, "We'll just try not to think about it while it is happening."

Words to Know

Binyan	been-<u>yahn</u>	building
Cheder	<u>cheh</u>-dair	room
Chadarim	chah-dahr-<u>eem</u>	rooms
Chalon	chah-<u>lohn</u>	window
Dirah	dee-<u>rah</u>	apartment
Ma'alit	mah-ah-<u>leet</u>	elevator
Makrer	mahk-<u>rair</u>	refrigerator
Mekom Chanayah	meh-<u>kohm</u> chah-na-<u>yah</u>	parking spot
Shati'ach	sha-<u>tee</u>-ach	rug
Shutaf (MS)	shoo-<u>tahf</u>	roommate
Shutafa (FS)	shoo-tah-<u>fah</u>	roommate
Tzehmach	<u>tzeh</u>-mach	plant

Commanding People: Do As I Say

Hebrew uses a special verb tense to make commands called **Tzivui** (tzee-*vooy*). Unfortunately, you probably hear this verb tense a lot around the office, and if you're *really unlucky,* around the house as well! This special verb tense is similar to the future tense, but the prefix is dropped. For example:

Tense	Hebrew	Pronunciation	Translation	Gender
Future tense	**Tishma**	teesh-*mah*	You will hear	(MS)
Command tense	**Sh'ma!**	sh*mah*	Hear!	(MS)
Future tense	**Tishme'i**	teesh-meh-*ee*	You will hear	(FS)
Command tense	**Shim'ee**	sheem-*ee*	Hear!	(FS)

In the command tense in the feminine singular and in the masculine plural, the vowels change just a bit. You can tell someone to finish up something like this:

G'mor! (*gmohr;* Finish up!) (MS)

Gimri! (geem-*ree;* Finish up!) (FS)

Gimru! (geem-*roo;* Finish up!) (for a bunch of people, male, female and mixed-gender)

Here's how you tell someone to sit:

Shev! (sh*ehv;* Sit!) (MS)

Sh'Vi (sh-*vee;* Sit!) (FS)

Sh'Voo (sh-*voo;* Sit!) (for a bunch of people, male, female, or mixed-gender)

If you want to tell someone *not* to do something, you use the word **Al** (ahl) in combination with the future tense. For example:

Al Tichtov! (ahl teech-*tohv;* Don't write!) (MS)

Al Tichtevi (ahl teech-te-*vee;* Don't write! (FS)

Al Tichtevu (ahl teech-te-*voo;* Don't write!) (for a bunch of people, male, female or mixed gender)

Fun & Games

Use the following word list to identify the pictured rooms. Check Appendix C for the answers.

Ambatia, Aron, Chadar Sheinah, Mitbach, Musach, Salon

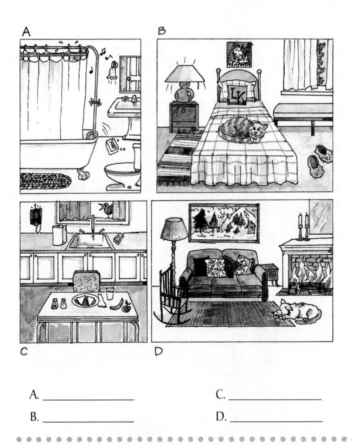

A. _____   C. _____

B. _____   D. _____

Part III
Hebrew on the Go

The 5th Wave
By Rich Tennant

"All the Hebrew I know comes from what I picked up at the corner deli. I think that's why they always gave us a pickle whenever we checked out of an Israeli hotel."

In this part . . .

1n this part, you can escape the daily grind and — in the words of Mark Twain — "throw off the bowlines. Sail away from the safe harbor. Catch the trade winds in your sails. Explore. Dream. Discover." Twain said, "Twenty years from now you will be more disappointed by the things you didn't do, than the ones you did do." So what are you waiting on? Do it. And do it in Hebrew. This chapter shows you how. **N'siah Tovah** (neh-see-ah *toh*-vah; Good travels!)

Chapter 11

Planning a Trip

In This Chapter

▶ Deciding where and when to go

▶ Exploring various countries and cities

▶ Arriving and leaving your destination

*Y*ou want to take a trip, but you don't know where to go. In this chapter, I give you some key Hebrew words and phrases that can help you decide where to visit and how to plan your trip.

For me, I think I'll take a **Chofesh** (*choh*-fehsh; vacation) after I'm done writing this book! And, the places I want to go! So many countries I want to see, so many things I want to do. I want to hike in Costa Rica, sail down the canals in Italy, sunbathe in Greece, and go on a safari in Africa. And oh yeah, I really want to go have tapas in Spain, see the museums in France, and gawk at all the tall blonde people in the Scandinavian countries. I'm game for just about anything! And did I mention India? **Nesiah Tovah** (neh-see-*ah* toh-*vah;* Happy traveling!)

Choosing Your Final Destination (And When You Want to Go)

Figuring out when you're going to take your trip is as important as choosing your destination. You won't be happy if you visit some place during the worst weather they have all year. Then again, maybe you want to because everything will be cheap! No matter when you go, a little planning is good. Table 11-1 shows the months when you may plan a vacation:

Table 11-1	Rattling Off the Months	
Hebrew	*Pronunciation*	*Translation*
Yanuar	*yan*-oo-ahr	January
Februar	*feb*-roo-ahr	February
Mehrtz	*mehrtz*	March
April	a-*preel*	April
Maye	m*ahye*	May
Yuni	*yoo*-nee	June
Yuli	*yoo*-lee	July
August	oh-*goost*	August
September	*sehp-tehm*-bear	September
October	*ohc-toh*-bear	October
November	*noh-vehm*-bear	November
Detzember	*deh-tzehm*-bear	December

Whittling down your choices — so many places you can go!

Then, of course, you have many **Aratzot** (ah-rahtz-*oht;* countries) you can choose to visit. When I travel, I am less interested in the **Atarei Tayarut** (ah-tah-*rey* tah-yah-*root;* tourist sites) and more interested in the **Tofa'ot Teva** (toh-fah-*oht teh*-vah; natural phenomenon) and the **Chaim Yom Yomi'im** (chah-*yeem* yohm-*yoh-mee-eem;* daily life) of the people who live there. Also, I always find it interesting to visit **Ir HaBirah** (eer hah-bee-*rah;* the capital city). Of the following countries in Table 11-2, where would you like to go?

Table 11-2	Names of Countries	
Hebrew	*Pronunciation*	*Translation*
Anglia	*ahng*-lee-*yah*	England
Artzot HaBrit	ahrtz-*oht* hah-*breet*	the United States
Germania	gayr-*mah*-nyah	Germany

Hebrew	Pronunciation	Translation
Hodu	*hoh*-doo	India
Italya	ee-*tahl*-yah	Italy
Meksiko	*mehk*-see-koh	Mexico
Mitzrayim	meetz-*rah*-yeem	Egypt
Polin	poh-*leen*	Poland
Russia	*roos*-yah	Russia
Schvaitz	sh-*vaitz*	Switzerland
S'farad	sfah-*rahd*	Spain
Shvedia	shuh-*vehd*-yah	Sweden
Sin	seen	China
Turkia	*toor*-kee-yah	Turkey
Tzarfat	tzar-*faht*	France
Yapan	yah-*pahn*	Japan
Yarden	yahr-*dehn*	Jordan
Yavan	yah-*vahn*	Greece

Making your way to Machtesh Ramon

One of the most amazing **Tofa'ot Teva** (toh-fah-*oht teh*-vah; natural phenomena) in Israel is the Machtesh Ramon, the largest crater in the world. When I first heard about this place and heard it was a crater, I immediately thought of the moon. However, the Machtesh Ramon isn't like the moon's craters, but rather a cave drained by a single **Wadi** (*wah*-dee; riverbed). You can find the Machtesh Ramon in the Negev Desert in Israel, a few hours south of the southern city of Beersheva. The Machtesh Ramon is home to many beautiful trees, shrubs, and flowers, such as **Chinoniot** (chee-noh-nee-*yoht*; daisies) and **Tziv'onim** (tzeev-oh-*neem*; tulips).

Many animals live there, including the **Ako** (ah-*koh*; ibex), **Namer** (nah-*mehr*; leopard), **Tzavua** (tzah-*voh*-ah; hyena), **Shual** (shoo-*ahl*; fox), and **Tzvi** (tzuh-*vee*; deer). Rock formations, fossils, and volcanic phenomenon — some as old as 220 million years — fill the place. The site also has an amazing museum. And if you like to hike, the Machtesh Ramon has some great trails. And if you really want to rough it, consider camping outdoors. At night, you can enjoy some incredible **Hitbonenut BaKochavim** (heet-boh-neh-*noot* bah-koh-chah-*veem*; stargazing) because the area has few lights and the air is crisp and clear.

The literal meaning of the Hebrew word for the United States **Artzot HaBrit** (ahrtz-*oht* hah-*breet*) is *the lands of the covenant*. A covenant is an unbreakable agreement between parties. In the case of the United States of America, the "covenant" is the Constitution.

Talkin' the Talk

Orli and Yoni are planning to travel. Orli wants to go to South America, but Yoni wants to go to India. (Track 22)

Yoni:	**Tov, Le'an Nos-im?** *tohv*, leh-*ahn* nohs-*eem*? Good. Where are we traveling?
Orli:	**Ani Hayiti Rotzah Linso'a L'Drom Amerika.** ah-*nee* hah-*yee*-tee roh-*tzah* leen-*soh-ah* leh-drohm ah-*meh*-ree-kah. I want to travel to South America.
Yoni:	**Davka, Ani Hayiti Rotzeh Linso'a L'Hodu.** dahv-*kah* ah-*nee* hah-*yee*-tee roh-*tzah* leen-*soh*-ah leh-*hoh*-doo. But I really want to travel to India.
Orli:	**Bo Nitpasher V'Nisa L'Shteihen.** boh neet-pah-*shehr* vuh-nee-*sah* luhsh-tay-*hehn*. Let's compromise and travel to both.

Finding your way around

In Hebrew, when you want to indicate direction, you add the sound "*ah*" to the end of certain common words, stressing the syllable before that ending. So instead of saying: **Ani Rotzah Lachzor La'Bayit** (ah-*nee* roh-*tzah* lach-*zohr* lah-*bah*-yeet; *Literally:* I want to return to the house), you can just say **Ani Rotzah Lachzor Ha'Baytah** (ah-*nee* roh-*tzah* lach-*zohr* hah-*bahy*-tah; something more like "I want to go home").

Use these words when trying to find your way around:

Noun of place	*Directional*
Achor (ah-*chohr;* backside)	**Achora** (ah-*chor*-ah; backwards)
Darom (Dah-*rohm;* south)	**Daroma** (dah-*roh*-mah; southwards)
Ha Aretz (hah-*ah*-rehtz; Israel)	**Artza** (*ahrtz*-ah; to Israel)
Ha-Chutz (Ha-*chootz;* outside)	**Ha-Chutza** (ha-*chootz*-ah; [to] outside)
Ha'Ir (hah-*eer;* the town)	**Ha'Irah** (hah-*eer*-ah; to town)
Kedem (*keh*-dehm; front)	**Kadima** (kah-*dee*-mah; forward)
Negev (*neh*-gehv; the Negev, south)	**Negba** (*nehg*-bah; southward)
Penim (p'neem; inside)	**Penima** (p-*nee*-mah; to the inside)
S'mol (smohl; left)	**S'mola** (*smoh*-lah; leftward)
Tzafon (tzah-*fohn;* north)	**Tzafona** (tzah-*foh*-nah; northwards)
Yamin (yah-*meen;* right)	**Yemina** (yah-*mee*-nah; rightward)

Packing

I love **Linso'a** (leen-soh-*ah;* to travel), but I hate **La'Aroz** (lah-ah-*rohz;* to pack)! I often wait until the last minute **La'Aroz** just before I am ready **La'Azov** (lah-ah-*zov;* to leave) my house for my **Tiyul** (tee-*yool;* trip). A bad **Hergel** (hehr-*gehl;* habit) I know. I want to share a tip my aunt taught me: Instead of **Lekapel** (leh-kah-*pehl;* folding; *Literally:* to fold) your **Begadim** (beh-gah-*deem;* clothes), **LeGalgel** (leh-gah-*gehl;* to roll) them instead! It really does save space in your **Mizvadah** (meez-vah-*dah;* suitcase)!

Words to Know

Chofesh	<u>choh</u>-fehsh	vacation
La'Aroz	lah-ah-<u>rohz</u>	to pack
La'Azov	lah-ah-<u>zohv</u>	to leave
Linso'a	leen-<u>soh</u>-ah	to travel
Mizvada	meez-vah-<u>dah</u>	suitcase
Tiyul	tee-<u>yool</u>	trip

Booking a trip

When you're ready to arrange your travel and your lodging, you may want to consider using a **Sochnut Nesi'ot** (sohch-*noot* neh-see-*oht;* travel agency). These professionals can arrange everything for you — your plane tickets, your hotel reservation, your car rental (if you need one), and even deals on complete tour packages. They're worth checking out. They can book you on a **Haflaga B'Yam** (hahf-lah-*gah* buh-*yahm;* cruise) or on a **Tiyul Me'urgan** (tee-*yool* meh-oor-*gahn;* organized tour). Maybe they can even get you a **Hanacha** (hah-nah-*chah;* discount).

Traveling internationally

If you're traveling abroad, then you have a host of additional things to consider. Make sure your **Darkon** (dahr-*kohn;* passport) is current and you've checked with the **Consulia** (kon-*soo*-lee-yah; counsulate) or the **Shagrirut** (shahg-ree-*root;* embassy) to see if you need a visa. When you cross the border of a country, you may have to go through **Meches** (*meh*-chehs; customs) and declare what you're bringing with you. And don't forget your **Hamcha'ot Nosim** (ham-chah-*oht* nohs-*eem;* traveler's checks)! See Chapter 12 for more words you can use when traveling.

Words to Know

Consulia	con-sool-yah	consulate
Darkon	dahr-kohn	passport
Haflaga B'Yam	hahf-lah-gah bah-yahm	cruise
Hamcha'Ot Nos'im	hahm-chah-oht nohs-eem	traveler's checks
Ir Birah	eer beer-ah	capital city
Meches	meh-chehs	customs
Shagrirut	shahg-ree-root	embassy
Tiyul Me'urgan	tee-yool meh-oohr-gahn	organized tour

Reciting the travelers' prayer

You find a **Tfilat Ha'Derech** (t-fee-*laht* hah-*dehr*-rech; travelers' prayer) in many Jewish **Siddurim** (see-doo-*reem;* prayerbooks) that Jews traditionally say any time they leave their own city. You also find this prayer on the back of keychains or in little cards you can stick in your wallet. In Israel, taxi drivers often hand out little cards with this prayer on it, with the other side of the card serving as a business card. Jews even recite a special **Tfilat Ha'Derech** for traveling on an airplane! The prayer beseeches God **She'Tolichenu L'Shalom** (sheh-toh-lee-*chay*-noo leh-shah-*lohm;* that we will be guided in peace) and **She'Tachziranu L'Veitanu B'Shalom** (sheh-tach-zea-*raye*-noo leh-vei-*teh*-noo beh-shah-*lohm;* and that we will return home in peace).

Coming and Going: Knowing Where You Are

You can announce your arrival in several ways. You can say **Ani Ba** (MS) or **Ani Ba'ah** (FS) (ah-*nee* bah or ah-*nee* bah-*ah;* I'm coming). You can also use the expression, **Ani Magiah** (MS) or **Ani Megiaah** (FS) (ah-*nee* mah-*gee-ah* or ah-*nee* mah-gee-*ah;* I'm arriving). When traveling in a group, after you've arrived somewhere, say **Higanu** (hee-*gah*-noo; We have arrived).

When you leave, you can say any of the following:

- ✔ **Ani Ozev** (ah-*nee* oh-*zehv;* I'm leaving.) (MS)

  Ani Ozevet (ah-*nee* oh-*zeh*-vet; I'm leaving.) (FS)

- ✔ **Ani Holech** (ah-*nee* hoh-*lech;* I'm going.) (MS)

  Ani Holechet (ah-*nee* hoh-*leh*-cheht; I'm going.) (FS)

- ✔ **Ani Zaz** (ah-*nee* zahz; I'm moving.) (MS)

- ✔ **Ani Zaza** (ah-*nee* zah-zah; I'm moving) (FS)

And then, of course, you can use that favorite, often-used Israeli expression **Yalla-Bye** (*yah*-lah *bye;* Let's go. Bye!) You may also want to say **Lehitra'ot** (leh-heet-rah-*oht;* See you soon!).

Talkin' the Talk

Jill has spent the past month visiting her cousin in Israel. Her cousin Polly has agreed to drive her to the airport. They're discussing when the plane will leave and what time they need to leave the apartment to arrive at the airport on time. (Track 23)

Polly: **Matai Ha'Tisa Shelach?**
mah-*tye* hah-tee-*sah* sheh-*lach*
When is your flight?

Jill: **Ha'Matos Mamri B'Taysha.**
hah-mah-*tohs* mahm-*ree* buh-*tay*-shah
The plane takes off at nine.

Polly: **Yesh Lach Et Kartis Ha'Tisa Ve'Ha'Darkon Shelach?**
yehsh lach eht kahr-*tees* hah-tee-*sah* veh-hah-dahr-*kohn* sheh-*lach*
Do you have your plane ticket and your passport?

Jill: **Ken, Yesh Li.**
kehn *yehsh*-lee
Yes, I have them.

Polly: **Tov. Ani Akpeetz Otach Od Me'at Le'Nemal Ha-te'ufa. Ani Lo Rotzah She'te'achri V'Tefasfesi Et Ha'tisa Shelach.**
tohv ah-*nee* ahk-*peetz* oh-*tach* ohd meh-*aht* leh-neh-*mahl* hah-teh-oo-*fah* ah-*nee* loh-roh-*tzah* sheh-teh-ach-*ree* ve-teh-fahs-feh-*see* eht hah-tee-*sah* sheh-*lach*
Good. I'll drop you by the airport soon. I don't want you to be late and miss your flight.

Words to Know

B'Zman	buhz-<u>mahn</u>	on time
Kartis Tisa	kahr-<u>tees</u> ti-<u>sah</u>	airline ticket
L'Hamri	leh-hahm-<u>ree</u>	to take off
Linkhot	leen-<u>chot</u>	to land
Matos	mah-<u>tohs</u>	airplane
Meuchar	meh-oo-<u>chahr</u>	late
Nemal Ha'Te'ufa	neh-<u>mahl</u> hah-tuh-oo-<u>fah</u>	airport
Tisa	tee-<u>sah</u>	flight

Discussing the Future: Verb Forms and Popular Expressions

When you want to say something in the future tense, for most Hebrew verbs, you add prefixes to the **Shoresh** (*shoh*-resh; verb root), and in some cases, you add suffixes as well. In the future tense you add the following prefixes and suffixes to the root:

I	**E**	eh
You (MS)	**Ti**	tee
You (FS)	**Ti**	tee
+ the suffix	**I**	ee
He	**Yi**	yee
She	**Ti**	tee
We	**Ni**	nee
You (MP/FP)	**Ti**	tee
+ the suffix	**U**	oo
They	**Yi**	yee
+ the suffix	**U**	oo

For example, conjugate the word **Lichtov** (leech-*tohv;* to write) in the future tense like this:

Ani Echtov (ah-*nee* ech-*tohv;* I will write.)

Atah Tichtov (ah-*tah* teech-*tohv;* You will write.) (MS)

At Tich'tevi (aht teech-teh-*vee;* You will write.) (FS)

Hu Yichtov (hoo yeech-*tohv;* He will write.) (MS)

He Tichtov (hee teech-*tohv;* She will write.) (FS)

Anachnu Nichtov (ah-nach-*noo* neech-*tohv;* We will write.)

Atem (MP)/**Aten Tichtevu** (FP) (ah-*tem*/ah-*ten* teech-teh-*voo;* You (plural, whether it is a bunch of guys, a bunch of gals, or some combination of the two!) will write.)

Hem (MP)/**Hen Yichtevu** (FP) (hem/hen yeech-teh-*voo;* They will write.)

Fun & Games

Fill in the missing words with one of three possible answers under each sentence. Have fun! Flip to Appendix C for the answers.

1. **Ani Rotzah _____ L'Anglia.**

   I want to travel to England.

   Lehishtazef, Linso'a, Lishtot

2. **Ani Rotzeh _____ B'Machtesh Ramon.**

   I want to hike in Machtesh Ramon.

   Lehaflig, Linso'a, L'Tayel

3. **Anachnu Rotzim _____ Al Ha'Kinneret.**

   We want to sail on the Kinneret.

   Lehaflig, L'Tayel, Linso'a

4. **Ha'Matos _____ B'Od Sha'ah.**

   The plane will take off in another hour.

   Yamrie, Yelech, Yichtov

5. **Yesh Lach Eht Ha' _____ Shelach?**

   Do you have your passport? (FS)

   Darkon, Kartis, Matos

Chapter 12

Getting Around: Flying, Driving, and Riding

In This Chapter

▶ Flying the friendly skies

▶ Finding ground transportation

▶ Being early, late, or right on time

▶ Expressing yourself with wishes and requests

Oy-vah-voye (oye-vah-*vohye;* Oh no!). I'm probably the last person in the world who should write this chapter. I get lost everywhere I go. It's a special talent I have, though this particular talent isn't very useful. So don't depend on me for directions. And, if you're traveling with me, plan on navigating — or plan on getting lost. But I am good for something: I can tell you how to say everything you need to get from here to there in Hebrew.

Getting Through the Airport

Here's the scene: You're about to leave the house to take a **Tisa Ben-leumit** (tee-*sah behn*-leh-oo-*meet;* international flight). **Kartis Tisa** (kahr-*tees* tee-*sah;* plane ticket)? Check. **Darkon** (dahr-*kohn;* passport)? Check. **Mizvada** (meez-vah-*dah;* suitcase)? Check. What else do you need? Nothing? Then you're ready to go. Traveling light is always your best bet!

Checking in

When you arrive at the **Nemal Ha'teufa** (neh-*mahl* hah-teh-oo-*fah;* airport) you usually head for the **Dalpack Rishum** (dahl-*pahk* ri-*shoom;* check-in counter) where you check your **Mizvada** (meez-vah-*dah;* luggage). The friendly **Pakid** (pah-*keed;* clerk) may have a few questions for you:

- **Ha'im Mishehu Lo Mukar Lecha Natan Lecha Mashehu?** (hah-*eem* mee-sheh-hoo loh moo-*kahr* leh-*chah* nah-*tahn* leh-*chah mah*-sheh-hoo; Has someone unknown to you given you anything?) (MS)

  Ha'im Mishehu Lo Mukar Lach Natan Lach Mashehu? (hah-*eem* mee-sheh-hoo loh moo-*kahr lahch* nah-*tahn* lach *mah*-sheh-hoo; Has someone unknown to you given you anything?) (FS)

- **Ha'im Arazta Et HaMizvada Shelchah?** (hah-*eem* ah-*rahz*-tah eht hah-meez-vah-*dah* shehl-*chah;* Did you pack your luggage?) (MS)

  Ha'im Arazt Et HaMizvada Shelach? (hah-*eem* ah-*rahzt* eht hah-meez-vah-*dah* shel-*ach;* Did you pack your luggage?) (FS)

- **Ha'im Ha'Mizvadot Hayu Etzlecha Me'Az She'Arazta Otam?** (hah-*eem* hah-meez-vah-*doht* hah-*yoo* ehtz-leh-*chah* mee-*ahz* sheh-ah-*rahz*-tah oh-*tahm;* Has your luggage been with you since you packed?) (MS)

  Ha'im Ha'Mizvadot Hayu Etzlech Me'Az She'Arazt Otam? (hah-*eem* hah-meez-vah-*doht* hah-*yoo* ehtz-*lech* mee-*ahz* sheh-ah-*rahzt* oh-*tahm;* Has your luggage been with you since you packed?) (FS)

After you pass this battery of questions, you walk through a **Megaleh Matachot** (meh-gah-*leh* mah-tah-*choht;* metal detector) and send your **Tarmilim** (tahr-mee-*leem;* carry-on luggage) through the **Machshir Rentgen** (mach-*sheer rehnt*-gehn; X-ray machine). After this final check, you should be ready to hop onto the plane.

Suffering through the flight

Are you a bit of a **Kvetch** (k-*vehch;* whiner) when you have to fly? If so, you may need all sorts of **Tziud** (tzee-y*ood;* supplies) to see you through your journey. You may need **Mastik** (*mahs*-teek; chewing-gum) and **Otmei Oznayim** (oht-*may* ohz-*nye*-eem; earplugs) to help you deal with the pressure in your ears, and perhaps some **Tipot L'enayim** (tee-*poht* leh-aye-*nah*-eem; eye drops) to combat all that dry cabin air. You can ask the **Dayal** (MS) or **Dayelet** (FS) (dah-*yahl* or dah-*yeh*-leht; flight attendant) for a **Karit** (kah-*reet*; pillow) and **Smichah** (s-mee-*chah*; blanket). Personally, I always bring my **Sidur** (see-*door*; prayer book) and say a little **T'fillah** (tfee-*lah*; prayer) before the **Matos** (mah-*tohs*; plane) **Mamri** (mahm-*ree*; takes-off).

Getting your feet back on the ground

B'ezrat HaShem (beh-ehz-*raht* hah-*shem*; With God's help), the plane will land safely. Then you can head off to your next destination. Gather all your belongings (please don't drop your briefcase on the little old lady's head as you remove it from the overhead bin), and you're ready **Laredet Me'ha'matos** (lah-*reh*-deht meh-hah-mah-*tohs*; to get off the plane). But not so fast! You're not out of the woods yet. You have to go through **Meches** (*meh*-chehs; customs) when you take an international flight. Someone will stamp your **Darkon.** Then you can collect your **Mizvada** (meez-vah-*dah*; luggage) and find ground transportation.

Reaching for a barf bag, and other emergencies

Sometimes you just don't wanna hear some words — especially on an airplane. But — **Chas V'Chalilah** (chahs veh-chah-*lee*-lah; heaven forbid) — in the unlikely event of a **Nechitat Cherum Al Ha'mayim** (neh-chee-*taht* cheh-*room* ahl hah-*mah*-yeem; emergency water landing), you need to know what to do. Pay attention to the **Hora'ot Bit'choniot** (hoh-rah-*oht* beet-choh- nee-*yoht*; safety instructions) and locate the nearest **Petach Cherum** (*peh*-tach che-*room*; emergency exit). The **Chagorat Hatzalah** (chah-goh-*raht* ha-tza-*lah*; life jackets) can usually be found under your **Kiseh** (key-*seh*; seat). The **Masechot Chamtzan** (mah-seh-*choht* cham-*tzahn*; oxygen mask) usually comes down **B'ofen Automati** (beh-*oh*-fehn oh-toh-*mah*-tee; automatically) from a compartment above.

Hopefully, you and a large body of water won't meet during your flight, and the worst event you'll be subjected to is a little **Mezeg Avir Bilti Yatziv** (*meh*-zehg ah-*veer* bil-*tee* yah-*tzeev*; unstable weather conditions) and perhaps a bit of **Ma'arbolot** (mah-ahr-boh-*loht*; turbulence). Fasten your **Chagorat Bitachon** (chah-goh-*raht* bee-tah-*chohn*; seatbelt) and try not to get too sick. But, if your stomach starts doing back flips, grab the **Sakit Haka'ah** (sah-*keet* hah-kah-*ah*; barf bag) in the seat pocket in front of you. **Tisah Ne'imah** (tee-*sah* neh-ee-*mah*; Have a nice flight!).

Words to Know

Bitachon	beeh-tah-_chohn_	security
Darkon	dahr-_kohn_	passport
Dayal (MS)	dah-_yahl_	flight attendant
Dayelet (FS)	dah-_yeh_-leht	flight attendant
Kartis	kahr-_tees_	ticket
La'Azov	lah-ah-_zohv_	to leave
Lehagiah	leh-hah-_gee_-ah	to arrive
Le'hamri	leh-ham-_ree_	to take off
Linchoht	leen-_choht_	to land
Matos	mah-_tohs_	airplane
Mizvadah	meez-vah-_dah_	luggage
Nemal Te'ufah	neh-mahl teh-oo-_fah_	airport
Tayas (MS)	tah-_yahs_	pilot
Tiyeset (FS)	tah-_yeh_-seht	pilot

Renting a Vehicle — and a Phone to Go with It

When you visit a different town, state, province, or country, the most convenient transportation option often is **Liskor Rechev** (lees-_kor_ reh-chehv; to rent) a vehicle. Most folks usually rent a **Mechonit** (meh-choh-_neet_; car), but in Israel, you can also rent an **Ofno'a** (ohf-_noh_-ah; motorcycle). To rent any vehicle, you need to present a valid **Rishayon Nehigah** (ree-shah-_yohn_ neh-hee-_gah;_ driver's license) and **Kartis Ashray** (kahr-tees ahsh-_rye;_ credit card). The clerk at the rental counter usually asks whether you want to purchase **Bitu'ach** (bee-_too_-ach; insurance) and informs you that you must accept liability if you decline it. And, if you put the pedal to the metal one time too many and get **Dochot** (doh-*choht;* tickets), you're responsible for paying those bills as well. So **Sah BiZhirut** (sah beez-hee-*root;* drive carefully).

When you drive around town, make sure that you stay in the same **Nativ** (nah-*teev;* lane) and don't weave through traffic. Pay attention to all the **Tamrurim** (tahm-roo-*reem;* traffic signs) and obey the **Ramzor** (rahm-*zohr;* traffic signal). Look both ways when you stop at a **Tzomet** *(tzoh*-meht; junction) and stop for all pedestrians — they have the **Z'chut K'dima** (z-*choot* kdee-*mah;* right of way) you know. Before you drive down any **Rechov** (reh-*chohv;* street) make sure that it isn't a **Rechov Chad Sitri** (reh-*chohv* chahd-seet-*ree;* one-way street). You don't want to drive in the wrong **Kivun** (kee-*voon;* direction). And, if you need to cover some major ground, forget taking a **Rechov,** and hop on a **K'vish Maheer** (*kveesh* mah-*heer;* expressway).

Renting a car

If you decide to rent a car, you need to find a **Chevrat Haskarat Rechev** (chehv-*raht* hahs-kah-*raht* reh-chehv; car-rental agency). You can often find these businesses right at the **Nemal Ha'teufa** (neh-*mahl* hah-teh-oo-*fah;* airport). Step right up, and an attendant greets you and asks you what kind of car you want to rent. He or she may say something like **Aizeh Sug Rechev Atah Rotzeh?** (MS) or **Aizeh Sug Recev At Rotzah?** (FS) (aye-*zeh* soog *reh*-chehv roh-*tzeh or* aye-*zeh* soog *reh*-chehv aht roh-*tzah;* What kind of vehicle would you like?) You can respond with any of the following:

- ✔ **Mechonit** (meh-choh-*neet;* car)
- ✔ **Mischarit** (mees-chah-*reet;* van)
- ✔ **Ofnoa** (ohf-*noh*-ah; motorcycle)
- ✔ **Heluchim Automatim** (hee-loo-*cheem* oh-toh-*mah*-teem; automatic transmission)
- ✔ **Mot Heluchim** (mot hee-loo-*cheem;* stick shift)

Hopefully, you know your own mind. The only thing you need is some Hebrew vocabulary so you can express it. If you want to rent a blue motorcycle, or if you're wondering whether you can get a car with a CD player, all you need to do is ask. Here are some handy-dandy phrases you may want to use:

- ✔ **Ani Rotzeh . . .** (ah-*nee* roh-*tzeh;* I want . . .) (MS)

  Ani Rotzah . . . (ah-*nee* roh-*tzah;* I want . . .) (FS)
- ✔ **Efshar . . .** (ehf-*shahr;* Is it possible . . . *or* May I . . .)
- ✔ **Efshar LeKabel . . .** (ehf-*shahr* leh-kah-*behl;* May I have . . .)

- **Haim Yesh . . .** (hah-*eem* yesh; Is there . . .)
- **Ten Li . . .** (tehn lee; Give me . . .) (MS)

  T'ni Li . . . (*tnee* lee; Give me . . .) (FS)

The clerk may also ask you about the terms of your rental contract. Expect to hear any of the following:

- **L'Kamah Z'man Atah Rotzeh Liskor Et Ha'Rechev?** (leh-*kah*-mah z-*mahn* ah-*tah* roh-*tzeh* lees-*kor* eht hah-*reh*-chehv; How long do you want to rent the vehicle?) (MS)

  L'Kamah Z'man At Rotzah L'iskor Et Ha'Rechev? (leh-*kah*-mah z-*mahn* aht roh-*tzah* lees-*kor* eht hah-*reh*-chehv; How long do you want to rent the vehicle?) (FS)

- **Matai Atah Rotzeh Liskor Et Ha'Rechev?** (mah-*tye* ah-*tah* roh-*tzeh* lees-*kor* eht hah-*reh*-chehv; When do you want to rent the vehicle?) (MS)

  Matai At Rotzah Liskor Et HaRechev? (mah-*tye* aht roh-*tzah* lees-*kor* eht hah-*reh*-chehv; When do you want to rent the vehicle?) (FS)

- **Eifo Atah Rotzeh Lehachzir Et Ha'Rechev?** (aye-*foh* ah-*tah* roh-*tzeh* le-hach-*zeer* eht hah-*reh*-chehv; Where do you want to return the vehicle?) (MS)

  Eifo At Rotzah Lehachzir Et Ha'Rechev? (aye-*foh* aht roh-*tzah* le-hach-*zeer* eht hah-*reh*-chehv; Where do you want to return the vehicle?) (FS)

To which you can reply:

- **Ani Rotzeh Liskor Et Ha'Rechev L . . .** (ah-*nee* roh-*tzeh* lees-*kor* eht hah-*reh*-chehv leh; I want to rent the vehicle for . . .) (MS)

  Ani Rotzah L'iskor Et Ha'Rechev L . . . (ah-*nee* roh-*tzah* lees-*kor* eht hah-*reh*-chehv leh; I want to rent the vehicle for . . .) (FS)

- **Ani Rotzeh Liskor Et Ha'Rechev B . . .** (ah-*nee* roh-*tzeh* lees-*kor* eht hah-*reh*-chehv beh; I want to rent the vehicle on . . .) (MS)

  Ani Rotzah Liskor Et Ha'Rechev B . . . (ah-*nee* roh-*tzah* lees-*kor* eht hah-*reh*-chehv beh; I want to rent the vehicle on . . .) (FS)

- **Ani Rotzeh Lehachzir Et Ha'Rechev B . . .** (ah-*nee* roh-*tzeh* lehach-zeer eht hah-*reh*-chehv beh; I want to return the vehicle at . . .) (MS)

  Ani Rotzah Lehachzir Et Ha'Rechev B . . . (ah-*nee* roh-*tzah* lehach-*zeer* eht hah-*reh*-chehv beh; I want to return the vehicle at . . .) (FS)

You're going to need some additional Hebrew vocab with the expressions I list above. Start off with the days of the week in Chapter 7.

Renting a phone

A **Pelehfohn** (*peh*-leh-fohn; cellphone) may be necessary when traveling abroad. Whenever I travel to Israel, I actually order my rental **Pelehfohn** in advance over the Internet. (My American cellphone won't work in Israel.) The company then sends it to me while I'm still in the United States, complete with a telephone number I can distribute to family and friends. You can rent a cellphone on the Internet at www.travelcell.com. Believe me, if you visit Israel, you'll want one. Israel is perhaps one of the most cellphone-addicted societies I have ever seen — some people even carry around two and talk on both at the same time. Two is a bit excessive, but you won't want to be without one. (For more on phone-talk, check out Chapter 9.)

Talkin' the Talk

Alon has just arrived in Tel Aviv. After going through customs, he stops by a car-rental agency and talks to an employee, a lovely woman named Sivan. (Track 24)

Alon: **Boker Tov. Ani Rotzeh Liskor Rechev.**
boh-kair *tohv.* ah-*nee* roh-*tzah* lees-*kor reh*-chehv.
Good morning. I would like to rent a car.

Sivan: **Eizeh Sug Rechev Atah Rotzeh?**
aye-*zeh* soog *reh*-chehv ah-*tah* roh-*tzeh?*
What kind of vehicle would you like?

Alon: **Ani Rotzeh Mechonit Bemechir Ha'Chi Zol She'Yesh.**
ah-*nee* roh-*tzeh* meh-choh-*neet.* hah-*chee zoh-la* sheh-*yehsh.*
I would like a car. The least expensive one that you have.

Sivan: **Atah Rotzeh Mot Hiluchim Oh Hiluchim Automatim?**
ah-*tah* roh-*tzeh* moht hee-loo-*cheem* oh hee-loo-*cheem* oh-toh-mah-*teem?*
Would you like a stick-shift or an automatic tranmission?

Alon: **Mot Hiluchim, B'vadai!**
moht hee-loo-*cheem*, beh-vah-*dye!*
A stick shift of course!

Sivan:	**L'Kamah Z'man Atah Rotzeh Liskor Et Ha'Rechev?**
	leh-*kah*-mah z'*mahn* ah-*tah* roh-*tzeh* lees-*kor* eht
	hah-*reh*-chehv?
	For how long would you like to rent the car?
Alon:	**L'Sh'vua'im.**
	leh-sh-voo-*ah*-yeem.
	For two weeks.

Words to Know

Chad-Sitri	chahd-seet-<u>ree</u>	one-way
K'vish Maheer	k-<u>veesh</u> mah-<u>heer</u>	expressway
Mechonit	meh-choh-<u>neet</u>	car
Nativ	nah-<u>teev</u>	lane
Ofnoa	ohf-<u>noh</u>-ah	motorcycle
Ramzor	rahm-<u>zohr</u>	traffic signal
Rechov	reh-<u>chohv</u>	street
Tzomet	<u>tzoh</u>-meht	junction
Z'chut Kdimah	z-<u>choot</u> k-dee-<u>mah</u>	right of way

CULTURAL WISDOM

Driving like an Israeli

Israelis are famous for their driving habits. So, if you drive in Israel, watch out for Israeli drivers who are known **Litz'ok** (leetz-*ohk;* to yell) and **Lekalel** (leh-kah-*lehl;* to swear) out the **Chalon** (chah-*lohn;* window) at the other drivers, lay on the **Tzofar** (tzoh-*fahr;* horn) whenever they hit **P'kakei T'nu'ah** (pkah-*kay* t-noo-*ah;* traffic) or an **Or Adom** (ohr ah-*dohm;* red light), and take plenty of illegal **P'niot Parsah** (p-nee-y*oht* pahr-*sah;* U-turns). Be careful because it's common practice to ignore all the **Tamrurim** (tahm-roo-*reem;* traffic signs), go faster than the **Mehirut Maksimalit Muteret** (meh-hee-*root* mahks-ee-*mah*-leet moo-*teh*-reht; speed limit), and **La'akohf** (lah-ah-*kohf;* pass) other cars whenever possible.

Navigating Public Transportation

Whether you're traveling or simply getting around your hometown, using **Tachbura Tziburit** (tach-boo-*rah* tzee-booh-*reet;* public transportation) is often an inexpensive and environmentally friendly way to go. Letting someone else do the driving is also a lot less stressful.

Traveling by taxi

When you leave the **Nemal Ha'teufa** (neh-*mahl* hah-teh-oo-*fah;* airport), you may decide to take a cab to your next destination. If you travel in Israel, you have the option of a **Sherut** (sheh-*root;* shared taxi) or a **Monit Special** (moh-*neet speh*-shl; special or private taxi). A **Sherut** is a great big taxi, often with two or three back seats. Between five and ten people can share them. They operate out of the airport and between central bus stations of major cities. Either way, the **Nahag** (nah-*hahg;* driver) happily takes your **Mizvada** (meez-vah-*dah;* luggage) and helps you to your seat. He or she may ask you **Le'an Atah Nose'ah?** (M) *or* **Le'an At Nosa'at?** (F) (leh-*ahn* ah-*tah/aht* noh-*seh*-ah/noh-*sah*-aht; Where are you traveling?). You can respond by saying **Ani Nose'ah L . . .** (M) *or* **Ani Nosa'at L . . .** (F) (ah-*nee* noh-*seh*-ah/noh-*sah*-aht luh; I'm traveling to . . .).

Moniyot (moh-nee-*yoht;* taxis) are a great and convenient way to get around. In Israel, if you want to flag one down, just point your index finger toward the ground. A **Monit** will pull right over. The **Nahag** may ask you whether you want a **Mechir** (meh-*cheer;* flat fee) or **Moneh** (moh-*neh;* meter). Responding with **Hishtamesh Ba'moneh** (heesh-tah-*mehsh* bah-moh-*neh;* Use the meter) is usually your best option. And when you arrive at your destination, be sure to ask for a **Kabalah** (kah-bah-*lah;* receipt).

Cabbies in Israel are notoriously friendly and often freely spout their opinions on anything — religion, politics, and the state of world peace. Talking to them is a great way to learn about the country and take the pulse of the people living there. Also, remember that tipping the driver isn't customary. So, when they quote you a price, you can give them exact change or expect **Odef** (*oh*-dehf; change) in return. (Check out Chapter 14 for the scoop on money matters.)

Watching the wheels on the bus go round and round

Riding on an **Autobus** (*oh*-toh-boos; bus) in Israel is a cultural experience. They go everywhere. If you're a frequent traveler on the bus system, you may want to get a **Kartisia** (kahr-tee-see-*yah;* bus ticket) that contains places where the **Nahag** (nah-*hahg;* driver) punches a hole every time you board the bus. Different **Kartisiot** (kahr-tee-see-y*oht;* bus tickets) exist for children, youths (ages 12 to 18), adults, and senior citizens. You also may want to consider a **Chodshi Chofshi** (chohd-*shee* chohf-*shee;* monthly bus pass) that you can just flash at the driver upon boarding. Or if you're just an occasional bus traveler, you can forget the tickets and passes all together and simply pay the fare.

In Israel, you place the fare in the bus driver's hand, and he makes **Odef** for you. Sometimes, if a lot of people are waiting at the **Tachanat Ha'autobus** (tah-chah-*naht* hah-*oh*-toh-boos; bus stop), the **Nehag Ha'autobus** (neh-*hahg* hah-oh-toh-*boos;* bus driver) also opens up the back door of the bus. People in the back pass their fare or their **Kartisia** to the front of the **Autobus.** Miraculously, the correct change and the correct bus ticket always come back to their rightful owner. It's an honor system, and it really works!

Folks in Israel tell a joke about a rabbi and an Israeli bus driver who, after living long and full lives, arrive in heaven. The rabbi is chagrined to discover that the bus driver has received a higher place in heaven than he has! So the rabbi marches right up to God to register a complaint. "God," the rabbi says, "how can this be? I've devoted my entire life to you, and yet a bus driver earns a higher place in heaven than I?" God looks at the rabbi and responds, "Look. It's this way. Whenever you started teaching, your congregants started sleeping. But whenever the bus driver started driving, his passengers started praying!"

Getting specific about the Israeli bus system

Although the Israeli bus system serves only a population slightly larger than 6 million, it operates 4,000 buses on thousands of scheduled routes and is the second largest bus system in the world, just after London Transport. Most of the buses in the country are run by a cooperative called *Egged,* which literally means *linked together,* but *Dan* serves the population in the greater Tel Aviv area. National poet Haim Nachman Bialik proposed the name *Egged* to epitomize the cooperative nature of the Jewish state. In the cooperative, members perform all duties to run the company, own a share of the company, and collectively make management decisions.

The cooperative was founded in 1933 as a merger between four other bus cooperatives. Then, during the times of the British Mandate before Israel's independence in 1948, the bus lines ran scheduled routes to Lebanon, Syria, Iraq, Trans-Jordan, and Egypt! Today, *Egged* is still a cooperative with 3,250 members and 4,550 salaried employees, serving a million domestic passengers a day.

Traveling on trains

The first **Rakevet** (rah-*kehv*-eht; railroad) in **Eretz Yisrael** (*eh*-rehtz yees-rah-*ehl;* the Land of Israel) was established in 1892. Then and throughout the years of Ottoman rule and the British Mandate, the **Passim** (pah-*seem;* tracks) reached all the way to **Mitzrayim** (meetz-*rah*-yeem; Egypt), **Suria** (*soor*-yah; Syria), and **Levanon** (leh-vah-*nohn;* Lebanon). Today in Israel the **Rakevet** is a popular (but limited) form of **Tachburah** (tach-booh-*rah;* transportation) with **Kavim** (kah-*veem;* lines) running regularly between Haifa and Tel Aviv, Tel Aviv and Jerusalem, Tel Aviv and Rechovot, and Haifa and Netanya.

Rakevet Yisrael (rah-*keh*-veht yees-rah-*ehl;* Israeli railways) has approximately 50 **Rakavot** (rah-kah-*voht;* trains), 70 **Rakavot Nosim** (rah-kah-*voht* noh-*s-eem;* passenger cars), and 1,300 **Rakavot Mit'an** (rah-kah-*voht* meet-*ahn;* freight cars). You can find a **Lu'ach Z'manim** (loo-*ach* z-mah-*neem;* schedule) at www.israrail.org.il, where you can also find **Mo'di'in** (moh-dee-*een;* information) about **Rakavot Nos'im.** The site features a **Mapat Kavei Nos'im** (mah-*paht* kah-*vay* nohs-*eem;* map of passenger lines) and **Tachanot Nos'im** (tah-chah-*noht* nohs-*eem;* passenger stations). These maps are sorted by **Ta'arich** (tah-ah-*reech;* date), **Tachanat Motza** (tah-chah-*naht* moh-*tzah;* departure station), and **Tachana sofit** (tah-chah-*nah* soh-*feet;* final station).

There's a children's song in Hebrew about a **Rakevet.** Just keep repeating these three lines:

> **Hinei Rakevet!**
> **He Mistovevet!**
> **Al Galgalim, Al Galgalim, Al Galgalim, Toot, Toot!**

> hee-*nay* rah-*kehv*-eht!
> hee mees-toh-*veh*-veht!
> ahl gahl-gah-*leem,* ahl gahl-gah-*leem,* ahl gahl-gah-*leem, toot, toot!*

> Here is a train!
> It goes around!
> On wheels, on wheels, on wheels, toot, toot!

Reading maps and schedules

If you need to read a **Mapah** (mah-*pah;* map) or a **Lu'ach Z'manim** (loo-*ahch* z-mah-*neem;* schedule), you may encounter some of these words:

- **Kav** (kahv; line)
- **Sha'ah** (shah-*ah;* hour)

✔ **Ta'arich** (tah-ah-*reech;* date)

✔ **Yom** (yohm; day)

✔ **Z'man** (zmahn; time)

✔ **Darom** (dah-*rohm;* south)

✔ **Ma'arav** (mah-ah-*rahv;* west)

✔ **Mizrach** (meez-*rahch;* east)

✔ **Tzafon** (tzah-*fohn;* north)

You'll need to tell time to interpret train schedules, so check out Chapter 7. And for more info on directions, take a look at Chapter 15.

Words to Know

Autobus	oh-toh-<u>boos</u>	bus
Luach Z'manim	loo-<u>ahch</u> z-mahn-<u>eem</u>	schedule
Mapah	mah-<u>pah</u>	map
Monit	moh-<u>neet</u>	taxi
Noseah (MS)	noh-<u>seh</u>-ah	travel
Nosa'at (FS)	noh-<u>sah</u>-aht	travel
Nehag (MS)	neh-<u>hahg</u>	driver
Odef	<u>oh</u>-dehf	change
Rakevet	rah-<u>keh</u>-veht	train
Sherut	sheh-<u>root</u>	shared taxi

Being Early or Late

Everyone seems to have their own internal clock. Some people are always **Mukdam** (mook-*dahm;* early), some people are always **Me'uchar** (meh-oo-*chahr;* late), and others are always **B'dikyuk Bazman** (bee-dee-*yook* bahz-*mahn;* exactly on time). But, if you're a person who is always late, and you have to catch a plane, train, or bus, you may want to consider changing your habits — if only for a day.

You can use some of the following phrases when you want to discuss such timely issues:

- **Ani Hayiti Bidiyuk BaZman.** (ah-*nee* hah-*yee*-tee bee-dee-y*ook* bahz-*mahn;* I was exactly on time.)

- **Ani Hikdamti.** (ah-*nee* heek-*dahm*-tee; I was early.)

- **Ani Hikdamti Otchah.** (ah-*nee* heek-*dahm*-tee oht-*chah;* I beat you *or* I was before you.) (MS)

   Ani Hikdamti Otach. (ah-*nee* heek-*dahm*-tee oh-*tach;* I beat you *or* I was before you.) (FS)

- **Ani Echarti.** (ah-*nee* e-*chahr*-tee; I was late.)

- **Slicha Al Ha'lchur.** (slee-*chah* ahl-hah-ee-*choor;* Excuse the lateness.)

- **Slicha Al Ha'lkuv.** (slee-*chah* ahl hah-ee-*koov;* Excuse the delay.)

Fun & Games

Find the perfect match. I've given you the questions in Hebrew and English, but the possible answers are only in Hebrew. Watch out! I've given one too many answers. You can find the solutions in Appendix C.

Questions:

1. **Aizeh Sug Rechev Atah Rotzeh?** (ay-*zeh* soog reh-*chehv* ah-*tah* roh-*tzeh;* What kind of vehicle do you want?)

2. **Matai Ha'Matos Mamri?** (mah-*tye* hah-mah-*tohs* mahm-*ree;* When does the plane take off?)

3. **Ha'im Yesh Lu'ach Z'manim Shel Ha'Rakevet?** (hah-*eem* yehsh *loo*-ahch z-mah-*neem* shehl hah-rah-*keh*-veht; Is there a train schedule?)

4. **Eifo Tachanat Ha'otobus?** (ay-*foh* tah-chah-*naht* hah-oh-toh-*boos;* Where is the bus station?)

5. **Le'an Atah Rotzeh Linso'a?** (leh-*ahn* ah-*tah* roh-*tzeh* leen-*soh-ah;* Where do you want to travel?)

Answers:

A. **Yesh Lu'ach Z'manim BaReshet.**

B. **Ani Rotzeh Mechonit K'tanah.**

C. **Ha'Autobus Nose'ah Mahair.**

D. **Ani Rotzeh Linso'a L'Yerushalayim.**

E. **Tachanat Ha'otobus BeMercaz Ha'Ir.**

F. **Ha'Matos Mamri BeSha'ah Shmoneh Baboker.**

Chapter 13

Checking into a Hotel

• •

In This Chapter

▶ Locating a hotel to spend the night

▶ Checking in

▶ Paying your bill when you leave

• •

*E*veryone likes to have a warm, comfy place to rest his or her head at night whenever traveling. In this chapter, I help you with the Hebrew vocabulary and phrases that you need to find a hotel, make reservations, inquire about your hotel's facilities, and check in and out so you can have a restful night of sleep.

Finding the Hotel That's Right for You

If you're looking for **Linah** (lee-*nah;* lodging), you may want to pick up a travel guide or hit the Internet to find out about accommodations. If you're feeling adventurous, you can wait until you get to your desired destination and take your chances. But if you're traveling during tourist season, be prepared to find a lot of "no vacancy" signs. A good way to find a hotel is to ask people you know if they can recommend a reliable place to stay. You can ask:

✔ **Atah Yachol Ahl Lehamlitz Linah Ba'Ezor?** (ah-*tah* yah-chohl leh-hahm-*leets* ahl lee-*nah* bah-eh-*zohr;* Can you recommend lodging in the area?) (MS)

At Yecholah Lehamlitz Ahl Linah BaEzor? (aht yeh-chohl-*lah* leh-hahm-*leets* ahl lee-*nah* bah-eh-*zohr;* Can you recommend lodging in the area?) (FS)

✔ **Atah Makir Malon Tov?** (ah-*tah* mah-*keer* mah-*lohn tohv;* Do you know of a good hotel?) (MS)

Aht Makirah Malon Tov? (aht mah-*keer*-ah mah-*lohn tohv;* Do you know of a good hotel?) (FS)

You may also want to specify the **Derug** (deh-*roog;* rating you want). Will only **Chamishah Kochavim** (chah-mee-*shah* koh-chah-*veem;* five stars) suffice or can you make do with something a little less **Mefo'ar** (meh-foh-*ahr;* luxurious)?

You can choose from all sorts of **Melonot** (meh-lohn-*oht;* hotels) with different kinds of **Ne'imot** (neh-eem-*oht;* amenities). In addition to the **Malon** (mah-*lohn;* hotel option), you also may consider staying at:

 ✔ **Achsaniyah** (ach-sah-nee-*yah;* a hostel)

 ✔ **Linah Kafrit** (lee-*nah* kahf-*reet;* a country house)

 ✔ **Zimmer** (*tsee*-mer; a bed and breakfast)

Making your reservations

If you're a planner, you probably want to book your room reservation in advance. But if you're a free spirit, then you probably have better luck finding an empty **Cheder** (*cheh*-dehr; room) in **Melonot** or **Achsaniot** (ahch-sah-nee-*yoht;* hostels) outside of **Mercaz Ha'Ir** (mehr-*kahz* hah-*eer;* the city center).

But whether you make your **Hazmanah** (hahz-mah-*nah;* reservation) in person or over the phone, you use the same expression: **Efshar LeHazmin Cheder?** (ehf-*shahr* leh-hahz-*meen cheh*-dehr?; May I reserve a room?).

If you want to reserve more than one room, insert the proper number: **Shnai Chadarim** (shu-*nay* chah-dah-*reem;* two rooms), **Shlosha Chadarim** (shuh-loh-*shah* chah-dahr-*eem;* three rooms), **Arba'ah Chadarim** (ahr-bah-*ah* chah-dahr-*eem;* four rooms), and so forth.

Of course, you also want to know if the **Malon** has a **Cheder Panui** (*cheh*-dehr pah-*nooy;* vacant room); and if the **Malon** has one **Mitah** (mee-*tah;* bed) or two **Mitot** (mee-*toht;* beds) in the room. And you want to inquire about the **Ta'arif** (tah-ah-*reef;* rate) for each night.

Before you call to make your reservation, you may want to read Chapter 9 to brush up on your phone conversation skills and also the sections for telling time and the days of the week in Chapter 7.

Words to Know

Cheder	<u>cheh</u>-dair	room
Hazmanah	hahz-mah-<u>nah</u>	reservation
Malon	mah-<u>lohn</u>	hotel
Mitah	mee-<u>tah</u>	bed
Ta'arif	tah-ah-<u>reef</u>	rate

Telling the receptionist how long you plan to stay

After you announce that you want to make a reservation, the person taking the reservation may have some questions for you. He or she will probably ask you:

> **L'Aizeh Ta'Arichim Atah Rotzeh Lehazmin Et Ha'Cheder?** (leh-*ay*-zeh tah-ah-ree-*cheem* ah-*tah* rot-*zeh* leh-haz-*meen* eht hah-*cheh*-dehr; For what dates would you like to reserve a room?) (MS)

> **L'Aizeh Ta'Arichim Aht Rotzah Lehazmin Et Ha'Cheder?** (leh-*ay*-zeh tah-ah-ree-*cheem* aht roh-*tzah* leh-haz-*meen* eht hah-*cheh*-dehr; For what dates would you like to reserve a room?) (FS)

Depending on your travel plans, you may want to respond by saying the following:

> ✔ **Ani Rotzeh Le'Hazmin Cheder L. . . Lailot.** (ah-*nee* roh-*tzeh* leh-hahz-*meen* cheh-dehr leh . . . lay-*loht;* I want to reserve a room for . . . nights.) (MS)

> **Ani Rotzah Le'Hazmin Cheder L. . . Lailot.** (ah-*nee* roh-*tzeh* leh-hahz-*meen* cheh-dehr leh . . . lay-*loht;* I want to reserve a room for . . . nights.) (FS)

> ✔ **Ani Rotzeh Le'Hazmin Cheder MiHa . . . L . . . B'Chodesh.** (ah-*nee* roh-*tzeh* leh-hahz-*meen* cheh-dehr meh-hah . . . le. . . buh *choh*-dehsh; I want to reserve a room from the . . . to the . . . of the month.) (MS)

> **Ani Rotzah Le'Hazmin Cheder MiHa . . . L . . . B'Chodesh.** (ah-*nee* roh-*tzah* leh-hahz-*meen* cheh-dehr meh-hah . . . le . . . buh *choh*-dehsh; I want to reserve a room from the . . . to the . . . of the month.) (FS)

✔ **Ani Rotzeh Le'Hazmin Cheder L . . . Lailot**. (ah-*nee* roh-*tzeh* leh-hahz-*meen cheh*-dehr leh . . . lay-*loht;* I want to reserve a room for . . . nights.) (MS)

Ani Rotzah Le'Hazmin Cheder L . . . Lailot. (ah-*nee* roh-*tzah* leh-hahz-*meen cheh*-dehr leh . . . lay-*loht;* I want to reserve a room for . . . nights.) (FS)

Specifying the kind of room you want

When you're making a reservation, the person taking your reservation will probably ask you what type of room you want, saying something like this:

Eizeh Sug Cheder Atah Rotzeh? (ay-*zeh* soog *cheh*-dehr ah-*tah* roh-*tzeh;* What kind of room would you like?) (MS)

Eizeh Sug Cheder At Rotzah? (ay-*zeh* soog *cheh*-dehr aht roh-*tzah;* What kind of room would you like?) (FS)

You can respond with any of the following:

✔ **Ani Rotzeh Et Ha'Penthouze** (ah-*nee* roh-*tzeh* eht hah-*pent*-houz; I would like the penthouse.) (MS)

Ani Rotzah Et Ha'Penthouze (ah-*nee* roh-*tzah* eht hah-*pent*-houz; I would like the penthouse.) (FS)

✔ **Ani Rotzeh Suitah Im Chadar Shenah V'Chadar Megurim** (ah-*nee* roh-*tzeh swee*-tah eem *chah*-dehr shay-*nah* veh-chah-*dahr* meh-goo-*reem;* I would like a suite with a bedroom and a living room.) (MS)

Ani Rotzah Suitah Im Chadar Shenaih V'Chadar Megurim (ah-*nee* roh-*tzah swee*-tah eem chah-*dahr* shay-*nah* veh-chah-*dahr* meh-goo-*reem;* I would like a suite with a bedroom and a living room.) (FS)

✔ **Ani Rotzeh Chadar Sheinah Bilvad** (ah-*nee* roh-*tzeh* chah-*dahr* shay-*nah* beel-*vahd;* I'd like a single bedroom.) (MS)

Ani Rotzah Chadar Sheinah Bilvad (ah-*nee* roh-*tzah* chah-*dahr* shay-*nah* beel-*vahd;* I'd like a single bedroom.) (FS)

✔ **Ani Rotzeh Cheder Im Shtei Mitot** (ah-*nee* roh-*tzeh cheh*-dehr eem shuh-*tay* mee-*toht;* I want a room with two beds.) (MS)

Ani Rotzah Cheder Im Shtei Mitot (ah-*nee* roh-*tzah cheh*-dehr eem shuh-*tay* mee-*toht;* I want a room with two beds.) (FS)

✔ **Ani Rotzeh Cheder Im Mitah Zugit** (ah-*nee* roh-*tzah cheh*-dehr eem mee-*tah* zoo-*geet;* I want a room with a double bed.) (MS)

Ani Rotzah Cheder Im Mitah Zugit (ah-*nee* roh-*tzah cheh*-dehr eem mee-*tah* zoo-*geet;* I want a room with a double bed.) (FS)

You may also want to inquire about the **Ne'imot** and **Sherutim** (sheh-root-*eem;* services) that come with the room. Start out by asking **Haim Yesh** (hah-*eem* yehsh . . .; Is there . . .); and then plug in any of the vocabulary in Table 13-1.

Table 13-1	Common Hotel Amenities	
Hebrew	*Pronunciation*	*English Translation*
Braichat Schiyah	bray-*chaht* - schee-*yah*	swimming pool
Chadar Kosher	chah-*dahr koh*-sher	weight room
Jacuzzi P'nimi	jah-*koo*-zee pnee-*mee*	an indoor Jacuzzi
Kasefet	kah-*sehf*-eht	a safe
Lul L'Tinok	lool leh-tee-*nohk*	a baby's playpen
Meezug Avir Mercazi	mee-*zoog* ah-*veer* mehr-kah-*zee*	central air conditioning
Migrash Tenis	meeg-*rahsh teh*-nees	tennis court
Mirpeset	meer-*peh*-seht	a balcony
Peh'ilut Bidur L'Yeladim	peh-ee-*luht* bee-*door* leh-yeh-lah-*deem*	children's activities
Sherut K'Visa	sheh-*root* kvee-*sah*	laundry service
Televizia Im K'Valim	teh-leh-*veez*-yah eem k'-vah-*leem*	television with cable

Rise and shine: Breakfasts at Israeli hotels

If you have never had breakfast in an Israeli hotel, you're in for a real treat! Most hotels in Israel serve a buffet breakfast as part of the service. At the buffet, you find an incredible spread of vegetables (yes, Israelis eat raw vegetables for breakfast — a healthy and delicious habit), fruits of all kinds, a wonderful display of Israeli milk products including yogurt and **Lebeh** (lehbehn; a delicious milk product) not found in North America, but common in the Middle East. You also can eat all sorts of breads, hard-boiled eggs, and for the North American palate . . . all kinds of cereal. But I recommend that when in Israel, do as the Israelis do and fill your plate with veggies, fruit, a bit of bread, and perhaps some yogurt. I can't think of a better way to start the day! **Bete'avon** (beh-teh-ah-*vohn;* Good appetite!)

Asking about the price

If you like the hotel and want to stay there, ask about the price: **Kamah Oleh Hah'Cheder?** (kah-*mah* oh-*leh* hah-*cheh*-dehr; How much does the room cost?)

You can also ask if the hotel offers a **Hanachah** (hah-nah-*chah;* discount) or **Mivtza** (meev-*tzah;* special or sale). Just talk to **Mehnahel HaMalon** (meh-nah-*hehl* hah-mah-*lohn;* the hotel manager). When you're traveling off-season, you sometimes can find some good deals!

Words to Know

Chadar Sheinah	chah-<u>dahr</u> shay-<u>nah</u>	bedroom
Hanachah	hah-nah-<u>chah</u>	discount
Mefo'ar	meh-foh-<u>ahr</u>	luxurious
Menahel Ha'Malon	meh-nah-<u>hehl</u> hah-mah-<u>lohn</u>	hotel manager
Mitah Zugit	mee-<u>tah</u> zoo-<u>geet</u>	double bed
Neimot	neh-ee-<u>moht</u>	amenities
Sherutim	sheh-roo-<u>teem</u>	services

Checking In: Names, Addresses, and Room Numbers

After you arrive at your hotel, go straight to the **Kabbalah** (kah-bah-*lah;* reception desk) to check in. Hopefully you've already reserved a room. If not, you just have to take your chances! If you're the planning-in-advance type and have indeed made reservations, you have to let the receptionist know by saying: **Ani Hizmanti Cheder** (ah-*nee* heez-*mahn*-tee *cheh*-dehr; I reserved a room).

Tell the receptionist your name by saying: **HaShem Sheli . . .** (hah-*shehm* sheh-*lee* . . .; My name is . . .)

The receptionist may also ask you your **Ofen HaTashlum** (oh-*fehn* hah-tahsh-*loom;* method of payment), including Mezuman (meh-zoo-*mahn;* cash), **Kartis Ashraai** (kahr-*tees* ash-*rye;* credit card), or **Hamcha'ah** (ham-chah-*ah;* check.) For more information on money, be sure to read Chapter 14.

Determining your length of stay

To confirm your reservation, the receptionist may ask you:

> **Le'Kamah Z'Man Atah Mitkonen) L'Hisha'er** (leh-kah-*mah* z-*mahn* ah-*tah* meet-koh-*nen* leh-hee-shah-*air;* How long are you planning to stay?) (MS)

> **Le'Kamah Z'Man At MitkonenetL'Hisha'er?** (leh-kah-*mah* z-*mahn* aht meet-koh-*nenet* leh-hee-shah-*air;* How long are you planning to stay? (FS)

You can respond by saying:

✔ **Ani Esha'er L . . .** (ah-*nee* eh-shah-*air* leh . . .; I'll stay for . . .)

✔ **Anachnu Nisha'er L . . .** (ah-*nach*-noo nee-shah-*air* leh . . . ; We'll stay for . . .)

Then you can just plug in any of the following:

✔ **L'Shavua Echad** (leh-shah-*voo*-ah eh-*chahd;* for one week)

✔ **L'Shloshah Yamim** (leh-shlo-*shah* yah-*meem;* for three days)

✔ **Rak Lilah Echad** (rahk *lye*-lah eh-*chahd;* just one night)

Take a look at Chapter 1 for more on counting in Hebrew.

Filling out the registration form

At some **Melonot,** the receptionist may ask you to provide your personal information on a **Tofes** (*toh*-fehs; form) as part of the registration process. If so, the receptionist may say: **Na Lemaleh Et HaTofes** (nah leh-mah-*leh* eht hah-*toh*-fehs; Please fill out this form).

You may have to provide some personal information on the **Tofes**. Table 13-2 shows some common information you might have to provide.

Table 13-2	Information to Know When You Check into a Hotel	
Hebrew	**Pronunciation**	**English Translation**
Chatimah	chah-teeh-*mah*	signature
Eizor Mikud	ay-*zohr* mee-*kood*	zip code
Eretz	*eh*-rehtz	country
Ir	eer	city
Le'om	leh-*ohm*	nationality
Mekom Leidah	meh-*kohm* lay-*dah*	birthplace
Miktso'a	meek-*tsoh*-ah	profession
Mispar Ha'Bayit	mees-*pahr* hah-*bah*-yeet	house number
Rechov	reh-*chohv*	street
Shem Mishpacha	shem meesh-pah-*chah*	last name (literally family name)
Shem Prati	shehm prah-*tee*	first name (literally private name)
Ta'arich Leidah	tah-ah-*reech* lay-*dah*	birthdate

Talkin' the Talk

 Yaniv has arrived at a hotel for a week's vacation. He goes to the **Pakid** (pah-*keed;* receptionist) to check in. (Track 25)

Yaniv: **Erev Tov! HaShem Sheli Yaniv. Ani Hizmanti Cheder.**
eh-rehv t*ohv!* hah-*shem* sheh-*lee* yah-*neev.* ah-*nee* heez-*mahn*-tee *cheh*-dehr.
Good evening! My name's Yaniv. I reserved a room.

Receptionist: **Nachon. Cheder Echad Im Mitah Zugit V'Ambatia. Na Lemaleh Et HaTofes.**
nah-*chohn.* *cheh*-dehr ech-*ahd* eem mee-*tah* zoo-*geet* veh-ahm-*baht*-yah. nah leh-mah-*leh* eht hah-*toh*-fehs.
Correct. One room with a double bed and a bathroom. Please fill out the form.

Yaniv:	**Ha'Im Yesh Lachem Brehcha V'Chadar Kosher?** hah-*eem* yaysh lah-*chehm* bray-*chah* veh-chah-*dahr* *koh*-shehr? Do you have a pool and a work-out room?
Receptionist:	**Bevadai. Henei Ha'Mafte'ach Shelcha. Ha'Cheder Shelcha Shlosh Me'ot V'Chamesh.** beh-vah-*dai*. hee-*nay* hah-mahf-*teh*-ach shehl-chah. hah-*cheh*-dehr shehl-*chah* sh-*lohsh* meh-*oht* veh-chah-*mesh*. Certainly. Here's your key. Your room is 305.
Yaniv:	**Todah Rabbah.** toh-*dah* rah-*bah*. Thank you very much.

Settling into your room

After you check in, the receptionist will let you know your room number, saying something like:

> **Mispar HaCheder Shelchah . . .** (mees-*pahr* hah-*cheh*-dehr shehl-*chah;* Your room number is . . .) (MS)

> **Mispar HaCheder Shelach . . .** (mees-*pahr* hah-*cheh*-dehr shehl-*ach;* Your room number is . . .) (FS)

Then **Sof Kol Sof** (*sohf* kohl *sohf;* finally) you'll be led to your room. You can **Lanuach** (lah-*noo*-ahch; rest)! Kick off your **Na'alayim** (nah-ah-*lah*-eem; shoes), and pour yourself a **Mashkeh Charif** (mahsh-*keh* chah-*reef;* drink) from the minibar. Maybe you want to order **Sherut Chadarim** (sheh-*root* chah-dahr-*reem;* room service). **Lehadlik Et Ha'Televizia** (leh-hahd-*leek* eht hah-teh-leh-*veez*-yah; flip on the television), or open the **Ha'Chalon** (hah-chah-*lohn;* window) and take in the beautiful **Nof** (nohf; view). **Shehut Ne'Ima** (sheh-*hoot* neh-ee-*mah;* Have a nice stay)!

When you want to hang out in your room and you don't want to be disturbed, hang the little door sign that bears the following message: **Na Lo Lehafriah!** (nah loh leh-hahf-*ree*-ah; Please do not disturb!)

Words to Know

Brehcha	bray-<u>chah</u>	pool
Kabbalah	kah-bah-<u>lah</u>	reception
Lanu'ach	lah-<u>noo</u>-ach	to rest, relax
Lemalech	leh-mah-<u>leh</u>	to fill out
Mafteach	mahf-<u>teh</u>-ach	key
Na Lo LeHafri-ah	nah-loh-leh-hahf-<u>ree</u>-ah	Please don't disturb!
Nof	nohf	view
Sherut Chadarium	sheh-<u>root</u> chah-dehr-<u>reem</u>	room service
Tofes	<u>toh</u>-fehs	form

Checking Out and Paying the Bill

You just enjoyed your stay at the hotel and now you need to hit the road. Whether you're there for business or pleasure, hopefully you used some of the **Ne'imot** (neh-ee-*moht;* amenities) and took in some of the sights. Now all you need to do is check out. Hebrew has no exact phrase that's comparable to the English term "to check out." You just say, **La'azov Et Ha'Malon** (lahtz-eht eht hah-mah-*lohn;* to leave the hotel). If you want to ask about a specific checkout time, you can say either of the following:

✔ **B'Aizoh Sha'ah Ani Tzarich La'Tzet Me'Ha'Cheder?** (buh-ay-*zoh* shah-*ah* ah-*nee* tzah-*reech* lah-*tzhet* meh-hah-*cheh*-dehr; At what time to I need to exit the room?) (MS)

B'Aizoh sha'ah ani tzarich la'tzet me'hacheder? Beh-eizoh shah-*ah* ah-*nee* tz-ree-*chah* lah-*tzhet* meh-hah-*cheh*-dehr; At what time to I need to exit the room?) (FS)

✔ **B'Aizoh Sha'ah Ani Tzarich La'Azov Et Ha'Cheder? ?** (buh-ay-*zoh* shah-*ah* ah-*nee* tzah-*reech* lah-ah-*zohv* eht hah-*cheh*-dehr; What time do I need to leave the room?) (MS)

TIP

B'Aizoh Sha'ah Ani Tzricha La'Azov Et Ha'Cheder? (buh-ay-*zoh* shah-*ah* ah-*nee* tz-*ree-chah* lah-ah-*zohv* eht hah-*cheh*-dehr; What time do I need to leave the room?) (FS)

Look at Chapter 5 for vocabulary about paying a bill.

Asking for your bill

When you're ready to leave, simply approach the **Kabbalah** (kah-bah-*lah;* reception desk) and let the receptionist know your intentions by saying:

Ani Ozev Et Ha'Malon (ah-*nee* oh-*zehv* eht hah-mah-*lohn;* I'm leaving the hotel.) (MS)

Ani Ozevet Et Ha'Malon (ah-*nee* oh-*zeh*-vet eht hah-mah-*lohn;* I'm leaving the hotel.) (FS)

Anachnu Ozvim Et Ha'Malon (ah-*nach*-nu ohz-*veem* eht hah-mah-*lohn;* We're leaving the hotel.) (MP/FP)

The **Pakid** (MS)/**Pekidah** (FS) (pah-*keed*/peh-kee-*dah;* receptionist) may begin preparing your **Cheshbon** (chehsh-*bohn;* bill). But you can also ask for it by saying **Efshar Lekabel Et Ha'Cheshbon B'Vakasha?** (ehf-*shahr* leh-kah-*behl* eht-hah-chehsh-*bohn* beh-vah-kah-*shah;* May I have the bill please?)

Asking about special charges

When you check out, you discover all those extra charges on your **Cheshbon**. For example, if you've ordered **Sherut Cheder** (sheh-*root cheh*-dehr; room service) every night, eaten the minibar out of house and home, or spent a lot of time chatting on the phone in your hotel room, prepare for a little shock! You can inquire about these little (and not-so-little) charges by asking **Ha'Im Hayu Aluyot Nosafot?** (hah-*eem* hah-*yoo* ah-loo-*yoht* noh-sah-*foht;* Were there extra charges?)

Leaving the hotel

If you want to hang around town after you've checked out, you can usually arrange to leave your luggage in the hotel storage. Just ask: **Efshar Le'HaSh-ir Et Ha'Mizvadot Sheli B'Ichsun Ha'Malon?** (ehf-*shahr* leh-hash-*ir* eht hah-meez-vah-*doht* sheh-*lee* beh-eech-*soohn* hah-mah-*lohn?;* May I leave my luggage in the hotel storage?)

In Hebrew, you can tell if something is plural if it has an ending of **Im** (eem) or **Ot** (oht). The **Im** is a masculine ending and the **Ot** is a feminine ending. For example:

- Take the feminine singular noun **Mizvada** (meez-vah-*dah;* luggage): Its plural form is **Mizvadot** (meez-vah-*doht;* luggage).

- The masculine singular noun **Tik** (teek; bag) becomes **Tikim** (teek-*eem;* bags) in the plural form.

When you return to the hotel to pick up your luggage, you can ask: **Efshar L'Kabel Et Ha'Mizvadot Sheli?** (ehf-*shahr* leh-kah-*behl* eht hah-meez-vah-*doht* sheh-*lee?;* May I have my luggage?)

In Hebrew, when you want to indicate ownership of something, you use the possessive adjective **Shel** (shehl) inflected with certain letters and vowels to indicate "mine," "ours," and so forth. For example:

Adjective	Pronunciation	Meaning
Sheli	sheh-*lee*	mine
Shelcha (MS)	shehl-*chah*	yours
Shelach (FS)	shehl-*ach*	yours
Shelo	sheh-*loh*	his
Shela	sheh-*lah*	hers
Shelanu	sheh-*lah*-noo	ours
Shelachem (MP or FP)	sheh-lah-*chem*	yours
Shalahen (FP)	sheh-lah-*hen*	yours
Shelachem (MP or FP)	sheh-lah-*chehm*	theirs
Shelachen (FP)	sheh-lah-*chehn*	theirs

Because possessives are adjectives, place them *after* the noun. Also when you place the possessive adjective *after* the noun, you need to place the **Hey** (hay; the Hebrew word for "the" or the *definite article*) in *front* of the noun. For example:

- **HaMizvadot Shelanu** (hah-meez-vah-*doht* sheh-*lah*-noo; our luggage)

- **HaMizvadot Shelachem** (hah-meez-vah-*doht* sheh-lah-*chehm;* your (plural) luggage)

- **HaMizvadot Shela** (hah-meez-vah-*doht* sheh-*lah;* her luggage)

- **HaMizvadot Sheli** (hah-*seh*-fehr sheh-*lee;* my luggage)

After you retrieve your **Mizvadot** (meez-vah-*doht;* luggage), you may ask the **Pakid** (MS)/**Pekidah** (FS) to call a cab by saying:

Atah Yachol LeHazmin Li Monit? (ah-*tah* yah-*chohl* leh-hahz-*meen* lee moh-*neet;* Can you call a cab for me?) (MS)

At Yecholah LeHazmin Li Monit? (aht yeh-chohl-*ah* leh-hahz-*meen* lee moh-*neet;* Can you call a cab for me?) (FS)

Talkin' the Talk

Yael and Yaniv (a woman and a man, respectively) are checking out of their hotel today after a week's stay. They go to the reception to check out.

Yael:	**Boker Tov! Anachnu Ozvim HaYom. Efshar L'Kabel Et HaCheshbon?**
	boh-kehr t*ohv*! ah-*nach*-noo ohz-*veem* hah-*yohm.* ehf-*shahr* leh-kah-*behl* eht hah-chehsh-*bohn*?
	Good morning! We're leaving today. May I have the bill?
Reception:	**Boker Or. Rak Rega, Ani Miyad Avi Lach Et HaCheshbon.**
	boh-kehr *ohr.* rahk *reh*-gah. ah-*nee* mee-*yahd* ah-*vee* lach eht hah-chesh-*bohn.*
	Morning light. One moment. I'll bring you the bill right away.
Yael:	**Todah Rabbah. Efshar L'hash'eer Et Ha'Mizvadot Shelanu BaMachsan Ad Ha'Erev?**
	toh-*dah* rah-*bah.* ehf-*shahr* leh-ha-sh-*ir* eht hah-meez-vah-*doht* sheh-*lah*-noo bah-mach-*sahn* ahd hah-*eh*-rehv?
	Thank you very much. May we leave our luggage in the storage until the evening?
Reception:	**B'vadai. Tachtemi Po B'Vakashah. Nesi'ah Tovah!**
	beh-vah-*dai.* tach-teh-*mee* poh beh-vah-*kah*-shah. neh-see-*ah* toh-*vah*!
	Certainly. Sign here please. Have a nice trip!

When someone says to you: **Boker Tov** (*boh*-kehr *tohv;* Good morning), respond by saying: **Boker Or** (*boh*-kehr *ohr;* Morning light).

Words to Know

Cheshbon	chehsh-_bohn_	bill
Kabbalah	kah-bah-_lah_	reception desk
La'Azov	lah-ah-_zohv_	to leave
La'Tzet	lah-_tzeht_	to exit
Machsan	mach-_sahn_	storage
Mizvada	meez-vah-_dah_	luggage
Nesiah Tovah!	neh-see-_ah_ toh-_vah_	Have a nice trip!

Fun & Games

Use the correct words from the word the word bank to complete the questions. The answers are in Appendix C.

Efshar, Hizmanti, Eizeh, Kahma, Ha'Im

1. _____ **Lekabel Et HaMizvadot Shelanu?** (May we have our luggage?)

2. _____ **Sug Cheder Atah Rotzeh?** (What kind of room would you like?)

3. **Ani** _____ **Cheder.** (I reserved a room.)

Chapter 14

Money, Money, Money

Some folks say money makes the world go 'round. Other people say that it's the root of all evil. But whatever it is, money is certainly part of everyone's lives in this postmodern, 21st-century world. In this chapter, I show you how to talk about the stuff that's been likened to the staff of life — bread and dough.

Going to the Bank

Ah, a trip to the **Bank** (bahnk; bank). Some people love it; others dread it. But however you feel about visiting your bank, the task is unavoidable at times. Maybe you only need to go to your local **Snif** (sneef; branch) to cash or deposit a **Hamcha'a** (hahm-chah-*ah;* check). Hopefully the **S'chum** (s-*choom;* amount) you **Lehafkid** (leh-haf-*keed;* to deposit) is larger than the amount you **Limshoch** (leem-*shohch;* to withdraw)! But often you have to go to a larger bank to take care of big monetary matters, like taking out a **Halva'ah** (hahl-vah-*ah;* loan) or — gasp — applying for a **Mashkanta** (mahsh-kahn-*tah;* mortgage). In this section, I give you some bank terms to help you with your banking communications.

Talking to tellers

So what do you need to do? Do you need to **Lehafkid Kesef** (leh-haf-*keed keh*-sehf; deposit money) into your **Cheshbon** (chesh-*bohn;* account) or **Limshoch** (leem-*shohch;* withdraw) it? Are you there to **Lehagish Bakasha** (leh-hah-*geesh* bah-kah-*shah;* apply for) a **Halva'ah** or a **Mashkanta**? Maybe you need to make a **Tashloom** (tash-*loom;* payment). Just ask the **Kaspar** (kahs-*pahr;* teller) what you need and he'll be happy to help you.

Here are some helpful phrases:

- **Ani Rotzeh Lifto'ach Cheshbon.** (ah-*nee* roh-*tzeh* leef-*toh*-ach chehsh-*bohn;* I want to open an account.) (MS)

  Ani Rotzah Lifto'ach Cheshbon. (ah-*nee* roh-*tzah* leef-*toh*-ach chehsh-*bohn;* I want to open an account.) (FS)

- **Ani Rotzeh Lehagish Bakasha Le'halva'ah.** (ah-*nee* roh-*tzeh* leh-hah-*geesh* bah-kah-*shah* leh-hal-vah-*ah;* I want to apply for a loan.) (MS)

  Ani Rotzah Lehagish Bakasha Le'halva'ah. (ah-*nee* roh-*tzah* leh-hah-*geesh* bah-kah-*shah* leh-hal-vah-*ah;* I want to apply for a loan.) (FS)

- **Ani Rotzeh Lehavir Kesf** (ah-*nee* roh-*tzeh* leh-hah-ah-*veer* keh-sehf; *Literally:* I want to transfer money; I want to wire money.) (MS)

  Ani Rotzah Leha'avir Kesef (ah-*nee* roh-*tzah* leh-hah-ah-*veer* *keh*-sehf; *Literally:* I want to transfer money; I want to wire money.) (FS)

- **Mah Ha'ribit?** (mah hah-ree-*beet;* What's the interest rate?)

- **Efshar Lachtom Al Ha'hamcha'a?** (ehf-*shahr* lach-*tohm* ahl hah-hahm-chah-*ah;* Can you sign this check?)

- **Matai Atah Yachol Leshalem?** (mah-*tye* ah-*tah* yah-*chohl* leh-shah-*lehm;* When can you make a payment?) (MS)

  Matai At Y'cholah Leshalem? (mah-*tye* aht yeh-choh-*lah* leh-shah-*lehm;* When can you make a payment?) (FS)

Instead of schlepping all the way to the bank, you can just use an ATM, which is called a **Kaspomat** (kahs-poh-*maht*) in Hebrew. I always get a big kick out of seeing Hebrew on the ATM screen. Here's this ancient, Biblical language, and it's at home in the modern world.

Counting your change

The **Shekel** (*sheh*-kehl) is the currency of Israel. The Israeli currency system is based on the **Shekel Chadash** (*sheh*-kehl chah-*dahsh;* New Israeli Shekel), which has been in circulation since 1985. The New Israeli Shekel (NIS) is made up of 100 **Agorot** (ah-goh-*roht;* the equivalent of $\frac{1}{100}$ of the currency, like a penny to the dollar. This is the plural form). Israel no longer mints the one **Agorah** (ah-goh-*rah*) coin, so most of the time **Odef** (*oh*-dehf; change) is rounded to the nearest five **Agorot** (ah-goh-*roht*). If the change is two **Agorot** or less the sum is rounded down. If the change is three **Agorot** or more, the change is rounded up.

Something old, something new: Israeli coins

Israeli **Matbe'ot** (maht-beh-*oht;* coins) offer an amazing tour of ancient Israelite history. Many of today's coins are imprints of ancient Israelite coins dating back to the first century of the Common Era or even earlier.

The five-**Agorot** (ah-goh-*roht*) coin is a replica of a coin from the fourth year of the war between the Jews and Rome, and it depicts symbols from the Jewish harvest holiday of **Sukkot** (soo-*koht*). The ten-**Agorot** coin bears the imprint of a coin issued by the Israelite empire between B.C.E. 40 and 37, the seven-branched candelabrum that once stood in the Jewish Temple in Jerusalem.

The **Chatzi-Shekel** (chahtz-*ee* sheh-*kehl;* half-sheckel) depicts a harp of an ancient Israelite

seal, and the **Shekel** (sheh-kehl; one-shekel coin) has an image of a lily and ancient Hebrew letters from a Judean coin from the Persian period (sixth to fourth centuries B.C.E.).

The five-**Shekel** coin shows a column typical of buildings in the anceint Israelite period between the tenth and seventh centuries B.C.E. The ten-**Shekel** coin — the most gorgeous in my opinion — a metal and copper coin depicting a palm tree with seven leaves and two baskets with dates, orginates from a coin minted in 69 c.e., the fourth year of the Jewish-Roman war, one year before the destruction of the Second Temple in Jerusalem.

In Hebrew, people refer to the word **Shekel Chadash** with the term **Shach** (shach) for short. This is generally used when talking about money in an official way, such as at the bank, or when people are discussing the economy.

Shekels come in denominations of ½, one, five, and ten-shekel coins. **Sh'tarot** (sh-tah-*roht;* bills) come in denominations of 10, 20, 50, 100, and 200 shekels.

Talkin' the Talk

Tamir goes to the bank to open an account. He talks with a bank employee who gets him started with a checking account and a credit card. (Track 26)

Tamir: **Boker Tov.**
boh-kehr tohv.
Good morning.

Clerk: **Boker Or. Efshar La'Azor L'cha?**
boh-kehr ohr. ehf-*shahr* lah-ah-*zohr* leh-*chah*?
Morning light. May I help you?

Tamir:	**Ken. Ani Rotzeh Lifto'ach Cheshbon Hamcha'oht V'Gam L'Hazmin Kartis Ashrei.**
	kehn. ah-*nee* roh-*tzeh* leef-*toh*-ach chehsh-*bohn* hahm-chah-*oht* veh-*gahm* leh-hahz-*meen* kahr-*tees* ash-*rye*.
	Yes. I would like to open a checking account and also order a credit card.
Clerk:	**B'vadai. Na Lemaleh Et Ha'Tofes ha'zeh.**
	beh-vah-*dai*. nah leh-mah-*leh* eht hah-*toh*-fehs hah-*zeh*.
	Certainly. Please fill out this form.
Tamir:	**Todah. Henei. Ani Milehti Et Ha'Tofes.**
	toh-*dah*. hee-*nay*. ah-*nee* mee-*leh*-tee eht hah *toh*-fehs.
	Thanks. Here it is. I filled out the form.
Clerk:	**Todah Rabbah Lecha. Atah Yachol Letzapot laHamcha'ot Ve'Kartis Ha'Ashrei B'Od Shlosha Shavuot.**
	toh-*dah* rah-*bah* leh-*chah*. ah-*tah* yah-*chohl* leh-tzah-*poht* lah-hamcha-*oht* veh-kar-*tees* hah-ash-*rahy* buh-*ohd* sh-loh-*shah* shah-voo-*oht*.
	Thank you very much. You can expect your checks and your credit card in the mail in three weeks.
Tamir:	**Yofie. Todah Rabbah.**
	yoh-fee. toh-*dah* rah-*bah*.
	Great. Thanks a lot.

Considering wealth in Jewish thought

When considering wealth, Judaism takes the middle road advocating neither asceticism nor excessive materialism. In a book of Jewish wisdom literature, *Pirke Avot* (peer-*kay* ah-*voht*; sayings of the ancestors), the ancient Rabbis asked, "Who is rich?" Their answer: Those who find contentment in their lot. The Rabbis also taught that where there is no flour, there is no Torah. This statement recognizes that physical needs and other practical matters must be met before spirituality can be possible.

Words to Know

bank	bahnk	bank
kesef	<u>keh</u>-sehf	money
halva'ah	hahl-vah-<u>ah</u>	loan
lehafkid	leh-hahf-<u>keed</u>	to deposit
lehashki'ah	leh-hahsh-<u>kee</u>-ah	to invest
limshoch	leem-<u>shohch</u>	to withdraw
mashkanta	mahsh-kahn-<u>tah</u>	mortgage
matbe'ah	maht-<u>beh</u>-ah	coin
odef	<u>oh</u>-dehf	change
s'chum	s-<u>choom</u>	amount
snif	sneef	branch
tashlum	tahsh-<u>loom</u>	payment

Jewish villages in Eastern Europe used to participate in a **Rosh HaShanah** (rohsh hah-shah-*nah;* New Year's) custom: One person would go door-to-door with a sack. Folks who could afford to put money in the sack did so, and people who needed money took it from the sack. The entire process was all completely anonymous. No one knew who gave money to or who took money from the sack. Everyone got what they needed, and no one was embarrassed. In this way, everyone in the **Kehillah** (keh-hee-*lah;* community) helped each other.

Changing Money

Whenever you travel — whether for business or pleasure — you usually have to exchange your money for the local currency. Most **Bankim** (*bahn*-keem; banks) accept dollars or **Hamcha'ot Nos'im** (hahn-chah-*ot* nohs-*eem;* traveler's checks) in return for the local currency in cash. You can usually spot a board with the **Sha'ar Chalifin** (*shah*-ahr chah-lee-*feen;* exchange rate). Just go straight up to the window and say:

Ani Rotzeh Lehamir Kesef. (ah-*nee* rohtz-*eh* leh-hah- *meer keh*-sehf; I want to exchange money.) (MS)

Ani Rotzah Lehamir Kesef (ah-*nee* rohtz-*ah* leh-hah-*meer keh*-sehf; I want to exchange money.) (FS)

Here are some additional phrases that may come in handy:

- **Ani Rotzeh Lehamir Dollarim Le'Shkalim.** (ah-*nee* roh-*tzeh* leh-hah-*meer* doh-lah-*reem* leh-sh-kahl-*eem;* I want to exchange dollars for shekels.) (MS)

  Ani Rotzah Lehamir Dollarim Le'Shkalim. (ah-*nee* roh-*tzah* leh-hah-*meer* doh-lah-*reem* lehsh-kah-*leem;* I want to exchange dollars for shekels.) (FS)

- **Mah Sha'ar Ha'chah-lifin?** (mah *shah*-ahr hah-chah-lee-*feen;* What's the exchange rate?)

- **Kamah Ha'Amlot?** (kah-*mah* hah ahm-*loht;* What are the fees?)

- **Atem Mekablim Hamcha'ot Nos'im?** (ah-*tehm* meh-kah-*bleem* hahm-chah-*oht* nohs-*eem;* Do you accept traveler's checks?) (MP)

When you exchange money or cash **Hamcha'aot Nos'im** (hahm-chah-*oht* nohs-*eem;* traveler's checks), you may be asked for your ID, so have your **Darkon** (dahr-*kohn;* passport) or some other form of **Teudat Zehut** (teh-oo-*daht* zeh-*hoot;* ID) ready. The **Kaspar** (kahs-*pahr;* teller) will ask you:

Ha'im Yesh Lecha Te'udat Zehut? (hah-*eem* yehsh leh-*chah* teh-oo-*daht* zeh-*hoot;* Do you have an identity card?) (MS)

Ha'im Yesh Lach Te'udat Zehut? (hah-*eem* yesh lach teh-oo-*daht* zeh-*hoot;* Do you have an identity card?) (FS)

If you want to ask someone to make change or break a large bill for you, the phrase you use is **Efshar Lifrot Li?** (ehf-*shahr* leef-*roht lee;* Can you break this for me?)

Talkin' the Talk

Eric, an American tourist in Israel, heads to the bank to change money.

Eric:	**Boker Tov. Ani Rotzeh Lehamir Dollarim Amerikanim Le'Shkalim B'vakashah. Mah Sha'ar Hachalifin?** *boh*-kehr tohv. ah-*nee* roh-*tzeh* leh-hah-*meer* doh-lah-*reem* ah-meh-ree-*kah*-neem leh-sh-*kah*-leem beh-vah-kah-*shah*. mah *shah*-ahr-ha-cha-lee-*feen?* Good morning. I want to exchange American dollars for shekels please. What's the exchange rate?

Teller:	**Boker Or. Sha'ar Ha'chalifin Hu Arba'ah Shkalim L'Dollar Echad.** *boh*-kehr ohr. *shah*-ahr ha-chah-lee-*feen* hoo ahr-bah-ah sheh-*kah*-leem leh-*doh*-lar e-*chad*. Morning light. The exchange rate is four shekels to the dollar.
Eric:	**Yofie. Ani Rotzeh Lehamir Arba Me'ot Dollarim B'hamcha'ot Nos'im L'Shkalim Chadashim.** *yoh*-fee. ah-*nee* roh-*tzeh* leh-hah-*meer* ahr-*bah* meh-*oht* doh-lah-*reem* beh-hahm-chah-*oht* nohs-*eem* lehsh-*kah*-leem chah-dah-*sheem*. Great. I want to exchange four hundred dollars in traveler's checks to New Israeli Shekels.
Teller:	**Ayn Be'aya. Yesh Lechah T'eudat Zehut?** ayn be-ah-y*ah*. yehsh leh-*chah* teh-oo-*daht* zeh-*hoot*? No problem. Do you have ID?
Eric:	**Ken. Henei Ha'Darkon Sheli.** kehn. hee-*nay* hah-dahr-*kohn* sheh-*lee*. Yes. Here's my passport.
Teller:	**Ve'Hinei Ha'Kesef Shelcha. Le'Arba Meot Dollarim Mekablim Elef V'Shesh Me'ot Shkalim Minus Esrim Shkalim La'Amla. Az Atah Mekabel Elef, Chamesh Me'ot u'Shmonim Shekalim Chadashim.** veh-hee-*nay* hah-*keh*-sehf shel-*chah*. leh-ahr-*bah* meh-*oht* doh-lah-*reem* meh-kah-*bleem* eh-lehf veh-shehsh meh-*oht* sheh-*kah*-leem mee-noos ehs-*reem* shkah-*leem* lah-ah-m-*lah*. ahz ah-*tah* meh-kah-*behl* eh-lehf, chah-*mehsh* meh-*oht* oosh-moh-*neem* sh-kah-*leem* chah-dah-*sheem*. And here is your money. For four hundred dollars you get one thousand and six hundred shekels minus twenty shekels for the transaction fee. So you get one thousand, five hundred and eighty New Israeli Shekels.
Eric:	**Todah Rabbah.** toh-*dah* rah-*bah*. Thanks a lot.

If you have a **Kartis Ashrei** (kahr-*tees* ahsh-*rye;* credit card), you can get cash at any **Kaspomat** (kahs-poh-*maht;* ATM), but watch out for, the **Amlah** (ahm-*lah;* fee)!

Words to Know

Amlah	ahm-<u>lah</u>	fee
Hamcha'a	hahm-chah-<u>ah</u>	check
Hamcha'ot Nos'im	hahm-chah-<u>oht</u> nohs-<u>eem</u>	traveler's checks
Kartis Ashrye	kahr-<u>tees</u> ahsh-<u>rye</u>	credit card
Kaspar	kahs-<u>pahr</u>	bank teller
Kaspomat	kahs-poh-<u>maht</u>	ATM
Sha'arei Chalifin	shah-ah-<u>ray</u> chah-lee-<u>feen</u>	exchange rates
Te'udat Zehut	teh-oo-<u>daht</u> zeh-<u>hoot</u>	ID

The Hebrew word for *charity* is **Tzdakah** (tzdah-*kah;* Literally: justice; right-eous giving). The Jewish concept of philanthropy is inherent in this word's meaning. While the Latin root for *charity* means *love* and is based on the idea of giving out of the goodness of one's heart, the Jewish concept of **Tzdakah** is based on equitable distribution of wealth. In Judaism, transferring wealth from those who earn it to those who need it is an obligation incumbent upon everyone. Even those who are dependent on receiving **Tzdakah** are obligated to give it.

Flowing with the Currency

If you're an avid traveler, you may have all kinds of currencies in your pocket. For example, you may have

- **Dinar** (dee-*nahr;* Jordanian dinar)
- **Dolar** (*doh*-lahr; the American or Canadian dollar)
- **Euro** (*yur*-oh; European euro; also pronounced *ey*-ro in Israel because Europe is pronounced ey-*ro*-pah)
- **Frank** (frank; Swiss frank)

✔ **Keter** (*keh*-tehr; Danish and Norwegian crown)

✔ **Lira** (*lee*-rah; British, Lebanese, and Egyptian pound)

✔ **Peso** (*pay*-soh; Mexican peso)

✔ **Rand** (rand; Saudi Arabian rand)

✔ **Yen** (yehn; Japanese yen)

✔ **Zloty** (*zloh*-tee; Polish zloty)

Using Credit Cards

Anywhere you go these days, you can pay for almost everything with **Kartisei Ashrye** (kahr-tee-*say* ahsh-*rye;* credit cards), and Israel is no exception. You can ask whether a particular establishment accepts **Kartisei Ashrye** by using either of the following questions:

✔ **Atem Mekablim Kartisei Ashrye?** (ah-*tehm* meh-kah-*bleem* kahr-tee-*say* ahsh-*rye;* Do you accept credit cards?)

✔ **Efshar L'Shalem Im Kartis Ashrye?** (ehf-*shahr* leh-shah-*lehm* eem kahr-*tees* ahsh-*rye;* May I pay with a credit card?)

Directing Your Objects

So you've got your verbs. Then you've got your nouns. Often, when you put them together in a sentence, you add another word that receives the action of the verb — the goal or result of the verb. This word is the direct object. For example, in the sentence, "Molly kicked the ball," *ball* is the direct object — the thing that got kicked (received the action of the verb).

Sometimes, you place a preposition between the verb and a definite noun (a noun that is preceded by the word *the,* for example, *the book,* as opposed to *a book,* which would be an indefinite noun — that's another story). Prepositions are one of the trickier things in Hebrew for English-speakers to master because the verbs that normally accompany prepositions in English aren't necessarily the same verbs that take prepositions in Hebrew.

The Hebrew prepositions are:

✔ **Al** (ahl; on)

✔ **Ben** (bayn; between)

✔ **B'** (buh; in *or* with)

✔ **Im** (eem; with)

✔ **K'** (kuh; like)

✔ **L'** (luh; to)

✔ **M'** (muh; from)

Another difficulty with prepositions is the fact that Hebrew *does* have an article **Et** (eht), for definite direct objects if the verb before it doesn't use a preposition, and it doesn't have an equivalent in English. **Et** is placed between a verb and a definite direct object. For example, **Ani Rotzeh Liknot Et HaKovah** (ah-*nee* roh-*tzeh* leek-*noht* eht hah-*koh*-vah; I want to buy the hat.) *Liknot* is the verb and ***HaKovah*** is the direct object. The **Et** between them tells you that the direct object is definite (*the* hat) and not indefinite (*a* hat). You don't use **Et** when the object is indirect. So if you want to buy *a* hat, but not any particular hat, you wouldn't use the article **Et**.

You also place the article **Et** in front of proper nouns, such as the name of a country. For example: **Ani Ohev Et Yisrael** (ah-*nee* oh-*hehv* eht yees-rah-*ehl;* I love Israel).

Think of **Et** as a road sign — Definite Direct Object Ahead (DDOA).

Finally, you can't assume that English verbs and their Hebrew equivalents take the same preposition. In English, you say, "that depends *on* blah, blah, blah," but in Hebrew you say, "that depends *with* blah, blah, blah." Similarly, we're proud *of* something in English, but proud *in/with* something in Hebrew. And so it is with many verbs, especially when the preposition refers to some abstract relationship, not something physical and concrete.

What verbs take which prepositions? As in English, the verb-preposition linking pattern is completely arbitrary. You just have to know this stuff. Table 14-1 includes a short list to get you started.

Table 14-1	Looking at Hebrew Prepositions	
Hebrew Verb + Preposition	*Pronunciation*	*Translation*
Lashevet Al	lah-*sheh*-veht al	to sit *on*
Laredet M'	lah-*reh*-deht meh	to descend *from*
Lefached M'	leh-fah-*chehd* meh	to be afraid *from*
Lehakshiv L'	leh-hahk-*sheev* leh	to listen *to*
Lehistakel B'	leh-his-tah-*kehl* beh	to look *in*

Hebrew Verb + Preposition	Pronunciation	Translation
Latet L'	lah-*teht* leh	to give *to*
La'azor L'	lah-ah-*zohr* leh	to help *to*
Lechakot L	leh-chah-*koht* leh	to wait *to*
Livchor B'	leev-*chohr* beh	to choose *in/with*
L'Shalem L'	leh-shah-*lehm* leh	to pay *to*
Lenagen B'	leh-nah-*gehn* beh	to play (a musical instrument) *with*
L'vakesh M'	leh-vah-*kehsh* meh	to request *from*
Linhog B'	leen-*hohg* beh	to drive *in*
Lagur B'	lah-*goor* beh	to live *in* a place or (*on*) a street
Lishlo'ach L'	leesh-*loh*-ahch leh	to send *to*
Lesaper L'	leh-sah-*pehr* leh	to tell *to*
Lishmor Al	leesh-*mohr* ahl	to guard *on*
L'tzavot Al	leh-tzah-*voht* ahl	to command *on*
Lehistakel Al	leh-hees-tah-*kehl* ahl	to look *upon*
Le'ha'amin B'	leh-hah-ah-*meen* beh	to believe *in/with*
Le'echoz B'	leh-eh-*chohz* beh	to grasp *with/in*
Le'ayem Al	leh-ah-*yehm* ahl	to threaten *on*
Le'esor Al	leh-eh-*sohr* ahl	to forbid *on*
Lehavdil Ben	leh-hahv-*deel* bein	to differentiate *between*
Lehityaded Im	leh-heet-yah-*dehd* eem	to befriend *with*
Lehitkatev Im	leh-heet-*kah*-tehv eem	to correspond *with*
Lehitmoded Im	leh-heet-moh-*dehd* eem	to cope *with*
Lehodot L'	leh-hoh-*doht* leh	to thank *to*
Lehagen Al	leh-hah-*gehn* ahl	to protect *on*
Lid'og L	leed-*ohg*	to worry *for*

Fun & Games

Write the correct English translation for the following Hebrew words:

1. **Ham-cha-ot Nos'im** _____

2. **Te'udat Zehut** _____

3. **Cheshbon** _____

4. **Boker Or** _____

5. **Sha'arei Hachalifin** _____

Chapter 15

Where Is the Western Wall? Asking Directions

. . . .

In This Chapter

▶ Requesting directions

▶ Offering directions

▶ Navigating North, South, East, and West

. . . .

*I*f you get lost, don't hesitate to ask for directions! Otherwise you may end up going in circles for hours, or end up in a place you don't want to be. So speak up and ask!

In this chapter, I give you the Hebrew words and phrases necessary for giving and asking directions. Where do you want to go? Is it **Rachok** (rah-*chohk;* far) or **Karov** (kah-*rohv;* near)? Do you want to take the **Autobus** (*oh*-toh-boos; bus) or can you **Lalechet Ba'Regel** (lah-*leh*-cheht bah-*reh*-gehl; walk)? This chapter also gives you the words so you can navigate a map, talk about various destinations, and discuss modes of transportation.

Making Sure You Don't Get Lost

Suppose you want to go to **HaKotel HaMa'Aravi** (hah-*koh*-tehl hah-mah-ah-rah-*vee;* the Western Wall). You know it is in the **Ha'Iir Ha'Atikah** (hah-eer hah-ah-tee-*kah;* Old City of Jerusalem), but you're not sure how to get there, and you certainly don't want to get lost! If you're a good navigator, you may want to consult a **Mapah** (mah-*pah;* map). But I never trust my map-reading skills. I get better results if I walk up to the nearest (and friendly-looking) stranger and **Levakesh Ezrah** (leh-vah-*kehsh* ehz-*rah;* ask for help).

Where in Hebrew is **Eifo** (*ay*-foh). Another Hebrew word, **Le'an** (leh-*ahn*), means "to where," as in "Where are you going?" or "Where is this bus going?" To ask for directions, first say, "**Slicha** (slee-*chah;* excuse me)," and then ask away:

- ✔ **Slicha, Eifo Ha ...**(slee-*chah ay*-foh *hah* . . .; Excuse me, where is the . . . ?)

- ✔ **Slicha, Eich Ani Yachol LeHagiah Le . . .**(slee-*chah,* eich ah-*nee* yah-chohl le-hah-*gee*-ah leh; Excuse me, how can I get to . . .?) (MS)

  Slicha, Eich Ani Yechola LeHagiah Le . . . (slee-*chah,* eich ah-*nee* yeh-*choh*-lah le-hah-*gee*-ah leh . . .; Excuse me, how can I get to . . .) (FS)

- ✔ **Slicha, Eifo Ani Yachol Limtzoh . . .** (slee-*chah ay*-foh ah-*nee* yah-*chohl* leem-*tzoh* . . .; Excuse me, where can I find . . .) (MS)

  Slicha, Eifo Ani Yechola Limtzoh . . . (slee-*chah ay*-foh ah-*nee* yeh-choh-*lah* leem-*tzoh* . . .; Excuse me, where can I find . . .) (FS)

Table 15-1 has several locations you may want to ask about finding.

Table 15-1	Looking for Locations	
Hebrew	*Pronunciation*	*Translation*
Beit Cholim	bayt choh-leem	hospital
Beit Knesset	bayt *kneh*-seht	synagogue
Do'ar	*doh*-ahr	post office
Kolno'a	kohl-*noh*-ah	cinema
Knesiya	kneh-see-*yah*	church
Misgad	mees-*gahd*	mosque
Nemal Ha'Te'ufa	neh-*mahl* hah-teh-oo-*fah*	airport
Tachanah	tah-chah-*nah*	station
Te'atron	teh-aht-*rohn*	theater

If you're lost, you can use one of these phrases (and using **Slicha** in these cases wouldn't hurt either):

- ✔ **Ani Halachti Le'Ibud.** (ah-*nee* hah-*lach*-tee leh-ee-*bood;* I got lost.)

- ✔ **Ani Ibadeti Et Ha'Tzafon.** (ah-*nee* ee-bah-de-*tee* eht hah-tzah-*fohn; Literally:* I lost the North.)

- ✔ **Ani Ta'iti Ba'Derech.** (ah-*nee* tah-*ee*-tee bah-*deh*-rech; I made a mistake along the way.)

Note: All the preceding phrases are gender-neutral because they're in the past tense for "I," which is the same whether the speaker is male or female.

If you're taking an **Autobus** (oh-toh-*boos;* bus), and want to know where it's going, you can ask **Le'an Ha'Autobus Nose'a?** (leh-*ahn* hah-*oh*-toh-boos noh-*seh*-ah; (to) Where is this bus going?)

If you're driving a car and want to know how to get somewhere, you can ask for directions:

- ✔ **Eich Ani Yachol Lehagiah L. . .** (eich ah-*nee* yah-*chohl* leh-hah-*gee*-ah leh . . .; How can I get to . . . ; *Literally:* to arrive at . . .) (MS)

  Eich Ani Yechola Lehagiah L . . . (eich ah-*nee* yeh-choh-*lah* leh-hah-*gee*-ah leh . . .; How can I get to . . .; *Literally:* to arrive at . . .) (FS)

If you want to ask others where they're going, the sentences are similar:

- ✔ **Le'an Ata Holech?** (leh-*ahn* ah-*tah* hoh-*lech*?; Where are you going?) (MS)

  Le'an At Holechet? (leh-*ahn* aht hoh-*leh*-cheht?; Where are you going?) (FS)

- ✔ **Le'an Atem Holchim?** (leh-*ahn* ah-*tem* hol-*cheem;* Where are you going?) (MP)

  Le'an Aten Holchot? (leh-*ahn* ah-*ten* hol-*chot;* Where are you going?) (FP)

- ✔ **Le'an Hem Holchim?** (leh-*ahn* hem hohl-*cheem?;* Where are they going?) (MP)

  Le'an Hen Holchot? (leh-*ahn* hen hohl-*choht?;* Where are they going?) (FP)

Words to Know

Beit Cholim	bayt choh-<u>leem</u>	hospital
Beit Knesset	bayt <u>kneh</u>-seht	synagogue
Doar	<u>doh</u>-ahr	post office
Kolno'a	kohl <u>noh</u>-ah	movie theater
Nemal Ha'Te'ufah	neh-<u>mahl</u> hah-teh-oo-<u>fah</u>	airport
Slicha	slee-<u>chah</u>	excuse me

Giving and Understanding Directions for Lost Souls

I remember how excited I was after tourists started asking me for directions when I lived in Jerusalem. At first, I thought it was because I had become so acculturated to the place people thought I was Israeli. Then I realized tourists asked me for directions because they could tell I spoke English.

Nonetheless, I did direct an Israeli or two while I lived there. Even today, years after I have moved back to the United States, I can still give walking directions on the streets of Jerusalem. I know the place like the back of my hand. Table 15-2 can help you give directions (or how to understand likely responses whenever you need to ask for directions).

Table 15-2	Giving and Understanding Directions	
Hebrew	*Pronunciation*	*Translation*
Al-Yad	ahl-*yahd*	next to
Bachutz	bah-*chootz*	outside
Bein	bayn	between
Bifnim	beef-*neem*	inside
La'Avor Et Ha	lah-ah-*vohr* eht hah	to pass the
Lach'tzot Et Ha'Kvish	lah-cha-*tzot* eht hahk-*veesh*	to cross the street
La'lechet Yashar	lah-*leh*-cheht yah-*shahr*	to go straight
Lema'la	leh-*mah*-lah	up
Lemata	leh-*mah*-tah	down
Lifnot Yamina Ba'Tzomet	leef-*noht* yah-*mee*-nah bah-*tzoh*-meht	to turn right at the junction
Mimul	mee-*mool*	across from
Mitachat	mee-*tah*-chaht	under
Po	poh	here
Sham	shahm	there

In Hebrew, you don't say "on the right" or "on the left" like in English. To indicate something is on the right side, you say: **BuTzad Yamin** (buh-*tzahd* yah-*meen*). To indicate something is on the left side, you say: **BuTzad Smol** (buh-*tzahd* s-*mohl*).

You can give directions in the infinitive, future, and command tenses. Using the infinitive is a more classical form of Hebrew. You hear the infinitive as well as the future and command tenses on the streets of Israel. Even though the command tense is technically correct, some people in Israel think using the imperative is somewhat rude, like something a teacher or a military commander would use, so they speak in future tense instead.

When you're giving or receiving directions, you may hear or make reference to various landmarks. For example, you may tell someone that they need to turn at a **Ramzor** (rahm-*zohr;* traffic light) or at a **Tzomet** *(tzoh-*meht; junction). If someone is walking, you may make reference to the **Midracha** (meed-rah-*chah;* sidewalk) or the **Kikar** (kee-*kahr;* square). Then again, if you're driving, someone may mention **HaK'vish HaRashi** (hah-k*veesh* hah-rah-*shee;* the main road) or a **Gesher** (*geh*-shehr; bridge).

Words to Know

Eich	ehch	how
Eifo	ay-<u>foh</u>	where
Gesher	<u>geh</u>-shehr	bridge
Kikar	kee-<u>kahr</u>	square
Kivun	kee-<u>voon</u>	direction
Le'An	leh-<u>ahn</u>	to where
Mapah	mah-<u>pah</u>	map
Midracha	meed-rah-<u>chah</u>	sidewalk
Ramzor	rahm-<u>zohr</u>	traffic light
Tzomet	<u>tzoh</u>-meht	junction

Talkin' the Talk

Sarah is in the Old City of Jerusalem looking for the Western Wall. She is in the Jewish Quarter and knows she is close, but she still can't find it. So she asks a woman for directions. (Track 27)

Sarah: **Slicha**
slee-*chah.*
Excuse me.

Woman: **Ken?**
kehn?
Yes?

Sarah: **Ani Halachti L'Ibud. Eifo Ani Yechola Limzto Et Ha'Kotel Ha'Ma'aravi?.**
ah-*nee* ha-*lach*-tee leh-ee-*bood.* ay-*foh* ah-*nee* yeh-choh-*lah* leem-*tzoh* eht hah-*koh*-tehl hah-mah-ah-rah-*vee?*
I'm lost. Where can I find the Western Wall?

Woman: **Zeh Lo Rachok. Tilchi Yashar, Yashar, Yashar, Ve'Az Tish'ali.**
zeh loh rah-*chohk* til-*chee* yah-*shahr*, yah-*shahr*, yah-*shahr* ve-*ahz* tee-shah-*lee.*
It's not far. Go straight, straight, straight, and then ask.

Sarah: **Todah.**
toh-*dah.*
Thanks.

Providing directions the Israeli way

Israelis are infamous for their way of giving directions. They commonly gesticulate wildly and say something like **Yashar, Yashar, Yashar Ad Ha'Sof!** (yah-*shahr*, yah-*shahr*, yah-*shahr*, ahd hah-*sohf;* straight, straight, straight until the end!) As if that's helpful. Or sometimes you even hear **Yashar, Yashar, Yashar Ve'Az Tishal!** (yah-*shahr*, yah-*shahr*, yah-*shahr*, veh-*ahz* teesh-*ahl;* straight, straight, straight and then ask). Which idiomatically speaking means "I don't know how to get there, but I'm too proud to admit it. So keep going in the direction you're going and then try asking again. Good luck."

Keeping North, South, East, and West Straight

When you're traveling around, it can be helpful if you know the cardinal points on the compass:

- **Darom** (dah-*rohm;* south)
- **Ma'arav** (mah-ah-*rahv;* west)
- **Mizrach** (meez-*rach;* east)
- **Tzafon** (tzah-*fohn;* north)

To describe where something is using the cardinal points, preface it with the preposition (and prefix!) **B . . .** (buh . . .), which means *on* or *in.* For example: **Ani BaMizrach** (ah-*nee* bah-meez-*rach;* I am in the East!)

If you want to say the Hebrew equivalent of northward, southward, and so on, you indicate direction by adding the Hebrew character that sounds like *hey* at the end of the word. For example:

- **Daroma** (dah-*roh*-mah; southward)
- **Ma'arava** (mah-ah-*rah*-vah; westward)
- **Mizracha** (meez-*rah*-chah; eastward)
- **Tzafona** (tzah-*foh*-nah; northward)

Libi BaMizrach, V'Anochi B'Sof Ma'Arav! (lee-*bee* bah-meez-*rach* veh-ah-noh-*chee* buh-*sohf* mah-ah-*rahv!;* "My heart is in the East, but I'm at the edge of the West!") These words are by the famous Jewish poet **Yehuda Ha'Levi** (yeh-hoo-*dah* hah-*leh*-vee) penned in 12th-century Spain. His poetry expressed the Jewish longing for Zion, the land of Israel. A prolific Hebrew poet, his "Songs of Zion" are among his most celebrated works.

Talkin' the Talk

Michael, an American tourist in Israel, wants to go to the shopping mall and doesn't know if he should walk or take the bus. So he asks a man on the street.

Michael: **Slicha. Eifo HaKanyon?**
slee-*chah.* ay-*foh* hah-kahn-*yohn?*
Excuse me. Where's the shopping mall?

Man:	**Zeh Mamash Rachok Mi'Po, B'Eizor Malcha.**
	zeh mah-*mahsh* rah-*chohk* mee-*poh* beh-ay-*zohr* *mahl*-chah.
	It's quite far from here, in the Malcha area.

Michael:	**Ani Yachol Lalechet BaRegel?**
	ah-*nee*. yah-*chohl* lah-*leh*-cheht bah-*reh*-gehl?
	Can I get there by foot?

Man:	**Lo. Zeh Rachok Midai. Tzarich Lakachat Autobus.**
	loh zeh rah-*chohk* mee-*dye*. tzah-*reech* lah-*kah*-chaht *oh*-toh-boos.
	No, it's too far. You need to take a bus.

Michael:	**Eizeh Autobus Nose'a Le'Sham?**
	ay-*zeh* *oh*-toh-boos noh-*seh*-ah leh-*shahm?*
	Which bus goes there?

Man:	**Atah Yachol Lakachat Kav Shesh. Ha'Tachana Bidiyuk Mimul Ha'Mashbir.**
	ah-*tah* yah-*chohl* lah-*kah*-chaht kahv *shehsh.* hah-tah-chah-*nah* bee-dee-*yook* mee-*mool* hah-mahsh-*beer.*
	You can take line six. The (bus) station is exactly across from the Mashbir (department store).

Michael:	**Todah Rabbah.**
	toh-*dah* rah-*bah*.
	Thanks a lot.

Fun & Games

• •

Fill in the blanks using the following words:

BaRegel, Eizeh, Ha'Kanyon, Le'an, Le'Ibud,

1. **Ani Halachti _____.**

   I got lost.

2. **Slicha. Eifo _____?**

   Excuse me, where is the shopping mall?

3. **_____ Ata Holech?**

   Where are you going?

4. **Ani Yachol Lalechet _____?**

   Can I get there by foot ?

5. **_____ Autobus Nose'a Le'Sham?**

   Which bus goes there?

• •

Chapter 16

Handling Emergencies

• •

In This Chapter

▶ Dealing with car trouble

▶ Talking to medical staff

▶ Knowing what to do after a thief strikes

• •

*I*nto each life some rain must fall, and sometimes it turns into a full-blown storm, in the form of an emergency, which is never fun. In this chapter, I talk about possible unfortunate incidents, and give you the vocabulary to deal with them if the need arises.

In an emergency situation, you call out for help to anyone who may hear, and you let everyone know that you need help now! Read the following list of useful Hebrew phrases to use when you need a helping hand:

✔ **Dachuf!** (dah-*choof;* It's urgent!)

✔ **Hatzilu!** (hah-*tzee*-loo; Rescue!)

✔ **Hitkashru LaMishtara!** (heet-kahsh-*roo* lah-meesh-tah-*rah;* Contact the police!)

✔ **Ta'azru Li, B'Vakasha!** (tah-ahz-*roo* lee beh-vah-kah-*shah;* Help me please!)

Tackling Your Uncooperative Car

Car trouble can be very frustrating. If your car is giving you fits, I hope you've just **Nigmar Ha'delek** (neeg-*mahr* hah-*deh*-lehk; run out of gas) or something minor (and annoying) like a **Teker BaGalgal** (*teh*-kehr bah-gahl-*gahl;* flat tire). I hope you didn't have **Te'uunat Drachim** (teh-oo-*naht* drah-*cheem;* an accident).

Driving a car can be perilous. Fasten your **Chagorat Betichut** (chah-goh-*raht* beh-tee-*choot;* seatbelt)! Use these basic Hebrew phrases to describe what has happened to your car:

- **HaMechonit Sheli Hitkalkelah.** (hah-meh-choh-*neet* sheh-*lee* heet-kahl-keh-*lah;* My car broke down.)
- **HaMechonit Sheli Nitke'Ah.** (hah-meh-choh-*neet* sheh-*lee* neet-keh-*ah;* My car is stuck.)
- **Hayta Te'unat Drachim.** (hahy-t*ah* teh-oo-*naht* drah-*cheem;* There was an accident.)
- **Nigmar Li Ha'Delek . . .** (neeg-*mahr lee* hah-*deh-* lehk; I ran out of gas.)
- **Yesh Li Punture (or, Teker** (teh-*kehr*) **BaGalgal . . .** (yehsh lee puhn-*tsher* bah-gahl-*gahl;* I have a flat tire.)

You also may need to communicate to emergency workers or bystanders if someone has been hurt or not:

- **Ani Beseder.** (ah-*nee* beh-*seh*-dehr; I'm okay.)
- **Ani Niftza'ti.** (ah-*nee* neef-*tzah*-tee; I've been injured.)
- **Mishehu Niftza.** (*mee*-sheh-*hoo* neef-*tzah;* Someone's been injured.)

Jews recite a special prayer called **Birkat HaGomel** (beer-*kaht* hah-goh-*mehl*) after surviving a dangerous situation. You can immediately recite it or go to a synagogue the very next Sabbath to recite it. The words are as follows:

> **Baruch Atah Adonai Eloheinu Melech Ha'Olam, Ha'Gomel L'Chayavim Tovot She'Gmalani Kol Tov.**
>
> bah-*rooch* ah-*tah* ah-doh-*naye* eh-loh-*hay*-noo *meh*-lehch hah-oh-*lahm* hah-goh-*mehl* leh-chah-yah-*veem* toh-*voht* sheh-gh-mah-*lah*-nee kohl tohv.
>
> Praised are you Eternal One our God, Ruler of the Cosmos, who does favors for those who need them, and has done so for me.

If you recite these words in the synagogue, at the traditional time during the Torah reading, the congregation will respond:

> **Mi She'G'malcha Kol Tov, Hu Yigmalcha Kol Tov Sela.**
>
> mee sheh-guh-mahl-*chah* kohl tohv hoo yeeg-mahl-*chah* kohl tohv *seh*-lah.
>
> May the One who has granted you goodness continue to do so!

If you find yourself in an emergency situation where you really need to talk shop with a **Mechonai** (meh-choh-*nye;* mechanic), refer to Table 16-1 for words that you may need.

Table 16-1	Helpful Words to Use with a Mechanic	
Hebrew	*Pronunciation*	*Translation*
Bataria Solela	bah-tah-*ree*-yah soh-leh-*lah*	battery
Blamim	blah-*meem*	brakes
Davsha	dav-*shah*	pedal
Delek	*deh*-lehk	gasoline
Galgalim	gahl-gah-*leem*	wheels
Hehgeh	*heh*-geh	steering wheel
Hiluchim	hee-loo-*cheem*	gears
Manof	mah-*nohf*	jack
Mafte'ach	mahf-*teh*-ach	key
Magavim	mah-gah-*veem*	windshield wipers
Mano'a	mah-*noh*-ah	engine
Masa'it Grar	mah-sah-*eet* grahr	tow truck
Matzmed	mats-*med*	clutch
Musach	moo-*sach*	garage
Shimsha	sheem-*shah*	windshield
Shemen	*sheh*-mehn	oil
Timsoret	teem-soh-*reht*	transmission
Tzmigim	tzmee-*geem*	tires

Talkin' the Talk

Tamir's car has broken down. He flags down a woman named Sigal for help.

Tamir: **Hatzilu! Hatzilu!**
hah-*tzee*-loo! hah-*tzee*-loo!
Help! Help!

Sigal: **Mah Karah?**
mah kah-*rah*?
What happened?

Tamir: **Ha'Mechonit Sheli Hitkalkelah.**
hah-meh-choh-*neet* sheh-*lee* heet-kahl-keh-*lah*.
My car has broken down.

Sigal: **Ptach Et Michseh Ha'Mano'a.**
pe-*tach* eht meech-*seh* hah-mah-*noh*-ah.
Open the hood.

Tamir: **At Y'chola LeTaken Et Zeh?**
aht yeh-choh-*lah* leh-tah-*kehn* eht zeh?
Can you fix it?

Sigal: **Lo. Ha'Chagorah Shelcha Nishbera. Hitkasher L'Musach.**
loh. hah-chah-goh-*rah* shehl-chah neesh-beh-*rah*.
heet-kah-*shehr* leh-moo-*sach*.
No. Your fanbelt is broken. Call a garage.

Words to Know

B'Seder	beh-<u>seh</u>-dehr	okay
Dachuf	dah-<u>choof</u>	urgent
Delek	<u>deh</u>-lehk	gasoline
Ezra	ehz-<u>rah</u>	help
Galgalim	gahl-gah-<u>leem</u>	wheels
Hazilu	hah-<u>tzee</u>-loo	rescue
Mano'a	mah-<u>noh</u>-ah	engine
Mechonit	meh-choh-<u>neet</u>	car
Musach	moo-<u>sahch</u>	garage
Shemen	<u>sheh</u>-mehn	oil
Tzmigim	tzmee-<u>geem</u>	tires

Doctor, Doctor: Give Me the News

Are you feeling a bit under the weather? Are you flummoxed and can't figure out what's wrong? Maybe you need to see the doctor. Doctors have studied medicine for many years and can help relieve your symptoms. Use these Hebrew words when talking to a doctor or nurse:

- **Ach** (ach; nurse) (MS)

  Achot (ach-*hoht;* nurse) (FS)
- **Beit Cholim** (bayt choh-*leem;* hospital)
- **Chadar Miyun** (chah-*dahr* mee-*yoon;* emergency room)
- **Rofeh** (roh-*feh;* doctor) (MS)

  Rof'ah (rohf-*ah;* doctor) (FS)

The knee bone's connected to the leg bone: Identifying your body parts

If you want to explain that some part of your body hurts, you can say **Koev Li Ha . . .** (koh-*ehv lee* hah; . . . hurts me), and then finish the sentence with the body part that hurts. Just take your pick from the Hebrew words in Table 16-2.

Table 16-2	Body Parts	
Hebrew	*Pronunciation*	*Translation*
Af	ahf	nose
Aynayim	ay-*nah*-eem	eyes
Berech	*beh*-rech	knee
Beten	*beh*-tehn	stomach
Chazeh	chah-*zeh*	chest
Etzem	*eh*-tzehm	bone
Gav	gahv	back
Karsol	kahr-*sohl*	ankle
Katef	kah-*tehf*	shoulder

(continued)

Table 16-2 *(continued)*

Hebrew	Pronunciation	Translation
Lev	lehv	heart
Ozen	*oh*-zehn	ear
Peh	peh	mouth
Re'ot	reh-*oht*	lungs
Regel	*reh*-gehl	leg
Rohsh	rohsh	head
Tzavar	tzah-*vahr*	neck
Zro'a	*zroh*-ah	arm

Be careful not to put the sentence in a different order, with the body part first, because then you'd have to conjugate the verb *aches* in the feminine form because the names of most parts of the body are feminine (with the exception of breasts — go figure).

Describing your symptoms

Poor baby! Not feeling well? Do you have a **Ke'ev-Rohsh** (keh-*ehv* rohsh; headache)? A **Ke'ev Beten** (keh-*ehv beh*-tehn; stomachache)? A **Chom** (chom; fever)? Have you **Hiketah** (hee-*keh*-tah; been throwing up) (MS)? Oy-vey. I hope you don't have the flu. Use some of these Hebrew words and phrases to describe your condition:

✔ **Ani Choleh.** (ah-*nee* choh-*leh;* I'm sick.) (MS)

   Ani Cholah. (ah-*nee* choh-*lah;* I'm sick.) (FS)

✔ **Ani Hikahti.** (ah-*nee* hee-keh-*tee;* I threw up.)

✔ **Ani Hitztananti.** (ah-*nee* heetz-tah-*nahn*-tee; I caught a cold.)

✔ **Ani Lo Margish Tov.** (ah-*nee* loh mahr-*geesh* tohv; I don't feel well.) (MS)

   Ani Lo Margisha Tov. (ah-*nee* loh mahr-gee-shah tohv; I don't feel well.) (FS)

✔ **Ani Allergi L . . .** (ah-*nee* ah-*lehr*-gee leh; I'm allergic to . . .) (MS)

   Ani Allergit L . . . (ah-*nee* ah-*lehr*-geet leh; I'm allergic to . . .) (FS)

✔ **Yesh Li Shilshul.** (yesh lee shil-*shool;* I have diarrhea.)

✔ **Yesh LiChom.** (yesh lee chohm; I have a fever.)

Explaining your unique medical needs

Doctors have a hard time treating you if they can't see the full picture. You must fill your doctor in on your medical history. If you're allergic to medication or have any other medical conditions, tell your doctor. Otherwise the results may be disastrous.

The Hebrew phrase **Yesh Li** (yesh *lee*), which translates as "I have" literally means "there is to me." For this reason, the following phrases are gender neutral. Both males and females can use them without changing the conjugation.

- **Ani B'Herayon.** (ah-*nee* buh-heh-rah-*yohn;* I'm pregnant.)
- **Yesh Li As'ma.** (yesh lee ahs-*mah;* I have asthma.)
- **Yesh Li Machala'at Nefila.** (yesh lee mah-chah-*laht* neh-fee-*lah;* I have epilepsy.)
- **Yesh Li Kotzev Lev.** (yesh lee koh-*tzehv-lehv;* I have a pacemaker.)
- **Yesh Li Sakeret.** (yesh lee sah-*keh*-reht; I have diabetes.)

Receiving a thorough examination

After you walk into the examination room, usually the nurse comes in, weighs you, and takes your **Chom** (chohm; temperature), **Dofek** (*doh*-fehk; pulse), and **Lachatz Dam** (*lah*-chahtz dahm; blood pressure). Then the doctor arrives and probably asks some of the following questions about your condition:

- **Eich Atah Margish?** (ehch ah-*tah* mahr-*geesh;* How do you feel?) (MS)

  Eich At Margisha? (ehch aht mahr-gee-*shah;* How do you feel?) (FS)
- **Mah Mafri'a L'cha?** (mah mah-*free*-ah luh-*chah;* What's bothering you?) (MS)

  Mah Mafri'a Lach? (mah mah-*free*-ah *lach;* What's bothering you?) (FS)
- **Ko'ev L'cha Mashehu?** (koh-*ehv* leh-*chah mah*-sheh-hoo; Does something hurt you?) (MS)

  Ko'ev Lach Mashehu? (koh-*ehv-lach mah*-sheh-hoo; Does something hurt you?) (FS)
- **Eifo Zeh Ko'ev L'cha?** (ay-*foh* zeh koh-*ehv* leh-*chah;* Where does it hurt you?) (MS)

  Eifo Zeh Ko'ev Lach? (ay-*foh* zeh koh-*ehv lach;* Where does it hurt you?) (FS)
- **Koev L'Cha Po?** (koh-*ehv* luh-*chah* poh; Does it hurt here?) (MS)

  Koev Lach Po? (koh-*ehv lach* poh; Does it hurt here?) (FS)

✔ **Kamah Z'Man Hirgashta Kacha?** (kah-*mah* z-*mahn* heer-*gahsh*-tah *kah*-chah; How long have you felt this way?) (MS)

Kamah Z'Man Hirgasht Kacha? (kah-*mah* z-*mahn* heer-*gahsht* kah-*chah;* How long have you felt this way?) (FS)

✔ **Ha'im Atah Allergi?** (hah-*eem* ah-*tah* ah-*lehr*-gee leh-*mah*-sheh-hoo; Are you allergic to anything?) (MS)

Ha'im At Allergit L'Mashehu? (hah-*eem* ah-*aht* ah-*lehr*-geet leh-*mah*-sheh-hoo; Are you allergic to anything?) (FS)

Take a look at Chapter 7 where I cover the days and weeks.

During the office visit, the doctor examines different body parts and asks for symptoms to determine a diagnosis. To prepare for the examination, he or she may ask you to do any of the following commands:

✔ **Na Lehorid Et Ha'Chultzah.** (nah leh-hoh-*reed* eht hah-chool-*tzah;* Please take off your shirt.)

✔ **Na Linshom.** (nah leen-*shom;* Please breathe.)

✔ **Na Le'hishta'el.** (leh-hish-tah-*ehl;* Please cough.)

✔ **Na Lishkav al HaGav.** (nah leesh-*kahv* ahl hah-*gahv;* Please lie down.)

✔ **Tiftach Et HaPeh.** (teef-*tach* eht hah-*peh;* Open your mouth.) (MS)

Tiftechi Et HaPeh. (teef-te*h*-chee eht hah-*peh;* Open your mouth.) (FS)

Paying attention to the diagnosis

After the doctor examines you, he or she will give a **Ivchun** (eev-*choon;* diagnosis). The following words are possible diagnoses:

✔ **Aba'abu'ot Ru'ach** (ah-*bah*-ah-boo-oht *roo*-ach; chicken pox)

✔ **Daleket** (dah-*leh*-keht; an infection)

✔ **Hitztanenut** (heetz-tah-neh-*noot;* a cold)

✔ **Sha'pa'at** (shah-*pah*-aht; the flu)

✔ **Tzahevet** (tzah-*hehv*-eht; jaundice)

You may want to ask: **Ha'Im Zeh Madbik?** (hah-eem zeh-mahd-*beek;* Is it contagious?). I hope you don't need a **Z'rikah** (zree-*kah;* injection) or a **Toch Vridi** (tohch-vree-*dee;* I.V.).

When people are ill, wish them a **Refu'ah Shleimah** (reh-foo-*ah* shuh-lay-*mah;* a complete recovery). If someone is quite ill, you can recite a **Misheberach L'Cholim** (mee-sheh-bay-*rach* leh-choh-*leem;* a special prayer for the sick) during the Torah service in synagogue on Monday, Thursday, or Saturday mornings.

Talkin' the Talk

Shulamit hasn't been feeling well. At the doctor's office, Shulamit asks her doctor if she can figure out what's wrong. (Track 28)

Shulamit: **Ani Lo Margisha Tov.**
ah-*nee* loh mahr-gee-*shah* tohv.
I don't feel well.

Doctor: **Mah Mafri'ah Lach?**
mah maf-ree-*ah* lach?
What's bothering you?

Shulamit: **Ko'ev Li Ha'Garon, HaRosh VeHa'Beten.**
koh-*ehv* lee hah-gah-*rohn* hah-rohsh veh-hah-*beh*-tehn.
My ears, head, and stomach hurt.

Doctor: **Mah Od?**
mah ohd?
What else?

Shulamit: **Ani Hiketi V'yehsh Li Shilshul.**
ah-nee hee-keh-tee veh-yesh lee sheel-*shool*.
I threw up and I also have diahrrea.

Doctor: **Tiftechi Eht HaPeh V'Tinshemi B'Vakasha.**
teef-teh-*chee* eht hah-*peh* veh-teen-sheh-*mee* beh-vah-kah-*shah*.
Open your mouth and breathe please.

Doctor: **Yesh Lach Shapa'at. Ani Roshemet Lach Mirsham. Ve'Gam At Tzricha LaNu'ach Shavua.**
yehsh lach shah-*pah*-aht. Ah-nee roh-*she*-meht lach meer-*shahm*. veh-gahm aht tzree-*chah* lah-*noo*-ach shah-*voo*-ah.
You have the flu. I'm writing you a prescription. And you also need to rest for a week.

Going to the pharmacy

Perhaps the doctor gives you a **Mirsham** (meer-*shahm;* prescription) and you need to go to the **Beit Mirkachat** (bayt meer-*kah*-chaht; pharmacy) to fill it. While you're there, you may want to pick up some of the following items:

- ✔ **Akamol** (ahk-ah-*mohl;* Israeli nonaspirin)
- ✔ **Asprin** (ahs-*preen;* aspirin)
- ✔ **Kadurey Sheyna** (kah-doo-*ray* shay-*nah;* sleeping pills)
- ✔ **Madchom** (mahd-*chohm;* thermometer)
- ✔ **Trufat Shi'ul** troo-*faht* shee-*ool;* cough medicine)
- ✔ **Tachboshet** (tahch-*boh*-sheht; bandage)
- ✔ **Tipot Shiul** (tee-*poht* shee-*ool;* cough drops)
- ✔ **Tavliot Neged Chumtziyut** (tahv-lee-*oht neh*-gehd choom-tzee-*yoot;* antacid tablet)

Talkin' the Talk

Prescription in hand, Shulamit goes to the nearest pharmacy to have her prescription filled.

Shulamit: **Shalom. Yesh Li Mirsham MiHaRofeh.**
shah-*lohm.* yesh lee meer-*shahm* me-hah-roh-*feh.*
Hello. I have a prescription from the doctor.

Pharmacist: **T'ni Li Et HaMirsham.**
t-*nee lee* eht hah-meer-*shahm.*
Give me the prescription.

Shulamit: **Henei. Efshar Lakachat Akamol Gam Ken?**
hee-*nay* ehf-*shahr* lah-*kah*-chat ah-kah-*mohl* gahm kehn?
Here it is. May I take Akamol (Israeli nonaspirin), too?

Pharmacist: **Bevadai. Henei Ha'Trufot Shelach G'veret. Kchi Shnei Kadurim Shalosh Pe'amim B'Yom Bemeshech Shavua.**
beh-vah-*dai.* hee-*nay* haht-roo-*foht* sheh-*lach* ge-*veh*-reht. *kchee* sh-*nay* kah-doo-*reem* pah-ah-*mah*-yeem buh-*yohm* be-*meh*-shech shah-*voo*-ah.
Certainly. Here's your medicine, Miss. Take two pills three times a day for a week.

Shulamit: **Todah Rabbah Lecha.**
toh-*dah* rah-*bah* leh-*chah.*
Thank you very much.

Doctor: **Ayn Be'ad Mah. Targishi Tov V'Refu'a Shleimah.**
ayn be'*ahd mah.* tahr-*gee*-shee tohv veh-reh-foo-*ah*
sh-lay-*mah.*
No problem. Feel better and have a complete recovery.

Words to Know

Ach (MS)	ahch	nurse
Achoht (FS)	ach-<u>hoht</u>	nurse
Beit Cholim	bayt choh-<u>leem</u>	hospital
Beit Mirkachat	bayt meer-<u>kah</u>-chat	pharmacy
Cherum	cheh-<u>room</u>	emergency
Cholah (FS)	choh-<u>lah</u>	sick
Choleh (MS)	choh-<u>leh</u>	sick
Chom	chohm	fever
Daleket	dah-<u>leh</u>-keht	infection
Dofek	<u>doh</u>-fehk	pulse
Kadurim	kah-door-<u>eem</u>	pills
Lachatz Dam	<u>lah</u>-chatz dahm	blood pressure
Mirsham	meer-<u>shahm</u>	prescription
Rofah (FS)	rohf-<u>ah</u>	doctor
Rofeh (MS)	rohf-<u>eh</u>	doctor
Trufot	troo-<u>foht</u>	medicine
Yesh Li	yesh <u>lee</u>	I have
Zrikah	zree-<u>kah</u>	shot

The Red Shield of David: Reaching out to others in need

The Israeli version of the Red Cross is the **Magen David Adom** (mah-*gehn* dah-*veed* ah-dohm), the Red Shield of David. If you're in Israel, use the following emergency phone numbers:

✔ **Mishtara** (meesh-tah-*rah;* police): 100

✔ **Ambulance** (*ahm*-boo-lahnce; ambulance): 101

✔ **Mechabey Esh** (meh-chah-*bay* esh; fire department): 102

Getting Help After You've Been Robbed

If you've ever walked out to your car to see that it was broken into, you know the sinking feeling in your stomach. I hope you never have to experience it. But if someone steals something from you, you can say: **Mishehu Ganav Li Et Ha . . .** (*mee*-sheh-hoo gah-*nahv* lee eht hah . . .; Someone stole my . . .).

If someone breaks into your car or your house, you say:

✔ **Partzu Li Eht Ha'Mechonit.** (pahr-*tzoo* lee eht hah-meh-choh-*neet;* My car has been broken into.)

✔ **Partzu Li La'Bayit.** (pahr-*tzoo* lee lah-*bye*-yeet; My house has been broken into.)

People will probably tell you to **Na Lifnot El Ha'Mishtara** (nah leef-*noht* ehl hah-meesh-tah-*rah;* go to the police).

Or what if your house — **Chas V'Chalilah** (chahs veh-*chah*-lee-*lah;* heaven forbid) — catches on fire. Call the **Mechabey Esh** (meh-chah-*bay* aysh; fire department) for **Kaba'im** (kah-bah-*eem;* fire fighters) to come and extinguish the **Esh** (aysh; fire).

Talkin' the Talk

Randy, an American tourist, was pickpocketed. Luckily, he sees a police officer and flags her down.

Randy: **Slicha Shoteret. Ganvu Li Et Ha'Arnak.**
slee-*chah* shoh-*tai*-reht, gahn-voo *lee* eht hah-ahr-*nahk*.
Excuse me, police officer. My wallet has been stolen.

Officer: **Matai Zeh Karah?**
mah-*tye* zeh kah-*rah*?
When did it happen?

Randy: **Bdiuk Achshav.**
beh-dee-*yook* ahch-*shahv*.
Just now.

Officer: **Hem Pag'u B'Cha?**
hehm, pah-*g*-oo buh-*chah*?
Did they hurt you?

Randy: **Lo Ani B'Seder.**
loh. ah-nee beh-*seh*-dehr.
No. I'm alright.

Words to Know

Arnak	ahr-<u>nahk</u>	wallet
Esh	aysh	fire
Lifrotz	lee-<u>frohtz</u>	to break into
Lignov	leeg-<u>nohv</u>	to steal
Kaba'i (MS)	kah-<u>bye</u>	firefighter
Kaba'im (FS)	kah-bah-<u>eem</u>	firefighter
Mechabey Esh	meh-chah-<u>bay</u> aysh	fire department
Mishtara	meesh-tah-<u>rah</u>	police station
Shotair (MS)	shoh-<u>tehr</u>	police officer
Shoteret (FS)	shoh-tehr-<u>reht</u>	police officer

Fun & Games

Using the words in the word bank, identify the body parts in Hebrew.

Aynayim, Beten, Gav, Katef, Ozen, Regel, Rohsh, Tzavar, Zro'a

A. _____   F. _____

B. _____   G. _____

C. _____   H. _____

D. _____   I. _____

E. _____   J. _____

Part IV
Sacred Hebrew

The 5th Wave   By Rich Tennant

"You don't have to tell me the kitchen's a spiritual center of the house. God knows I pray for a good matzah kugel every Passover."

In this part . . .

Hebrew, often called The Holy Tongue, is the language of Jewish prayers, holidays, and sacred texts. This part introduces you to some specifically religious vocabulary, enabling you to unlock the wisdom of Judaism's sacred texts and holy days.

Chapter 17

Let's Get Biblical

The Hebrew Bible comprises three parts: "The Torah," which consists of the five books of Moses (Genesis, Exodus, Leviticus, Numbers, and Deuteronomy); "The Prophets" or **Nevi'im** (neh-vee-*eem*), which include Judges, Joshua, Samuel, Kings as well as the prophets, such as Isaiah, Jeremiah, Amos, and others; and finally "The Writings" or **Ketuvim** (keh-too-*veem*), which include the Psalms, the Song of Songs, Ruth, and other Biblical writings. Together, these sections are called the **Tanach** (tah-*nahch*) in Hebrew. Calling the Hebrew Bible the "Old Testament" is a misnomer because that term is a Christian concept. Refer to the Jewish Biblical cannon either by its Hebrew name, the **Tanach,** or simply "the Hebrew Bible."

Although the Modern Hebrew you may hear spoken on the streets of Tel Aviv and around the world bears much similarity with its Biblical progenitor, you can notice a few differences. Comparing Modern Hebrew with Biblical Hebrew is like comparing modern English with its Shakespearian cousin. They're the same language, but different.

In this chapter, I introduce you to a few of the key features of Biblical Hebrew to help you understand the world's best-selling book in its original language.

Figuring Out the Word Order in Biblical Hebrew

The first difference in Biblical Hebrew is word order. Although in Modern Hebrew the noun or pronoun often starts a sentence, in Biblical Hebrew, a verb often takes the lead. Table 17-1 shows a couple of examples.

Table 17-1	Checking Out Biblical Word Order
Modern Hebrew	**Biblical Hebrew**
HaShem Amar El B'nei Yisrael (hah-*shem* ah-*mahr* ehl buh-*nay* yees-rah-*ehl;* The Eternal One Said to the Children of Israel)	**VaYomer HaShem El Bnai Yisrael Le'emor . . .** (vah-yoh-*mehr* hah-*shehm* ehl buh-*nay* yees-rah-*ehl* leh-eh-*mohr; Literally:* Said the Eternal One to the Children of Israel, saying)
Melech Chadash Kam B'Mitzrayim She'Lo Yada Et Yosef (meh-*lehch* chah-*dahsh* kahm buh-meez-*rah*-yeem sheh-*loh*-yah-*dah* eht yoh-*sehf;* a new king arose in Egypt that did not know Joseph.)	**VaYakam Melech-Chadash Al-Mitzrayim Asher Lo'Yada Et Yosef** (vah-*yah*-kahm meh-lehch-chah-*dahsh* ahl-meetz-*rah*-yeem ah-*sher* loh-yah-*dah* eht yoh-*sehf;* [There] Arose a new king over Egypt that did not know Joseph) (Exodus 1:8)

Biblical Hebrew possesses something unique called the **Vav Hahipuch** (vahv hah-hee-*pooch*), what I like to call *the amazing reversing Vav.* You place the **Vav Hahipuch** in front of a past-tense verb, and the verb "magically" changes to the future tense. Place it in front of a future-tense verb, and the verb amazingly changes to the past tense. For example: **HaKimoti** (hah-kee-*moh*-tee) means, "I established." But if you put *the amazing reversing Vav* in front, **Ve'Hakimoti** (veh-hah-kee-*moh*-tee) means, "I will establish" as in this verse:

> **Ve'Hakimoti Et Briti Beyni U'Veincha . . .** (veh-hah-kee-*moh*-tee eht bree-*tee* bay-*nee* oo-vayn-*chah;* I will establish my covenant between me and you . . .) (Genesis: 17:7)

Look at another example. **Shinantam** means, "taught them." But with *the amazing reversing Vav* in front, **V'Shinantam** becomes "you shall teach them" as in this verse:

> **V'Shinantam L'Vanecha** (veh-shee-nahn-*tahm* leh-vah-*neh*-chah; You shall teach them to your children . . .) (Deuteronomy 6:7)

Note: Sometimes, in addition to its role in changing verb tense, the **Vav Hahipuch** does double-duty and means *and.*

Clipped verbs are another phenomenon in Biblical texts. You get a clipped verb when the end letter *hey* disappears. This happens often when a verb is paired with a **Vav Hahipuch.**

For example, the Hebrew verb for "he will see" is **Yir'eh** (yeer-*eh;* he will see). An example of this verb "getting clipped" with a **Vav Hahipuch** is: **Va'Yar** (vah-*yahr;* he saw). Watch closely because three things happen:

1. First the *hey* (which is represented with **eh**) drops off.

2. Then, because the *hey* dropped off, the vowel under the *yod* (represented by the **Y**) changes from an "*ee*" sound to an "*ah*" sound.

3. Finally, an *amazing reversing Vav* is added to the front of the word, changing it from past tense to future tense.

Table 17-2 shows some common Biblical verbs with **Vav Hahipuch**. I put an asterisk next to clipped verbs.

Table 17-2	Looking At Biblical Verbs	
Hebrew	**Pronunciation**	**Translation**
Vayelech	vah-yee-*lech*	he went
*Vayar	vah-*yahr*	he saw
Vayehi	vah-yeh-*hee*	it came to pass
*Vaya'as	vah-*yah*-ahs	he made
*Vayar	vah-yahr	he saw
*Vaya'an	vah-*yah*-ahn	he answered
Va'ta'an	vah-*tah*-ahn	she answered
*Vayetzav	vah-yeh-*tzahv*	he commanded
*Vayetzeh	vah-yeh-*tzeh*	he went out
Vatetze	vah-tey-*tzeh*	she went out
Ve'ahavta	vuh-ah-hahv-*tah*	you shall love
Ve'shinantam	vuh-shee-nahn-*tahm*	you (MP/FP) shall teach them
V'Shamru	vuh-shahm-*roo*	they will guard
V'Hakimoti	veh-hah-kee-*moh*-tee	I will establish

Words to Know

B'nai Yisrael	buh-nay yees-rah-_ehl_	children of Israel
Briti	bree-_tee_	my covenant
L'Vaneicha	leh-vah-_neh_-chah	to your children
Melech	_meh_-lehch	king
Mitzrayim	meetz-_rah_-yeem	Egypt
Ve'Shinantam	veh-shee-_nahn_-tam	you shall teach them
Vayakam	vah-yah-_kahm_	arose
VaYomer	vah-_yoh_-mehr	he said
Yisrael	yees-rah-_ehl_	Israel

Emphasizing When God Really Meant It

Sometimes when the Bible says something, it _really_ means it. And because the Bible doesn't have italics, it uses a special tense called the emphatic tense (or emphatic verb construct) to show when God meant business. The word to be emphasized is repeated, and during the second repetition a suffix of **un** (_oon_) or **ot** (_ot_) is added. See if you can find them in the following passages:

ShaMor Tishmarun Et Mitzvot-Hashem Eloheichem (sha-_mohr_ teesh-mah-_roon_ eht meetz-_voht_ hah-_shehm_ eh-loh-hay-_chehm;_ You shall _surely keep_ the commandments of the Eternal One your God.) (Deuteronomy 6:17)

VaYomer HaNachash El HaIshah Lo Mot Tamutun (vah-_yoh_-mehr hah-nah-_chahsh_ ehl hah-ee-_shah_ loh moth tah-moot-_toon;_ The snake said to the woman, you are _absolutely not going to die_.) (Genesis: 3:4)

Biblical text also demonstrates emphasis by placing the command form of a verb in front of the future-tense verb (see Appendix A for more examples of future tense). For example:

VaYetzav HaShem Eloheem Al Ha'Adam Le'emor MiKol Etz HaGan achol Tochal. U'Me'Etz Ha'Da'At Tov VaRah Lo Tochel Mimenu Ki B'Yom Achl'Cha Mimenu Mot Tamut.

vah-yeh-*tzahv* hah-*shehm* eh-loh-*heem* ahl-hah-ah-*dahm* leh-eh-*mohr* mee-*kohl* ehtz hah-*gahn* ah-*chohl* toh-*chehl*, oo-meh-*ehtz* hah-*dah*-aht tohv vah-*rah* loh toh-*chahl* mee-*meh*-noo kee buh-*yohm* och-leh-*chah* mee-*meh*-noo moht tah-*moot*.

God the Eternal One commanded the human being saying from all the trees in the garden you can absolutely eat. But from the Tree of Knowing Good and Evil you shall not eat from it, for on the day of your eating (it) you will absolutely die. (Genesis 2:16-17)

The Hebrew word for the first human being **Adam** (hah-ah-*dahm*) is connected to the Hebrew word for earth **Adamah** (ah-dah-*mah*) from which the human being was created. According to rabbinic wisdom, this being was initially neither male nor female and was actually a hermaphrodite. Hence, calling this creature "a man" is a bit of a misnomer. Better translations are either "human being" or "earthling."

Words to Know

Eitz	*ehtz*	tree
HaGan	hah-*gahn*	the garden
Ishah	ee-*shah*	woman
Le'emor	leh-eh-*mohr*	saying
Mitzvot	meetz-*voht*	commandments
Mot Tamut	moht tah *moot*	you shall die
Nachash	nah-*chahsh*	snake
Shamor	shah-*mohr*	you shall keep, guard
Tochel	toh-*chehl*	you shall eat
VaYetzav	vah-yeh-*tzahv*	commanded
VaYomer	vah-yoh-*mehr*	said

Naming the books of the Bible

The books of the Hebrew Bible have Hebrew names of course! While this list is by no means exhaustive, I list the Hebrew names of the books with which you may be most familiar.

Hebrew	Pronounciation	Translation
Bereisheit	buh-reh-*sheet*	Genesis
Shemot	sh-*moht*	Exodus
Vayikra	vah-yee-*krah*	Leviticus
Bamidbar	bah-meed-*bahr*	Numbers
D'Varim	duh-var-*reem*	Deuteronomy
Yehoshua	yeh-hoh-*shoo-ah*	Joshua
Shoftim	shohf-*teem*	Judges
M'lachim	m-lah-*cheem*	Kings
Yesha'ayahu	yeh-sha-ah-*yah*-hoo	Isaiah
Yirmiah(hu)	yeer-mee-*yah*-(hoo)	Jeremiah
Tehilim	teh-hee-*leem*	Psalms
Mishlei	meesh-*lay*	Proverbs
Shir HaShirim	sheer hah-shee-*reem*	The Song of Songs
Kohelet	koh-*heh*-leht	Ecclesiastes

Wishing, Intending, and Prohibiting

In Biblical texts, when the text wants to indicate the speakers' wishes or intends for something to happen (as in, "and it shall come to pass") an *ah* or an *eh* will be added at the end of the word. This tense is called *cohortive*. For example:

Eten (eh-*tehn;* I will give) becomes **Etna,** which is hard to translate into English properly, but it means, "I really intend to give." When you see the *a* or *ah* at the end of the verb, it means, "I really intend to do this thing I'm saying I'm gonna' do!" Don't be confused by the **V'** in the following passage. It's not an amazing reversing **Vav,** but a regular old **V** which translates as *and.*

> **V'Etna Vriti Beni U'Veinecha . . .** (veh-eht-*nah* vree-*tee* bay-*nee* oo-vayn-neh-chah . . .; And I *really will give* my covenant between me and you (between your children) . . .) (Genesis:17:2)

In another example, **Haged** means "tell," and it is in a command form. You add two things to this verb. First, add the **a** at the end which again, is hard to translate into English, but basically when you see it, it means, *"I really want you to do this thing I'm asking you to do!"* To soften it, **Na** is added in this case, which means "please" (how very polite!) Take a look at the example of this phenomena in action:

> **Hagida-Na Lanu B'Asher Le'Mi Ha'Rah'ah Ha'Zot . . .** (hah-*gee*-dah-*nah lah*-noo bah-ah-*shehr* leh-*mee* hah-rah-*ah* hah-*zoht;* Tell us please on whose account is this evil . . .) (Jonah 1:8)

Biblical Hebrew expresses prohibitions by using the Hebrew word for "no," **Lo** (*loh*) or **Al** (*ahl*) plus the imperfect tense. For example, **Lo Tirtzach** (loh teer-*tzahch;* Don't murder) (Exodus 20:13). In general, **Lo** is for general prohibitions (for example, don't murder), while **Al** is used for forbidding a specific action, such as **Al Tishlach Yad'cha** (ahl teesh-*lahch* yahd-*chah;* do not lay; *Literally*: stretch out your hand). (Genesis: 22:12)

Deciphering One-Word Wonders

Sometimes a word only occurs, or appears, once in the Hebrew Bible. These words are called **Hapax Legomena** (hah-*pahx* leh-goh-meh-*nah*). They are special, because if they only occur once, we can't be certain what they mean in their Biblical contexts, which, of course, leaves plenty of room for the imagination! Some of the more famous **Hapax Legomena** include:

- ✔ **Tohu Va'Vohu** (*toh*-hoo-vah-*voh*-hoo): From Genesis 1:2 — The earth was **Tohu Va'Vohu** over the surface of the deep and a wind from God sweeping over the water.

    What does **Tohu Va'Vohu** mean? Scholars have written many volumes, but no one knows for sure. But the New Jewish Publication Society translates it as "unformed and void."

- ✔ **Sulam** (soo-*lahm*): From Genesis 28:12 — He had a dream; a **Sulam** was set on the ground and its top reached to the sky, and angels of God were going up and down on it.

    What's a **Sulam**? Nobody knows as it appears just once in the Hebrew Bible, but the New Jewish Publication Society translates it as "stairway." Gunther Plaut's commentary in *The Torah: A Modern Commentary* (published by the UAHC press) indicates that the word can also be translated as "ladder" or "ramp" and notes, "The **Sulam** in Jacob's dream reflects an ancient belief in a cosmic bond between heaven and earth."

You can search up more one-word wonders in an amazing reference book called a *Concordance,* (compiled by Avraham Even-Shoshan and published by Kiryat-Sefer Ltd, Jerusalem) which lists every word and phrase in the Hebrew Bible in its alphabetical order and shows exactly where it appears throughout the **Tanach.** If you want to go into further depth with Biblical Hebrew, I recommend the following book: *Grammatical Concepts 101 for Biblical Hebrew: Learning Biblical Hebrew Grammatical Concepts through English Grammar* by Gary A. Long, published by Hendrickson Publishers.

Counting Down the Greatest Biblical Hits

Many people have a list of their favorite Biblical quotations. In the following list, I share some of mine with you.

- **Shlach Et Ami Ve'Ya'avduni** (sh-*lahch* eht ah-*mee* vuh-yah-ahv-*doo*-nee; Let My people go, so that they might serve Me.) (Exodus 10:43)

- **V'Shamru B'nei Yisrael Et HaShabbat, La'Asot Et HaShabbat LeDorotam, Beini U'Vein B'Nei Yisrael Ot Hee L'Olam** (veh-shahm-*roo* buh-*nay* yees-rah-*ehl* eht hah-shah-*baht* bay-*nee* oo-*vayn* buh-*nay* yees-rah-*ehl* oh *tee* leh-oh-*lahm;* The Children of Israel shall guard the Sabbath, making the Sabbath for generations. Between Me and the Children of Israel, it shall be a sign forever.) (Exodus 31:16)

- **Ze'ev V'Taleh Yir'u K'Echad V'Aryeh K'Bakar Yochal Teven . . . Lo Yere'u V'Lo Yashchitu B'Chol Har Kodshi** (zuh-*ehv* vuh-tah-*leh* yeer-*oo* keh-eh-*chahd* veh-ahr-*yeh* kuh-bah-*kahr* yoh-*chahl teh*-vehn . . . loh yah-*reh*-oo veh-loh-yash-*chee*-too buh-*chohl* har kohd-*shee;* The wolf and the lamb shall eat together. And the lion shall eat straw like the fox . . . You shall not hurt or destroy in all my Holy Mountain.) (Isaiah 65:25)

- **V'Chitetu Charvotam L'Itim V'Chanitotayhem L'Mazmerot** (vuh-chee-teh-*too* chahr-voh-*tahm* leh-ee-*teem* veh-chah-*nee*-toh-*thei-hehm* leh-mahz-meh-*roht;* They shall beat their swords into plough shares, their spears into pruning hooks.) (Isaiah 2:4)

- **VaYigal KaMayim Mishpat U'Tzdakah KeNachal Eitan** (vah-yee-*gahl* kuh-*mah*-yeem meesh-*paht* oo-tzeh-dah-*kah* kuh-*nah*-chahl ay-*tahn;* Let law and order flow like water, justice like a strong stream.) (Amos 5:24)

- **Matzati Et She'Ahava Nafshi** (mah-*tzah*-tee eht sheh-ah-hah-*vah* nahf-*shee;* I have found the one my soul loves.) (Song of Songs 3:4)

- **Ani L'Dodi V'Dodi Li** (ah-*nee* leh-doh-*dee* vuh-doh-*dee* lee; I am my beloved's and my beloved is mine.) (Song of Songs 6:3)

✔ **Mayim Rabim Lo Yuchlu L'Chabot Et HaAhava U'Neharot Lo Yishtefuha** (*mah*-yeem rah-*beem* loh yooch-*loo* leh-chah-*boht* eht hah-ah-hah-*vah* oo-neh-hah-*rot* loh yeesh-teh-*foo*-hah; Many waters cannot extinguish love nor can rivers drown it out.) (Song of Songs 8:7)

✔ **Ki El Asher Tilchi Elech U'Va'Asher Talini Alin, Amech Ami V'Eloheich Elohei** (kee ehl ah-*shehr* tehl-*chee* eh-*lech* oo-vah-ah-*shehr* tah-*lee*-nee ah-*leen* ah-*mech* ah-*mee* veh-eh-loh-*hye*-eech eh-loh-*hye;* For wherever you go, I will go, wherever you lodge, I will lodge, your people shall be my people, and your God, my God.) (Ruth 1: 16)

✔ **Lakol Z'Man V'Et L'Chol Chefetz Tachat Ha'Shahmayim.** (lah-*kohl* zuh-*mahn* veh-*eht* leh-*chohl* cheh-fehtz *tah*-chaht hah-shah-*mye*-eem; For everything there is a season, and there is a time for every purpose under heaven.) (Ecclesiastes 3:1)

Words to Know

Ahava	ah-hah-<u>vah</u>	love
Am	<u>ahm</u>	people
Dod (MS)	<u>dohd</u>	beloved
L'Olam	leh-oh-<u>lahm</u>	forever
Mayim	<u>mah</u>-yeem	water
Mishpat	meesh-<u>paht</u>	law
Nachal	<u>nah</u>-chahl	river
Nefesh	<u>neh</u>-fehsh	soul
Ot	<u>oht</u>	sign
Rav	<u>rahv</u>	great
Tzadakah	tz-dah-<u>kah</u>	justice

Fun & Games

I've hidden the Hebrew names for some books of the Bible in this word search. I've given you the English names to let you know which ones you're looking for. The answers are in Appendix C.

Deuteronomy	Joshua	Numbers
Exodus	Judges	Proverbs
Genesis	Leviticus	Psalms

```
M  B  A  M  I  D  B  A  R  T
I  A  R  K  I  Y  A  V  I  E
S  H  O  F  T  I  M  E  S  H
H  A  U  H  S  O  H  E  Y  I
L  S  C  B  M  S  F  B' A  L
E  D' H  L  I  H  M  H  F  I
I  A  G  E  R  E  T  C  T  M
D' V  R  H  A  M  S  V  O  E
T  E  F  S  V  O  H  D  C  Y
B  M  H  I  D' T  M  B  S  A
```

Chapter 18

Like a Prayer

Most people yearn to respond to the wonders around them. Jews express this yearning in prayer and blessings directed toward God. Judaism has prayers and blessings for almost every occasion and event, from the ridiculous to the sublime, that reveals a core teaching of Judaism — that even the daily and seemingly mundane tasks of our lives offer opportunities for encountering the Divine. In this chapter, I give you some basic vocabulary so you can understand these different prayers and blessings, and I tell you how to navigate your way through the Jewish prayer book. Finally, I give you some tips on ways to make all the blessings and prayers more meaningful.

Blessing the Basics

Rabbis have taught that the nature and purpose of blessing can be found in understanding the word itself. The Hebrew word for blessing, **Bracha** (brah-*chah*), comes from the root that contains the characters *beit, resh,* and *chaf.* Other Hebrew words that share this root are:

> ✔ **Birkayim** (beer-*kah*-yeem; knees)
>
> ✔ **Breicha** (bray-*chah;* pool)

What's the connection? We bend our **Birkayim** to honor an important dignitary, such as a king, queen, or president. A **Bracha** is similar, because it's a way of honoring God. When we jump into a **Breicha,** the water can shock us and wake us up. It also surrounds us completely. So too, when we recite a **Bracha,** we wake up to blessings around us and remind ourselves that the Divine is everywhere. We must acknowledge God's presence around us: here, between you, others, the tree, the rock, and everywhere!

Judaism teaches that all creation — humanity, nature, animals, and the cosmos — emanate from One Divine Source. All is connected. Judaism teaches that to enjoy anything — food, beauty in nature, or a momentous occasion — without acknowledging its Divine Source in the form of a blessing is akin to thievery!

Deciphering the blessing formula

Judaism, being the ritualized religion that it is, has a formula upon which blessings are built. Most blessings start out with three basic parts:

- **Baruch** (bah-*rooch;* Blessed or Praised): The first part of the blessing, which offers blessings and praise.

- **Atah Adonai** (ah-*tah* ah-doh-*naye;* You God): The second part of the blessing formula, which includes God's ineffable name.

- **Eloheinu Melech Ha'Olam** (eh-loh-*hay*-noo *meh*-lech hah-oh-*lahm;* Our God and Ruler of the Cosmos): The third part of the blessing formula, which acknowledges that our God is a universal God, a God of all peoples. This portion of the blessing reminds us that because all people are connected to God, they all must be treated justly.

After the **Baruch Atah Adonai Eloheinu Melech Ha'Olam,** you can add whatever blessing is specific to the occasion. See the section, "Identifying some basic blessings," later in this chapter for examples of blessings that can follow this beginning.

In Jewish tradition, Jews no longer pronounce the name of God. During the times when the ancient Temple stood in Jerusalem, only once a year, on Yom Kippur, would the High Priest utter God's name. Today, in fact, God's name — spelled with the four Hebrew characters *yud, hey, vav,* and another *hey* — is considered so holy that it often isn't written, and instead abbreviated with the characters *yud, yud.* So how do you pronounce it? Many Jewish communities opt to address God as **Adonai** (ah-doh-*naye*), which literally means "My Lord" or "My Master." Newer traditions speak of God as **Yah** (yah), a sound that has no particular meaning, or **Shecheinah** (sheh-chee-*nah*), which means *God's presence.* Some say that the four letters of God's name correspond to the various tenses of the verb *to be* — the infinitive, present, past, and future. In other words, God is the Eternal One, beyond all time and space. I use this translation of God's name in this book.

Words to Know

Atah	ah-<u>tah</u>	You (divine)
Baruch	bah-<u>rooch</u>	bless/praise
Eloheinu	eh-loh-<u>hey</u>-noo	our God
Ha'Olam	hah-oh-<u>lahm</u>	the Cosmos
Melech	<u>meh</u>-lech	Ruler (divine)

Years before Albert Einstein (who was Jewish, by the way) posited his theory of relativity and the time-space continuum, the Hebrew language intuited this universal truth. The Hebrew word **Olam** (oh-*lahm*), which I translate as *cosmos,* contains within it the concepts of infinity in both time and space. In Modern Hebrew, **L'Olam** (leh-oh-*lahm*) means *forever* and **Olam** (oh-*lahm*) means *world* or *universe*. These two concepts of time and space are embedded in the same Hebrew word **Olam**, revealing an understanding that time and space are indeed connected.

Identifying some basic blessings

Judaism has a blessing for almost everything. Most blessings begin with the basic blessing formula: **Baruch Atah Adonai Eloheinu Melech Ha'Olam** . . . (bah-*rooch* ah-*tah* ah-doh-*naye* eh-loh-*hey*-noo *meh*-lech hah-oh-*lahm meh*-lech hah-oh-*lahm;* Praise are You Eternal One Ruler of the Cosmos) and then conclude with words specific to a particular blessing depending on the circumstance. The following paragraphs tell you some common times to say blessings and the words you need to say them.

Before eating bread

Before eating bread, you follow the basic blessing beginning with **HaMotzi Lechem Min Ha'aretz** (hah-moh-*tzee leh*-chem meen hah-*ah*-rehtz; who brings forth bread from the earth). So the entire blessing looks like this.

בָּרוּךְ אַתָּה יְיָ אֱלֹהֵינוּ מֶלֶךְ הָעוֹלָם

הַמּוֹצִיא לֶחֶם מִן הָאָרֶץ.

Baruch Atah Adonai, Eloheinu Melech Ha'Olam HaMotzi Lechem Min Ha'Aretz.

bah-*rooch* ah-*tah* ah-doh-*naye* eh-loh-*hey*-noo *meh*-lech hah-oh-*lahm* hah-moh-*tzee* leh-chem meen hah-*ah*-rehtz.

Blessed are You, Eternal One our God, Universal Presence, who brings forth bread from the earth.

Before drinking wine

Before you drink wine, you finish the basic blessing with **Boreh P'ri HaGafen** (boh-*reh* puh-*ree* hah-*gah*-fehn; who creates the fruit of the vine). The whole blessing in Hebrew is:

בָּרוּךְ אַתָּה יְיָ אֱלֹהֵינוּ מֶלֶךְ הָעוֹלָם בּוֹרֵא פְּרִי הַגָּפֶן.

Baruch Atah Adonai, Eloheinu Melech Ha'Olam Borei Pri HaGafen.

bah-*rooch* ah-*tah* ah-doh-*naye* eh-loh-*hey*-noo *meh*-lech hah-oh-*lahm* boh-*ray* puh-*ree* hah-gah-*fehn*.

Blessed are You, Eternal One our God, Universal Presence, who creates the fruit of the vine.

Over Sabbath candles

Over Sabbath candles you follow the basic blessing phrase with **Asher Kidshanu B'mitzvotav V'tzivanu L'hadlik Ner Shel Shabbat** (ah-*shair* keed-*shah*-noo buh-meetz-voh-*tahv* veh-tzee-*vah*-noo leh-hahd-*leek* nair shehl shah-*baht;* who made us holy with Divine commandments and commanded us to kindle Shabbat lights). It looks like this in Hebrew:

בָּרוּךְ אַתָּה יְיָ אֱלֹהֵינוּ מֶלֶךְ הָעוֹלָם

אֲשֶׁר קִדְּשָׁנוּ בְּמִצְוֹתָיו וְצִוָּנוּ לְהַדְלִיק נֵר

שֶׁל שַׁבָּת. (שֶׁל יוֹם טוֹב.)

Baruch Atah Adonai, Eloheinu Melech Ha'Olam, Asher Kid'Shanu B'Mitzvotav V'tzivanu L'hadlik Ner Shel Shabbat.

bah-*rooch* ah-*tah* ah-doh-*naye* eh-loh-*hey*-noo *meh*-lech hah-oh-*lahm* ah-*shair* keed-*shah*-noo buh-meetz-voh-*tahv* veh-keed-*shah*-noo leh-hahd-*leek* nair shehl shah-*baht*.

Blessed are You, Eternal One our God, Universal Presence, who sanctifies us with paths of holiness and gives us the festival lights.

For special occasions

During special occasions, birthdays, and holidays, upon eating the first fruit of its season, you conclude the basic blessing with **Sh'hecheyanu, V'Kiyemanu, V'Higianu LaZman HaZeh** (sheh-heh-cheh-*yah*-noo ve-kee-yah-*mah*-noo veh-hee-gee-*ah*-noo lahz-*mahn* hah-*zeh;* who has kept us alive, sustained us, and enabled us to reach this season). This prayer looks like this in Hebrew:

בָּרוּךְ אַתָּה יְיָ אֱלֹהֵינוּ מֶלֶךְ הָעוֹלָם

שֶׁהֶחֱיָנוּ וְקִיְמָנוּ וְהִגִּיעָנוּ לַזְּמַן הַזֶּה.

Baruch Atah Adonai, Eloheinu Melech Ha'Olam, Sh'hecheyanu, V'Kiyemanu, V'Higianu LaZman HaZeh.

bah-*rooch* ah-*tah* ah-doh-*naye* eh-loh-*hay*-noo *meh*-lech hah-oh-*lahm* sheh-heh-cheh-yah-noo veh-kee-*yeh-mah*-noo veh-hee-gee-ah-*noo* lahz-*mahn* hah-*zeh.*

Blessed are You, Eternal One our God, Universal Presence, who keeps us in life always, who supports the unfolding of our uniqueness, and who brings us to this very moment for blessing.

Before reading the Torah

During a regular *Shabbat* service, anyone in the congregation can be asked to recite a blessing before the reading of the Torah. (Don't worry; usually you know this in advance.) Usually, this blessing is chanted responsively with the other members of the congregation.

If you're called to recite the blessing, walk up to the **Bima** (*bee*-mah; podium) when the Rabbi calls your name. If you're wearing a **Tallit** (tah-*leet;* prayer shawl), the Rabbi or Torah reader will point to the word of the Torah scroll where he or she will be reading. In most traditional services, you're supposed to take the **Tzitzit** (tzee-*tzeet;* fringes) of the corner of your **Tallit** and touch them to the word in the scroll and then to your lips as an expression of your love for the Torah before beginning the blessing.

Recite the first line, and listen for the congregation's response. Then repeat their response and recite the last line of the blessing.

בָּרְכוּ אֶת יְיָ הַמְבֹרָךְ:

בָּרוּךְ יְיָ הַמְבֹרָךְ לְעוֹלָם וָעֶד:

בָּרוּךְ אַתָּה יְיָ אֱלֹהֵינוּ מֶלֶךְ הָעוֹלָם

אֲשֶׁר בָּחַר בָּנוּ מִכָּל הָעַמִּים

וְנָתַן לָנוּ אֶת תּוֹרָתוֹ: בָּרוּךְ אַתָּה יְיָ נוֹתֵן הַתּוֹרָה:

[Person saying the blessing] **Barchu Et Adonai Hamvorach.**

bahr-*choo* eht ah-doh-*naye* hahm-voh-*rahch.*

Praise the Eternal One, the one who is blessed!

[Congregation] **Baruch Adonai Hamvorach L'Olam Va'ed.**

bah-*rooch* ah-doh-naye ham-voh-*rahch* leh-oh-*lahm* vah-*ehd.*

The Eternal One is blessed forever and ever.

[Person saying the blessing] **Baruch Atah Adonai, Eloheinu Melech Ha'Olam, Asher Bachar Banu MiKol Ha'Amim, Ve'Natan Lanu Et Torato. Baruch Atah Adonai Notein HaTorah.**

bah-*rooch* ah-*tah* ah-doh-*naye* eh-loh-*hay*-noo *meh*-lehch hah-oh-*lahm* ah-*shehr* bah-*chahr bah*-noo mee-*kohl* hah-ah-*meem* veh-nah-*tahn lah*-noo eht toh-*rah*-toh. Bah-*rooch* ah-*tah* ah-doh-*naye* noh-*tehn* hah-toh-*rah.*

Praised are You, Eternal One, Our God Ruler of the Cosmos, who chose us from among the nations, and gave us Divine (*Literally:* his) Torah. Praised are You Eternal One, giver of Torah.

After reading the Torah

When the Torah reading is finished, the Rabbi or reader points to the final word of the passage. Once again you touch the scroll with the **Tzitzit** of your **Tallit** and bring the **Tzitzit** to your lips before reciting the following blessing in its entirety:

בָּרוּךְ אַתָּה יְיָ אֱלֹהֵינוּ מֶלֶךְ הָעוֹלָם

אֲשֶׁר נָתַן לָנוּ תּוֹרַת אֱמֶת

וְחַיֵּי עוֹלָם נָטַע בְּתוֹכֵנוּ:

בָּרוּךְ אַתָּה יְיָ נוֹתֵן הַתּוֹרָה:

Baruch Atah Adonai, Eloheinu Melech Ha'Olam, Asher Natan Lanu Toraht Emet, Ve'Chayai Olam Natah B'Tocheinu. Baruch Atah Adonai, Notein HaTorah.

bah-*rooch* ah-*tah* ah-doh-*naye* eh-loh-*hay*-noo *meh*-lehch hah-oh-*lahm* ah-*shehr* nah-*tahn lah*-noo toh-*raht* eh-*meht* veh-chah-*yay* oh-*lahm* nah-*tah* beh-toh-*chay*-noo bah-*rooch* ah-*tah* ah-doh-*naye* noh-*tehn* hah-toh-*rah.*

Praised are You Eternal One, Our God Ruler of the Cosmos, Who chose us from all the nations, and gave us Divine (*Literally:* his) Torah. Praised are You, Eternal One, giver of Torah.

When witnessing the wonder of nature

Finally, when witnessing the awe of nature, such as lightning, high mountains, or great rivers, finish the blessing with **Oseh Ma'aseh B'reishit** (oh-*seh* mah-ah-*seh* buh-ray-*sheet;* maker of works of creation). The next time you experience the wonder of nature, try this prayer.

בָּרוּךְ אַתָּה יְיָ אֱלֹהֵינוּ מֶלֶךְ הָעוֹלָם

עֹשֶׂה מַעֲשֵׂה בְרֵאשִׁית.

Baruch Atah Adonai, Eloheinu Melech Ha'Olam, Oseh Ma'aseh B'reishit.

bah-*rooch* ah-*tah* ah-doh-*naye* eh-loh-*hay*-noo *meh*-lehch hah-oh-*lahm* oh-seh mah-ah-*seh* beh-reh-*sheet.*

Blessed are You, Eternal One our God, Universal Presence, who makes the works of Creation.

After a meal

The traditional blessing after a meal is called the **Birkat HaMazon** (beer-*kaht* hah-mah-*zohn*) — the blessing for nourishment. Often referred to in the United States as simply the **Birkat,** this blessing celebrates the experience of being filled, nourished, and supported by food and by the universe in which the food grows. The purpose of **Birkat HaMazon** is to universalize this experience and affirm that it's available to everyone. (***Note:*** This version is shortened.)

בָּרוּךְ אַתָּה יְיָ אֱלֹהֵינוּ מֶלֶךְ הָעוֹלָם הַזָן אֶת הָעוֹלָם כֻּלוֹ בְּטוּבוֹ

בְּחֵן בְּחֶסֶד וּבְרַחֲמִים הוּא נוֹתֵן לֶחֶם לְכָל בָּשָׂר כִּי לְעוֹלָם

חַסְדוּ. וּבְטוּבוֹ הַגָּדוֹל תָּמִיד לֹא חָסַר לָנוּ וֹאַל יֶחְסַר לָנוּ

מָזוֹן לְעוֹלָם וָעֶד. בַּעֲבוּר שְׁמוֹ הַגָּדוֹל כִּי הוּא אֵל זָן

וּמְפַרְנֵס לְכֹל וּמֵטִיב לְכֹל וּמֵכִין מָזוֹן לְכָל בְּרִיּוֹתָיו

אֲשֶׁר בָּרָא. בָּרוּךְ אַתָּה יְיָ הַזָן אֶת הַכֹּל.

Baruch Atah Adonai, Eloheinu Melech Ha'Olam, HaZan et Ha'Olam Bkulo, B'tuvo, B'chen B'chesed Uv'rachamim, Hu Notaen Lechem L'chol Basar, Ki L'olam Chas'do. Uv'tuvo HaGadol, Tamid Lo Chasar Lanu, V'al Yechsar Lanu Mazon L'olam Va'ed. Ba'-avur sh'mo Ha'Gadol, Ki Hu Ayl Zahn U'Mfarnes LaKol, U'Mechin Mazon L'chol B'ri'otav Asher Bara. Baruch Atah Adonai, HaZan Et HaKol.

bah-*rooch* ah-*tah* ah-doh-*naye* eh-loh-*hey*-noo *meh*-lehch hah-oh-*lahm* hah-*zahn* eht hah-oh-*lahm* buh-koo-*loh* buh-too-*voh* buh-*chehn*-buh-*cheh*-sehd oo-veh-rah-chah-*meem*, hoo noh-*tehn* *leh*-chehm luh-*chol* bah-*sahr* kee leh-oh-*lahm* chahs-*doh*. oov-too-*voh* hah-gah-*dohl* tah-*meed* loh chah-*sahr* lah-noo veh-*ahl* yehch-*sahr* lah-noo mah-*zohn* leh-oh-*lahm* vah-*ehd*. bah-ah-*voor* sh-*moh* hah-gah-*dohl* kee-hoo ehl zahn oom-fahr-*nehs* buh-ree-oh-*tahv* ah-*shehr* bah-*rah*. *bah*-rooch ah-*tah* ah-doh-*naye* hah-*zahn* eht hah-*kohl*.

Blessed are You, Eternal One our God, Ruling Presence of the Universe, who nourishes the entire universe in Goodness; who with grace, with loving kindness, and with mercy, provides nourishment for all flesh, with everlasting loving kindness. In that great goodness we have not lacked and may we never lack nourishment evermore. For the sake of God's great name, because God nourishes and sustains all, and prepares food for all creatures which God created. Blessed are You, Eternal One, who nourishes all.

Words to Know

Boreh	boh-<u>reh</u>	creates
Brit	breet	covenant
Dor	dohr	generation
Echad	eh-<u>chahd</u>	One
El	ehl	God
Ha'Adamah	hah-ah-dah-<u>mah</u>	the earth
Ha'Gafen	hah-gah-<u>fehn</u>	the vine
Halleluyah	hah-leh-loo-<u>yah</u>	praise God
Kadosh	kah-<u>dohsh</u>	holy
Mizonot	mee-zoh-<u>noht</u>	foods
Ner	nehr	candle
Shem	shehm	name
Yisrael	yees-rah-<u>ehl</u>	Israel
Z'chor	zuh-<u>chohr</u>	remember

Spiritually Speaking: Figuring Your Way Around the Prayer Book

You may understand a little Hebrew now, but you still may not know heads from tails when you walk into services at your local synagogue. In this section, I cover some of the basic rubrics of the Jewish prayer service. I talk about the **Sh'ma** (shuh-*mah*) prayer and the blessings that surround it, which Jews recite daily in the morning and at the evening prayer service. I also spend some time on the central Jewish prayer of **Amidah** (ah-mee-*dah*) known also as **Ha'Tefillah** (hah-tfee-*lah;* the prayer), which appears in the three prayer services — morning, noon, and evening — and has both weekday and Sabbath versions. Finally, I take a look at some concluding prayers recited in all the services.

Hebrew is an incredibly easy language to read. The hardest part, after getting used to the letters, is remembering to read from right to left. In most cases, you read the consonant letter first and the vowel below it, and then you go back up to the consonant again. See Chapter 1 for a discussion of the Hebrew alphabet.

If you want some practice reading, check out: `http://ejemm.com/aleph/`. It's an online course in Hebrew reading and Jewish values. It has fun interactive activities and audio so you can hear the sounds of the letters. It'll get you reading Hebrew in no time!

The choreography of prayer

If you ever attended football games in high school, you're probably familiar with the chant, "Lean to the left, lean to the right, stand up, sit down, fight, fight, fight!" Jewish prayer services are somewhat similar (with respect to standing up and sitting down at least). At times you stand, other times you sit, and you even turn to the left and the right. You stand whenever the ark containing the Torah scrolls is open, and during the **Barchu** (bahr-*choo;* the call to worship), during the silent recitation of the **Amidah** (ah-mee-*dah*), and for the first three blessings during its repetition. You also stand during the **Aleinu** (ah-ley-*noo*), which is part of the concluding prayers of the service.

During the **Kedushah** (kdoo-*shah;* sanctification), which is the third blessing in the **Amidah,** not only do you get to stand, but you also get to stand on your toes and sway from side-to-side, like the angels of which the prayer speaks. You also stand during the **Chatzi Kadish** (chah-*tzee* kah-*deesh;* a prayer that Jews say when transitioning from one portion of the service to another). During the **Kadish Yatom** (kah-deesh yah-*tohm;* the mourners Kaddish) those not mourning the loss of a close relative usually sit down while those in mourning rise. However, some Reform congregations have all the congregants rise and recite the prayer in memory of those who lost their lives in the Holocaust and have no one to recite the prayer for them.

The Sh'ma and her blessings

The **Sh'ma** (shuh-*mah*) is known as the watchword of the Jewish faith as it affirms the unity of the universe rooted in the belief in One God. The prayer has its origins in the Torah and literally speaks to the Jewish people saying: Listen up, people of Israel! The Eternal One is our God, the Eternal One is One!

שְׁמַע יִשְׂרָאֵל יְיָ אֱלֹהֵינוּ יְיָ אֶחָד.

Sh'ma Yisrael: Adonai Eloheinu Adonai Echad.

sh-*mah* yees-rah-*ehl* ah-doh-*naye* eh-loh-*hay*-noo ah-doh-*naye* eh-chahd.

Listen, Israel: The Eternal is our God, the Eternal is One.

You can say the **Sh'ma** anytime throughout the day. These words are the last expressions a Jew is to speak before dying, and these words are contained in daily prayers and are included in the prayer upon retiring for the night. This prayer calls upon people to hear that which awakens the deeper love and compassion of their beings — to hear the deeper message that all is one.

When you want to say these prayers in Hebrew, remember that the *ch* transliteration is a guttural sound, like clearing your throat. When you see the letter *i*, it's pronounced *ee* like in the word *feet*. The *e* sounds like *eh*, and the *o* is a short *o*.

The **Sh'ma** is introduced by the call to worship, the **Barchu** (bahr-*choo*), and then is surrounded by different blessings in the morning and evening service. In the morning, the **Yotzer Or** (yoh-*tzehr* ohr) prayer, which speaks of how Divine Energy creates the world anew each day precedes the **Sh'ma.** The **Ahava Rabbah** (ah-hah-*vah* rah-*bah*), which speaks of God's love for the people of Israel as demonstrated by revealing to them divine law, follows. In the evening, the blessings before the **Sh'ma** are on similar themes.

The second paragraph of the **Sh'ma** is often referred to as the **V'ahavta** (ve-ah-*hahv*-tah; you shall love), although it is technically part of the same prayer. (***Note:*** The preceding prayer is an abridged version.)

וְאָהַבְתָּ אֵת יְיָ אֱלֹהֶיךָ בְּכָל לְבָבְךָ וּבְכָל נַפְשְׁךָ וּבְכָל

מְאֹדֶךָ: וְהָיוּ הַדְּבָרִים הָאֵלֶּה אֲשֶׁר אָנֹכִי מְצַוְּךָ הַיּוֹם עַל

לְבָבֶךָ: וְשִׁנַּנְתָּם לְבָנֶיךָ וְדִבַּרְתָּ בָּם בְּשִׁבְתְּךָ בְּבֵיתֶךָ וּבְלֶכְתְּךָ

בַדֶּרֶךְ וּבְשָׁכְבְּךָ וּבְקוּמֶךָ: וּקְשַׁרְתָּם לְאוֹת עַל יָדֶךָ

וְהָיוּ לְטֹטָפֹת בֵּין עֵינֶיךָ: וּכְתַבְתָּם

עַל מְזֻזוֹת בֵּיתֶךָ וּבִשְׁעָרֶיךָ:

V'ahavta et Adonai Elohecha, B'chol L'vav'cha, Uv'chol Naf'sh'cha, Uv'chol M'odecha. V'hayu Had'varim Ha'eleh, Asher Anochi M'tzav'cha HaYom, ahl L'va-vecha. V'she-nan-tam L'vanecha, V'debarta Bahm, B'shiv'T'cha B'vay'-techa, Uv'lech-t'cha VaDerech, Uv'shoch'b'cha Uv'kumecha. Uk'shartam L'ot Ahl Ya'decha, V'hayu L'to-tafot Bayn Aynecha. Uch'tavtam Ahl m'zuzot Baytecha, U'visharecha.

veh-ah-hahv-*tah eht* ah-doh-*naye* eh-lo-*heh*-chah buh-*chohl* leh-vahv-*chah* oov-*chohl* nahf-sheh-*chah* oov-*chohl* meh-oh-*deh*-chah. veh-hah-yoo hahd-vah-*reem* ha-*ay*-leh ah-*shehr* ah-noh-*chee* meetz-ahv-*chah* hah-yohm ahl leh-vah-veh-*chah.* veh-shee-nahn-*tam* leh-vah-*neh*-chah veh-dee-*bahr*-tah-bahm, buh-sheev-teh-*chah* buh-vay-*teh*-chah oo-veesh-ah-*reh*-cha.

Then you will love the Lord your God with all your heart, with all your soul, and with all your resources. Let these words, which I command you today, be upon your heart. Repeat them to your children, and speak of them when you sit in your house, when you walk on the way, when you lie down and when you rise up. Bind them as a sign upon your arm and let them be for frontlets between your eyes. Write them on the doorposts of your house and upon your gates.

The **V'ahavta** contains commandments to affix a **Mezuzah** (meh-zoo-*zah;* words from the Torah written on a parchment and placed within a container) to one's door, to pray with **Tefillin** (teh-fee-*leen;* little boxes containing Biblical verses strapped to the head and forearm), to wear a **Tallit** (tah-*leet;* prayer shawl), and to teach one's children about God and God's laws. The prayer also talks about the causal relations between one's actions and one's fate. If one follows the natural and divine laws of the universe, one will surely enjoy prosperity. But if one doesn't, misery is sure to follow.

The **Mi-Chamocha** (mee-chah-*moh*-chah), a prayer that recalls God's redemption of the Hebrew slaves from Egypt, follows the **Sh'ma** in both the morning and evening. In the evenings, the **Mi-Chamocha** is followed by an additional prayer called the **Hashkieveinu** (hahsh-kee-*vay*-noo), which asks that God shelter us under his divine wing, keep us safe throughout the night, and grant us peace.

Jews recite certain prayers, such as the **Barchu** (bahr-*choo*) and the **Amidah** (ah-mee-*dah*), facing east toward Zion. When you're in Israel, you face toward Jerusalem. And when you're in Jerusalem, you face toward **Har HaBayit** (hahr hah-*bah*-yeet; the Temple Mount), the remnant of the ancient Holy Temple of Jerusalem. Jewish tradition has it that not only is **Har HaBayit** the site of the ruins of the Holy Temple, it also was the site upon which Abraham, Judaism's patriarch, nearly sacrificed his son Isaac, and the spot upon which creation of the world began. Some legends claim that on this spot Jacob had his famous dream of a ladder ascending to heaven with angels upon it. In the Talmud, this spot is called the **Tabur Ha'aretz** (tah-*boor* hah-*ah*-rehtz; navel of the world) and is considered to be the connecting point between the earthly world and the heavenly world. The site remains the most holy site in the Jewish world today, and the focus of many Jewish prayers.

Prayer gear

During prayer services men, and in some liberal congregations women, may wear a head-covering called a **Kippah** (kee-*pah*) which demonstrates reverence to God. During morning services adults in the congregation — just men in traditional settings, and men and women in more liberal settings — may wear a **Talit** (tah-*leet*), which is a four-cornered garment with fringes on its corners. The fringes are tied in such a way that they number 613, the number of **Mitzvot** (meetz-*voht*) a Jew is commanded to observe. The basis for this custom is the Torah itself which states **"VeAsu Lahem Tzit-tzit al Kanfei Bigdeihem L'Dorotam"** (veh-ah-*soo* lah-*hem* tzeet-*tzeet* ahl kahn-*fey* beeg-day-*hem* leh-doh-roh-*tam;* and you shall make for yourself fringes on the corners of your garments for all generations). During weekday morning services, but not on the Sabbath, men — and in more liberal settings women — will don **Tefillin** (teh-fee-*leen*) which are little boxes containing Biblical verses strapped to the head and forearm. The orgins of this custom can be found in the Torah as well which states **"Uk'shartam L'Ot Al Yadecha, VeHayu Le'totafot Bein Aynecha"** (ook shahr-*tahm* le'*oht* ahl yahd-eh-*chah* veh-hah-*yoo* leh-toh-tah-*foht* bayn aye-neh-*chah;* And you shall make them as a sign upon your hand, as a symbol between your eyes").

Words to Know

Barchu	bahr-<u>choo</u>	raise
Choshech	choh-<u>shehch</u>	darkness
Echad	eh-<u>chahd</u>	one
Lev	lehv	heart
L'Olam Va'Ed	oh-<u>lahm</u> vah-<u>ehd</u>	forever and ever
Nefesh	<u>neh</u>-fehsh	soul
Or	ohr	light
Sh'ma	sh-<u>mah</u>	listen
Yotzer	yoh-<u>tzehr</u>	creates

Dissecting the Standing Prayer

Known as the Standing Prayer, the **Amidah** (ah-mee-*dah*) consists of three parts:

- **Shevach** (*sheh*-vahch; praise)
- **Bakashah** (bah-kah-*shah;* petition)
- **Hoda'ah** (hoh-dah-*yah;* thanks)

The **Shevach** section consists of a prayer called the **Avot** (ah-*voht*) that invokes the Jewish ancestors. In Orthodox prayer books, **Avraham** (ahv-rah-*hahm;* Abraham), **Yitzhak** (yeetz-*chahk;* Isaac), and **Ya'akov** (yah-ah-*kohv;* Jacob) are mentioned. In Conservative, Reform, Reconstructionist, and Renewal prayer books, the matriarchs **Sarah** (sah-*rah;* Sarah), **Rivkah** (reev-*kah;* Rebecca), **Rachel** (rah-*chehl;* Rachel), and **Leah** (lay-*ah;* Leah) are also invoked.

The second blessing in the **Shevach** section praises God as a mighty hero, healer of the sick and redeemer of captives. The third blessing, the **Kedushah** (keh-doo-*shah*), speaks of God's holiness.

Choosing the sight for the Holy Temple of Jerusalem

A Jewish legend tells of two siblings who farmed a plot of land together. One of the siblings was married with children, while the other sibling was single and had no children. One night after the wheat harvest, the married sibling sat awake deep in thought. "I am married with children," the married sibling thought. "But my sibling is all alone. It's not fair that I should have all this wheat to myself when I have so many people to take care of me. I am going to sneak some of my wheat into my sibling's pile." So in the darkness of the night, the married sibling did so.

Coincidentally, that same night, the single sibling sat up pondering way into the night. "I am single, I've got just myself to worry about," the single sibling thought. "But my sibling has to worry about a spouse and children! It's not fair

that I should have so much just for me. I am going to sneak some of my wheat into my sibling's pile." So in the darkness of the night, the single sibling did so.

In the morning, both siblings were puzzled when their piles of wheat were unchanged. So the process repeated itself again, and again, night after night, until the siblings finally ran into each other; each carrying sheaves of wheat to the other's side of the field. When they realized what the other had done, they embraced and wept.

God looked down upon this scene of love, harmony, and sharing, and decreed that on that very spot should the Holy Temple of Jerusalem be built, as a symbol of such values. And that spot remains, the most venerated spot in the Jewish world today.

On weekdays, the **Bakashah** section asks God for all sorts of "goodies": **Binah** (bee-*nah;* wisdom), **T'shuva** (tuh-shoo-*vah;* repentance), **Slicha** (suh-lee-*chah;* forgiveness), **Ge'ulah** (geh-oo-*lah;* redemption), **Refu'ah** (reh-foo-*ah;* healing), **Kibbutz Galuyot** (kee-*bootz* gahl-loo-*yoht;* the ingathering of the Jewish exiles to Israel), and **Tzedek** (*tzeh*-dehk; justice), just to name a few. On the Sabbath, Jews replace the petitionary prayers with a blessing praising the Sabbath day.

The **Amida** concludes with the **Hoda'ah** section, words of gratitude to God, a beseeching to God to hear our prayer, and a prayer for peace.

A prayer for peace

At the beginning of the 19th century, Rabbi Nachman of Bratslav wrote one particularly moving prayer for peace. Many synagogues in Israel and the Jewish Diaspora recite it, and Israeli children study it as part of their third-grade curriculum.

Yehi Ratzon Milfanecha Adonoi Eloheinu V'Elohei Avoteinu
SheTevtel Milchamot U'Shifihut Damim Min HaOlam.
V'Tamshich Shalom Gadol V'Niflah Ba'Olam
V'Lo Yisa Goi El Goi Cherev V'Lo Yilmadu Od Milchamah
Rak Yakiru V'Yedu Kol Yoshvei-Tevel Ha'Emet La'Amito.
Asher La Banu LaZeh Ha'Olam Bishveil Riv U'Machloket
V'Lo Bishveil Sinah V'Kinah, V'Kintur U'Shfichut Damim,
Rak Banu La'Olam K'dai Le'Hakir Otcha Titbarech LaNetzach.
U'V'Chen Trachem Aleinu, Vikuyam Banu Mikra SheKatuv:
VeNatati Shalom Ba'Aretz U'Sh'chavtem V'Ayn Machrid
V'Hishbati Chaya Ra'ah Min Ha'Aretz V'Cherev Lo Ta'Avor B'Artzchem
VaYigal KaMayim Mishpat, U'Tzadakah K'Nachal Eitan.
Ki Mal'ah Ha'Aretz De'ah Et-Adonoi KaMayim LaYam M'chasim.

May it be your will Eternal One our God and God of our ancestors that war and bloodshed will cease.
That a great, wonderful peace will envelope the whole world,
And nation will not lift up sword against nation, and neither shall they learn war any more.
Only will all the inhabitants of the earth become acquainted with and know this truth:
We did not come into this world for fighting or quarrels,
And not for hatred, zealotry, destruction or spilling of blood.
Rather, we have only come into the world to know you God and to praise you forever.
So, please have mercy upon us, and fulfill the promise written in Scriptures:
I will grant peace to the land. You shall lie down and none shall be afraid.
I will rid the land of vicious beasts and the sword shall not cross your lands.
Justice will swell up like water, righteousness like a mighty stream.
And all of the earth shall be filled with the knowing of the Eternal One as the water fills the sea.

Concluding prayers

The **Aleinu** (ah-*lay*-noo), which affirms the unique destiny of the Jewish people and looks forward to the day when all peoples of the world are united in peace and harmony, and the **Kadish Yatom** (kah-*deesh* yah-*tohm;* mourner's prayer) conclude Jewish prayer services. This prayer is actually in Aramaic, which is also written in Hebrew letters. Many congregations also add prayers for the State of Israel and prayers for peace.

Praying for peace

Because peace is such a central concept in Judaism, you can choose from many prayers for peace. The morning, afternoon, and evening **Amida** (ah-mee-*dah*) all conclude with a prayer for peace. Many congregations in Israel and across the Jewish Diaspora include a prayer for peace during the Torah service or at the conclusion of the morning prayer service.

To see and hear these prayers check out: www.learnhebrewprayers.com.

Making Prayer Meaningful

If you've mastered the Hebrew in the Jewish prayers, you've won half the battle. The other half of the battle is finding meaning in those prayers. And it isn't always easy. The rabbi of my synagogue in Jerusalem, Rabbi Levi Weiman-Kelman of *Kol HaNeshamah* said in his essay, *An Introduction to Prayer,* "Praying is a lot like playing jazz. Sometimes we all pray in harmony, other times we pray at our own rhythm, at our own volume. Jewish tradition explores the inner meaning of the words through interpretation, and ancient sacred texts stay alive when each generation reinterprets them."

While the focus of this book is **Ivrit** (eev-*reet;* Hebrew) rather than **T'fillah** (tuh-fee-*lah;* prayer), I want to guide you to some books that may make your prayer experience more spiritually satisfying. Some books I suggest are:

- ✔ *To Pray as a Jew.* Rabbi Hayim Halevy Donin wrote this classic work. This book covers the basic structure of the Orthodox prayer service and explains what to do when.

- ✔ *The Way Into Jewish Prayer.* Author Lawrence Hoffman reveals the spirituality and wisdom inherent in Jewish prayer, and the *who, what, why, when,* and *how* of Jewish prayer.

- ✔ *My People's Prayer Book.* Published by Jewish Lights Publishing, this series of books, each devoted to a different part of the Jewish prayer service, includes traditional prayer texts. It also includes pages of commentary from different scholars and rabbis.

Fun & Games

Pick your favorite blessing or prayer from the ones I present in this chapter. Try to write it in Hebrew on the following lines:

_____

_____

_____

_____

_____

_____

Chapter 19

Sacred Time, Sacred Space

· ·

In This Chapter

▶ Taking a peek inside a synagogue

▶ Holy words for holy days

· ·

In Judaism, a blessing exists that praises God for distinguishing between the holy and the everyday (or *profane*). Both the holy and the everyday are important in life. A majority of this book focuses on the everyday stuff, but at times, the holy and the everyday converge. In this chapter, I talk a bit about the sacred places of Jewish worship, and I give you some particular Hebrew vocabulary used during sacred times of the year.

Going to a Synagogue

In Hebrew, a *synagogue* is called a **Beit Knesset** (bayt *kneh*-seht; *Literally:* house of gathering). In traditional synagogues, you may find a **Mechitza** (meh-*chee*-tzah; divider between the men and women's sections), but in other synagogues, men and women sit together. The *pulpit* is called a **Bimah** (bee-*mah*). The **Aron HaKodesh** (ah-*rohn* hah-*koh*-desh; holy ark) is the special ark, or closet, that holds the Torah scrolls at the front of the synagogue. The ark is placed on the eastern side of the synagogue facing toward Zion and Jerusalem. The eternal light hanging above the **Aron HaKodesh** is called the **Ner Tamid** (nehr tah-*meed*). The **Ner Tamid** is always lit, symbolizing the eternity of God.

You can find synagogues on almost every street corner in Israel, as well as in the Diaspora (Jewish communities around the world). Synagogues are primarily places of worship, but as the name implies (the literal translation of the Hebrew word is *house of gathering*), they're the center of much of Jewish communal life. Congregants go to synagogues not only for prayer and religious study, but also for meals, celebrations, and community events. Traditionally, on weekdays, three prayer services are held each day: **Shacharit** (shah-chah-*reet;* the morning service), **Mincha** (meen-*chah;* the afternoon service), and **Ma'ariv** (mah-ah-*reev;* the evening service). Additionally, Torah services are held on Monday, Thursday, and Sabbath (Saturday) mornings, when the Torah is read aloud.

Looking at Christian churches in Israel

Many **K'nesiot** (kneh-see-*yoht;* churches) dot the landscape in Israel, including **Knessiyat HaKever** (kneh-see-y*aht* hah-*keh*-vehr; Church of the Holy Sepulcher) in the Old City of Jerusalem, where Christian faithful believe Jesus was buried. Adherents of many different streams of **Natzrut** (nahtz-*root;* Christianity) share this **K'nesiah** (Kneh-see-*yah;* church). You can see them all in action if you visit this church on **Chag HaMolad** (chahg hah-moh-*lahd;* Christmas), one of the holiest days of the **HaShanah HaNotzrit** (hah-shah-*nah* hah-nohtz-*reet;* Christian year). The Hebrew word for Christian is **Notzri** (nohtz-*ree*), which comes from **Natzeret** (nah-*tzeh*-reht; the city of Nazareth).

Checking Out Holy Words for Holy Days

The calendar you're probably most familiar with — the Gregorian or civil calendar — is a solar calendar based on the number of days necessary for the earth to revolve around the sun. The Jewish **Luach** (*loo*-ahch; calendar) is both a lunar and a solar calendar, officially called *luni-solar,* which sounds just about right because it's kinda' loony. Each month follows the phases of the moon. A month begins when the moon is just a sliver facing left in the night sky. A full moon occurs on the 15th of every month, and then towards the end of each month, the moon shrinks back into a sliver and disappears once again.

The Jewish year consists of 12 months, which are either 29 or 30 days long. A pure lunar calendar is 354 days, 11 days short of a complete solar rotation. So the Jewish calendar adds an extra month to 7 out of every 19 years, which allows it to be guided by the patterns of the moon but still keep pace with the seasons of the sun so that the Jewish holidays always fall roughly in the same season. That's why **Rosh HaShanah** (rohsh-hah-shah-*nah;* Jewish New Year) always falls roughly in the fall, **Chanukkah** (*chah*-noo-kah) falls generally in the winter, and **Pesach** (peh-*sahch;* Passover) comes each year in the spring. In the following sections, I provide a brief introduction to important Jewish holidays and some of the Hebrew vocabulary that accompanies them. To find out more about Jewish holidays, check out *Judaism For Dummies* (David Blatner and Ted Falcon, Wiley).

Shabbat: The Sabbath

Of central importance to the Jewish week, the **Shabbat** (shah-*baht;* Jewish Sabbath) is ushered in with **Hadlakat Nerot** (hahd-lah-kaht neh-*roht;* candle-lighting), **Brachot** (brah-*choht;* blessings), and **Shira** (shee-*rah;* song). The dinner table is covered with a **Mapah Levanah** (mah-*pah* leh-vah-*nah;* white table cloth), and people recite **Brachot** over the **Challah** (chah-*lah;* braided egg bread) and **Yayin** (*yah*-yin; wine) at the beginning of **Aruchat HaShabbat** (ah-roo-*chaht* hah-shah-*baht;* the festive Sabbath meal).

The lighting of candles ushers in many Jewish holidays — including the Jewish New Year and Passover. Candle-lighting marks the transitional moment between the profane and the sacred. Candles also serve a practical purpose: According to traditional practice, turning on a light or striking a match after the holiday begins is forbidden. **Yayin,** a symbol of joy in Judaism, is also used to usher in holy days. The two loaves of **Challah** symbolize the two portions of manna Jews were given on Fridays in the Sinai wilderness so they wouldn't need to search for food on the Sabbath day. The table itself is considered a mini-altar, reminiscent of the altar in the **Beit HaMikdash** (bayt hah-meek-*dahsh;* Holy Temple) that stood in Jerusalem many years ago. Jews dip their **Challah** in **Melach** (*meh*-lahch; salt) just as the holy priests in the **Beit HaMikdash** once did during the ritual offerings that took place there.

Shabbat is devoted to **Menuchah** (meh-noo-*chah;* rest), **Tefillah** (tuh-fee-*lah;* prayer), **Iyun** (ee-*yun;* contemplation), and **Z'man Mishpachti** (z-mahn meesh-pahch-*tee;* family time). The traditional greeting on the Jewish Sabbath is **Shabbat Shalom** (shah-*baht* shah-*lohm;* A peaceful Sabbath). **Shabbat** lasts for 25 hours from sunset Friday evening until sundown Saturday night when the sun has completely set in the night sky and three **Kochavim** (koh-chah-*veem;* stars) can be seen.

The holy day of **Shabbat** is ushered out with a ceremony called **Havdallah** (hahv-dah-*lah; Literally:* differentiation) where **Brachot** are said over **B'samim** (beh-sah-*meem;* spices), a **Ner Havdallah** (nehr hahv-dah-*lah;* braided Havdallah candle), and **Yayin** or another "important drink of the society." (In the summer, I like to use beer. Some people use orange juice, coffee, or even hard liquor!) The braided candle with its many wicks represents the complexity of the regular workweek, which is returning and beginning anew. The sweet smell of the **B'samim** is meant to comfort us as the peaceful **Shabbat** departs and tide us over until it returns again. When **Shabbat** is over, it's customary to wish people a **Shavu'a Tov** (shah-*voo*-ah *tohv;* good week).

Rosh HaShanah: The Jewish New Year

Rosh HaShanah (rohsh hah-shah-*nah;* Jewish New Year) literally means the *head of the year.* This holiday is also called **Yom HaZikaron** (yohm hah-zee-*kah-rohn;* Day of Memory) and **Yom HaDin** (yohm hah-*deen;* Day of Judgment). The Jewish New Year ushers in a ten-day contemplative period known as **Yamim Nora'im** (yah-*meem* noh-rah-*eem;* Awesome Days). Jews mark **Rosh HaShanah** with a festive meal during which they serve a round **Challah** (chah-*lah;* braided egg bread) along with other symbolic foods such as **Dag** (dahg; fish), **Gezer** (*geh*-zehr; carrots), and **Rimonim** (ree-moh-*neem;* pomegranates). These foods symbolize the fertility, luck, and plenty that we hope will be ours in the new year ahead. And the all-time-favorite tradition, dipping **Tapuchim** (tah-poo-*cheem;* apples) in **D'vash** (duh-*vahsh;* honey), symbolizes hope for a sweet new year.

During this holy and intense time of the year, folks engage in acts of **Tefillah** (tuh-fee-*lah;* prayer), **Teshuva** (teh-shoo-*vah;* repentance), and **Tzedakah** (tzeh-dah-*kah;* righteous acts and giving). Traditional greetings include **Shanah Tovah** (shah-*nah* toh-*vah;* A good year), **Shanah Tovah U'Metukah** (shah-*nah* toh-*vah* oo-meh-too-*kah;* A good and sweet year), and **Le'Shanah Tovah Tikatevu** (leh-shah-*nah* toh-*vah* tee-kah-*tay-voo*), which means *A good year and may we be written in the Book of Life.*

Yom Kippur: The Day of Atonement

Yom Kippur (yohm kee-*poor;* Day of Atonement) caps off **Yamim Nora'im** (yah-*meem* noh-rah-*eem;* Awesome Days). (Check out the "Rosh HaShanah: The Jewish New Year" section earlier in this chapter.) **Yom Kippur,** the most solemn day on the Jewish calendar, is marked by **Tzom** (tzohm; fasting) and **Slichot** (slee-*choht;* penitential prayers) and ends with a long, loud **Shofar** (shoh-*fahr;* blast) traditionally sounded using a ram's horn. The traditional greeting for this holy day is **G'mar Chatimah Tovah** (gmahr chah-tee-*mah* toh-*vah;* May you be sealed in for a good year).

Sukkot: The Fall Harvest Festival

The holiday of **Sukkot** (soo-*koht;* holiday of booths), which falls five days after Yom Kippur, actually has many names reflecting its many meanings. It's called **Sukkot** in honor of the **Sukkot** (*Literally:* booths) that Jews build on this holiday to commemorate the ancient Hebrews who lived in **Sukkot** in the Sinai wilderness for 40 years after the exodus from Egypt.

After breaking the fast of **Yom Kippur,** the tradition is to rush outside and begin building a **Sukkah** (soo-*kah;* temporary hut) for **Sukkot.** People generally build these **Sukkot** in their backyard, or on their patio if they don't have a backyard, by themselves or with the help of friends and family. Building a **Sukkah** and living in it for the duration of this seven-day festival is among the central observances, along with gathering **Arba'at Ha'Minim** (ahr-*bah*-aht hah-mee-*neem;* four species) — a **Lulav** (loo-*lahv;* palm branch), an **Aravah** (ahr-ah-*vah;* willow branch), **Hadas** (hah-*dahs;* myrtle) and **Etrog** (eh-*trohg;* citron) — and shaking them. You can buy these four species in a Jewish store already bound together, and then you can ritually shake them each day and carry them in the parades that happen in the synagogue each morning of this holiday.

This holiday is also called **Chag Ha'Asif** (chahg hah-ah-s*eef;* harvest holiday) because it celebrates the fall harvest, **Z'man Simchatenu** (z-*mahn* seem-chaht-*tay*-noo; season of our joy), and people sometimes simply call it **HeChag** (cheh-*chahg;* holiday).

On this holiday, you traditionally greet fellow celebrants with a hearty **Chag Sameach** (chahg sah-*may*-ach; Happy holiday) during the first two days and the last day of the festival. During the in-between days known as **Chol HaMoed** (chohl hah-moh-*ehd*), you wish others a **Moed Tov** (moh-*ehd tohv;* Good holiday — L*iterally:* good time).

Sh'mini Atzeret and Simchat Torah: Praying for Rain and Rejoicing in the Torah

Shmini Atzeret (shmee-*nee* ah-*tzeh*-reht) and **Simchat Torah** (seem-*chat* toh-*rah*) cap off the weeklong **Sukkot** festival (see the "Sukkot: The Fall Harvest Festival" section earlier in this chapter). **Shmini Atzeret** ushers in the rainy season in Israel with a special **T'fillat Hageshem** (teh-fee-*laht* hah-*geh*-shem; prayer for rain) asking God for just enough rain to be a **Bracha** (brah-*chah;* blessing) but not so much that it's a **Klalah** (klah-*lah;* curse).

Simchat Torah marks the end and beginning of the yearly Torah reading cycle. In Israel and the Reform Jewish communities of the Diaspora, folks celebrate **Shmini Atzeret** and **Simchat Torah** as one holiday, but in Orthodox and Conservative Jewish communities in the Diaspora, they're celebrated as two different holidays on two consecutive days. The traditional greeting for these holidays is **Chag Same'ach** (chahg sah-*meh*-ach; Happy holiday).

Words to Know

Chag	chahg	holiday
Nerot	neh-roht	candles
Rosh HaShanah	rohsh hah-shah-nah	Jewish New Year
Shabbat	shah-baht	Sabbath
T'fillah	tuh-fee-lah	prayer
T'shuvah	tuh-shoo-vah	repentance
Tzedakah	tzeh-dah-kah	righteous giving
Yayin	yah-yin	wine
Yom Kippur	yohm kee-poor	Day of Atonement

Chanukah: The Jewish Festival of Lights

During the darkest nights of the year shines one of the most beloved Jewish holidays, **Chanukah** (*chah*-noo-kah; *Literally:* dedication), otherwise known as **Chag HaUrim** (chahg hah-oo-*reem;* Festival of Lights). **Chanukah** celebrates the victory of the Jews over their Assyrian rulers who desecrated the Holy Jewish Temple and sought to outlaw the practice of Judaism. **Chanukah** also celebrates the Jewish rededication of the Holy Temple and their dedication to Jewish values and ways of life. Jews celebrate the eight-day holiday by lighting **Nerot** (nay-*roht;* candles) in a special **Chanukah** candelabra called a **Chanukiah** (chah-noo-kee-*yah*), adding one each night of the festival.

The candles symbolize the container of oil found in the Temple that was enough to burn for one day in the **Menorah** (meh-noh-*rah;* candelabra) but instead burned for eight. The **Nerot** are lit by a helper candle called the **Shamash** (shah-*mahsh*). The **Shamash** gives light to the other candles without diminishing its own, which reveals an important spiritual truth: When you share, you create abundance.

Traditional foods include **Levivot** (leh-vee-voht; *latkes,* potato pancakes) and **Sufganiot** (soof-gah-nee-*yoht;* jelly doughnuts), reminiscent of the container of oil found in the Temple. Spinning the **Sevivon** (seh-vee-*vohn;* dreidle, the special Chanukah top) is also part of the celebration. In Israel, the **Sevivon** has four sides with the Hebrew letters *nun, gimmel, hey,* and *peh,* which stand for the words **Nes** (nehs; miracle), **Gadol** (gah-*dohl;* great), **Haya** (hah-*yah;* happened), and **Poh** (poh; here) spelling out *a great miracle happened here.* But, in the Jewish Diaspora, the *peh* is replaced with *shin* because a great miracle happened **Sham** (shahm; there) — in Israel.

Traditional greetings for this holiday include **Chag Chanukah Sameach** (chahg chah-noo-*kah* sah-*may*-ach; Happy Chanukkah) and **Chag Urim Sameach** (chahg oo-*reem* sah-*meh*-ach; Happy Holiday of Lights).

Tu BiShevat: The Birthday of the Trees

Even the trees have a holiday on the Jewish calendar! This post-biblical holiday, known by its date, **Tu BiShevat** (tu-bee-sheh-*vaht*), the 15th of **Shevat** (sheh-*vaht;* the Hebrew month of Shevat), was originally a holiday for tax purposes. Today it has grown into a holiday celebrating **Etzim** (eh-*tzeem;* trees) and **Teva** (*teh*-vah; nature).

Of growing popularity are **Tu BiShevat** *seders* (ritual meals) modeled after the traditional Passover meal. These ritual meals, conceptualized by Jewish mystics, involve eating different types of fruits and nuts and drinking from four different-shaded cups of wine and grape juice. The first cup is all white wine symbolizing winter. The second cup is white wine with a drop of red wine symbolizing the earth's awakening with spring. The third cup is half-red and half-white symbolizing the ripening harvest during summertime. And the final cup is a cup of red wine symbolizing the fullness of the fall harvest.

In Israel, schoolchildren plant trees to celebrate **Tu BiShevat.** If you're not in Israel, it's customary to buy a tree in Israel that the **Keren Kayemet L'Yisrael** (*keh*-rehn kah-*yeh*-meht leh-yees-rah-*ehl;* Jewish National Fund) plants. You can buy one by calling the Jewish National Fund at 800-542-8733 or visiting the organization's Web site at www.jnf.org.

Purim: A Jewish Mardi Gras

Purim (poo-*reem*) is a favorite among children because they get to dress up in **Tachposot** (tahch-poh-*soht;* costumes) when they come to synagogue. Adults in the congregation chant from the **Megilat Esther** (meh-gee-*laht* ehs-*tehr;* Scroll of Esther), telling the story of the wicked Haman (hah-*mahn*) and the brave Queen Esther (ehs-*tahr*). Debauchery reins in the synagogue as children and adults alike drown out the villain's name with **Ra'ah-shanim** (rah-ah-shah-*neem;* noisemakers).

Other hallmarks of **Purim** include a festive **Se'udah** (seh-oo-*dah;* meal), **Matanot Le'evyonim** (mah-tah-*noht* leh-ehv-yoh-*neem;* gifts to the poor), and **Mishlo'ach Manot** (meesh-*loh*-ach mah-*noht;* little gift packages) containing the traditional Purim pastry — **Oznei Haman** (ohz-*nay* hah-*mahn*) — and other tasty treats. **Oznei Haman** literally translates as *Haman's ears* (although in other traditions they're considered to be Haman's hat) as a way of making fun of the villain of the Purim story. These customs originate from the Scroll of Esther itself, which states that the day the Jewish people were saved from the wicked Haman was to be a day of feasting and gift giving.

Words to Know

Chanukah	chah-noo-<u>kah</u>	Chanukah
Etz	ehtz	tree
Nes	nehs	miracle
Purim	poo-<u>reem</u>	Purim
Ra'ashan	rah-ah-<u>shahn</u>	noisemaker
Sevivon	seh-vee-<u>vohn</u>	dreidle
Teva	<u>teh</u>-vah	nature

Pesach: Passover

Pesach (*peh*-sahch; Passover) is a springtime holiday that celebrates the Hebrew Exodus from **Mitzrayim** (meetz-*rah*-eem; Egypt) when they fled the oppression of the Egyptian pharaoh and began their return to **Eretz Yisrael** (*eh*-rehtz yees-rah-*ehl;* the Land of Israel) by crossing the Sinai wilderness.

A frenzied spring-cleaning project with a spiritual component in which traditional Jewish households rid themselves of **Chametz** (chah-*mehtz;* leavened food products) ushers in this holiday of renewal. The night before the holiday begins, adults hide pieces of **Chametz** throughout the house. Children then search the darkened house for **Chametz** with the aid of a candle, feather, and spoon in a ritual called **Bedikat Chametz** (beh-dee-*kaht* chah-*mehtz*). The candle provides light in a darkened house; the feather is used to sweep the **Chametz** into the spoon. Then the **Chametz** is thrown away or burned the next day.

Families hold a traditional Passover meal called the **Seder** (*seh*-dehr; *Literally:* order) in which participants read the Passover story from a book called the **Hagaddah** (hah-gah-*dah; Literally:* the telling), drink four cups of **Yayin** (*yah*-yeen; wine), and eat other symbolic foods such as **Matzah** (mah-*tzah;* unleavened bread), **Karpas** (kahr-*pahs;* parsley), **Charoset** (chah-*roh*-seht; a food symbolic of brick mortar that different Jewish communities make with different ingredients, including apples, walnuts, and dates), **Beitzah** (bay-*tzah;* egg), and **Maror** (mah-*rohr;* bitter herbs). The **Matzah** is reminiscent of the bread the Hebrew slaves quickly made before their departure from Egypt and therefore didn't have time to let rise. The **Maror** recalls the bitterness of slavery. The **Charoset,** which is quite tasty, recalls the mortar that the enslaved Hebrews used to make bricks. And the **Beitzah** and the **Karpas** evoke the hope of this springtime holiday.

Yom HaShoah V'Ha'G'vurah: Holocaust Remembrance Day

Yom HaShoah (yohm hah-shoh-*ah;* Holocaust Remembrance Day) memorializes the tragedy of the Jews who were systematically murdered as part of Hitler's Final Solution. The Holocaust killed six million Jewish people (including a million and half children), destroying one-third of world Jewry. World Jewry chose to commemorate this dark time in our history on the Hebrew date of the 27th of **Nissan** (**Nissan** is a Hebrew month in the spring), the date of the Warsaw-ghetto uprising against the Nazis.

Jews mark the day with solemn speeches, memorial candles, and a special **Tekes** (*teh*-kehs; ceremony) that features the reading of victim's names at Israel's Holocaust memorial, **Yad VaShem** (yahd vah-*shehm*). In Israel, a siren sounds at 10 a.m., and the Israeli population stops their activities and stands at attention for the duration of the siren. Each year, Jewish youth conduct a March of the Living at the death camps in Poland and follow it with a trip to Israel for Israel's Independence Day the following week.

Yom HaZikaron: Israeli Memorial Day

Yom HaZikaron (yohm hah-zee-kah-*rohn*) is a solemn and sad day on the Jewish calendar. This day memorializes individuals who have fallen in Israel's **Milchamot** (meel-chah-*moht;* wars). Ceremonies and visits to **Har Hertzl** (hahr *hehr*-tzehl; Mount Hertzl), Israel's main military cemetery, mark this remembrance. This holiday falls one week after **Yom HaShoah.** As on **Yom HaShoah,** a siren wails at 10 a.m. At this time, all of Israel stands silently at attention in memorial to the lives that were lost.

Yom HaAtzma'ut: Israeli Independence Day

Like so much in Jewish history, the bitter is mixed with the sweet. At the close of **Yom HaZikaron,** a siren sounds marking the end of the day of mourning and ushering in the celebration of Israel's independence. In Israel, the day is marked by **Zikukim** (zee- *koo-keem;* fireworks), **Al Ha'Esh** (ahl hah-*ehsh;* barbeques), dancing in the streets, and general revelry.

Lag B'Omer: The 33rd Day of the Omer

A somewhat obscure day on the Jewish calendar, this date is the 33rd day of a counting period between **Pesach** and **Shavuot** (shah-voo-*oht;* Festival of Weeks) called the **Omer** (*oh-*mehr). **Lag B'Omer** is a traditional time for a ceremonial first cutting of a baby's hair called **Chalakah** (chah-lah-*kah*) and **Chatunot** (chah-too-*noht;* weddings). The day also commemorates the end of a plague that sickened many students of a famous first-century rabbi, Rabbi Akiva. As such, outdoor revelry and that Israeli favorite, **Al Ha'Esh** (ahl hah-*ehsh;* barbeques), mark the day.

Shavuot: The Festival of Weeks

Shavuot (shah-voo-*oht*), often translated as the *Feast of Weeks,* celebrates the high point of the Jewish calendar year: the giving of the **Torah** (toh-*rah;* Torah) on **Har Sinai** (hahr see-*naye;* Mount Sinai) to the **Am Yisrael** (ahm yees-rah-*ehl;* Jewish people). Jews celebrate the holiday with an all-night study session called **Tikkun Leil Shavuot** (tee-*koon* layl shah-voo-*oht*) and the reading of the **Aseret HaDibrot** (ah-seh-*reht* hah-deeb-*roht;* Ten Commandments) at a sunrise service. Dairy products are the food of choice for this holiday. Flowers and greenery decorate the synagogue in this happy late-spring holiday that also celebrates the **Chitah** (chee-*tah;* wheat harvest) and the **Bikurim** (bee-koo-*reem;* first fruit of the season) in Israel.

Tisha B'Av: The Ninth of Av

A somber day on the Jewish calendar, **Tish'a B'Av** (teesh-*ah* beh-*ahv;* the ninth of Av) commemorates the destruction of the **Beit HaMikdash** (bayt hah-meek-*dahsh;* Holy Temple) in Jerusalem in 356 B.C.E. and 70 C.E.. Other calamities that occurred on this day include the expulsion of the Jews from England in 1290 C.E., the expulsion of the Jews from Spain in 1492 C.E., and the mobilization of the Russian army in 1914, which led to World War I (which some people believe ultimately led to the Holocaust and the destruction of a third of the Jews in the world).

A dawn-to-dusk **Tzom** (tzohm; fast), readings of the **Eicha** (ay-*chah;* Book of Lamentations), and other rituals of **Evel** (*eh*-vehl; mourning) mark the day. On this solemn day, it's traditional *not* to greet anyone. As *Judaism For Dummies* (David Blatner and Ted Falcon, Wiley) notes, "This day raises important themes for today's Jews — loss, exile, and the desire to return home."

Tu B'Av: The Holiday of Love

Six days after **Tish'a B'Av** (teesh-*ah* beh-*ahv*) comes **Tu B'Av** (too beh-*ahv;* 15 of Av), a joyous holiday of hope and love. Tradition holds that during the time of the **Beit HaMikdash** (bayt hah-meek-*dahsh;* Holy Temple), young women wishing to marry exchanged white garments (so that no one could tell the rich women from the poor women) and danced in the light of the full **Yare'ach** (yah-*reh*-ach; moon) while men who wanted to get married danced after them in search of a **Kallah** (kah-*lah;* bride).

Today in Israel, a musical "love festival" at the shores of the **Kinneret** (kee-*neh*-reht; Sea of Galilee) marks the day. This holiday signals the beginning of the end of the year — **Rosh HaShanah** being a mere six weeks away. At this time, people begin to sign cards and other correspondences with the traditional New Year's greeting, **L'Shanah Tovah Tikatevu** (leh-shah-*nah* toh-*vah* tee-kah-*teh*-voo; May you be written and sealed for a good year).

Words to Know

Chametz	chah-<u>mehtz</u>	leaven
Chitah	chee-<u>tah</u>	wheat
Evel	eh-<u>vehl</u>	mourning
Har Sinai	hahr see-<u>nah</u>-ye	Mount Sinai
Maror	mah-<u>rohr</u>	bitter herbs
Tzom	tzohm	fast
Zikaron	zee-kah-<u>rohn</u>	memory

Fun & Games

All right. Now it's time to see how festive you're feeling. Match the holiday in the first column to the English term in the second column by drawing a line between the terms. The answers are in Appendix C.

Yom HaZikaron	Jewish New Year
Pesach	Awesome Days
Shavuot	Israeli Memorial Day
Rosh HaShanah	Day of Atonement
Yom Kippur	Holocaust Remembrance Day
Yom HaShoah	Festival of the Weeks
Shabbat	The Jewish Sabbath
Yamim Noraim	Passover

Part V
The Part of Tens

The 5th Wave   By Rich Tennant

"Saaay - I have an idea. Why don't we turn down the lights, put on some soft music, and curl up with the Talmud tonight?"

In this part . . .

This part is **Katzar Aval La'inyan** (kah-*tzhar* ah-*vahl* lah-in-*yahn;* short and to the point). It gives you several practical tips you can use as you immerse yourself in the wonderful world of Hebrew. I give you ten good tips for learning Hebrew. They worked for me, and I bet they'll work for you. Then I provide ten popular Hebrew expressions you're likely to encounter in the Jewish Diaspora (lands outside Israel), and ten Israeli expressions that'll have you sounding like a native. I also tip you off to some cool and interesting reading about the incredible Hebrew language. And last but certainly not least, read the Ten Commandments in Hebrew. It doesn't get much better than that.

Chapter 20

Ten Ways to Pick Up Hebrew Quickly

In This Chapter

▶ Eating like an Israeli

▶ Using the power of the mouse

▶ Taking a field trip

*Y*ou picked up this book, which is a great start to getting a handle on Hebrew. Now you want to pick up the Hebrew language as quickly as possible. I don't blame you. Hebrew is an amazing language, and mastering it can open doors to incredible and sacred ancient literature, modern poetry and prose, wonderful music, and conversation with native Israelis. You can speak the oldest living language spoken today. That's quite an accomplishment. In this chapter, I outline ten tips (okay, you caught me — eleven tips) to help you move closer to your admirable goal.

Read Hebrew Food Labels

Reading food labels is a great (and tasty) way to learn all sorts of words. Ask your friends in Israel to send you some stuff, or go to a store that sells Israeli products. Kosher stores in Jewish areas and many stores that sell Middle Eastern goods generally carry Israeli products. For example, the Armenian shop on my way home from work sells a lot of Israeli products. You can also order Israeli products online. One Web site I find particularly useful is Israeli Wishes site at `www.israeliwishes.com`. You can find the famed **Bamba Bisli** (*bahm*-bah *bees*-lih; snack/cereal) and all kinds of Israeli goodies. Plus you can always ask your local store to carry Israeli products. Go white and blue.

Visit an Israeli Restaurant

If you're lucky enough to live in an area with an Israeli restaurant, check it out — not only for the opportunity to speak Hebrew but also for the delicious food. You can order your grub in Hebrew, and you can also chat with the staff. They probably speak Hebrew as well as the Hebrew-speaking clientele.

Read Hebrew Publications

Several Hebrew publications are geared to the beginning Hebrew reader. My favorite is *Sha'ar La'Matchil,* an easy-to-read Hebrew weekly newspaper published by the Israeli Board of Education. You can order the paper by e-mailing Izi Aviv at yediothads@nyc.rr.com or calling 718-793-7713. You also may want to check out *La'Mishpacha,* a monthly magazine geared toward the adult Hebrew beginner. You can order this publication by logging on to the Internet and visiting http://hist-ivrit.org/lamishp/lamorder.htm. And if you're feeling up to the challenge of a whole book, the Gesher series offers short stories written in easy-to-understand Hebrew with Hebrew-English translations provided for the trickier words. You can order these books by visiting this Web site: http://wisdomcalls.com/Students/GesherHebrew.asp.

Check Out Israeli Videos, TV, Movies, and Music

Constant exposure to a language will help you acquire it. One way to increase your language-interaction time is to watch Hebrew movies and television programs. You can order Israeli television programs on DVD via the Internet (www.drishatshalom.com). The DVDs come with or without English subtitles. You can also have Israeli TV beamed right into your home. The Israeli Network (Internet: www.theisraelinetwork.com) offers 24-hour programming with live news broadcasts daily. For movies, go to your local video store and ask that they stock Israeli movies (for a list of recommendations see Chapter 7). Listening to Hebrew music is also a great way to learn the language. Pick up some CDs of the most popular artists such as David Broza, Yehuda Polliker, Rita, Ahinoam Nini, Ivri Leder, and Rami Kleinstein. Children's music is also great. (For more on Jewish music, check out www.tara.com online.)

Sing Hebrew Songs and Prayers

If you want to take a low-tech approach to picking up Hebrew more quickly, go to a traditional synagogue to reinforce your language efforts. Just open up the **Siddur** (see-*door;* prayer book) and follow right along. You'll be amazed at the results.

Listen to Hebrew Radio Programs

Several radio stations across North America offer weekly Hebrew programs. You can also access Israel radio from the Net. Want to listen to the news in easy Hebrew? Check out www.a7.org/hebrew/newspaper/news/easyhebnews.htm.

Surf the Internet

As an astute reader, you've probably noticed that I include a lot of Internet sites with my other tips in this chapter. That's because you can find Hebrew galore on the Net. To learn more about the history of the Hebrew language don't miss the official Web site of the Academy of the Hebrew Language (http://hebrew-academy.huji.ac.il/english.html). Jacob Richman has put together an amazing list of Hebrew learning sites that you can find on the Web (www.jr.co.il/hotsites/j-hebrew.htm). Among my favorites are a site that teaches you the best of Israeli slang (www.learnhebrew.org.il) and an online English-Hebrew dictionary (www.dictionary.co.il). You won't want to miss out on the Web site of the National Center for Hebrew Language (www.ivrit.org) or the Web site of the Hebrew Language and Culture Association — The Histardrut Ivrit of America (www.hebrewusa.org). And don't forget www.hebrewresources.com, a site chock-full of resources to help you learn, study, and speak Hebrew. **Glisha Ne'imah!** (guh-lee-*shah* neh-ee-*mah;* Happy surfing!).

Join the Hebrew Lovers Society

With membership in the Hebrew Lovers Society, sponsored by the National Center for Hebrew Language (NCHL), you get a newsletter, and you can stay up to date on Hebrew programs in North America. Membership is just $25 a year. To join send your check to the NCHL at 633 Third Ave., 21st Floor, New York, New York 10017. Or you can log on to www.ivrit.org, click on the membership form, fill it out, print it out, and send it in. Are you a phone person? If so, just give these folks a call at 212-339-6023.

Hang a Few Hebrew Magnets and Posters

Consistent visual exposure to print promotes language acquisition, so fill up your home with Hebrew. You can get posters with Hebrew print from your local Jewish bookstore, or order them online at www.israeliposters.co.il. Hebrew magnetic poetry makes a great addition to your fridge. You can purchase poetry magnets on the Web at www.hebrewmagnets.co.il. The magnet Web site also contains a glossary with English translations of all the words included in the kit, so a stop at this site is a great way to add to your growing vocabulary.

Take a Hebrew Class

Nothing beats a good Hebrew class. Synagogues, Jewish community centers, and centers for adult education often offer Hebrew language courses. For something more intensive, you can check out your local university to see if non-degree-seeking students are allowed to take certain classes. If you're lucky enough to live near a Jewish institution of higher learning, such as the Jewish Theological Seminary, Hebrew Union College-Jewish Institute of Religion, Baltimore Hebrew College, or the University of Judaism, take a Hebrew class at one of these fine institutions. But better yet, take a Hebrew **Ulpan** (ool-*pahn;* immersion course). Israel history of absorbing many immigrants and teaching them Hebrew has led to the perfection of the art of language acquisition and the creation of language-immersion courses called **Ulpan** (*Literally:* studio). You can find an **Ulpan** in North America or in Israel. Among the best in Israel are Ulpan Akiva in Netanya, Ulpan Etzion in Jerusalem, and my alma matter, the Hebrew University of Jerusalem. If you can't get to a class, Hebrew College offers Hebrew study online at www.hebrewcollege.edu. For a complete list of Hebrew **Ulpan,** check out this Internet link: www.ivrit.org/html/ulpan/ulpan.html.

Travel to Israel

You can't choose a better way to learn a language than to immerse yourself in it. And the best place to immerse yourself in Hebrew is Israel. Even if you travel at a time when the security situation is a bit precarious, you can do a few things to mitigate the risk (and I do hope you won't let that stop you).

If you go on an organized tour, the tour organizers will take extra measures to keep you secure, including having an armed guard with the group at all times. And, of course, it helps to simply be alert: Report unattended bags immediately (don't ever pick them up). Keep an eye out for anyone who seems suspicious or nervous, wears a coat or a jacket when it's not appropriate, or has a waist that seems a little "bulky." But again, please don't let my security advice scare you. Go!

Many options for visiting Israel exist including guided tours and extended stays. If you're Jewish and between the ages of 18 and 26, a wonderful organization called birthright israel (Internet: www.birthrightisrael.com) offers all-expense-paid 10-day educational tours to help Jewish youth become acquainted with their ancestral homeland. If you want to get off the beaten path, take a trip with the Society for Protection of Nature in Israel. If you choose this option, take a tour meant for Israelis, and you'll be immersed in Hebrew. If you're still feeling green and want to extend your stay, check out this program called the Green Kibbutzim Semester (Internet: www.livingroutes. com/programdetails/greenkibbutz/overview.html) or the Arava Institute of Environmental Studies (http://arava.org).

Speaking of *kibbutzim* — those communal agricultural villages — you have many options for volunteering at one if that's your goal. If you'd like to try your hand at living in Israel — and you'd like to make a positive difference while you are there — think about Interns for Peace (Internet: (www.internsforpeace. org), an organization that works for coexistence between Jewish and Arab communities, or Project Oztma (www.projectotzma.com), which combines learning with fieldwork in disadvantaged communities in Israel.

Are you looking for intensive Jewish study? You have plenty of options, including the Pardes Institute of Jewish Studies (Internet: www.pardes.org.il) and Beit Midrash: A Liberal Yeshivah (Internet: www.huc.edu/bmaly). Of course, all the major universities — the Hebrew University of Jerusalem, Tel Aviv University, University of Haifa, Ben-Gurion University of the Negev, and Bar Ilan University — have programs for foreign students. You can go for a summer, a semester, or the whole year.

As the first Prime Minister of Israel, David Ben-Gurion, said, "At least . . . come to Israel to study!"

Chapter 21

Ten Books on Hebrew You Just Gotta Have

. . . .

In This Chapter
▶ Checking out the letters
▶ Adding some yoga to your Hebrew
▶ Tracing the history

. . . .

*I*f you're like me, you're a real book fiend. Although I wrote *Hebrew For Dummies* to fulfill your every basic Hebrew need, I also want to help you take your Hebrew to the next level. Check out these amazing books if you want to delve even deeper into the wonderful world of Hebrew language.

Hebrew: The Eternal Language

Hebrew: The Eternal Language (by William Chomsky, Jewish Publication Society) is a gem of a book that tells the amazing story of the Hebrew language from its birth in the Near Eastern cradle of civilization to its use as a modern, thriving language in the state of Israel today. This fascinating story illuminates how Hebrew encapsulates the unique experiences and ideas of the Jewish people.

The Tongue of the Prophets: The Life Story of Eliezer Ben Yehuda

The Tongue of the Prophets: The Life Story of Eliezer Ben Yehuda (by Robert St. John, Greenwood) reads like a novel, and it should. The story of Eliezer Ben Yehuda seems almost too incredible to be true. Meet the man who revived Hebrew into the modern, spoken language it is today.

The Hebrew Alphabet: A Mystical Journey

This beautiful little book, *The Hebrew Alphabet: A Mystical Journey* (by Edward Hoffman, illustrations by Karen Silver, Chronicle Books), unlocks the mysteries of the Hebrew letters. Accompanied by stunning illustrations of the Hebrew alphabet, this book reveals how the Hebrew letters can be used as tools for spiritual development, based on the work of 11th-century Jewish mystic Rabbi Abraham Abulafia.

Aleph-Bet Yoga: Embodying the Hebrew Letters for Physical and Spiritual Well-Being

Feel stressed out? *Aleph Bet Yoga: Embodying the Hebrew Letters for Physical and Spiritual Well-Being* (by Steven A. Rapp, Jewish Lights) will help calm your nerves. Yoga meets Hebrew in this work that combines the poses of Hatha yoga with the shapes of the Hebrew alphabet. Each position is shown with a Hebrew verse and an English reflection for meditation.

The Word: The Dictionary that Reveals the Hebrew Source of English

Some say Hebrew is the mother of all languages. *The Word: The Dictionary that Reveals the Hebrew Source of English* (by Isaac E. Mozenson, SPI Books) sets out to prove it. By tracing the etymology of hundreds of everyday words, Mozenson exposes the possible Hebrew origins of these words. A fascinating journey.

How the Hebrew Language Grew

How the Hebrew Language Grew (by Edward Horowitz, KTAV) not only tells the great history of the Hebrew language, but it also explains the basic structure and vocabulary. An easy and fascinating read.

Modern Hebrew: An Essential Grammar

For you grammar geeks, *Modern Hebrew: An Essential Grammar* (by Lewis Gilinert, Routledge) is unparalleled. This concise book makes the complexities of Hebrew grammar simple.

Hebrew Verb Tables

Hebrew Verb Tables (by Asher Talmon and Ezri Uval, Tamir Publishers) is a comprehensive book that lets you to conjugate any Hebrew verb anywhere. The late Ezri Uval was also my teacher at the Hebrew Union College-Jewish Institute of Religion in Jerusalem. May his memory be a blessing.

Poems of Jerusalem and Love Poems

Poems of Jerusalem and Love Poems (by Yehuda Amichai, Sheap Meadow Press) is a gorgeous collection of poems about the two favorite subjects of Israel's premier poet, Yehuda Amichai's — love and Jerusalem. This bilingual edition can help you pick up some Hebrew and expose you to Israel's most beloved poet. A gifted poet and a talented teacher, Yehuda Amichai taught foreign students at the Hebrew University of Jerusalem in the latter part of his career. I had the pleasure of studying with him. Yehuda Amichai died in September 2000. May his memory be a blessing.

Hebrew-English/English-Hebrew Dictionaries

You shouldn't be without a good dictionary. The hardback "Alcalay" (*The Complete English Hebrew/Hebrew English Dictionary Volumes I, II, III,* by Reuben Alcalay, Massada Press) dictionary is the most comprehensive Hebrew-English/English-Hebrew dictionary available. The *Multi-Dictionary* (*Multi-Dictionary: Bilingual Learner's Dictionary, English-Hebrew, Hebrew-English,* Lauden-Weinbach), known in Hebrew as the **Rav Milon** (rahv mee-*lohn*), is a close second. It contains excellent tables and lists. As for pocket dictionaries, Ben-Yehuda's dictionary (*Ben Yehuda's Pocket English-Hebrew/Hebrew-English Dictionary,* by Ehud Ben Yehuda and David Weinstein, Pocket Books) is my dictionary of choice.

In the words of the great sage Shammai, "Make your study a fixed habit; otherwise, you will never study." And in the words of his rival, the great sage Hillel, "Now, go and study!"

Chapter 22

Ten Favorite Hebrew Expressions

*E*ven outside Israel, Hebrew is an important part of Jewish life. Throughout history, the Jewish people have continued to hold on to the language of their native land. Today, although the majority of the world's Hebrew speakers live in Israel, about a million Hebrew speakers live outside of the state of Israel, most of them in North America. Even if they don't speak Hebrew fluently, most Jews know a Hebrew phrase or two. Here are ten Hebrew phrases you're likely to hear in Jewish communities both inside and outside of Israel.

Mazal Tov

(mah-*zahl tohv; Literally:* A good sign.)

This phrase is used to mean *congratulations*. Guests shout it at Jewish weddings when the groom stomps on a glass, breaking it in memory of the destruction of the Temple in Jerusalem and as a reminder that the world is still broken today. You can also say **Mazal Tov** to someone on other happy occasions — a birthday, a Bar or Bat Mitzvah, a new job, or an engagement. Here's something funny: In Israel, whenever someone accidentally breaks a glass or a dish in a restaurant, the entire restaurant shouts out **Mazal Tov** in unison.

B'Karov Etzlech

(buh-kah-*rohv* ehtz-*lehch; Literally:* Soon so shall it be by you.) (FS)

This expression is a good way to respond when someone wishes you a hearty **Mazal Tov.** Its most common use is by brides in response to their single women friends congratulating them on their wedding, but you can use it in any circumstance. If you want to say **B'Karov Etzlech** to a guy, you should say **B'Karov Etzlecha** (buh-kah-*rohv* ehtz-leh-*chah*).

Titchadesh

(teet-chah-*dehsh; Literally:* You shall be renewed.) (MS)

This is a nice thing to say to males when they make a new purchase, whether they've bought clothing, a new car, or a new house. If you're speaking to a girl or woman you should say **Titchadshi** (teet-chahd-*shee*). To a group of people, say **Titchadshu** (teet-chahd-*shoo*).

B'Teavon

(buh-tay-ah-*vohn; Literally:* With appetite.)

B'Teavon is the Hebrew equivalent of *bon appetit!* A host may say this when presenting a dish, and a waiter or waitress may say it to customers in a restaurant. When you dine with someone, you can say this phrase to each other before digging in. When I was at Jewish camp as a child, the counselors used this phrase at the beginning of meals to signal to the campers that we could begin eating. Ah, yummy camp food . . . **B'Teavon!**

B'Ezrat HaShem

(beh-ehz-*raht* hah-*shehm; Literally:* With help of the Name.)

In religiously observant circles, Jews often refer to the Holy One (God that is) as **HaShem,** which literally means *the Name.* Because God's name is so precious, you never even recite it in prayer, let alone in conversation. But sometimes, you do want to talk about God in the course of conversation, so religiously observant folks mention God by referring to **HaShem.** People often use this phrase when they speak about the future and want God's help. For example, this book will be successful, **B'Ezrat HaShem.**

Yishar Koach

(yih-shahr koh-*ach; Literally:* Straight power.)

You can use this expression when you want to say, *good for you, way to go,* or *more power to you* when someone has accomplished something. People often use this phrase in the synagogue after someone has received an honor such as leading a portion of the prayer service or reading Torah. The proper response to this phrase is **Baruch Teheyeh** (bah-*rooch* teeh-hee-*yeh*) to a guy and **Brucha Teeheyi** (bh-roo-*chah* tee-hee-*yee*) to a girl or a woman. Both phrases mean *you shall be blessed.*

Dash

(dahsh; Regards)

Dash is an acronym for **Drishat Shalom** (duh-ree-shaht shah-lohm), which literally means *wishings* or *demands of peace.* **Dash** is used to mean *regards.* You ask someone to send **Dash** just like you'd ask to someone to send your regards. For the full Hebrew phrase, use either of the following:

- **Timsor Lo Dash Mimeni** (teem-*sohr* loh dahsh mee-*mehn*-nee; Send him my regards.)
- **Timseri La Dash Mimeni** (teem-seh-*ree* lah dahsh mee-*mehn*-nee; Send her my regards.)

You can also send *warm regards* with **Dash Cham** (dahsh *chahm*).

Nu

(nuuuuuuu; How did it go?)

This phrase has no literal translation into English. After a friend has gone out on a hot date the night before, when your mother has an important interview, or when your child has a big test at school, you'll probably want to inquire about how everything went. So you say **Nu?** expectantly and wait for a reply.

Kol HaKavod

(kohl hah-kah-*vohd; Literally:* All of the respect.)

You can use this little phrase when you want to say *all right, way to go,* or *a job well done.* You've almost finished reading this chapter, **Kol HaKavod!**

L'Chaim

(lecha'*im; Literally:* To life.)

L'Chaim is one of my favorite Jewish expressions because I believe that it reveals a lot about the Jewish approach to life. The phrase is not *to a good life, to a healthy life,* or even *to a long life.* It is simply *to life,* recognizing that life is indeed good and precious and should always be celebrated and savored. **L'Chaim!**

Chapter 23

Ten Great Israeli Phrases

. . . .

In This Chapter

▶ Commenting on politicians

▶ Eating ice cream

▶ Keeping a positive attitude

. . . .

Modern Hebrew is a wonderfully colorful language, and the expressions I list in this chapter demonstrate that fact. So, if you want to sound like a real native speaker, use these phrases correctly, and you're sure to impress.

Mah Pitom

(mah peet-*ohm; Literally:* What suddenly.)

This expression is the Hebrew equivalent of "What'cha talkin' 'bout Willis?" Use it to express surprise and disagreement. You can also use it to modestly object to a compliment. So, if someone says to you, "You must be the greatest Hebrew speaker that ever lived," you can reply with **Mah Pitom.**

Yesh G'vul L'Chol Ta'alul

(yehsh guh-*vool* leh-*chohl* tah-ah-*lool; Literally:* There's a limit to all mischievousness.)

Truer words have never been spoken. Frequently used with children when their behavior has gotten out of hand, this phrase can also be used with adults — particularly politicians. What do you think of the antics of the mayor? Out of control? **Yesh G'vul L'Chol Ta'alul.** You can also use the beginning of this phrase, **Yesh G'vul,** which means *there's a limit,* to mean simply *enough already.*

Pa'am Shlishit Glidah

(pah-*ahm* shlee-*sheet* glee-*dah*; *Literally:* The third time, ice cream!)

I first heard this phrase from my Hebrew professor at UCLA, Yonah Sabar, when I ran into him on campus twice in the same day. Apparently you say this phrase when you run into someone unexpectedly twice in one day, suggesting that, if this coincidence happens a third time, you'll both sit down to ice cream. Israel is a small country, so you'd expect to see people sitting and chowing down on ice cream all the time.

Im K'var, Az K'var

(eem-*kvahr*, ahz *kvahr*; *Literally:* If already, then already.)

This little number is the Israeli equivalent of *just do it* or *you might as well do it.* You're planning a trip to London, England. But, while you're on the Continent, you decide to extend your trip to France, Italy, and Spain. After all, you're already in Europe, so **Im K'var Az K'var.**

B'Shum Panim VaOfen Lo

(buh-*shoom* pah-*neem* vah-*oh*-fehn loh; *Literally:* In no face and manner.)

This is the Israeli equivalent of *no way José* or *in no way, shape, or form.* Say it when you really mean it — like when your teenage son or daughter wants to go to an all-night coed slumber party (with no parents around) at the school troublemaker's house. Yeah right. **B'Shum Panim Va'Ofen Lo.**

Stam

(stahm; *Literally:* Plain.)

This is one of those Hebrew phrases I just wish we had in English. It's so useful. Israelis usually pronounce it by stretching out the *a,* as in *staaaaaaaam.* In response to the question, "Why did you do that?" you can say **Staaaam** (just because). You can use it to emphasize a word, as in the phrase **Hu Stam Tipesh** (hoo stahm tee-*pehsh;* He's just plain stupid). You can use this phrase to mean *nothing,* as in "What are you doing?" **Stam.** Or you can use it as *just kidding.* "Hey did you know the sky is falling?" **Staaaaam!** A great all-purpose word.

Betach

(*beh*-tahch; *Literally:* Certainly.)

Here's an expression that's classically Israeli. Like **Stam,** Israelis pronounce it by elongating the *a,* as in *betaaaach.* Use it emphatically when the answer is obvious and you want to say something like *but of course.* Did you enjoy reading *Hebrew For Dummies?* **Betach!**

Chaval Al HaZ'man

(cha-*val* al-haz-*mahn; Literally:* A waste of time.)

This one's a little counterintuitive. Although it literally means *a waste of time,* Israelis use it to mean the opposite: Something is great, huge, or fantastic. I didn't believe it either until I heard it all over Israel. So what do you think of this book? I hope reading it has been figuratively, but *not* literally, **Chaval Al HaZ'man!**

Chazak V'Amatz

(chah-*zahk* veh-aeh-*mahtz; Literally:* Be strong and courageous.)

This phrase is one of my favorite Israeli expressions because it comes straight from the Bible — a true testament to the power those ancient words have over our lives today. It's from the first chapter of the Book of Joshua (Joshua 1:6) when God speaks to Joshua (who's getting ready to lead the people Israel over the river Jordan and into the Promised Land). **Chazak V'Amatz Ki Atah Tanchil Et Ha'Am** (chah-*zahk* veh-eh-*mahtz* kee ah-*tah* tahn-*cheel* eht hah-*ahm;* Be strong and courageous for you shall lead the nation!). Incidentally, President Clinton quoted these words in one of his speeches in the fall of 1995. Today Israelis use it like *you can do it.* I say this to my friends when they're going through a rough time or facing a big challenge.

Yehiyeh Tov

(yih-hee-*yeh tohv; Literally:* It will be good; things will get better.)

This quintessential Israeli phrase has been used since before Israel was officially declared a state. Israelis have seen tough times, but through it all, they continue to hold on to their optimism and belief that, even in the most difficult of times, things will get better. Jews throughout the world share their dream of an Israel at peace with its neighbors. The dream, and phrase, is rooted in the Judaic vision of a world where peace and harmony exist among all peoples, countries, and regions. **Yehiyeh Tov.**

Chapter 24

The Ten Commandments in Hebrew

*O*ne of the coolest things about knowing Hebrew is being able to read the Bible in its original form. And what could be cooler than reading the Ten Commandments in their orginal language? Kind of gives you chills, doesn't it? The English phrase *Ten Commandments,* itself, is a bit interesting because Hebrew uses the term **Aseret HaDibrot** (ah-sehr-*reht* hah-dee-bh-*roht;* The Ten Statements).

Thousands of years after they were first spoken, the Ten Commandments still remain a cornerstone of many societies. Revolutionary in their time, they established shared commitments — rather than shared interests — as the basis of society. And like the laws of nature, these laws of morality come with serious consequences when broken. As actor/director Cecil De Mille said, "We cannot really break the law; we can merely break ourselves against the law." And without further ado, here they are.

Anochi Adonai Elohecha.

ah-noh-*chee* ah-doh-*naye* eh-loh-*heh*-chah.

I am the Lord your God.

Lo Yehiyeh Lecha Elohim Acherim. Lo Ta'aseh Le'chah Pesel.

loh yeh-hee-*yeh* leh-*chah* eh-loh-*heem* ah-*cheh*-reem. loh tah-ah-*seh* leh-*chah peh*-sehl.

You shall have no other god before Me. You shall not make for yourself a graven image.

Lo Tisa Et Shem Adonai Elohecha La'Shav.

loh tee-*sah* eht shehm ah-doh-*naye* eh-loh-*heh*-cha lah-*shahv*.

You shall not swear falsely by the name of the Eternal One your God.

Z'chor Et Yom HaShabbat L'Kodsho.

zchohr eht yohm hah-shah-*baht* leh-kohd-*shoh*.

Remember the Sabbath Day and keep it holy.

Kabed Et Avicha V'Et Imecha.

kah-*behd* eht ah-*vee*-chah veh-eht ee-*meh*-chah.

Honor your father and mother.

Loh Tirtzach.

loh teehr-*tzahch*.

You shall not murder.

Lo Tin'af.

loh teen-*ahf*.

You shall not commit adultery.

Lo Tignov.

loh teeg-*nohv*.

You shall not steal.

Lo Ta'aneh Bere'acha Ed Shaker.

loh tah-ah-*neh* be-ray-ah-*chah* ehd shah-*kehr*.

You shall not bear false witness against your neighbor.

Lo Tachmod.

loh tahch-*mohd*.

You shall not covet.

Appendix A

Verb Tables

. . . .

*F*or each verb in this appendix, I give you its infinitive form, present tense, past tense, future tense, and imperative mood (command form). This list isn't exhaustive, but you can make yourself understood if you use any of the common verbs in the following tables.

You may wonder why the present tense in the following tables only has four forms. Traditionally, Hebrew had no present tense per se, but, under the influence of European languages and because 19th century Jewish immigrants felt a need for a present tense, Modern Hebrew developed something to serve as present tense — the four forms I show in these tables. When you use the present tense, keep in mind that it expresses continuous action or state of being, such as *I am writing* rather than simply *I write*.

The apostrophes (') you see in the following tables indicate where the Hebrew character you would use to write that syllable would be silent — if you were writing in Hebrew characters.

Le'ehov (to love)

Present Tense		
'ohev (MS)		'ohavim (MP)
'ohevet (FS)		'ohavot (FP)

	Past Tense	Future Tense	Imperative Mood (Command)
I	'ahavti	'ohav	
You (MS)	Ahavta	T'ohav	Ehov
You (FS)	Ahavt	Tohavi	Ahavi
He	Ahav	Yohav	
She	Ahava	Tohav	
We	Ahavnu	Nohav	
You (MP)	Ahavtem	Tohavu	Ahavu
You (FP)	Ahavten	Tohavu	Ahavu
They	Ahavu	Yohavu	

Le'Echol (to eat)

Present Tense	
'ochel (MS)	'ochlim (MP)
'ochelet (FS)	'ochlot (FP)

	Past Tense	Future Tense	Imperative Mood (Command)
I	'achalti	'ochal	
You (MS)	'achalta	To'chal	Echol
You (FS)	'achlt	To'chli	Ichli
He	'achal	Yo'chal	
She	'achla	To'chal	
We	'achalnu	No'chal	
You (MP)	'achaltem	To'chlu	Ichlu
You (FP)	'achalten	To'chlu	Ichlu
They	'achlu	Yo'chlu	

Lo'mar (M) / Le'emor (F) (to say)

Present Tense	
'omer (MS)	'omrim (MP)
'omeret (FS)	'omrot (FP)

	Past Tense	Future Tense	Imperative Mood (Command)
I	'amarti	'omar	
You (MS)	'amarta	To'mar	'emor
You (FS)	'amart	To'mri	'imri
He	'amar	Yo'mar	
She	'amra	To'mar	
We	'amarnu	No'mar	
You (MP)	'amartem	To'mru	'imru
You (FP)	'amarten	To'mru	'imru
They	'amru	Yo'mru	

LaVoh (to come; to arrive)

Present Tense	
Ba (MS)	Ba'im (MP)
Ba'a (FS)	Ba'ot (FP)

	Past Tense	Future Tense	Imperative Mood (Command)
I	Ba'ti	'avo	
You (MS)	Ba'ta	Tavo'	Bo'
You (FS)	Ba't	Tavo'i	Bo'i
He	Ba'	Yavo'	
She	Ba'a	Tavo	
We	Ba'nu	Navo	
You (MP)	Ba'tem	Tavo'u	Bo'u
You (FP)	Ba'ten	Tavo'u	Bo'u
They	Ba'u	Yavo'u	

LaGur (to live; to dwell)

Present Tense	
Gar (MS)	Garim (MP)
Garah (FS)	Garot (FP)

	Past Tense	Future Tense	Imperative Mood (Command)
I	Garti	Agur	
You (MS)	Garta	Tagur	Gur
You (FS)	Gart	Taguri	Guri
He	Gar	Yagur	
She	Gara	Tagur	
We	Garnu	Nagur	
You (MP)	Gartem	Taguru	Guru
You (FP)	Garten	Taguru	Guru
They	Garu	Yaguru	

Lalachet (to go; to walk)

Present Tense		
Holech (MS)		Holchim (MP)
Holechet (FS)		Holchot (FP)

	Past Tense	Future Tense	Imperative Mood (Command)
I	Halachti	'elech	
You (MS)	Halachta	Telech	Lech
You (FS)	Halacht	Telchi	Lechi
He	Halach	Yelech	
She	Halcha	Telech	
We	Halachnu	Nelech	
You (MP)	Halachtem	Telchu	Lechu
You (FP)	Halachten	Telchu	Lechu
They	Halchu	Yelchu	

Lizkor (to remember)

Present Tense		
Zocher (MS)		Zochrim (MP)
Zocheret (FS)		Zochrot (FP)

	Past Tense	Future Tense	Imperative Mood (Command)
I	Zacharti	'ezkor	
You (MS)	Zacharta	Tizkor	Zachor
You (FS)	Zachart	Tizkeri	Zichri
He	Zachar	Yizkor	
She	Zachra	Tizkor	
We	Zacharnu	Nizkor	
You (MP)	Zachartem	Tizkeru	Zichru
You (FP)	Zacharten	Tizkeru	Zichru
They	Zachru	Yizkeru	

Lachzor (to return)

Present Tense	
Chozer (MS)	Chozrim (MP)
Chozeret (FS)	Chozrot (FP)

	Past Tense	Future Tense	Imperative Mood (Command)
I	Chazarti	Echzor	
You (MS)	Chazarta	Tachzor	Chazor
You (FS)	Chazart	Tachzeri	Chizri
He	Chazar	Yachzor	
She	Chazra	Tachzor	
We	Chazarnu	Nachzor	
You (MP)	Chazartem	Tachzeru	Chizru
You (FP)	Chazarten	Tachzeru	Chizru
They	Chazru	Yachzeru	

Lachshov (to think)

Present Tense	
Choshev (MS)	Choshvim (MP)
Choshevet (FS)	Choshvot (FP)

	Past Tense	Future Tense	Imperative Mood (Command)
I	Chashavti	Echshov	
You (MS)	Chashavta	Tachshov	Chashov
You (FS)	Chashvt	Tachshevi	Chishvi
He	Chashav	Yachshov	
She	Chashva	Tachshov	
We	Chashavnu	Nachshov	
You (MP)	Chashavtem	Tachshevu	Chishvu
You (FP)	Chashavten	Tachshevu	Chishvu
They	Chashvu	Yachshevu	

Lada'at (to know)

Present Tense	
Yode'a (MS)	Yod'im (MP)
Yoda'at (FS)	Yod'ot (FP)

	Past Tense	Future Tense	Imperative Mood (Command)
I	Yada'ti	'eda	
You (MS)	Yada'ta	Teda'	Da'
You (FS)	Yada't	Ted'i	D'ee
He	Yada'	Yeda'	
She	Yad'ah	Teda'	
We	Yada'nu	Neda'	
You (MP)	Yada'tem	Ted'u	D'u
You (FP)	Yada'ten	Ted'u	D'u
They	Yad'u	Yed'u	

Linso'a (to travel)

Present Tense	
Nose'ah (MS)	Nos'im (MP)
Nosa'at (FS)	Nos'ot (FP)

	Past Tense	Future Tense	Imperative Mood (Command)
I	Nasa'ti	'esa'	
You (MS)	Nasa'ta	Tisa'	Sa'
You (FS)	Nasa't	Tis'i	S'i
He	Nasa'	Yisa'	
She	Nas'ah	Tisa'	
We	Nasa'nu	Nisa'	
You (MP)	Nasa'tem	Tis'u	S'u
You (FP)	Nasa'ten	Tis'u	S'u
They	Nas'u	Yis'u	

Liknot (to buy)

Present Tense		
Koneh (MS)		Konim (MP)
Konah (FS)		Konot (FP)

	Past Tense	Future Tense	Imperative Mood (Command)
I	Kaniti	'ekneh	
You (MS)	Kanita	Tikneh	Kneh
You (FS)	Kanit	Tikni	K'ni
He	Kanah	Yikneh	
She	Kan'ta	Tikneh	
We	Kanu	Nikneh	
You (MP)	Kanitem	Tiknu	K'nu
You (FP)	Kaniten	Tiknu	K'nu
They	Kanu	Yiknu	

Likro (to read; to call; to call out)

Present Tense		
Kore' (MS)		Kor'im (MP)
Kore't (FS)		Kor'ot (FP)

	Past Tense	Future Tense	Imperative Mood (Command)
I	Kara'ti	'ekrah	
You (MS)	Kara'ta	Tikrah	Kra
You (FS)	Kara't	Tikre'i	Kir'i
He	Kara'	Yikra'	
She	Kar'ah	Tikra'	
We	Kara'nu	Nikra'	
You (MP)	Kara'tem	Tikre'u	Kir'u
You (FP)	Kara'ten	Tikre'u	Kir'u
They	Kar'u	Yikre'u	

Lishmo'a (to hear)

Present Tense			
Shome'a (MS)		Shom'im (MP)	
Shoma'at (FS)		Shom'ot (FP)	

	Past Tense	Future Tense	Imperative Mood (Command)
I	Shama'ti	'eshma	
You (MS)	Shama'ta	Tishma	Shema'
You (FS)	Shama't	Tishme'i	Shim'i
He	Shama'	Yishma'	
She	Sham'ah	Tishma'	
We	Shama'nu	Nishma'	
You (MP)	Shama'tem	Tish'me'u	Shim'u
You (FP)	Shama'ten	Tish'me'u	Shim'u
They	Sham'u	Yish'me'u	

Lishtot (to drink)

Present Tense			
Shoteh (MS)		Shotim (MP)	
Shotah (FS)		Shotot (FP)	

	Past Tense	Future Tense	Imperative Mood (Command)
I	Shatiti	'shteh	
You (MS)	Shatita	Tishteh	Shteh
You (FS)	Shatit	Tishti	Shti
He	Shata	Yishteh	
She	Shatetah	Tishteh	
We	Shatinu	Nishteh	
You (MP)	Shatitem	Tishtu	Shtu
You (FP)	Shatiten	Tishtu	Shtu
They	Shatu	Yishtu	

Hebrew-English Mini-Dictionary

A

abba (ah-*bah*) m: father

ach (ahch) m: brother

ach/achot (ahch/ach-*oht*) m/f: nurse

achyanit (ach-yahn-*eet*) f: niece

achot (ah-*choht*) f: sister

achyan (ach-*yahn*) m: nephew

adin/adina (ah-*deen*/ah-*deen-ah*) m/f: gentle

adon (ah-*dohn*) m: sir

af (ahf): nose

afarsek (ah-fahr-*sehk*) m: peach

afudah: (ah-foo-*dah*) f: sweater

agam (ah-*gahm*) m: lake

agvania (ahg-vah-nee-*yah*) f: tomato

akavich (ah-kah-*veesh*) m: spider

al-yad (ahl-*yahd*): next to

ambatia (ahm-*baht*-yah) f: bathroom

anan (ah-*nahn*) m: cloud

ananas (*ah*-nah-*nahs*) m: pineapple

anglit (ahn-*gleet*): English (language)

anivah (ah-nee-*vah*) f: necktie

aravit (ah-rah-*veet*) f : Arabic

arieh (ahr-*yeh*) m: lion

aron (ah-*rohn*) m: closet

artzot habrit (ahr-*tzoht* hah-*breet*) f: United States

aruchat boker (ah-roo-*chaht boh*-kehr) f: breakfast

aruchat erev (ah-roo-*chaht eh*-rehv) f: dinner

aruchat tzohorayim (ah-roo-*chaht* tzoh-ho-*rah*-yeem) f: lunch

ashir/ashira (ah-*sheer*/ah-shee-*rah*) m/f: rich

atzuv/atzuvah (ah-*tzoov*/ah-tzoo-*vah*) m/f: sad

autobus (*oh*-toh-boos) m: bus

avatiach (ah-vah-*tee*-ach) m: watermelon

aviv (ah-*veev*) m: spring (season)

avodah (ah-voh-*dah*) f: work

ayin (*ah*-yeen) f: eye

ayn (ayn): there isn't

B

ba'al (*bah*-ahl) m: husband

bachutz (bah-*chootz*): outside

barak (bah-*rahk*) m: lightning

bari/b'ri'ah (bah-*ree*/bree-*ah*) m/f: healthy

basar (bah-*sahr*) m: meat

bat-dod (baht-*dohd*) f: cousin

bevakasha (beh-vah-kah-*shah*): please

bayit (*bah*-yeet) m: house

begadim (beh-gah-*deem:*) m: clothes

beged yam (*beh*-gehd *yahm*) m: bathing suit

beit cholim (beht choh-*leem*) m: hospital

beitzim (bay-*tzeem*) f: eggs

ben-dod (behn-*dohd*) m: cousin

berech (*beh*-rech) f: knee

beten (*beh*-tehn) f: stomach

beyn (been) m: between

binyan (been-*yahn*) m: building

bitachon (bee-tah-*chohn*) m: security

boker (*boh*-kehr) m: morning

breicha (bray-*chah*) f: pool

b'seder (beh-*seh*-dher): okay

b'teavon! (beh-teh-ah-*vohn*): good appetite!

bubah (boo-*bah*) f: doll

bul (bool) m: stamp

C

chacham/chachamah (chah-*chahm*/chah-*chah*-mah) m/f: smart

chagorah (chah-goh-*rah*) f: belt

chalav (chah-*lahv*) m: milk

chalifa (chah-lee-*fah*) f: suit

chalon (chah-*lohn*) m: window

cham/chamah (*chahm*/chah-*mah*) m/f: hot

chanut (chah-*noot*) f: store

chatif (chah-*teef*) m: snack

chatimah (chah-tee-*mah*) f: signature

chatul (chah-*tool*) m: cat

chatza'it (chah-tzah-*eet*) f: skirt

chayot (chah-*yoht*) f: animals

chazak/chazakah (chah-*zahk*/chah-zah-*kah*) m/f: strong

chazia (chah-zee-*yah*) f: bra

chadar sheinah (chah-*dahr* shay-*nah*) m: bedroom

cheshbon (chehsh-*bohn*) m: bill

chof yam (chohf *yahm*) m: beach

chofesh, chufsha (choh-*fehsh*, choof-*shah*) m/f: vacation

choref (*choh*-rehf) m: winter

chulzah (chool-*tzah*) f: shirt

D

dachuf (dah-*choof*): urgent

dag (dahg) m: fish

dakah (ah-*kah*) f: minute

darkon (dahr-*kohn*) m: passport

darom (dah-*rohm*) m: south

davka (*dahv*-kah): spitefully

delek (*deh*-lehk) m: fuel

delet (*deh*-leht) f: door

devek (*deh*-vehk) m: glue

dira (dee-*rah*) f: apartment

d'li (dlee) m: bucket

doar (*doh*-ahr) m: mail

dod (dohd) m: uncle

dodah (*doh*-dah) f : aunt

dov (dohv) m: bear

E

efes (*eh*-fehs): zero

eich (ech): how

eifo (ay-*foh*): where

eizeh (ay-*zeh*): which

emek (*eh*-mehk) m: valley

emesh (*eh*-mehsh) m: last night

emet (eh-*meht*) m: truth

esek (*eh*-sehk) m: business

et (ayt) m: pen

etmol (eht-*mohl*) m: yesterday

etz (etz) m: tree

G

gader (gah-*dehr*) m: fence

gag (*gahg*) m: roof

galgiliot (gahl-gee-lee-*yoht*) f: in-line skates

gan chayot (gahn chah-*yoht*) m: zoo

gar/garah (gahr/*gahr*-ah) m/f: live (dwell)

garbayim (gahr-baye-*eem*) m: socks

garinim (gahr-ee-*neem*) m: seeds

gav (gahv) m: back

gezer (*geh*-zehr) m: carrot

gis (*gees*) m: brother-in-law

gisa (gee-*sah*) f: sister-in-law

glidah (glee-*dah*) f: ice cream

g'vinah (gvee-*nah*) f: cheese

g'vul (gvool) m: border

H

hanacha (hah-nah-*chah*) f: discount

har (hahr) m: mountain

henei (hee-*nay*): here is

hoda'a (hoh-dah-*ah*): message

horim (hoh-*reem*) m: parents

I

ima (*ee*-mah) f: mother

iparon (ee-pah-*rohn*) m: pencil

ir bira (eer bee-*rah*) f: capital city

ir (eer) f: city

ishah (ee-*shah*) f: wife

iton (ee-*tohn*) m: newspaper

itona'i/itona'it (ee-toh-*nay*/ee-toh-nah-*eet*) m/f: journalist

itz tapuzim (meetz tah-poo-*zeem*) m: orange juice

ivrit (eev-*reet*) f: Hebrew

J

juke (jook) m: bug

K

kacha-kacha (*kah*-chah *kah*-chah): so-so

kachol (kah-*chohl*) m: blue

kadur regel (kah-*door reh*-gehl) m: soccer

kadur (kah-*door*) m: ball

kadur-sal (kah-door *sahl*) m: basketball

kaf (kahf) m: tablespoon

kafa'fa/k'fafot (kfah-*fah*/kfah-*foht*) f: glove, gloves

kan (kahn): here

kanyon (ken-*yohn*) m: shopping mall

kapit (kah-*peet*) f: team

kar/karah (kahr/kah-*rah*) m/f: cold

kartis ashrei (kahr-*tees* ahsh-*rye*) m: credit card

kartis (kahr-*tees*) m: ticket

kaspomat (kahs-poh-*maht*) m: ATM

katan/k'tanah (kah-*tahn*/ktah-*nah*) m/f: little

katef (kah-*tehf*) f: shoulder

katom (kah-*tohm*) m: orange (fruit)

kayitz (*kah*-yeetz) m: summer

kef (kehf) m: fun

kehilla (keh-hee-*lah*) f: community

kelev (*keh*-lehv) m: dog

ken (kehn): yes

kesef (*keh*-sehf) m: money

keshet (*keh*-sheht) m: restroom

kior (kee-*yohr*) m: sink

kipah (kee-*pah*) f: yarmulke

kir (keer) m: wall

kis (kees) m: pocket

kisei (kee-*seh*) m: chair

kislofon (*ksee*-loh-fohn) m: xylophone

kochav (koh-chahv) m: star

kof (kohf) m: monkey

korot chaim (koh-*roht* chah-*yeem*) m: resume

kos (kohs) m: cup

kovah (*koh*-vah) m: hat

ktzat (ktzaht): (a) little

k'visa (kvee-*sah*) f: laundry

L

lamah (*lah*-mah): why

lavan (lah-*vahn*) m: white

lean (leh-*ahn*): (to) where

lemala (leh-*mah*-lah): up

lematah (leh-*mah*-tah): down

lev (lehv) m: heart

lifnei (leef-*nay*): before

lo (loh): no

luach (*loo*-ahch) m: calendar

M

ma'afiah (mah-ah-feey-*ah*) f: bakery

ma'alit (mah-ah-*leet*) f: elevator

ma'arav (mah-ah-*rahv*) m: west

machak (*mah*-chahk) m: eraser

machar (mah-*chahr*) m: tomorrow

machartayim (mach-rah-*tah*-yeem) m: day-after-tomorrow

machberet (mach-*beh*-reht) f: notebook

machshev (mahch-*shehv*) m: computer

maduah (mah-*doo*-ah): why

mafteach (mahf-*teh*-ach) m: key

magafayim (mah-gah-*fah*-yeem) m: boots

magevet (mah-*geh*-veht) f: towel

mah (mah): what

malon (mah-*lohn*) m: hotel

mamash (mah-*mahsh*): quite

mapah (mah-*pah*) f: tablecloth

mapit (mah-*pete*) f: napkin

marak (mah-*rahk*) m: soup

mas (mahs) m: tape

maskoret (mahs-*koh*-reht) f: salary

masrek (mahs-*rehk*) m: comb

matai (mah-*tye*): when

matateh (mah-tah-*teh*) f: broom

matos (mah-*tohs*) m: airplane

mayim (*mah*-yeem) m: water

mazgan (mahz-*gahn*) m: air conditioner

mazleg (mahz-*lehg*) m: fork

michansayim (mich-nah-*sah*-yeem) m: pants

me'il (meh-*eel*) m: coat

melafefon (meh-lah-feh-*fohn*) m: cucumber

meltzar (mehl-*tzahr*) m: waiter

meltzarit (mehl-*tzah-reet*) f: waitress

me'od (meh-*ohd*): very

metria (mee-tree-*yah*) f: umbrella

me'uchar (meh-oo-*chahr*) m: late

mezeg avir (*meh*-zehg ah-*veer*) m: weather

mi (mee): who

midbar (meed-*bahr*) m: desert

mikrogal (*meek*-roh-gahl) m: microwave

mishkafay shemesh (meesh-kah-*fay* sheh-mehsh) m: sunglasses

mishkafayim (meesh-kah-*fah*-yeem) m: eyeglasses

mishpacha (meesh-pah-*chah*) f: family

mispar (mees-*pahr*) m: number

misrad (mees-*rahd*) m: office

mitachat (mee-*tah*-chaht): under

mitah (mee-*tah*) f: bed

mitbach (meet-*bahch*) m: kitchen

mitzaryim (meetz-*rah*-eem) f: Egypt

metzuyan (meh-tzoo-*yahn*) m: excellent

mivreshet (meev-*reh*-sheht) f: brush

mizrach (meez-*rahch*): east

mizvada (meez-vah-*dah*) f: suitcase

mochonit (meh-cho-*neet*) f: car

moreh/morah (moh-*reh*/moh-*rah*) m/f: teacher

motze'ei shabbat (motzeh-*ay* shah-*baht*): Saturday night

mukdam (mook-*dahm*): early

musach (moo-*sahch*) m: garage

N

na (nah): please

na'al/na'alyim (*nah*-ahl/nah-ahl-*lye*-eem) f: shoe, shoes

nachon (nah-*chohn*): correct

nahar (nah-*hahr*) m: river

naknikiah (nahk-nee-kee-*yah*) f: hot dog

nemal ha'teufa (neh-*mahl* hah-tef-oo-*fah*) m: airport

nechda (nech-*dah*) f: granddaughter

neched (*neh*-chehd) m: grandson

nudnik/nudnikit (*nood*-neek/*nood*-nee-keet) m/f: pest

O

ochel (*oh*-chehl) m: food

of (ohf) m: chicken

or (ohr) m: skin

orech din/orachat din (oh-*rehch* deen/oh-reh-chet *deen*) m/f: lawyer

orez (*oh*-rehz) m: rice

ozen (*oh*-zehn) f: ear

ozev/ozevet (oh-*zehv*/oh-*zeh*-veht) m/f: depart

P

panim (pah-*neem*) f: face

parvar (pahr-*vahr*) m: suburb

peh (peh) m: mouth

pelafon (*peh*-leh-fohn) m: cell phone

peel (peel) m: elephant

pinah (pee-*nah*) f: corner

poh (poh): here

prachim (prah-*cheem*) m: flowers

p'santer (psahn-*tehr*) m: piano

R

rachok/rechokah (rah-*chohk*/reh-choh-*kah*) m/f: far

rechov (reh-*chohv*) m: street

rah (rah) m: bad

rak (rahk): only

ramzor (rahm-*zohr*) m: traffic light

rentgen (*rehnt*-gehn) m: X-ray

rav/raba (rahv/rah-*bah*) m/f: rabbi

regel (*reh*-gehl) f: leg

rehut (ree-*hoot*) m: furniture

rich-rach (*reech*-rahch) m: zipper

rikud (ree-*kood*) m: dance (noun)

ritzpa (reetz-*pah*) f: floor

rofeh/rofah (roh-*feh*/rohf-*ah*) m/f: doctor

rosh (rohsh) m: head

rotev (*roh*-tehv) m: sauce

ruach (*roo*-ach) m: wind

S

saba (*sah*-bah) m: grandfather

safa (sah-*fah*) f: language

safsal (sahf-*sahl*) f: bench

sakin (sah-*keen*) m: knife

sal (sahl) m: basket

salat (sah-*laht*) m: salad

same'ach/s'mecha (sah-*meh*-ach/smeh-*chah*) m/f: happy

sandalim (sahn-dah-*leem*) m: sandals

sapah (sah-*pah*) f: couch

savta (*sahv*-tah) f: grandmother

segol (seh-*gohl*) m: purple

sela (*seh*-lah) f: rock

seret davik (*seh*-reht dah-*veek*) m: tape

seret (*seh*-reht) m: movie

sha'ah (shah-*ah*) f: hour

shabbat (shah-*baht*) f: Saturday

shachor (shah-*chohr*) m: black

shalom (shah-*lohm*): peace

sham (shahm): there

shamayim (shah-*mye*-eem) m: sky

shanah (shah-*nah*) f: year

sha'on (shah-*ohn*) m: watch

shatiach (shah-*tee*-ach) m: rug

shavua (shah-*voo*-ah) m: week

shezif (sheh-*zeef*) m: plum

shekdim (shkeh-*deem*) f: almonds

sheket (*sheh*-keht): quiet

sheleg (*sheh*-lehg) m: snow

shem (shehm) m: name

shemesh (*sheh*-mehsh) f: sun

shilshom (shil-*shohm*) m: day-before-yesterday

shir (sheer) m: song

shniyah (shnee-*yah*) f: second (in time)

shoter/shoteret (shoh-*tehr*/shoh-teh-*reht*) m/f: police officer

shulchan (shool-*chahn*) m: sweater

sicha (see-*chah*) f: conversation

simla (seem-*lah*) f: dress

siyur (see-*yoor*) m: tour

slicha (slee-*chah*): excuse (me)

smartoot (smahr-*toot*) m: rain

s'mol (smohl) m: left

sof hashavua (sohf hah-shah-*voo*-ah): weekend

stav (stahv): fall (season)

sukaria (soo-kahr-*yah*) f: candy

sus (soos) m: horse

T

tachsheetim (tahch-shee-*teem*) f: jewelry

tachtonim (tahch-toh-*neem*) m: underwear

tafrit (tahf-*reet*) f: menu

ta'im (tah-*eem*) m: delicious

tanor (tah-*noor*) m: oven

tapuach adamah (tah-*poo*-ahch ah-dah-*mah*) m: potato

tapuach (tah-*poo*-ach) m: apple

tapuz (tah-*pooz*) m: orange:(color)

tari/t'riah (tah-*ree*/tree-*yah*) m/f: fresh

telefone (*teh*-leh-fohn) m: telephone

televizia (teh-leh-veez-*yah*) f: television

teras (*tee*-rahs) m: corn

tered (*teh*-rehd) m: spinach

teva (*teh*-vah) m: nature

tikra (teek-*rah*) f: ceiling

tipesh/tipshah (tee-*pesh*/teep-*shah*) m/f: stupid

tiyul (tee-*yool*) m: hiking

t'munot (tmoo-*noht*) f: pictures

todah (toh-*dah*): thanks

tov/tovah (*tohv*/toh-*vah*) m/f: good

tzafon (tzah-*fohn*): north

tzahov (tzah-*hohv*) m: yellow

tza'if (tzah-*eef*) m: scarf

tza'ir/tza'irah (tzah-*eer*/tzeh-ee-*rah*)
m/f: young

tzalachat (tzah-*lah*-chaht) f: plate

tza'meh/tze'me'ah (tzah-*meh*/ tzmeh-*ah*)
m/f: thirsty

tzavar (tzah-*vahr*) m: neck

tzevet (*tzeh*-veht) f: team

tzipur (tzee-*pohr*) m: bird

tzohorayim (tzoh-hoh-*rah*-yeem) m: noon

U

ugah (oo-*gah*) f: cake

ugiah (oo-gee-*yah*) f: cookie

V

vered (*veh*-rehd) m: rose

varod (vah-*rohd*) m: pink

Y

yad (yahd) f: hand

yafeh/yahfa (yah-*feh*/yah-*fah*) m/f: pretty

yakar/yakara (yah-*kahr*/yeh-*kha-rah*)
m/f: expensive

yam (yahm) m: ocean

yamin (yah-*meen*) m: right

yarok (yah-*rohk*) m: green

yashar (yah-*shahr*) m: straight

yayin (*yah*-yeen) m: wine

yerakot (yeh-rah-*koht*) m: vegetables

yesh (yesh): there is

yisrael (yees-rah-*ehl*) f: Israel

yom chamishi (yohm chah-mee-*shee*):
Thursday

yom revi'i (yohm reh-vee-*ee*)
m: Wednesday

yom shishi (yohm shee-*shee*) m: Friday

yom shlishi (yohm shuh-lee-*shee*)
m: truth

yom (yohm) m: day

Z

zol (zohl) m: inexpensive

English-Hebrew Mini-Dictionary

A

air conditioner: **mazgan** (mahz-*gahn*) m

airplane: **matos** (mah-*tohs)* m

airport: **namal ha'teufa** (neh-*mahl* hah-tef-oo-*fah*) m

almonds: **shekdim** (sh-kay-*deem*) f

animals: **chayot** (chah-*yoht*) f

apartment: **dira** (dee-*rah*) f

apple: **tapuach** (tah-*poo*-ach) m

apricot: **mish-mish** (mish-*mesh*) m

Arabic: **aravit** (ah-rah-*veet*) f

ATM: **kaspomat** (kahs-poh-*maht*) m

aunt: **dodah** (*doh*-dah) f

B

back: **gav** (gahv) m

bad: **rah** (rah) m

bakery: **ma'afiah** (mah-ah-feey-ah) f

ball: **kadur** (kah-*door*) m

basketball: **kadur-sal** (kah-door *sahl*) m

basket: **sal** (sahl) m

bathing suit: **beged yam** (*beh*-gehd yahm) m

bathroom: **ambatia** (ahm-baht-*yah*) f

beach: **chof yam** (chohf *yahm*) m

bear: **dov** (dohv) m

bed: **mitah** (mee-*tah*) f

bedroom: **chedar sheinah**:(chah-*dahr* shay-*nah*) m

before: **lifnei** (leef-*nay*)

belt: **chagorah** (chah-goh-*rah*) f

bench: **safsal** (sahf-*sahl*) f

between: **bein** (beyn) m

bill: **cheshbon** (chehsh-*bohn*) m

bird: **tzipur** (tzee-*pohr*) m

black: **shachor** (shah-*chohr*) m

blue: **kachol** (kah-*chohl*) m

boots: **magafayim** (mah-gah-*fah*-yeem) m

border: **g'vul** (gvool) m

bra: **chazia** (chah-zee-*yah*) f

breakfast: **aruchat boker**:(ah-roo-*chaht* boh-kehr) f

broom: **matateh** (mah-tah-*teh*) f

brother: **ach** (ahch) m

brother-in-law: **gis** (gees) m

brush: **mivreshet** (meev-*reh*-sheht) f

bucket: **d'li** (dlee) m

bug: **juke** (jook) m

building: **binyan** (been-*yahn*) m

bus: **autobus** (oh-toh-*boos*) m

business: **esek** (*eh*-sehk) m

C

cake: **ugah** (oo-*gah*) f

calendar: **luach** (*loo*-ahch) m

candy: **sukaria** (soo-kahr-*yah*) f

capital city: **ir bira** (eer bee-*rah*) f

car: **mochonit** (meh-cho-*neet*) f

carrot: **gezer** (*geh*-zehr) m

cat: **chatul** (chah-*tool*) m

ceiling: **tikra** (teek-*rah*) f

cell phone: **pelafon** (*peh*-leh-fohn) m

chair: **kisei** (kee-*seh*) m

cheese: **g'vinah** (gvee-*nah*) f

chicken: **of** (ohf) m

city: **ir** (eer) f

closet: **aron** (ah-*rohn*) m

clothes: **begadim** (bgah-*deem*) m

cloud: **anan** (ah-*nahnv*) m

coat: **me'il** (meh-*eel*) m

cold: **kar/karah** (kahr/kah-*rah*) m/f

comb: **masrek** (mahs-*rehk*) m

community: **kehilla** (keh-hee-*lah*) f

computer: **machshev** (mahch-*shehv*) m

conversation: **sicha** (see-*chah*) f

cookie: **ugiah** (oo-gee-*yah*) f

corn: **teras** (*tee*-rahs) m

corner: **pinah** (pee-*nah*) f

correct: **nachon** (nah-*chohn*)

couch: **sapah** (sah-*pah*) f

cousin:**bat-dod** (baht-*dohd*) f

cousin: **ben-dod** (behn-*dohd*) m

credit card: **kartis ashrei** (kahr-*tees* ahsh-*rye*) m

cucumber: **melafefon** (meh-lah-feh-*fohn*) m

cup: **kohs** (kohs) m

D

dance: (noun) **rikud** (ree-*kood*) m

day: **yom** (yohm) m

day-after-tomorrow: **machratayim** (mahch-rah-*tah*-yeem) m

day-before-yesterday: **shilshom** (shil-*shohm*) m

delicious: **ta'im** (tah-*eem*) m

depart: **ozev/ozevet** (oh-*zehv*/oh-*zeh*-veht) m/f

desert: **midbar** (meed-*bahr*) m

dinner: **aruchat erev** (ah-roo-*chaht eh*-rehv) f

discount: **hanacha** (hah-nah-*chah*) f

doctor: **rofeh/rofah** (roh-*feh*/rohf-*ah*) m/f

dog: **kelev** (*keh*-lehv) m

doll: **bubah** (boo-*bah*) f

door: **delet** (*deh*-leht) f

down: **lematah** (leh-*mah*-tah)

dress: **simla** (seem-*lah*) f

E

ear: **ozen** (oh-*zehn*) f

early: **mukdam** (mook-*dahm*)

east: **mizrach** (meez-*rahch*)

eggs: **beitzim** (bay-*tzeem*) f

Egypt: **mitzaryim** (meetz-*rye*-eem) f

elephant: **pil** (peel) m

elevator: **ma'alit** (mah-ah-*leet*) f

English (language): **anglit** (ahn-*gleet*)

eraser: **machak** (*mah*-chahk) m

excellent: **mitzuyan** (meh-tzoo-*yahn*) m

excuse (me): **slicha** (slee-*chah*)

expensive: **yakar/yakara** (yah-*kahr*/yeh-*kha-rah*) m/f

eye: **ayin** (*ah*-yeen) f

eyeglasses: **mishkafayim** (meesh-kah-*fah*-yeem) m

F

face: **panim** (pah-*neem*) f

fall (season): **stav** (stahv)

family: **mishpacha** (meesh-pah-*chah*) f

far: **rachok/rachokah**:(rah-*chohk*/
reh-*choh-kah*) m/f

father: **abba** (*ah*-bah) m

fence: **gader** (gah-*dehr*) m

fish: **dag** (dahg) m

floor: **ritzpa** (reetz-*pah*) f

flowers: **prachim** (prah-*cheem*) m

food: **ochel** (*oh*-chehl) m

fork: **mazleg** (mahz-*lehg*) m

fresh: **tari/t'riah** (tah-*ree*/tree-*yah*) m/f

Friday: **yom shishi** (yohm shee-*shee*) m

fuel: **delek** (*deh*-lehk) m

fun: **kef** (kehf) m

furniture: **rehut** (ree-*hoot*) m

G

garage: **musach** (moo-*sahch*) m

gentle: **adin/adina** (ah-*deen*/ah-*dee-
nah*) m/f

glove, gloves: **k'fa'fa/k'fafot**:(kfah-
fah/kfah-*foht*) f

glue: **devek** (*deh*-vehk) m

good appetite!: **b'teavon!** (beh-teh-
ah-*vohn*)

good: **tov/tovah** (*tohv*/toh-*vah*) m/f

granddaughter: **nechda** (nech-*dah*) f

grandfather: **saba** (*sah*-bah) m

grandmother: **savta** (*sahv*-tah) f

grandson: **neched** (*neh*-chehd) m

green: **yarok** (yah-*rohk*) m

H

hand: **yad** (yahd) f

happy: **sameach/s'micha**:(sah-meh-*ach*/
smeh-*chah*) m/f

hat: **kovah** (*koh*-vah) m

head: **rosh** (rohsh) m

healthy: **bari/b'ri'ah** (bah-*ree*/
bree-*ah*) m/f

heart: **lev** (lehv) m

Hebrew: **ivrit** (eev-*reet*) f

here is: **henei** (hee-*nay*)

here: **poh** (poh)

hiking: **tiyul** (tee-*yool*) m

horse: **sus** (soos) m

hospital: **beit cholim** (beht choh-*leem*) m

hot dog: **naknikiah** (nahk-nee-kee-*yah*) f

hot: **cham/chamah**:(*chahm*/cha-*mah*) m/f

hat: **kovah** (*koh*-vah) m

hotel: **malon** (mah-*lohn*) m

hour: **sha'ah** (shah-*ah*) f

house: **bayit** (*bah*-yeet) m

how: **eich** (ech)

husband: **ba'al** (*bah*-ahl) m

I

ice cream: **glidah** (guh-lee-*dah*) f

inexpensive: **zol** (zohl) m

in-line skates: **galgiliot** (gahl-gee-lee-*yoht*) f

spitefully: **davka** (*dahv*-kah)

Israel: **yisrael** (yees-rah-*ehl*) f

J

jewelry: **tachsheetim** (tahch-shee-*teem*) f

journalist: **itona'i/itona'it**:(ee-toh-*nay*/
ee-toh-nah-*eet*) m/f

K

key: **mafteach** (mahf-*teh*-ach) m

kitchen: **mitbach** (meet-*bahch*) m

knee: **berech** (*behr*-ech) f

knife: **sakin** (sah-*keen*) m

L

lake: **agam** (ah-*gahm*) m

language: **safa** (sah-*fah*) f

last night: **emesh** (*eh*-mehsh) m

late: **me'uchar** (meh-oo-*chahr*) m

laundry: **k'visa** (kvee-*sah*) f

lawyer: **orech din/orechet din** (oh-*rehch deen*/oh-reh- cheht *deen*) m/f

left: **s'mol** (smohl) m

leg: **regel** (*reh*-gehl) f

lightning: **barak** (bah-*rahk*) m

(a) little: **ktzat** (ktzaht)

little: **katan/k'tanah:**(kah-*tahn*/ ktah-*nah*) m/f

lion: **arieh** (ahr-*yeh*) m

live: (dwell) **gar/garah** (gahr/*gahr*-ah)

lunch: **aruchat tzohorayim** (ah-roo-*chaht* tzoh-ho-*rah*-yeem) f

M

mail: **doar** (*doh*-ahr) m

meat: **basar** (bah-*sahr*) m

menu: **tafrit** (tahf-*reet*) f

message: **hoda'a** (hoh-dah-*ah*)

microwave: **mikrogal** (*meek*-roh-gahl) m

milk: **chalav** (chah-*lah*) m

minute: **dakah** (dah-*kah*) f

money: **kesef** (*keh*-sehf) m

monkey: **kof** (kohf) m

morning: **boker** (*boh*-kehr) m

mother: **ima** (*ee*-mah) f

mountain: **har** (hahr) m

mouth: **peh** (peh) m

movie: **seret** (*seh*-reht) m

N

name: **shem** (shehm) m

napkin: **mapit** (mah-*pete*) f

nature: **teva** (*teh*-vah) m

neck: **tzavar** (tzah-*vahr*) m

necktie: **anivah** (ah-nee-*vah*) f

nephew: **achyan** (ach-*yahn*) m

newspaper: **iton** (ee-*tohn*) m

next to: **al-yad** (ahl-*yahd*)

niece: **achaynit** (ach-yah-*neet*) f

no: **lo** (loh)

noon: **tzohorayim** (tzoh-hoh-*rah*-yeem) m

north: **tzafon** (tzah-*fohn*)

nose: **af** (ahf)

notebook: **machberet** (mahch-*beh*-reht) f

number: **mispar** (mees-*pahr*) m

nurse: **ach/achot** (*ahch*/ah-*choht*) m/f

O

ocean: **yam** (yahm) m

office: **misrad** (mees-*rahd*) m

okay: **b'seder** (beh-*seh*-dehr)

only: **rak** (rahk)

orange juice: **mitz tapuzim** (meetz tah-poo-*zeem*) m

orange: (fruit) **katom** (kah-*tohm*) m

orange: (color) **tapuz** (tah-*pooz*) m

outside: **bachutz** (bah-*chootz*)

oven: **tanor** (tah-*noor*) m

P

pants: **michansayim** (mich-nah-*sah*-yeem) m

parents: **horim** (hoh-*reem*) m

passport: **darkon** (dahr-*kohn*) m

patio: **mirpeset** (meer-*peh*-seht) f

peace: **shalom** (shah-*lohm*)

peach: **afarsek** (ah-fahr-*sehk*) m

pen: **et** (eht) m

pencil: **iparon** (ee-pah-r*ohn*) m

pest: **nudnik/nudnikit**:(*nood*-neek/ *nood*-nee-keet) m/f

piano: **p'santer** (psahn-*tehr*) m

pictures: **t'munot** (tmoo-*noht*) f

pineapple: **ananas** (*ah*-nah-nahs) m

pink: **varod** (vah-*rohd*) m

plate: **tzalachat** (tzah-*lah*-chaht) f

please: **bevakasha** (beh-vah-kah-*shah*)

please: **na** (nah)

plum: **shezif** (sheh-*zeef*) m

pocket: **kis** (kees) m

police officer: **shoter/shoteret**: (shoh-*tehr*/ shoh-teh-*reht*) m/f

pool: **breicha** (buh-ray-*chah*) f

potato: **tapuach adamah**:(tah-*poo*-ahch ah-dah-*mah*) m

pretty: **yafeh/yahfa** (yah-*feh*/ yah-*fah*) m/f

purple: **segol** (seh-*gohl*) m

Q

quiet: **sheket** (*sheh*-keht)

quite: **mamash** (mah-*mahsh*)

R

rabbi: **rav/raba** (rahv/rah-*bah*) m/f

rag: **smartoot** (smahr-*toot*) m

rain: **geshem** (*geh*-shehm) m

rainbow: **keshet** (*keh*-sheht) m

red: **adom** (ah-*dohm*) m

refrigerator: **makrair** (mahk-*rehr*) m

restroom: **sherutim** (sheh-roo-*teem*) m

resume: **korot chaim** (koh-*roht* chah-*yeem*) m

rice: **orez** (*oh*-rehz) m

rich: **ashir/ashira** (ah-*sheer*/ ah-*shee-rah*) m/f

right: **yamin** (yah-*meen*) m

river: **nahar** (nah-*hahr*) m

rock: **sela** (seh-*lah*) f

roof: **gag** (gahg) m

rose: **vered** (*veh*-rehd) m

rug: **shatiach** (shah-*tee*-ach) m

S

sad: **atzuv/atzuvah**:(ah-*tzoov*/ ah-tzoo-*vah*) m/f

salad: **salat** (sah-*laht*) m

salary: **maskoret** (mahs-*koh*-reht) f

sandals: **sandalim** (sahn-dah-*leem*) m

Saturday night: **motz'ay shabbat**: (moh-tz*eh-ay*/shah-*baht*)

Saturday: **shabbat** (shah-*baht*) f

sauce: **rotev** (*roh*-tehv) m

scarf: **tza'if** (tzah-*eef*) m

second: (in time) **shniyah** (shnee-*yah*) f

security: **bitachon** (bee-tah-*chohn*) m

seeds: **garinim** (gahr-ee-*neem*) m

shirt: **chulzah** (chool-*tzah*) f

shoe, shoes: **na'al/na'alyim**:(*nah*-ahl/ nah-ah-*lah*-yeem) f

shopping mall: **kenyon** (ken-*yohn*) m

shoulder: **katef** (kah-*tehf*) f

signature: **chatimah** (chah-tee-*mah*) f

sink: **kior** (kee-*yohr*) m

sir: **madon** (ah-*dohn*) m

sister: **achot** (ah-*choht*) f

sister-in-law: **gisa** (gee-*sah*) f

skin: **or** (ohr) m

skirt: **chatza'it** (chah-tzah-*eet*) f

sky: **shamayim** (shah-mah-*eem*) m

smart: **chacham/chachamah** (chah-*chahm*/chah-chah-mah) m/f

snack: **chatif** (chah-*teef*) m

snow: **sheleg** (*sheh*-lehg) m

soccer: **kadur regel** (kah-*door reh*-gehl) m

socks: **garbayim** (gahr-bah-*eem*) m

song: **shir** (sheer) m

so-so: **kacha-kacha** (*kah*-chah *kah*-chah)

soup: **marak** (mah-*rahk*) m

south: **darom** (dah-*rohm*) m

spider: **akavich** (ah-*kah*-veech) m

spinach: **tered** (*teh*-rehd) m

spring (season): **aviv** (ah-*veev*) m

stairs: **madregot** (mahd-dreh-*goht*) f

stamp: **bul** (bool) m

star: **kochav** (koh-*chahv*) m

stomach: **beten** (*beh*-tehn) f

store: **chanut** (chah-*noot*) f

straight: **yashar** (yah-*shahr*) m

street: **rachov** (reh-*chohv*) m

strong: **chazak/chazakah** (chah-*zahk*/chah-*zahk*) m/f

stupid: **tipesh/tipshah** (tee-*pesh*/teep-*shah*) m/f

suburb: **parvar** (pahr-*vahr*) m

suit: **chalifa** (chah-lee-*fah*) f

suitcase: **mizvada** (meez-vah-*dah*) f

summer: **kayitz** (*kah*-yeetz) m

sun: **shemesh** (*sheh*-mehsh) f

sunglasses: **mishkafay shemesh** (meesh-kah-*fay sheh*-mehsh) m

sweater: **afudah** (ah-foo-*dah*) f

T

table: **shulchan** (shool-*chahn*) m

tablecloth: **mapah** (mah-*pah*) f

tablespoon: **kaf** (kahf) m

tape: **seret devik** (*seh*-reht *deh*-veek) m

teacher: **moreh/morah** (moh-*reh*/moh-*rah*) m/f

team: **tzevet** (*tzeh*-veht) f

teaspoon: **kapit** (kah-*peet*) f

telephone: **telefone** (*teh*-leh-fohn) m

television: **televizia** (teh-leh-*veez*-yah) f

thanks: **todah** (toh-*dah*)

there is: **yesh** (yesh)

there isn't: **ayn** (ayn)

there: **sham** (shahm)

thirsty: **tza'meh/tze'me'ah** (tzah-*meh*/tzmeh-*ah*) m/f

Thursday: **yom chamishi** (yohm chah-mee-*shee*)

ticket: **kartis** (kahr-*tees*) m

tomato: **agvania** (ahg-vah-nee-*yah*) f

tomorrow: **machar** (mah-*chahr*) m

tour: **siur** (see-*yoor*) m

towel: **magevet** (mah-*geh*-veht) f

traffic light: **ramzor** (rahm-*zohr*) m

tree: **etz** (etz) m

truth: **emet** (*eh*-meht) m

Tuesday: **yom shlishi** (yohm shlee-*shee*) m

U

umbrella: **metria** (mee-tree-*yah*) f

uncle: **dod** (dohd) m

under: **mitachat** (mee-*tah*-chaht)

underwear: **tachtonim** (tahch-toh-*neem*) m

United States: **artzot habrit** (ahr-*tzoht* hah-*breet*) f

up: **lemala** (leh-*mah*-lah)

urgent: **dachuf** (dah-*choof*)

V

vacation: **chofesh, chufsha** (*choh*-fehsh, choof-*shah*) m/f
valley: **emek** (*eh*-mehk) m
vegetables: **yerakot** (yeh-rah-*koht*) m
very: **me'od** (meh-*ohd*)

W

waiter: **meltzar** (mehl-*tzahr*) m
waitress: **meltzarit** (mehl-*tzah-reet*) f
wall: **kir** (keer) m
watch: **sha'on** (shah-*ohn*) m
water: **mayim** (*mah*-eem) m
watermelon: **avatiach** (ah-vah-*tee*-ach) m
weather: **mezeg avir** (*meh*-zehg ah-*veer*) m
Wednesday: **yom revi'i** (yohm reh-vee-ee) m
week: **shavua** (shah-*voo*-ah) m
weekend: **sof hashavua** (sohf hah-shah-*voo*-ah)
west: **ma'arav** (mah-ah-*rahv*)m
what: **mah** (mah)
when: **matai** (mah-*tye*)
where: **eifo** (*ay*-foh)
(to) where: **lean** (leh-*ahn*)
which: **eizeh** (ay-*zeh*)
white: **lavan** (lah-*vahn*) m
who: **mi** (mee)

why: **lamah** (*lah*-mah)
why: **maduah** (mah-*doo*-ah)
wife: **ishah** (ee-*shah*) f
wind: **ruach** (*roo*-ach) m
window: **chalon** (chah-*lohn*) m
wine: **yayin** (*yah*-yeen) m
winter: **choref** (*choh*-rehf) m
work: **avodah** (ah-voh-*dah*) f

X

X-ray: **rantgen** (*rehnt*-gehn) m
xylophone: **ksilofon** (ksee-loh-*fohn*) m

Y

yarmulke: **kipah** (kee-*pah*) f
year: **shanah** (shah-*nah*) f
yellow: **tzahov** (tzah-*hohv*) m
yes: **ken** (kehn)
yesterday: **etmol** (eht-*mohl*) m
young: **tza'ir/tza'irah** (tzah-*eer*/tzeh-ee-*rah*) m/f

Z

zero: **efes** (*eh*-fehs)
zipper: **rich-rach** (*reech*-rahch) m
zoo: **gan chayot** (gahn chah-*yoht*) m

Appendix C

Answer Key

Chapter 1: You Already Know Some Hebrew

בּ

Makes a *B* sound as in *boat*.

צ

Makes a hard *Tz* sound as the double *zz* in *pizza*. In this book, I represent it with *tz*.

ג

Makes a *G* sound as in *girl*.

ו

Makes a *V* sound as in *video*.

ל

Makes an *L* sound as in *lemon*.

ר

Makes the *R* sound as in *round*. Roll it like a Spanish *R*, and pronounce it from the back of your throat.

שׁ

Makes a *Sh* sound as in *show*.

כ

Makes a strong guttural *H* sound.

Chapter 2: The Nitty Gritty: Basic Hebrew Grammar

1. **Hu Rotzeh Et Mechonit Nachon? / Ha'im Hu Rotzeh Et Mechonit?**

2. **Yesh Magevet Nachon? / Ha'im Yesh Magevet?**

Chapter 3: Shalom, Shalom! Meeting and Greeting

1. how 2. where 3. why 4. what 5. when 6. who

Chapter 4: Getting to Know You: Making Small Talk

A. **Aba** (father) B. **Ima** (mother) C. **Achot** (sister) D. **Ach** (brother)
E. **Savtah** (grandmother)

Chapter 5: Eat! Eat! You're So Thin!

Kapit (spoon), **Mapah** (tablecloth), **Mapit** (napkin), **Marak** (soup), **Mazleg** (fork),
Of (chicken), **Sakin** (knife), **Yayin** (wine)

Chapter 6: Going Shopping

A. **Kovah** (hat)

B. **Tza'if** (scarf)

C. **Kfafot** (gloves)

D. **Megafayim** (boots)

E. **Mitria** (umbrella)

F. **Simla** (dress)

G. **Chultzah** (shirt)

H. **Me'il Katzar** (jacket)

I. **Chagorah** (belt)

J. **Michnasyim** (pants)

K. **Garbayim** (socks)

L. **Na'alyim** (shoes)

M. **Mishkafay-Shemesh** (sunglasses)

N. **Beged Yam** (bathing suit)

O. **Sandalim** (sandals)

Chapter 7: Having Fun Hebrew Style

Kelev (dog), **Chatul** (cat), **Arieh** (lion), **Peel** (elephant), **Tzipor** (bird), **Parah** (cow), **Sus** (horse), **Tarnegol** (rooster), **Dag** (fish), **Sus Ha'Ye'or** (hippo)

Chapter 8: Enjoying Your Free Time: Hobbies, Sports, and Other Fun Activities

S'Chiya (swimming), **Kadur-Regel** (soccer), **Rikud** (ballet), **Tiyul** (hiking),
Kadur-Basis (baseball)

Chapter 9: Talking on the Phone

1. C (Speaking.) 2. B (Certainly.) 3. A (He's not here right now.)

Chapter 10: At the Office and Around the House

A. **Ambatia** B. **Chadar Sheinah** C. **Mitbach** D. **Salon**

Chapter 11: Planning a Trip

1. **Linso'a** 2. **L'Tayel** 3. **Lehaflig** 4. **Yamrie** 5. **Darkon**

Chapter 12: Getting Around: Flying, Driving, and Riding

1. B 2. G 3. A 4. F 5. E

Chapter 13: Checking into a Hotel

1. **Efshar** 2. **Eizeh** 3. **Hizmanti**

Chapter 14: Money, Money, Money

1. traveler's checks 2. I.D. 3. account 4. Morning light (good morning) 5. exchange rate

Chapter 15: Where Is the Western Wall? Asking Directions

1. **Le'lbud** 2. **Ha'Kenyon** 3. **Le'an** 4. **BaRegel** 5. **Eizeh**

Chapter 16: Handling Emergencies

A. **Rohsh** B. **Beten** C. **Tzavar** D. **Gav** E. **Ozen** F. **Zro'a** G. **Aynayim**
H. **Regel** I. **Katef**

Chapter 17: Let's Get Biblical

Chapter 18: Like a Prayer

There's no correct answer for this one. Hope you had fun trying to write in
Hebrew! Keep practicing and it'll get easier.

Chapter 19: Sacred Time, Sacred Space

Yom HaZikaron (Israeli Memorial Day)

Pesach (Passover)

Shavuot (Festival of the Weeks)

Rosh HaShanah (Jewish New Year)

Yom Kippur (Day of Atonement)

Yom HaShoah (Holocaust Remembrance Day)

Shabbat (The Jewish Sabbath)

Yamim Noraim (Awesome Days)

Appendix D

On the CD

System Requirements

Note that this CD is audio-only — just pop it into your CD player (or whatever you use to listen to music CDs).

If you're listening to the CD on your computer, make sure that your computer meets the minimum system requirements in the following list. If your computer doesn't match up to most of these requirements, you may have problems using the CD.

✔ A PC with a Pentium or faster processor; or a Mac OS computer with a 68040 or faster processor

✔ Microsoft Windows 95 or later; or Mac OS system software 7.6.1 or later

✔ At least 32MB of total RAM installed on your computer; for best performance, we recommend at least 64MB

✔ A CD-ROM drive

✔ A sound card for PCs; Mac OS computers have built-in sound support

✔ Media Player, such as Windows Media Player or Real Player

If you need more information on the basics, check out these books published by Wiley Publishing, Inc.: *PCs For Dummies,* by Dan Gookin; *Macs For Dummies,* by David Pogue; *iMacs For Dummies* by David Pogue; *Windows 95 For Dummies, Windows 98 For Dummies, Windows 2000 Professional For Dummies, Microsoft Windows ME Millennium Edition For Dummies,* all by Andy Rathbone.

Track Listing

Following is the list of the tracks that appear on this book's audio CD, which you can find inside the back cover of this book.

Track 1: Introduction and basic Hebrew sounds (Chapter 1)

Track 2: Saying a quick hello to a friend (Chapter 3)

Track 3: Asking for names and introducing yourself (Chapter 3)

Track 4: Making introductions (Chapter 3)

Track 5: Asking about family members (Chapter 4)

Track 6: Chatting about the weather (Chapter 4)

Track 7: Talking about professions (Chapter 4)

Track 8: Welcoming a friend to dinner and talking about the food (Chapter 5)

Track 9: Shopping for vegetables (Chapter 5)

Track 10: Asking the waiter for the check (Chapter 5)

Track 11: Making sure you're dressed for the snow (Chapter 6)

Track 12: Going to the beach (Chapter 6)

Track 13: Asking for the time (Chapter 7)

Track 14: Figuring out what to do for fun (Chapter 7)

Track 15: Discussing your hobby (Chapter 8)

Track 16: Talking about sports (Chapter 8)

Track 17: Starting a basic phone conversation (Chapter 9)

Track 18: Making a business call (Chapter 9)

Track 19: Asking to borrow things (Chapter 10)

Track 20: Talking about work (Chapter 10)

Track 21: Looking for an apartment (Chapter 10)

Track 22: Planning to travel (Chapter 11)

Track 23: Catching a plane (Chapter 11)

Track 24: Renting a car (Chapter 12)

Track 25: Checking into a hotel (Chapter 13)

Track 26: Going to the bank (Chapter 14)

Track 27: Asking for directions (Chapter 15)

Track 28: Explaining symptoms of illness (Chapter 16)

Troubleshooting

If you still have trouble installing the items from the CD, please call the Customer Service phone number at 800-762-2974 (outside the U.S.: 317-572-3993) or send email to techsupdum@wiley.com. Wiley Publishing Inc. provides technical support only for installation and other general quality control items; for technical support on the applications themselves, consult the program's vendor or author.

Index

• *N* •

Wiley Publishing, Inc.
End-User License Agreement